ÉCRITS

A SELECTION

❯❯❮❮

By Jacques Lacan
in Norton Paperback

ÉCRITS: A SELECTION
FEMININE SEXUALITY
THE FOUR FUNDAMENTAL CONCEPTS
OF PSYCHO-ANALYSIS

JACQUES LACAN

ÉCRITS

A SELECTION

TRANSLATED FROM THE
FRENCH BY
ALAN SHERIDAN

W · W · NORTON & COMPANY

New York · London

W. W. Norton & Company, Inc., 500 Fifth Avenue, New York, N.Y. 10110
W. W. Norton & Company Ltd., 37 Great Russell Street, London WC1B 3NU

Library of Congress Cataloging in Publication Data

Lacan, Jacques, 1901-
Écrits.

Bibliography: p.
Includes indexes.
1. Psychoanalysis—Addresses, essays, lectures.
BF173.L14213   1977   150'.19'5   77-22309
ISBN 0-393-01129-1
ISBN 0-393-30047-1   PBK
7 8 9 0

Contents

✦✦✦

Translator's note

⋙⋘

This selection of nine essays, representing well under a half of the material contained in the *Écrits*, is Lacan's own.

The Classified Index of Major Concepts and the Commentary on the Graphs are based on those prepared by Jacques-Alain Miller for the original French edition of the *Écrits*.

I am indebted to George Gross, Baudouin Jourdan and Stuart Schneiderman for their help with many of the difficulties presented by this uniquely difficult work.

I should also like to acknowledge assistance from the Arts Council of Great Britain.

The short glossary below is not intended to provide adequate definitions of concepts. To do so would be quite alien to the nature of Lacan's work, which is peculiarly resistant to interpretation of a static, defining kind. Though rooted in Freudian psychoanalysis, Lacan's concepts have evolved over the years to meet the requirements of a constant reformulation of psychoanalytic theory. They are best understood, therefore, operationally, at work in a number of different contexts. However, some of the terms do call for comment, if only by way of introduction. This, with the assistance of Jacques-Alain Miller, I have attempted to provide. In certain cases, however, Lacan has preferred that a term be left entirely unglossed, on the grounds that any comment would prejudice its effective operation.

The first italicized word in brackets in each entry is Lacan's French word, the second, where necessary, Freud's German. It is assumed that the reader is familiar with the terminology of 'classical' Freudian psychoanalysis.

AGENCY (*instance, Instanz*). Lacan's use of the term '*instance*' goes well beyond Freud's '*Instanz*'. It represents, one might say, an exploitation of the linguistic possibilities of the French equivalent of Freud's German term. In the absence of any exact equivalent of Lacan's French term, one is thrown back to the term used by Freud's English translators, 'agency'. In Freud, the reference is most often to the three 'agencies' of the id, ego and superego. In Lacan, one must bear in mind the idea of an 'acting upon', even 'insistence', as in the title of the essay, 'L'instance de la lettre'.

COUNTERPART (*le semblable*). This notion of the 'specular ego' was first developed in the essay, 'The Mirror Stage'.

DEMAND (*demande*). See DESIRE.

DESIRE (*désir; Wunsch, Begierde, Lust*). The *Standard Edition* translates Freud's '*Wunsch*' as 'wish', which corresponds closely to the German word. Freud's French translators, however, have always used '*désir*', rather than '*voeu*', which corresponds to '*Wunsch*' and 'wish', but which is less widely used in current French. The crucial distinction between '*Wunsch*' and 'wish', on the one hand, and '*désir*', on the other, is that the German and English words are limited to individual, isolated acts of wishing, while the French has the much stronger implication of a continuous force. It is this implication that Lacan has elaborated and placed at the centre of his psychoanalytic theory, which is why I have rendered '*désir*' by 'desire'. Furthermore, Lacan has linked the concept of 'desire' with 'need' (*besoin*) and 'demand' (*demande*) in the following way.

The human individual sets out with a particular organism, with certain biological needs, which are satisfied by certain objects. What effect does the acquisition of language have on these needs? All speech is demand; it presupposes the Other to whom it is addressed, whose very signifiers it takes over in its formulation. By the same token, that which comes from the Other is treated not so much as a particular satisfaction of a need, but rather as a response to an appeal, a gift, a token of love. There is no adequation between the need and the demand that conveys it; indeed, it is the gap between them that constitutes desire, at once particular like the first and absolute like the second. Desire (fundamentally in the singular) is a perpetual effect of symbolic articulation. It is not an appetite: it is essentially excentric and insatiable. That is why Lacan co-ordinates it not with the object that would seem to satisfy it, but with the object that causes it (one is reminded of fetishism).

DRIVE (*pulsion, Trieb*). Lacan reinstates a distinction, already clear in Freud, between the wholly psychical *pulsion* (*Trieb*) and *instinct* (*Instink*), with its 'biological' connotations. As Lacan has pointed out,

Freud's English translators blur this distinction by translating both terms as 'instinct'.

ENUNCIATION (*énonciation*). The distinction between '*énoncé*' and '*énonciation*' is a common one in contemporary French thinking. '*Énoncé*', which I translate as 'statement', refers to the actual words uttered, '*énonciation*' to the act of uttering them.

IMAGINARY, SYMBOLIC, REAL (*imaginaire, symbolique, réel*). Of these three terms, the 'imaginary' was the first to appear, well before the Rome Report of 1953. At the time, Lacan regarded the 'imago' as the proper study of psychology and identification as the fundamental psychical process. The imaginary was then the world, the register, the dimension of images, conscious or unconscious, perceived or imagined. In this respect, 'imaginary' is not simply the opposite of 'real': the image certainly belongs to reality and Lacan sought in animal ethology facts that brought out formative effects comparable to that described in 'the mirror stage'.

The notion of the 'symbolic' came to the forefront in the Rome Report. The symbols referred to here are not icons, stylized figurations, but signifiers, in the sense developed by Saussure and Jakobson, extended into a generalized definition: differential elements, in themselves without meaning, which acquire value only in their mutual relations, and forming a closed order – the question is whether this order is or is not complete. Henceforth it is the symbolic, not the imaginary, that is seen to be the determining order of the subject, and its effects are radical: the subject, in Lacan's sense, is himself an effect of the symbolic. Lévi-Strauss's formalization of the elementary structures of kinship and its use of Jakobson's binarism provided the basis for Lacan's conception of the symbolic – a conception, however, that goes well beyond its origins. According to Lacan, a distinction must be drawn between what belongs in experience to the order of the symbolic and what belongs to the imaginary. In particular, the relation between the subject, on the one hand, and the signifiers, speech, language, on the other, is frequently contrasted with the imaginary relation, that between the ego and its images. In each case, many problems derive from the relations between these two dimensions.

The 'real' emerges as a third term, linked to the symbolic and the imaginary: it stands for what is neither symbolic nor imaginary, and remains foreclosed from the analytic experience, which is an experience of speech. What is prior to the assumption of the symbolic, the real in its 'raw' state (in the case of the subject, for instance, the organism and its biological needs), may only be supposed, it is an algebraic x. This Lacanian concept of the 'real' is not to be confused with reality, which is perfectly knowable: the subject of desire knows no more than that, since for it reality is entirely phantasmatic.

The term 'real', which was at first of only minor importance, acting as a kind of safety rail, has gradually been developed, and its signification has been considerably altered. It began, naturally enough, by presenting, in relation to symbolic substitutions and imaginary variations, a function of constancy: 'the real is that which always returns to the same place'. It then became that before which the imaginary faltered, that over which the symbolic stumbles, that which is refractory, resistant. Hence the formula: 'the real is the impossible'. It is in this sense that the term begins to appear regularly, as an adjective, to describe that which is lacking in the symbolic order, the ineliminable residue of all articulation, the foreclosed element, which may be approached, but never grasped: the umbilical cord of the symbolic.

As distinguished by Lacan, these three dimensions are, as we say, profoundly heterogeneous. Yet the fact that the three terms have been linked together in a series raises the question as to what they have in common, a question to which Lacan has addressed himself in his most recent thinking on the subject of the Borromean knot (*Séminaire* 1974–75, entitled 'R.S.I.').

JOUISSANCE (*jouissance*). There is no adequate translation in English of this word. 'Enjoyment' conveys the sense, contained in *jouissance*, of enjoyment of rights, of property, etc. Unfortunately, in modern English, the word has lost the sexual connotations it still retains in French. (*Jouir* is slang for 'to come'.) 'Pleasure', on the other hand, is pre-empted by '*plaisir*' – and Lacan uses the two terms quite differently. 'Pleasure' obeys the law of homeostasis that Freud evokes in 'Beyond the Pleasure Principle', whereby, through discharge, the psyche seeks the lowest possible level of tension. '*Jouissance*' transgresses this law and, in that respect, it is *beyond* the pleasure principle.

KNOWLEDGE (*savoir, connaissance*). Where 'knowledge' renders '*connaissance*', I have added the French word in brackets. Most European languages make a distinction (e.g. Hegel's *Wissen* and *Kenntnis*) that is lost in English. In modern French thinking, different writers use the distinction in different ways. In Lacan, *connaissance* (with its inevitable concomitant, '*méconnaissance*') belongs to the imaginary register, while *savoir* belongs to the symbolic register.

LACK (*manque*). '*Manque*' is translated here as 'lack', except in the expression, created by Lacan, '*manque-à-être*', for which Lacan himself has proposed the English neologism 'want-to-be'.

LURE (*leurre*). The French word translates variously 'lure' (for hawks, fish), 'decoy' (for birds), bait (for fish) and the notion of 'allurement' and 'enticement'. In Lacan, the notion is related to '*méconnaissance*'.

MÉCONNAISSANCE. I have decided to retain the French word. The sense is of a 'failure to recognize', or 'misconstruction'. The concept is central to Lacan's thinking, since, for him, knowledge (*connaissance*) is inextricably bound up with *méconnaissance*.

NAME-OF-THE-FATHER (*nom-du-père*). This concept derives, in a sense, from the mythical, symbolic father of Freud's *Totem and Taboo*. In terms of Lacan's three orders, it refers not to the real father, nor to the imaginary father (the paternal imago), but to the symbolic father. Freud, says Lacan, was led irresistibly 'to link the appearance of the signifier of the Father, as the author of the Law, to death, even to the murder of the Father, thus showing that although this murder is the fruitful moment of the debt through which the subject binds himself for life to the Law, the symbolic Father, in so far as he signifies this Law, is certainly the dead Father' (*Écrits*, 'Of a question preliminary to any possible treatment of psychosis').

NEED (*besoin*). See DESIRE.

OBJET PETIT a. The '*a*' in question stands for '*autre*' (other), the concept having been developed out of the Freudian 'object' and Lacan's own exploitation of 'otherness'. The '*petit a*' (small 'a') differentiates the object from (while relating it to) the '*Autre*' or '*grand Autre*' (the capitalized 'Other'). However, Lacan refuses to comment on either term here, leaving the reader to develop an appreciation of the concepts in the course of their use. Furthermore, Lacan insists that '*objet petit* a' should remain untranslated, thus acquiring, as it were, the status of an algebraic sign.

OTHER (*Autre, grand Autre*). See OBJET PETIT a.

PLEASURE (*plaisir*). See JOUISSANCE.

REAL (*réel*). See IMAGINARY.

STATEMENT (*énoncé*). See ENUNCIATION.

SYMBOLIC (*symbolique*). See IMAGINARY.

WANT-TO-BE (*manque-à-être*). See LACK.

Bibliographical note

⪢⪡

The mirror stage as formative of the function of the I
Le stade du miroir comme formateur de la fonction du Je. An earlier version, entitled simply *Le stade du miroir*, was delivered at the fourteenth International Psychoanalytical Congress, held at Marienbad in August 1936 under the chairmanship of Ernest Jones. An English translation of this version appeared in *The International Journal of Psychoanalysis*, vol. 18, part I, January, 1937, under the title, '*The Looking-glass Phase*'. A much revised later version was delivered at the sixteenth International Psychoanalytical Congress, in Zurich on July 17, 1949. It was published in the *Revue française de psychanalyse*, no. 4, October–December, 1949, pp. 449–55. The present translation is of the later version.

Aggressivity in psychoanalysis
L'aggressivité en psychanalyse. A theoretical report presented to the eleventh Congrès des psychanalystes de langue française, Brussels, May 1948. Published in the *Revue française de psychanalyse*, no. 3, July–September, 1948, pp. 367–88.

The function and field of speech and language in psychoanalysis
Fonction et champ de la parole et du langage en psychanalyse. Report to the Rome Congress held at the Istituto di Psicologia della Università di Roma, 26 and 27 September, 1953. Published in *La Psychanalyse*, P.U.F., vol. 1, 1956, pp. 81–166.

The Freudian thing
La chose freudienne ou Sens du retour à Freud en psychanalyse. Amplification of a lecture given at the Neuro-Psychiatric Clinic, Vienna, November of 1955. First appeared in *L'Évolution psychiatrique*, no. 1, 1956, pp. 225–52.

The agency of the letter in the unconscious or reason since Freud
L'instance de la lettre dans l'inconscient ou la raison depuis Freud. Delivered
on 9 May, 1957, in the Amphithéâtre Descartes of the Sorbonne, Paris,
at the request of the Philosophy Group of the Fédération des étudiants ès
Lettres. Written version dated 14–16 May, 1957. Published in *La Psych-*
analyse, vol. 3, P.U.F., 1957, pp. 47–81.

On a question preliminary to any possible treatment of psychosis
D'une question préliminaire à tout traitement possible de la psychose. Based
on the author's seminar for the first two semesters of the year 1955–6.
Written December 1957–January 1958. Published in *La Psychanalyse*,
vol. 4, P.U.F., 1959, pp. 1–50.

The signification of the phallus
La Signification du phallus. Lecture given in German under the title
Die Bedeutung des Phallus at the Max-Planck Institute, Munich, at the
invitation of Professor Paul Matussek, 9 May, 1958.

The direction of the treatment and the principles of its power
La direction de la cure et les principes de son pouvoir. First report to the
Colloque international de Royaumont, 10–13 July, 1958, at the invitation
of the Société française de psychanalyse. Published in *La Psychanalyse*,
vol. 6, P.U.F., 1961, pp. 149–206.

The subversion of the subject and the dialectic of
desire in the Freudian unconscious
Subversion du sujet et dialectique du désir dans l'inconscient freudien.
Delivered at a conference entitled 'La Dialectique', held at Royaumont,
19–23 September, 1960, at the invitation of Jean Wahl.

ONE

The mirror stage as formative of the function of the I as revealed in psychoanalytic experience

Delivered at the 16th International Congress of
Psychoanalysis, Zürich, July 17, 1949

༺༻

The conception of the mirror stage that I introduced at our last congress, thirteen years ago, has since become more or less established in the practice of the French group. However, I think it worthwhile to bring it again to your attention, especially today, for the light it sheds on the formation of the *I* as we experience it in psychoanalysis. It is an experience that leads us to oppose any philosophy directly issuing from the *Cogito*.

Some of you may recall that this conception originated in a feature of human behaviour illuminated by a fact of comparative psychology. The child, at an age when he is for a time, however short, outdone by the chimpanzee in instrumental intelligence, can nevertheless already recognize as such his own image in a mirror. This recognition is indicated in the illuminative mimicry of the *Aha-Erlebnis*, which Köhler sees as the expression of situational apperception, an essential stage of the act of intelligence.

This act, far from exhausting itself, as in the case of the monkey, once the image has been mastered and found empty, immediately rebounds in the case of the child in a series of gestures in which he experiences in play the relation between the movements assumed in the image and the reflected environment, and between this virtual complex and the reality it reduplicates – the child's own body, and the persons and things, around him.

This event can take place, as we have known since Baldwin, from the age of six months, and its repetition has often made me reflect upon the startling spectacle of the infant in front of the mirror. Unable as yet to walk, or even to stand up, and held tightly as he is by some support, human or artificial (what, in France, we call a '*trotte-bébé*'), he nevertheless overcomes, in a flutter of jubilant activity, the obstructions of his support and, fixing his attitude in a slightly leaning-forward position, in order to hold it in his gaze, brings back an instantaneous aspect of the image.

For me, this activity retains the meaning I have given it up to the age of eighteen months. This meaning discloses a libidinal dynamism, which has hitherto remained problematic, as well as an ontological structure of the human world that accords with my reflections on paranoiac knowledge.

We have only to understand the mirror stage *as an identification*, in the full sense that analysis gives to the term: namely, the transformation that takes place in the subject when he assumes an image – whose predestination to this phase-effect is sufficiently indicated by the use, in analytic theory, of the ancient term *imago*.

This jubilant assumption of his specular image by the child at the *infans* stage, still sunk in his motor incapacity and nursling dependence, would seem to exhibit in an exemplary situation the symbolic matrix in which the *I* is precipitated in a primordial form, before it is objectified in the dialectic of identification with the other, and before language restores to it, in the universal, its function as subject.

This form would have to be called the Ideal-I,[1] if we wished to incorporate it into our usual register, in the sense that it will also be the source of secondary identifications, under which term I would place the functions of libidinal normalization. But the important point is that this form situates the agency of the ego, before its social determination, in a fictional direction, which will always remain irreducible for the individual alone, or rather, which will only rejoin the coming-into-being (*le devenir*) of the subject asymptotically, whatever the success of the dialectical syntheses by which he must resolve as *I* his discordance with his own reality.

The fact is that the total form of the body by which the subject anticipates in a mirage the maturation of his power is given to him only as *Gestalt*, that is to say, in an exteriority in which this form is certainly more constituent than constituted, but in which it appears to him above all in a contrasting size (*un relief de stature*) that fixes it and in a symmetry that inverts it, in contrast with the turbulent movements that the subject feels are animating him. Thus, this *Gestalt* – whose pregnancy should be regarded as bound up with the species, though its motor style remains scarcely recognizable – by these two aspects of its appearance, symbolizes the mental permanence of the *I*, at the same time as it prefigures its alienating destination; it is still pregnant with the correspondences that unite the *I* with the statue in which man projects himself, with the phantoms that dominate him, or with the automaton in which, in an ambiguous relation, the world of his own making tends to find completion.

Indeed, for the *imagos* – whose veiled faces it is our privilege to see in outline in our daily experience and in the penumbra of symbolic efficacity[2] – the mirror-image would seem to be the threshold of the visible world, if we go by the mirror disposition that the *imago of one's own body* presents in hallucinations or dreams, whether it concerns its individual features, or even its infirmities, or its object-projections; or if we observe the role of the mirror apparatus in the appearances of the *double*, in which psychical realities, however heterogeneous, are manifested.

That a *Gestalt* should be capable of formative effects in the organism is attested by a piece of biological experimentation that is itself so alien to the idea of psychical causality that it cannot bring itself to formulate its results in these terms. It nevertheless recognizes that it is a necessary condition for the maturation of the gonad of the female pigeon that it should see another member of its species, of either sex; so sufficient in itself is this condition that the desired effect may be obtained merely by placing the individual within reach of the field of reflection of a mirror. Similarly, in the case of the migratory locust, the transition within a generation from the solitary to the gregarious form can be obtained by exposing the individual, at a certain stage, to the exclusively visual action of a similar image, provided it is animated by movements of a style sufficiently close to that characteristic of the species. Such facts are inscribed in an order of homeomorphic identification that would itself fall within the larger question of the meaning of beauty as both formative and erogenic.

But the facts of mimicry are no less instructive when conceived as cases of heteromorphic identification, in as much as they raise the problem of the signification of space for the living organism – psychological concepts hardly seem less appropriate for shedding light on these matters than ridiculous attempts to reduce them to the supposedly supreme law of adaptation. We have only to recall how Roger Caillois (who was then very young, and still fresh from his breach with the sociological school in which he was trained) illuminated the subject by using the term '*legendary psychasthenia*' to classify morphological mimicry as an obsession with space in its derealizing effect.

I have myself shown in the social dialectic that structures human knowledge as paranoiac[3] why human knowledge has greater autonomy than animal knowledge in relation to the field of force of desire, but also why human knowledge is determined in that 'little reality' (*ce peu de réalité*), which the Surrealists, in their restless way, saw as its limitation. These reflections lead me to recognize in the spatial captation manifested in the mirror-stage, even before the social dialectic, the effect in man of an organic insufficiency in his natural reality – in so far as any meaning can be given to the word 'nature'.

I am led, therefore, to regard the function of the mirror-stage as a particular case of the function of the *imago*, which is to establish a relation between the organism and its reality – or, as they say, between the *Innenwelt* and the *Umwelt*.

In man, however, this relation to nature is altered by a certain dehiscence at the heart of the organism, a primordial Discord betrayed by the signs of uneasiness and motor unco-ordination of the neo-natal months. The objective notion of the anatomical incompleteness of the pyramidal system and likewise the presence of certain humoral residues of the maternal organism confirm the view I have formulated as the fact of a real *specific prematurity of birth* in man.

It is worth noting, incidentally, that this is a fact recognized as such by embryologists, by the term *foetalization*, which determines the prevalence of the so-called superior apparatus of the neurax, and especially of the cortex, which psycho-surgical operations lead us to regard as the intra-organic mirror.

This development is experienced as a temporal dialectic that decisively projects the formation of the individual into history. The *mirror stage* is a drama whose internal thrust is precipitated from insufficiency to anticipation – and which manufactures for the subject, caught up in the lure of spatial identification, the succession of phantasies that extends from a fragmented body-image to a form of its totality that I shall call orthopaedic – and, lastly, to the assumption of the armour of an alienating identity, which will mark with its rigid structure the subject's entire mental development. Thus, to break out of the circle of the *Innenwelt* into the *Umwelt* generates the inexhaustible quadrature of the ego's verifications.

This fragmented body – which term I have also introduced into our system of theoretical references – usually manifests itself in dreams when the movement of the analysis encounters a certain level of aggressive disintegration in the individual. It then appears in the form of disjointed limbs, or of those organs represented in exoscopy, growing wings and taking up arms for intestinal persecutions – the very same that the visionary Hieronymus Bosch has fixed, for all time, in painting, in their ascent from the fifteenth century to the imaginary zenith of modern man. But this form is even tangibly revealed at the organic level, in the lines of 'fragilization' that define the anatomy of phantasy, as exhibited in the schizoid and spasmodic symptoms of hysteria.

Correlatively, the formation of the *I* is symbolized in dreams by a fortress, or a stadium – its inner arena and enclosure, surrounded by marshes and rubbish-tips, dividing it into two opposed fields of contest where the subject flounders in quest of the lofty, remote inner castle whose form (sometimes juxtaposed in the same scenario) symbolizes the id in a quite startling way. Similarly, on the mental plane, we find realized the structures of fortified works, the metaphor of which arises spontaneously, as if issuing from the symptoms themselves, to designate the mechanisms of obsessional neurosis – inversion, isolation, reduplication, cancellation and displacement.

But if we were to build on these subjective givens alone – however little we free them from the condition of experience that makes us see them as partaking of the nature of a linguistic technique – our theoretical attempts would remain exposed to the charge of projecting themselves into the unthinkable of an absolute subject. This is why I have sought in the present hypothesis, grounded in a conjunction of objective data, the guiding grid for a *method of symbolic reduction.*

It establishes in the *defences of the ego* a genetic order, in accordance with the wish formulated by Miss Anna Freud, in the first part of her great work, and situates (as against a frequently expressed prejudice) hysterical repression and its returns at a more archaic stage than obsessional inversion and its isolating processes, and the latter in turn as preliminary to paranoic alienation, which dates from the deflection of the specular *I* into the social *I.*

This moment in which the mirror-stage comes to an end inaugurates, by the identification with the *imago* of the counterpart and the drama of primordial jealousy (so well brought out by the school of Charlotte Bühler in the phenomenon of infantile *transitivism*), the dialectic that will henceforth link the *I* to socially elaborated situations.

It is this moment that decisively tips the whole of human knowledge into mediatization through the desire of the other, constitutes its objects in an abstract equivalence by the co-operation of others, and turns the I into that apparatus for which every instinctual thrust constitutes a danger, even though it should correspond to a natural maturation – the very normalization of this maturation being henceforth dependent, in man, on a cultural mediation as exemplified, in the case of the sexual object, by the Oedipus complex.

In the light of this conception, the term primary narcissism, by which analytic doctrine designates the libidinal investment characteristic of that moment, reveals in those who invented it the most profound awareness of semantic latencies. But it also throws light on the dynamic opposition between this libido and the sexual libido, which the first analysts tried to define when they invoked destructive and, indeed, death instincts, in order to explain the evident connection between the narcissistic libido and the alienating function of the *I*, the aggressivity it releases in any relation to the other, even in a relation involving the most Samaritan of aid.

In fact, they were encountering that existential negativity whose reality is so vigorously proclaimed by the contemporary philosophy of being and nothingness.

But unfortunately that philosophy grasps negativity only within the limits of a self-sufficiency of consciousness, which, as one of its premises, links to the *méconnaissances* that constitute the ego, the illusion of autonomy to which it entrusts itself. This flight of fancy, for all that it draws, to an unusual extent, on borrowings from psychoanalytic experience, culminates in the pretention of providing an existential psychoanalysis.

At the culmination of the historical effort of a society to refuse to recognize that it has any function other than the utilitarian one, and in the anxiety of the individual confronting the 'concentrational'[4] form of the social bond that seems to arise to crown this effort, existentialism must be judged by the explanations it gives of the subjective impasses that have indeed resulted from it; a freedom that is never more authentic than when it is within the walls of a prison; a demand for commitment, expressing the impotence of a pure consciousness to master any situation; a voyeuristic–sadistic idealization of the sexual relation; a personality that realizes itself only in suicide; a consciousness of the other than can be satisfied only by Hegelian murder.

These propositions are opposed by all our experience, in so far as it teaches us not to regard the ego as centred on the *perception–consciousness system*, or as organized by the 'reality principle' – a principle that is the expression of a scientific prejudice most hostile to the dialectic of knowledge. Our experience shows that we should start instead from the *function of méconnaissance* that characterizes the ego in all its structures, so markedly articulated by Miss Anna Freud. For, if the *Verneinung*

[handwritten: Act of P seeking favor by using flattery]

represents the patent form of that function, its effects will, for the most part, remain latent, so long as they are not illuminated by some light reflected on to the level of fatality, which is where the id manifests itself.

We can thus understand the inertia characteristic of the formations of the *I*, and find there the most extensive definition of neurosis – just as the captation of the subject by the situation gives us the most general formula for madness, not only the madness that lies behind the walls of asylums, but also the madness that deafens the world with its sound and fury.

The sufferings of neurosis and psychosis are for us a schooling in the passions of the soul, just as the beam of the psychoanalytic scales, when we calculate the tilt of its threat to entire communities, provides us with an indication of the deadening of the passions in society.

At this junction of nature and culture, so persistently examined by modern anthropology, psychoanalysis alone recognizes this knot of imaginary servitude that love must always undo again, or sever.

For such a task, we place no trust in altruistic feeling, we who lay bare the aggressivity that underlies the activity of the philanthropist, the idealist, the pedagogue, and even the reformer.

In the recourse of subject to subject that we preserve, psychoanalysis may accompany the patient to the ecstatic limit of the '*Thou art that*', in which is revealed to him the cipher of his mortal destiny, but it is not in our mere power as practitioners to bring him to that point where the real journey begins.

⟫⟫⟪⟪

Notes

1. Throughout this article I leave in its peculiarity the translation I have adopted for Freud's *Ideal-Ich* [i.e., 'je-idéal'], without further comment, other than to say that I have not maintained it since.

2. Cf. Claude Lévi-Strauss, *Structural Anthropology*, Chapter X.

3. Cf. 'Aggressivity in Psychoanalysis', p. 8 and *Écrits*, p. 180.

4. '*Concentrationnaire*', an adjective coined after World War II (this article was written in 1949) to describe the life of the concentration-camp. In the hands of certain writers it became, by extension, applicable to many aspects of 'modern' life [Tr.].

TWO

Aggressivity in psychoanalysis

Theoretical report presented to the 11th Congrès
des Psychanalystes de langue française,
Brussels, mid-May 1948

⧽⧽⧼⧼

The preceding report concerned the use we make of the notion of aggressivity in the clinic and in therapy. It remains to me to prove to you whether or not this notion can be developed into a concept capable of scientific use, that is to say, capable of objectifying facts of a comparable order in reality, or, more categorically, of establishing a dimension of experience whose objectified facts may be regarded as variables.

All of us here share an experience based upon a technique, a system of concepts to which we remain faithful, partly because this system was developed by the man who opened up to us all the ways to that experience, and partly because it bears the living mark of the different stages of its elaboration. That is to say, contrary to the dogmatism that is sometimes imputed to us, we know that this system remains open both as a whole and in several of its articulations.

These gaps seem to focus on the enigmatic signification that Freud expressed in the term *death instinct*, which, rather like the figure of the Sphinx, reveals the aporia that confronted this great mind in the most profound attempt so far made to formulate an experience of man in the register of biology.

This aporia lies at the heart of the notion of aggressivity, the importance of whose role in the economy of the psyche we are only just beginning to realize.

This is why the question of the metapsychological nature of the death tendencies is continually being discussed by our theoreticians, not without contradiction, and often, it must be admitted, in a somewhat formalist way.

I would just like to make a few remarks, propose a number of theses on the subject. They are the fruit of years of reflexion on the veritable aporia of the doctrine, and of the feeling that I have on reading many of these theoretical studies of our responsibility in the present evolution of psychology in the laboratory and as treatment. I am thinking, on the one hand, of the researches of the so-called behaviourists, who, it seems to me, owe their best results (slender as they often are in comparison with the apparatus with which they surround themselves) to the often implicit use they make of categories introduced into psychology by psychoanalysis; and, on the other hand, I am thinking of the kinds of treatment, given to both adults and children, that might be grouped together under the heading *psychodramatic* treatment, and which seeks its efficacity in the abreaction that it tries to exhaust on the level of play, and in which, again, classical psychoanalysis provides the principal underlying notions.

⤞⤞⤝⤝

Thesis I: *Aggressivity manifests itself in an experience that is subjective by its very constitution.*

It would be useful to return to the phenomenon of psychoanalytic experience. In approaching first principles, this reflexion is often omitted.

It can be said that psychoanalytic action is developed in and through verbal communication, that is, in a dialectical grasp of meaning. It presupposes, therefore, a subject who manifests himself as such to the intention of another.

It cannot be objected that this subjectivity must necessarily be obsolete according to the ideal fulfilled by physics, which eliminates it by means of the recording apparatus – though it cannot, incidentally, avoid the possibility of personal error in the reading of the result.

Only a subject can understand a meaning; conversely, every phenomenon of meaning implies a subject. In analysis a subject offers himself as being capable of being understood, and indeed *is* capable of being understood: introspection and supposedly projective intuition do not constitute here the vitiations of principle that a psychology, taking its first steps along the path of science, has regarded as insuperable. This would be to create an obstacle out of abstractly isolated moments of the dialogue, when one should be concerning oneself with its movement: it was Freud's great merit to have taken risks in this direction, and then to have overcome them with a rigorous technique.

Can his results form the basis of a positive science? Yes, if the experience is verifiable by everyone. But this experience, constituted between two subjects one of whom plays in the dialogue the role of ideal impersonality (a point to which I shall return later), may, once it is completed, and providing that it fulfils the conditions of efficiency that may be required of any special research, be resumed by the other subject with a third subject. This apparently initiatory way is simply a transmission by recurrence, which should cause surprise to no one, since it springs from the very bipolar structure of all subjectivity. Only the speed of diffusion of the experience is affected by it, and although its restriction to a particular cultural area may be a matter of dispute, everything would indicate that its results may be sufficiently relativized to provide a generalization capable of satisfying the humanitarian postulate that is inseparable from the spirit of science.

>>><<

Thesis II: *Aggressivity in experience is given to us as intended aggression and as an image of corporal dislocation, and it is in such forms that it shows itself to be efficient.*

The analytic experience allows us to feel the pressure of intention. We read it in the symbolic meaning of symptoms, as soon as the subject throws off the defences by which he disconnects them from their relations with his daily life and his history, in the implicit finality of his behaviour and his rejections, in his unsuccessful acts, in the avowal of his privileged phantasies, and in the riddles of his dream life.

We can measure it partly in the demanding tone that sometimes underlies his whole discourse, in his unfinished sentences, his hesitations, his inflexions and his slips of the tongue, in the inaccuracies of his descriptions of events, irregularities in his application of the analytic rule, late arrivals at sessions, calculated absences, and often in recriminations, reproaches, phantasmic fears, emotional reactions of anger, attempts at intimidation; the true acts of violence being as rare as the combination of circumstances that has led the patient to the doctor, and his transformation, accepted by the patient himself, in a convention of dialogue, would lead one to expect.

The efficacity proper to this aggressive intention is manifest: we constantly observe it in the formative action of an individual on those dependent on him; intended aggressivity gnaws away, undermines, disintegrates; it castrates; it leads to death: 'And I thought you were impotent!' growled a mother, suddenly transformed into a tigress, to her son, who, with great difficulty, had admitted to her his homosexual tendencies. And one could see that her permanent aggressivity as a virile woman had had its effect; I have always found it impossible, in such cases, to divert the blows away from the analytic enterprise.

This aggressivity is exercised within real constraints of course. But we know from experience that it is no less effective when given expression: a severe parent is intimidating by his or her very presence, and the image of the Punisher scarcely needs to be brandished for the child to form it. Its effects are more far-reaching than any act of brutality.

After the repeated failures of classical psychology to account for these mental phenomena, which, using a term whose expressive value is confirmed by all its semantic acceptations, we call images, psychoanalysis made the first successful attempt to operate at the level of the concrete reality that they represent. This was because it set out from their formative function in the subject, and revealed that if the transient images determine such individual inflexions of the tendencies, it is as variations of the matrices that those other specific images, which we refer to by the ancient term of *imago*, are constituted for the 'instincts' themselves.

Among these *imagos* are some that represent the elective vectors of aggressive intentions, which they provide with an efficacity that might be called magical. These are the images of castration, mutilation, dismemberment, dislocation, evisceration, devouring, bursting open of the body, in short, the *imagos* that I have grouped together under the apparently structural term of *imagos of the fragmented body*.

There is a specific relation here between man and his own body that is manifested in a series of social practices – from rites involving tattooing, incision, and circumcision in primitive societies to what, in advanced societies, might be called the Procrustean arbitrariness of fashion, a relatively recent cultural innovation, in that it denies respect for the natural forms of the human body.

One only has to listen to children aged between two and five playing, alone or together, to know that the pulling off of the head and the ripping open of the belly are themes that occur spontaneously to their imagination, and that this is corroborated by the experience of the doll torn to pieces.

We must turn to the works of Hieronymus Bosch for an atlas of all the aggressive images that torment mankind. The prevalence that psychoanalysis has discovered among them of images of a primitive autoscopy of the oral and cloacal organs has engendered the forms of demons. These are to be found even in the ogee of the *angustiae* of birth depicted in the gates of the abyss through which they thrust the damned, and even in the narcissistic structure of those glass spheres in which the exhausted partners of the garden of delights are held captive.

These phantasmagorias crop up constantly in dreams, especially at the point when analysis appears to be turning its attention on the most fundamental, most archaic fixations. I remember the dream of one of my patients, whose aggressive drives took the form of obsessive phantasies; in the dream he saw himself driving a car, accompanied by the woman with whom he was having a rather difficult affair, pursued by a flying-fish, whose skin was so transparent that one could see the horizontal liquid level through the body, an image of vesical persecution of great anatomical clarity.

These are all initial givens of a *Gestalt* proper to aggression in man: a *Gestalt* that is as much bound up with its symbolic character as with the cruel refinement of the weapons he makes, at least at the earlier, craft-stage of his industry. It is this imaginary function that I should now like to elucidate.

I should state at the outset that to attempt a Behaviourist reduction of the analytic process – to which a concern for rigour, quite unjustified in my view, seems to impel some of us – is to deprive it of its most important subjective givens, of which the privileged phantasies are the witnesses in consciousness, and which have enabled us to conceive of the identification-forming *imago*.

⋆⋆⋆⋆

Thesis III: *The springs of aggressivity decide the reasons that motivate the technique of analysis.*

In itself, dialogue seems to involve a renunciation of aggressivity; from Socrates onwards, philosophy has always placed its hope in the triumph of reason. And yet ever since Thrasymachus made his stormy exit at the beginning of the *Republic*, verbal dialectic has all too often proved a failure.

I have emphasized that the analyst cured even the most serious cases of madness through dialogue; what virtue, then, did Freud add to it?

The rule proposed to the patient in analysis allows him to advance in a blind intentionality that has no other purpose than to free him from an illness or an ignorance whose very limits he is unaware of.

His voice alone will be heard for a time whose duration remains at the discretion of the analyst. In particular, it will soon become apparent, indeed confirmed, that the analyst refrains from offering any kind of advice or trying to influence the patient in any particular direction. This constraint would seem to run counter to the desired end, and so must be justified by some deeper motive.

What, then, lies behind the analyst's attitude? The concern to provide the dialogue with a participant who is as devoid as possible of individual characteristics; we efface ourselves, we deprive the speaker of those expressions of interest, sympathy, and reaction that he expects to find on the face of the listener, we avoid all expression of personal taste, we conceal whatever might betray them, we become depersonalized, and try to represent for the other an ideal of impassibility.

In such behaviour we express not simply the apathy that we must have brought about in ourselves if we are to understand our subject, nor are we simply preparing the oracular form that our interpretative intervention must take against this background of inertia.

We wish to avoid the trap that already lies concealed in the appeal, marked by the eternal pathos of faith, that the patient addresses to us. It carries a secret within itself. 'Take upon yourself,' the patient is telling us, 'the evil that weighs me down; but if you remain smug, self-satisfied, unruffled as you are now, you won't be worthy of bearing it.'

What appears here as the proud revenge of suffering will show its true face — and sometimes at a moment decisive enough to enter the 'negative therapeutic reaction' that interested Freud so much — in the form of that resistance of *amour-propre*, to use the term in all the depth given it by La Rochefoucauld, and which is often expressed thus: 'I can't bear the thought of being freed by anyone other than myself.'

Of course, at a deeper level of emotional demand, it is participation in his illness that the patient expects from us. But it is the hostile reaction that guides our prudence, and which inspired Freud to be on his guard against any temptation to play the prophet. Only saints are sufficiently detached from the deepest of the common passions to avoid the aggressive reactions to charity.

As to presenting our own virtues and merits by way of example, the only person I have known to resort to such reactions was some establishment figure, thoroughly imbued with the idea, naïve as it was austere, of his own apostolic value; I well remember the fury he unleashed.

In any case, such reactions should hardly surprise us analysts; after all, do we not point out the aggressive motives that lie hidden in all so-called philanthropic activity?

Yet we must bring into play the subject's aggressivity towards us, because, as we know, these intentions form the negative transference that is the initial knot of the analytic drama.

This phenomenon represents in the patient the imaginary transference on to our person of one of the more or less archaic *imagos*, which, by an effect of symbolic subduction, degrades, diverts, or inhibits the cycle of such behaviour, which, by an accident of repression, has excluded from the control of the ego this or that function or corporal segment, and which, by an action of identification, has given its form to this or that agency of the personality.

It can be seen that the slightest pretext is enough to arouse the aggressive intention, which reactualizes the *imago*, which has remained permanent at the level of symbolic overdetermination that we call the subject's unconscious, together with its intentional correlation.

Such a mechanism often proves to be extremely simple in hysteria: in the case of a girl suffering from astasia–abasia, who for months had resisted various kinds of therapeutic suggestion, my person was immediately identified with a combination of the most unpleasant features that the object of a passion represented for her; it should be added that her passionate feelings were fairly strongly marked by an element of delusion. The subjacent *imago* was that of her father, and it was enough for me to remark that she had lacked paternal support (a lack which I knew had dominated her biography in highly dramatic fashion) for her to be cured of her symptom, without, it might be said, her having understood anything, or her morbid passion being in any way affected.

These knots are more difficult to break, we know, in obsessional neuroses, precisely because of the well-known fact that its structure is intended particularly to disguise, to displace, to deny, to divide, and to subdue the aggressive intention, by means of a defensive decomposition very similar in principle to that illustrated by the stepping and staggering techniques employed in military fortification at the time of Louis XIV – indeed, a number of my patients have themselves resorted to metaphors of military fortification to describe the workings of their own defences.

As to the role of aggressive intention in phobia, it is, as it were, manifest.

It is no bad thing, then, to reactivate such an intention in psychoanalysis.

What we try to avoid by our technique is allowing the patient's

aggressive intention to find the support of an idea of our person sufficiently elaborated for it to be able to be organized in those reactions of
opposition, negation, ostentation, and lying that our experience has
shown us to be the characteristic modes of the agency of the ego in
dialogue.

I am characterizing this agency here not by the theoretical construction
that Freud gives of it in his metapsychology, namely, as the *perception-
consciousness* system, but by the phenomenological essence that he recognizes as being in experience the most constant attribute of the ego, namely,
Verneinung, the givens of which he urges us to appreciate in the most
general index of a prejudicial inversion.

In short, we call ego that nucleus given to consciousness, but opaque
to reflexion, marked by all the ambiguities which, from self-satisfaction
to 'bad faith' (*mauvaise foi*), structure the experience of the passions in
the human subject; this 'I' who, in order to admit its facticity to existential
criticism, opposes its irreducible inertia of pretences and *méconnaissances*
to the concrete problematic of the realization of the subject.

Far from attacking it head-on, the analytic maieutic adopts a round-
about approach that amounts in fact to inducing in the subject a controlled
paranoia. Indeed, it is one of the aspects of analytic action to operate the
projection of what Melanie Klein calls *bad internal objects*, a paranoiac
mechanism certainly, but one that is here highly systematized, filtered, as
it were, and properly checked.

It is the aspect of our *praxis* that corresponds to the category of
space, however little it embraces that imaginary space in which the
dimension of the symptoms that structures them as excluded islets, inert
scotomas, or parasitical compulsions in the functions of the person is
developed.

To the other dimension, the temporal, corresponds anxiety and its
effects, whether patent as in the phenomenon of flight or inhibition, or
latent as when it appears only with the motivating *imago*.

Again, let us repeat, this *imago* is revealed only in so far as our attitude
offers the subject the pure mirror of an unruffled surface.

But let us imagine what would take place in a patient who saw in his
analyst an exact replica of himself. Everyone feels that the excess of
aggressive tension would set up such an obstacle to the manifestation of
the transference that its useful effect could only be brought about extremely slowly, and this is what sometimes happens in the analysis of
prospective analysts. To take an extreme case, if experienced in the form

of strangeness proper to the apprehensions of the *double*, this situation would set up an uncontrollable anxiety on the part of the analysand.

⟩⟩◄◄

Thesis IV: *Aggressivity is the correlative tendency of a mode of identification that we call narcissistic, and which determines the formal structure of man's ego and of the register of entities characteristic of his world.*

The subjective experience of analysis immediately inscribes its results in concrete psychology. Let us indicate simply what it brings to the psychology of the emotions by showing the signification common to states as diverse as phantasmatic fear, anger, active sorrow, or psychasthenic fatigue.

To pass now from the subjectivity of intention to the notion of a tendency to aggression is to make the leap from the phenomenology of our experience to metapsychology.

But this leap manifests nothing more than a requirement of thought which, in order to objectify the register of aggressive reactions, and given its inability to seriate this leap in a quantitative variation, must understand it in a formula of equivalence. This is the use we make of it in the notion of *libido*.

The aggressive tendency proves to be fundamental in a certain series of significant states of the personality, namely, the paranoid and paranoiac psychoses.

In my work I have emphasized that one could co-ordinate by their strictly parallel seriation the quality of the aggressive reaction to be expected from a particular form of paranoia with the stage of mental genesis represented by the delusion that is symptomatic of this same form. A relation that appears even more profound when – I have shown this in the case of a curable form, self-punishing paranoia – the aggressive act resolves the delusional construction.

Thus the aggressive reaction is seriated in a continuous manner, from the sudden, unmotivated outburst of the act, through the whole gamut of belligerent forms, to the cold war of interpretative demonstrations, paralleled by imputations of noxiousness which, not to mention the obscure *kakon* to which the paranoid attributes his alienation from all living contact, rising in stages from a motivation based on the register of a highly primitive organicism (poison), to a magical one (evil spells), a telepathic one (influence), a lesional one (physical intrusion), an abusive one (distortion of intention), a dispossessive one (appropriation of secrets), a profanatory one (violation of intimacy), a juridical one (prejudice), a persecutive one (spying and intimidation), one involving prestige (defamation and attacks on one's honour), and revenge (damage and exploitation).

I have shown that in each case this series, in which we find all the successive envelopes of the biological and social status of the person, retains the original organization of the forms of the ego and of the object, which are also affected by this series in their structure, even to the spatial and temporal categories in which the ego and the object are constituted, experienced as events in a perspective of mirages, as affections with something stereotypical about them that suspends the workings of the ego/object dialectic.

Janet, who demonstrated so admirably the signification of feelings of persecution as phenomenological moments in social behaviour, did not explore their common character, which is precisely that they are constituted by a stagnation of one of these moments, similar in their strangeness to the faces of actors when a film is suddenly stopped in mid-action.

Now, this formal stagnation is akin to the most general structure of human knowledge: that which constitutes the ego and its objects with attributes of permanence, identity, and substantiality, in short, with entities or 'things' that are very different from the *Gestalten* that experience enables us to isolate in the shifting field, stretched in accordance with the lines of animal desire.

In fact, this formal fixation, which introduces a certain rupture of level, a certain discord between man's organization and his *Umwelt*, is the very condition that extends indefinitely his world and his power, by giving his objects their instrumental polyvalence and symbolic polyphony, and also their potential as defensive armour.

What I have called paranoic knowledge is shown, therefore, to correspond in its more or less archaic forms to certain critical moments that mark the history of man's mental genesis, each representing a stage in objectifying identification.

By simple observation we can obtain a glimpse of these different stages in the child's development. A Charlotte Bühler, an Elsa Köhler, and, following in their footsteps, the Chicago School have revealed several levels of significative manifestations; but only the analytic experience can give them their true value by making it possible to reintegrate the subjective relation into them.

The first level shows us that experience of oneself in the earliest stage of childhood develops, in so far as it refers to one's counterpart, from a situation experienced as undifferentiated. Thus about the age of eight months, we see in these confrontations between children (which, if they are to be fruitful, must be between children whose age differential is no more than two and a half months) those gestures of fictitious actions by which a subject reconducts the imperfect effort of the other's gesture by confusing their distinct application, those synchronies of spectacular captation that are all the more remarkable in that they precede the complete co-ordination of the motor apparatuses that they bring into play.

Thus the aggressivity that is manifested in the retaliations of taps and blows cannot be regarded solely as a playful manifestation of the exercise of strengths and their employment in the mapping of the body. It must be understood in an order of broader co-ordination: one that will subordinate the functions of tonic postures and vegetative tension to a social relativity – in this regard, one might mention Wallon's remarkable work, which has drawn our attention to the prevalence of such a social relativity in the expressive constitution of the human emotions.

Furthermore, I believed myself that I could show that on such occasions the child anticipates on the mental plane the conquest of the functional unity of his own body, which, at that stage, is still incomplete on the plane of voluntary motility.

What we have there is a first captation by the image in which the first stage of the dialectic of identifications can be discerned. It is linked to a *Gestalt* phenomenon, the child's very early perception of the human form, a form which, as we know, holds the child's interest in the first months of life, and even, in the case of the human face, from the tenth day. But what demonstrates the phenomenon of recognition, which involves subjectivity, are the signs of triumphant jubilation and playful discovery that characterize, from the sixth month, the child's encounter with his image in the mirror. This behaviour contrasts strikingly with the indifference shown even by animals that perceive this image, the chimpanzee, for example, when they have tested its objectal vanity, and it becomes even more apparent when one realizes that it occurs at an age when the child, as far as instrumental intelligence is concerned, is backward in relation to the chimpanzee, which he catches up with only at eleven months.

What I have called the *mirror stage* is interesting in that it manifests the affective dynamism by which the subject originally identifies himself with the visual *Gestalt* of his own body: in relation to the still very profound lack of co-ordination of his own motility, it represents an ideal unity, a salutary *imago*; it is invested with all the original distress resulting from the child's intra-organic and relational discordance during the first six months, when he bears the signs, neurological and humoral, of a physiological natal prematuration.

It is this captation by the *imago* of the human form, rather than an *Einfühlung* the absence of which is made abundantly clear in early infancy, which, between the ages of six months and two and a half years, dominates the entire dialectic of the child's behaviour in the presence of his similars. During the whole of this period, one will record the emotional reactions and the articulated evidences of a normal transitivism. The child who strikes another says that he has been struck; the child who sees another fall, cries. Similarly, it is by means of an identification with the other than he sees the whole gamut of reactions of bearing and display, whose structural ambivalence is clearly revealed in his behaviour, the slave being identified with the despot, the actor with the spectator, the seduced with the seducer.

There is a sort of structural crossroads here to which we must accommodate our thinking if we are to understand the nature of aggressivity in man and its relation with the formalism of his ego and his objects. It is in this erotic relation, in which the human individual fixes upon himself an image that alienates him from himself, that are to be found the energy and the form on which this organization of the passions that he will call his ego is based.

This form will crystallize in the subject's internal conflictual tension, which determines the awakening of his desire for the object of the other's desire: here the primordial coming together (*concours*) is precipitated into aggressive competitiveness (*concurrence*), from which develops the triad of others, the ego and the object, which, spanning the space of specular communion, is inscribed there according to a formalism proper to itself that so dominates the affective *Einfühlung* that a child of that age may mistake the identity of the most familiar people if they appear in an entirely different context.

But if the ego appears to be marked from its very origin by this aggressive relativity – in which minds lacking in objectivity might recognize the emotional erections caused in an animal solicited, incidentally, in the course of its experimental conditioning, by a desire – how can one not conceive that each great instinctual metamorphosis in the life of the individual will once again challenge its delimitation, composed as it is of a conjunction of the subject's history and the unthinkable innateness of his desire?

This is why, except at a limit that even the greatest geniuses have never been able to approach, man's ego can never be reduced to his experienced identity; and in the depressive disruptions of the experienced reverses of inferiority, it engenders essentially the mortal negations that fix it in its formalism. 'I am nothing of what happens to me. You are nothing of value.'

And the two moments, when the subject denies himself and when he charges the other, become confused, and one discovers in him that paranoiac structure of the ego that finds its analogue in the fundamental negations described by Freud as the three delusions of jealousy, erotomania, and interpretation. It is the especial delusion of the misanthropic '*belle âme*', throwing back on to the world the disorder of which his being is composed.

Subjective experience must be fully enabled to recognize the central nucleus of ambivalent aggressivity, which in the present stage of our culture is given to us under the dominant species of *resentment*, even in its earliest aspects in the child. Thus, because he lived at a similar time, without having to suffer from a behaviourist resistance in the sense that we ourselves do, St Augustin foreshadowed psychoanalysis when he expressed such behaviour in the following exemplary image: '*Vidi ego et expertus sum zelantem parvulum: nondum loquebatur et intuebatur pallidus amaro aspectu conlactaneum suum*' (I have seen with my own eyes and known very well an infant in the grip of jealousy: he could not yet speak, and already he observed his foster-brother, pale and with an envenomed stare). Thus, with the *infans* (pre-verbal) stage of early childhood, the situation of spectacular absorption is permanently tied: the child observed, the emotional reaction (pale), and this reactivation of images of primordial frustration (with an envenomed stare) that are the psychical and somatic co-ordinates of original aggressivity.

Only Melanie Klein, working on the child at the very limit of the appearance of language, dared to project subjective experience back to that earlier period when observation enables us nevertheless to affirm its dimension, in the simple fact for example that a child who does not speak reacts differently to punishment or brutality.

Through her we know the function of the imaginary primordial enclosure formed by the *imago* of the mother's body; through her we have the cartography, drawn by the children's own hands, of the mother's internal empire, the historical atlas of the intestinal divisions in which the *imagos* of the father and brothers (real or virtual), in which the voracious aggression of the subject himself, dispute their deleterious dominance over her sacred regions. We know, too, the persistence in the subject of this shadow of the *bad internal objects*, linked with some accidental *association* (to use a term that we should accept in the organic sense that it assumes in our experience, as opposed to the abstract sense that it retains in Humean ideology). Hence we can understand by what structural means the re-evocation of certain imaginary *personae*, the reproduction of certain situational inferiorities may *disconcert* in the most strictly predictable way the adult's voluntary functions: namely, their fragmenting effect on the *imago* of the original identification.

By showing us the primordiality of the 'depressive position', the extreme archaism of the subjectification of a *kakon*, Melanie Klein pushes back the limits within which we can see the subjective function of identification operate, and in particular enables us to situate as perfectly original the first formation of the superego.

But it is of particular importance to define the orbit within which, as far as our theoretical reflexion is concerned, are ordered the relations – by no means all elucidated – of guilt tension, oral noxiousness, hypochondriacal fixation, even that primordial masochism that we exclude from our field of study, in order to isolate the notion of an aggressivity linked to the narcissistic relation and to the structures of systematic *méconnaissance* and objectification that characterize the formation of the ego.

To the *Urbild* of this formation, alienating as it is by virtue of its capacity to render extraneous, corresponds a peculiar satisfaction deriving from the integration of an original organic disarray, a satisfaction that must be conceived in the dimension of a vital dehiscence that is constitutive of man, and which makes unthinkable the idea of an environment that is preformed for him, a 'negative' libido that enables the Heraclitean notion of Discord, which the Ephesian believed to be prior to harmony, to shine once more.

When speaking of the problem of repression, Freud asks himself where the ego obtains the energy it puts at the service of the 'reality principle' – we need look no further.

There can be no doubt that it derives from the 'narcissistic passion', if, that is, one conceives of the ego according to the subjective notion that I am proposing here, as conforming with the register of my experience.

The theoretical difficulties encountered by Freud seem to me in fact to derive from the mirage of objectification, inherited from classical psychology, constituted by the idea of the *perception/consciousness* system, in which Freud seems suddenly to fail to recognize the existence of everything that the ego neglects, scotomizes, misconstrues in the sensations that make it react to reality, everything that it ignores, exhausts, and binds in the significations that it receives from language: a surprising *méconnaissance* on the part of the man who succeeded by the power of his dialectic in forcing back the limits of the unconscious.

Just as the senseless oppression of the superego lies at the root of the motivated imperatives of conscience, the passionate desire peculiar to man to impress his image in reality is the obscure basis of the rational mediations of the will.

The notion of aggressivity as a correlative tension of the narcissistic structure in the coming-into-being (*devenir*) of the subject enables us to understand in a very simply formulated function all sorts of accidents and atypicalities in that coming-into-being.

I shall now say something about how I conceive of the dialectical relation with the function of the Oedipus complex. In its normal state, this complex is one of sublimation, which designates precisely an identificatory reshaping of the subject, and, as Freud wrote when he felt the need for a 'topographical' co-ordination of the psychical dynamisms, a *secondary identification* by introjection of the *imago* of the parent of the same sex.

The energy for that identification is provided by the first biological upsurge of genital libido. But it is clear that the structural effect of identification with the rival is not self-evident, except at the level of fable, and can only be conceived of if the way is prepared for it by a primary identification that structures the subject as a rival with himself. In fact, the note of biological impotence is met with again here, as is the effect of anticipation characteristic of the genesis of the human psyche, in the fixation of an imaginary 'ideal', which, as analysis has shown, decides the conformity of the 'instinct' to the physiological sex of the individual. A point, let it be said in passing, whose anthropological implications cannot be too highly stressed. What concerns us here is the function that I shall call the pacifying function of the ego ideal, the connexion between its libidinal normativity and a cultural normativity bound up from the dawn of history with the *imago* of the father. Here, obviously, lies the import that Freud's work, *Totem and Taboo*, still retains, despite the mythical circularity that vitiates it, in so far as it derives from the mythological event, the murder of the father, the subjective dimension that gives this event meaning, namely, guilt.

Freud shows us, in fact, that the need to participate, which neutralizes the conflict inscribed after the murder in the situation of rivalry between the brothers, is the basis of the identification with the paternal Totem. Thus the Oedipal identification is that by which the subject transcends the aggressivity that is constitutive of the primary subjective individuation. I have stressed elsewhere how it constitutes a step in the establishment of that distance by which, with feelings like respect, is realized a whole affective assumption of one's neighbour.

Only the antidialectical mentality of a culture which, in order to be dominated by objectifying ends, tends to reduce all subjective activity to the being of the ego, can justify the astonishment of a Van den Steinen when confronted by a Bororo who says: 'I'm an ara.' And all the sociologists of 'the primitive mind' busy themselves around this profession of identity, which, on reflexion, is no more surprising than declaring, 'I'm a doctor' or 'I'm a citizen of the French Republic', and which certainly presents fewer logical difficulties than the statement, 'I'm a man', which at most can mean no more than, 'I'm like he whom I recognize to be a man, and so recognize myself as being such.' In the last resort, these various formulas are to be understood only in reference to the truth of 'I is an other', an observation that is less astonishing to the intuition of the poet than obvious to the gaze of the psychoanalyst.

Who, if not us, will question once more the objective status of this 'I', which a historical evolution peculiar to our culture tends to confuse with the subject? This anomaly should be manifested in its particular effects on every level of language, and first and foremost in the grammatical subject of the first person in our languages, in the 'I love' that hypostatizes the tendency of a subject who denies it. An impossible mirage in linguistic forms among which the most ancient are to be found, and in which the subject appears fundamentally in the position of being determinant or instrumental of action.

Let us leave aside the critique of all the abuses of the *cogito ergo sum*, and recall that, in my experience, the ego represents the centre of all the *resistances* to the treatment of symptoms.

It was inevitable that analysis, after stressing the reintegration of the tendencies excluded by the ego, in so far as they are subjacent to the symptoms that it tackled in the first instance, and which were bound up for the most part with the *failures* of Oedipal identification, should eventually discover the 'moral' dimension of the problem.

And, in a parallel fashion, there came to the forefront the role played by the aggressive tendencies in the structure of the symptoms and of the personality, on the one hand, and, on the other, all sorts of conceptions that stressed the value of the liberated libido, one of the first of which can be attributed to French psychoanalysts under the register of *oblativity*.

It is clear, in effect, that genital libido operates as a supersession, indeed a blind supersession, of the individual in favour of the species, and that its sublimating effects in the Oedipal crisis lie at the origin of the whole process of the cultural subordination of man. Nevertheless, one cannot stress too strongly the irreducible character of the narcissistic structure, and the ambiguity of a notion that tends to ignore the constancy of aggressive tension in all moral life that involves subjection to this structure: in fact no notion of oblativity could produce altruism from that structure. And that is why La Rochefoucauld could formulate his maxim, in which his rigour matches the fundamental theme of this thought, on the incompatibility of marriage and sexual pleasure (*délices*).

We would allow the sharpness of our experience to become blunted if we deluded ourselves, if not our patients, into believing in some kind of pre-established harmony that would free of all aggressive induction in the subject the social conformisms made possible by the reduction of symptoms.

And the theoreticians of the Middle Ages showed another kind of penetration, by which the problem of love was discussed in terms of the two poles of a 'physical' theory and an 'ecstatic' theory, each involving the re-absorption of man's ego, whether by re-integration into a universal good, or by the effusion of the subject towards an object without alterity.

This narcissistic moment in the subject is to be found in all the genetic phases of the individual, in all the degrees of human accomplishment in the person, in an earlier stage in which it must assume a libidinal frustration and a later stage in which it is transcended in a normative sublimation.

This conception allows us to understand the aggressivity involved in the effects of all regression, all arrested development, all rejection of typical development in the subject, especially on the plane of sexual realization, and more specifically with each of the great phases that the libidinal transformations determine in human life, the crucial function of which has been demonstrated by analysis: weaning, the Oedipal stage, puberty, maturity, or motherhood, even the climacteric. And I have often said that the emphasis that was placed at first in psychoanalytic theory on the aggressive turning round of the Oedipal conflict upon the subject's own self was due to the fact that the effects of the complex were first perceived in *failures* to resolve it.

There is no need to emphasize that a coherent theory of the narcissistic phase clarifies the fact of the ambivalence proper to the 'partial drives' of scoptophilia, sadomasochism, and homosexuality, as well as the stereo-typed, ceremonial formalism of the aggressivity that is manifested in them: we are dealing here with the often very little 'realized' aspect of the apprehension of others in the practice of certain of these perversions, their *subjective* value, in actual fact very different from that given to them in the existential reconstructions, striking though they be, of a Sartre.

I should also like to mention in passing that the decisive function that we attribute to the *imago* of one's own body in the determination of the narcissistic phase enables us to understand the clinical relation between the congenital anomalies of functional lateralization (left-handedness) and all forms of inversion of sexual and cultural normalization. This reminds one of the role attributed to gymnastics in the 'beautiful and good' ideal of education among the Ancient Greeks and leads us to the social thesis with which I will conclude.

꘏꘏꘏꘏

Thesis V: *Such a notion of aggressivity as one of the intentional co-ordinates of the human ego, especially relative to the category of space, allows us to conceive of its role in modern neurosis and in the 'discontents' of civilization.*

All I wish to do here is to open up a perspective on to the verdicts that our experience allows us in the present social order. The pre-eminence of aggressivity in our civilization would be sufficiently demonstrated already by the fact that it is usually confused in 'normal' morality with the virtue of strength. Understood, and quite rightly, as significant of a development of the ego, its use is regarded as indispensable in society, and so widely accepted in moral practice that in order to appreciate its cultural peculi-arity one must penetrate into the effective meaning and virtues of a practice like that of *yang* in the public and private morality of the Chinese.

If necessary, the prestige of the idea of the struggle for life would be sufficiently attested by the success of a theory that could make our think-ing accept a selection based only on the animal's conquest of space as a valid explanation of the developments of life. Indeed, Darwin's success seems to derive from the fact that he projected the predations of Victorian society and the economic euphoria that sanctioned for that society the social devastation that it initiated on a planetary scale, and to the fact that it justified its predations by the image of a laissez-faire of the strongest predators in competition for their natural prey.

Before Darwin, however, Hegel had provided the ultimate theory of the proper function of aggressivity in human ontology, seeming to prophecy the iron law of our time. From the conflict of Master and Slave, he deduced the entire subjective and objective progress of our history, revealing in these crises the syntheses to be found in the highest forms of the status of the person in the West, from the Stoic to the Christian, and even to the future citizen of the Universal State.

Here the natural individual is regarded as nothingness, since the human subject is nothingness, in effect, before the absolute Master that is given to him in death. The satisfaction of human desire is possible only when mediated by the desire and the labour of the other. If, in the conflict of Master and Slave, it is the recognition of man by man that is involved, it is also promulgated on a radical negation of natural values, whether expressed in the sterile tyranny of the master or in the productive tyranny of labour.

We all know what an armature this profound doctrine has given to the constructive Spartacism of the Slave recreated by the barbarism of the Darwinian century.

The relativization of our sociology by the scientific collection of cultural forms that we are destroying in the world, and also the analyses, bearing genuinely psychoanalytic marks, in which the wisdom of a Plato shows us the dialectic common to the passions of the soul and the city, may enlighten us as to the reason for this barbarism. What we are faced with, to employ the jargon that corresponds to our approaches to man's subjective needs, is the increasing absence of all those saturations of the superego and ego ideal that are realized in all kinds of organic forms in traditional societies, forms that extend from the rituals of everyday intimacy to the periodical festivals in which the community manifests itself. We no longer know them except in their most obviously degraded aspects. Furthermore, in abolishing the cosmic polarity of the male and female principles, our society undergoes all the psychological effects proper to the modern phenomenon known as the 'battle between the sexes' – a vast community of such effects, at the limit between the 'democratic' anarchy of the passions and their desperate levelling down by the 'great winged hornet' of narcissistic tyranny. It is clear that the promotion of the ego today culminates, in conformity with the utilitarian conception of man that reinforces it, in an ever more advanced realization of man as individual, that is to say, in an isolation of the soul ever more akin to its original dereliction.

Correlatively, it seems, for reasons, I mean, whose historical contingency rests on a necessity that certain of our preoccupations make it possible to perceive, we are engaged in a technical enterprise at the species scale: the problem is knowing whether the Master/Slave conflict will find its resolution in the service of the machine, for which a psychotechnique that is already proving rich in ever more precise applications will be used to provide space-capsule pilots and space-station supervisors.

The notion of the role of spatial symmetry in man's narcissistic structure is essential in the establishment of the bases of a psychological analysis of space – however, I can do no more here than simply indicate the place of such an analysis. Let us say that animal psychology has shown us that the individual's relation to a particular spatial field is, in certain species, mapped socially, in a way that raises it to the category of subjective membership. I would say that it is the subjective possibility of the mirror projection of such a field into the field of the other that gives human space its originally 'geometrical' structure, a structure that I would be happy to call *kaleidoscopic*.

Such, at least, is the space in which the imagery of the ego develops, and which rejoins the objective space of reality. Yet does it offer us a place of rest? Already in the ever-contracting 'living space' in which human competition is becoming ever keener, a stellar observer of our species would conclude that we possessed needs to escape that had very strange results. But does not the conceptual area into which we thought we had reduced the real later refuse to lend its support to physicist thinking? Thus, by extending our grasp to the confines of matter, will not this 'realized' space, which makes the great imaginary spaces in which the free games of the ancient sages moved seem illusory to us, vanish in its turn in a roar of the universal ground?

Nevertheless, we know where our adaptation to these needs proceeds from, and that war is proving more and more to be the inevitable and necessary midwife of all progress in our organization. Certainly the mutual adaptation of adversaries, opposed in their social systems, seems to be progressing towards a competition of forms, but one may well wonder whether it is motivated by an acceptance of necessity, or by that identification of which Dante in the *Inferno* shows us the image in a fatal kiss.

In any case, it would not appear that the human individual, as material for such a struggle, is absolutely without defect. And the detection of 'internal bad objects', responsible for reactions (which may prove extremely costly in machinery) of inhibition and forward flight, a detection that has recently been put to use in the selection of shock troops, fighter forces, parachute and commando troops, proves that war, after teaching us a great deal about the genesis of the neuroses, is proving too demanding perhaps in the quest for ever more neutral subjects in an aggressivity where feeling is undesirable.

Nevertheless, we have a few psychological truths to contribute there too: namely the extent to which the so-called 'instinct of self-preservation' deflects into the vertigo of the domination of space, and above all the extent to which the fear of death, the 'absolute Master', presupposed in consciousness by a whole philosophical tradition from Hegel onwards, is psychologically subordinate to the narcissistic fear of damage to one's own body.

I believe that there is some point in stressing the relation existing between the dimension of space and a subjective tension, which in the 'discontents' (*malaise*) of civilization intersects with that of anxiety, approached so humanely by Freud, and which is developed in the temporal dimension. The temporal dimension, too, should enlighten us as to the contemporary significations of two philosophies that seem to correspond to those already referred to: that of Bergson, for its naturalistic inadequacy, and that of Kierkegaard for its dialectical signification.

Only at the intersection of these two tensions should one envisage that assumption by man of his original splitting (*déchirement*), by which it might be said that at every moment he constitutes his world by his suicide, and the psychological experience of which Freud had the audacity to formulate, however paradoxical its expression in biological terms, as the 'death instinct'.

In the 'emancipated' man of modern society, this splitting reveals, right down to the depths of his being, a neurosis of self-punishment, with the hysterico-hypochondriac symptoms of its functional inhibitions, with the psychasthenic forms of its derealizations of others and of the world, with its social consequences in failure and crime. It is this pitiful victim, this escaped, irresponsible outlaw, who is condemning modern man to the most formidable social hell, whom we meet when he comes to us; it is our daily task to open up to this being of nothingness the way of his meaning in a discreet fraternity – a task for which we are always too inadequate.

THREE

The function and field of speech and language in psychoanalysis

Report to the Rome Congress held at the Istituto
di Psicologia della Università di Roma
26 and 27 September 1953

❧❧❧❧

Preface

'In particular, it should not be forgotten that the division into embryology,
anatomy, physiology, psychology, sociology and clinical medicine does not
exist in nature and there is only one discipline: a *neurobiology* to which observation obliges us to add the epithet *human* when it concerns us.' (Quotation chosen
as an inscription on an Institute of Psychoanalysis in 1952)

Before proceeding to the report itself, something should be said of the
surrounding circumstances. For they had some effect on it.

The theme was suggested to the author as the basis of the customary
theoretical report for the annual meeting of the society, which, at that
time, represented psychoanalysis in France. For eighteen years, this
society had pursued what had become a venerable tradition under the
title 'Congrès des Psychanalystes de langue française', then, for two
years this congress had been extended to psychoanalysts speaking any
of the Romance languages (Holland being included out of linguistic
tolerance). The Congress in question took place in Rome in September.

Meanwhile, serious disagreements led to a secession in the French
group. These disagreements came to a head on the occasion of the foundation of an 'institute of psychoanalysis'. The group that had succeeded in
imposing its statutes and programme on the new institute was then heard
to declare that it would prevent the member who, with others, had tried
to introduce a different conception into the institute, from speaking at
Rome, and it tried every means in its power to do so.

Yet it did not seem to those who, as a result, had founded the new
Société française de Psychanalyse that they were under any obligation to
deprive the majority of the students, who had rallied to their teaching, of
the forthcoming event, or even to hold it elsewhere than in the eminent
place for which it had been planned.

The generous sympathy that had been shown them by the Italian group meant that they could hardly be regarded as unwelcome guests in the Universal City.

As far as I was concerned, I felt considerably emboldened, however unequal I proved to be to the task of speaking about speech, by a certain connivance inscribed in the place itself.

Indeed, I recalled that well before the glory of the world's most elevated throne had been established, Aulus Gellius, in his *Noctes Atticae* gave to the place called *Mons Vaticanus* the etymology *vagire*, which designates the first stammerings of speech.

If, then, my speech was to be nothing more than a *vagitus*, an infantile cry, at least it would be an auspicious moment to renovate the foundations that this discipline of speech derives from language.

Moreover, this renovation derived too much meaning from history for me to avoid breaking with the traditional style that places a 'report' somewhere between a compilation and a synthesis, and not give it the ironical style of a radical questioning of the foundations of that discipline.

Since my listeners were those same students who expect us to speak, it was above all for them that I fomented my speech, in order to renounce, for their sake, the rules that are observed between augers by which meticulousness of detail is passed off as rigour, and rule confused with certainty.

Indeed, in the conflict that led them to the present outcome, it was realized that their autonomy as subjects had been ignored to such an exhorbitant degree that the primary requirement sprang from a reaction against the permanent tone that had permitted this excess.

The fact is that a vice was revealed that went well beyond the local circumstances that triggered off this conflict. The mere fact that one could claim to regulate the training of psychoanalysts in so authoritarian a fashion posed the question as to whether the established modes of this training did not produce the paradoxical result of maintaining them perpetually as minors.

Certainly the highly organized initiatory forms which, for Freud, were a guarantee that his doctrine would be transmitted are justified in the situation of a discipline that can survive only by maintaining itself at the level of an integral experience.

But have these forms not led to a dispiriting formalism that discourages initiative by penalizing risk, and turns the reign of the opinion of the learned into a principle of docile prudence in which the authenticity of research is blunted before it finally dries up?

The extreme complexity of the notions we use has the effect that in no other field does a mind run a greater risk, in exposing his judgement, of discovering his true capacities.

But this ought to have the result of making our first, if not sole, concern the formulation of theses through the elucidation of principles.

The severe selection that is, indeed, necessary cannot be left to the endless postponements of a fastidious co-optation, but should be based on the fecundity of concrete production and the dialectical testing of contradictory views.

For me, this does not imply that any particular value is to be placed on divergence. On the contrary, we were not in the least surprised to hear at the London International Congress – where, because we had failed to follow the prescribed forms, we had come as beggars – a personality well disposed towards us, deplore the fact that we could not justify our secession on the grounds of some doctrinal disagreement. Does this mean that an association that is supposed to be international should have any other purpose than the maintenance of the principle of the community of our experience?

It is no doubt an open secret that it's a long time since this was the case, and it was with no sense of scandal that to the impenetrable M. Zilboorg, who, setting our case aside, insisted that no secession should be acceptable except on the basis of a scientific dispute, the penetrating M. Wälder could reply that if we were to confront the principles in which each of us believed his experience was based our walls would dissolve very quickly into the confusion of Babel.

Our own opinion is, that if we do innovate, nothing is to be gained by taking credit for it.

In a discipline that owes its scientific value solely to the theoretical concepts that Freud forged in the progress of his experience – concepts which, by continuing to be badly criticized and yet retaining the ambiguity of the vulgar tongue, benefit, with a certain risk of misunderstanding, from these resonances – it would seem to me to be premature to break with the tradition of their terminology.

But it seems to me that these terms can only become clear if one establishes their equivalence to the language of contemporary anthropology, or even to the latest problems in philosophy, fields in which psychoanalysis could well regain its health.

In any case, I consider it to be an urgent task to disengage from concepts that are being deadened by routine use the meaning that they regain both from a re-examination of their history and from a reflexion on their subjective foundations.

That, no doubt, is the teacher's prime function – the function from which all others proceed, and the one in which the price of experience is best inscribed.

If this function is neglected, meaning is obscured in an action whose effects are entirely dependent on meaning, and the rules of psychoanalytic technique, by being reduced to mere recipes, rob the analytic experience of any status as knowledge and even of any criterion of reality.

For nobody is less demanding than a psychoanalyst as to what provides the status of his action, which he himself is not far from regarding as magical. This is because he is incapable of situating it in a conception of his field that he would not dream of according to his practice.

The epigraph with which I have adorned this preface is a rath r fine example.

Indeed, it accords with a view of analytic training rather like that of a driving-school which, not content with claiming the unique privilege of issuing the driving licence, also imagines that it is in a position to supervise the making of the car.

This comparison may or may not be valid, but it is as valid as those current in our most serious conventicles, which, because they originated in my address to the fools, do not even have the savour of a practical joke perpetrated by initiates, but seem none the less to be given currency by virtue of their pompous ineptitude.

They begin with the well-known comparison between the candidate who allows himself to get involved at too early a stage in practice and the surgeon who operates without sterilization, and they go on to the tear-jerking comparison between those unfortunate students divided in their loyalties to disputing masters and children caught up in their parents' divorce.

No doubt this latest born comparison seems to me to be inspired by the respect due to those who have indeed been subjected to what, moderating my thought, I will call a pressure to teach, which has put them severely to the test, but one may also wonder on hearing the tremulous tones of the masters whether the bounds of childishness have not, without warning, been pushed back to the point of foolishness.

Yet the truths contained in these clichés are worthy of more serious examination.

As a method based on truth and the demystification of subjective camouflages, does psychoanalysis display an excessive ambition to apply its principles to its own corporation: that is, to psychoanalysts' views of their role in relation to the patient, their place in intellectual society, their relations with their peers and their educational mission?

Perhaps, by reopening a few windows to the daylight of Freud's thought, this report will allay the anguish that some people feel when a symbolic action becomes lost in its own opacity.

However, in referring to the circumstances surrounding this speech, I am not trying to blame its all too obvious inadequacies on the haste with which it was composed, since its meaning, as well as its form, derives from that same haste.

Moreover, I have shown, in an exemplary sophism of intersubjective time, the function of haste in logical precipitation, where truth finds its unsupersedable condition.

Nothing is created without a sense of urgency; urgency always produces its supersession in speech.

But nor is there anything that does not become contingent when the moment for it comes to man, when he can identify in a single reason the course he chooses and the disorder he denounces, in order to understand its coherence in the real and anticipate by his certainty the action that weighs them against one another.

⸙⸙⸙⸙

Introduction

'We are going to determine that while we are still at the aphelion of our matter, for, when we arrive at the perihelion, the heat will be capable of making us forget it.'

(Lichtenberg)

' "Flesh composed of suns. How can such be?" exclaim the simple ones.'
(R. Browning, *Parleying with certain people*)

Such is the fright that seizes man when he unveils the face of his power that he turns away from it even in the very act of laying its features bare. So it has been with psychoanalysis. Freud's truly Promethean discovery was such an act, as his works bear witness; but that discovery is no less present in each humble psychoanalytic experience conducted by any one of the labourers formed in his school.

One can trace over the years this decline of interest in the functions of speech and in the field of language. This decline is responsible for the 'alterations in aim and technique' that are now acknowledged within the psychoanalytic movement, and whose relation to the general lessening of therapeutic effectiveness is nevertheless ambiguous. In fact the emphasis on the resistance of the object in current psychoanalytic theory and technique must itself be subjected to the dialectic of analysis, which cannot fail to recognize in this emphasis an alibi of the subject.

Let us try to outline the topography of this shift of emphasis. If we examine the literature that we call our 'scientific activity', the present problems of psychoanalysis fall clearly under three headings:

(a) The function of the imaginary, as I shall call it, or, to put it more simply, that of phantasies in the technique of the psychoanalytic experience and in the constitution of the object at the various stages of psychical development. The original impetus in this area came from the analysis of children, and from the fertile and tempting field offered to the attempts of researchers by access to the formation of structures at the preverbal level. It is there, too, that the culmination of this impetus is now inducing a return in the same direction by posing the problem of what symbolic status is to be given to phantasies in their interpretation.

(b) The concept of the libidinal object relations which, by renewing the idea of the progress of the treatment, is quietly altering the way in which it is conducted. Here the new perspective took its departure from the extension of the psychoanalytic method to the psychoses and from the momentary opening up of the psychoanalytic technique to data based on different principles. At this point psychoanalysis merges with an existential phenomenology – one might say, with an activism animated by charity. There again, a clear-cut reaction is taking place in favour of a return to the technical pivot of symbolization.

(c) The importance of the counter-transference and, correlatively, of the training of the analyst. Here the emphasis has resulted from the difficulties arising in the termination of the treatment, together with those that occur when the training analysis results in the introduction of the candidate into the practice of analysis. And the same oscillation can be observed in each case. On the one hand, the being of the analyst is shown, not without courage, to be a by no means negligible factor in the results of the analysis – and even a factor in the effects of the analysis that should, towards the end, be brought out into the open. On the other hand, it is put forward no less forcefully that no solution is possible except by an ever more thorough exploration of the mainsprings of the unconscious.

Besides the pioneer activity that they are manifesting on three different frontiers, these three problems have one thing in common with the vitality of the psychoanalytic experience that sustains them. This is the temptation for the analyst to abandon the foundation of speech, and this precisely in areas where, because they border on the ineffable, its use would seem to require a more than usually close examination: that is to say, childhood training by the mother, Samaritan-type aid, and dialectical mastery. The danger indeed becomes great if, on top of this, he abandons his own language in favour of others already established about whose compensations for ignorance he knows very little.

We would truly like to know more about the effects of symbolization in the child, and psychoanalysts who are also mothers, even those who give our loftiest deliberations a matriarchal air, are not exempt from that confusion of tongues by which Ferenczi designated the law of the relationship between the child and the adult.[1]

Our wise men's ideas about the perfect object relation are somewhat uncertainly conceived, and, when expounded, they reveal a mediocrity that does the profession no honour.

There can be little doubt that these effects – where the psychoanalyst resembles the type of modern hero famous for his vain exploits in situations entirely beyond his control – could be corrected by a proper return to a field in which the analyst ought to be past master: the study of the functions of speech.

But, since Freud, it seems that this central field of our domain has been left fallow. Note how he himself refrained from venturing too far into its outlying parts: he discovered the libidinal stages of the child through the analysis of adults and intervened in little Hans's case only through the mediation of his parents. He deciphered a whole section of the language of the unconscious in paranoid delusion, but used for this purpose only the key text that Schreber left behind in the volcanic debris of his spiritual catastrophe. On the other hand, however, he rose to a position of complete mastery as far as the dialectic of this work and the traditional view of its meaning were concerned.

Does this amount to saying that if the master's place remains empty, it is not so much the result of his own passing as that of an increasing obliteration of the meaning of his work? To convince ourselves of this, we have surely only to ascertain what is going on in the place he vacated.

A technique is being handed on in a cheerless manner, reticent to the point of opacity, a manner that seems terrified of any attempt to let in the fresh air of criticism. It has in fact assumed the air of a formalism pushed to such ceremonial lengths that one might well wonder whether it does not bear the same similarity to obsessional neurosis that Freud so convincingly defined in the observance, if not in the genesis, of religious rites.

When we consider the literature that this activity produces to feed on, the analogy becomes even more marked: the impression is often that of a curious sort of closed circuit in which the *méconnaissance* of the origin of the terms produces the problem of making them agree with each other, and in which the effort to solve this problem reinforces the original *méconnaissance*.

In order to get to the causes of this deterioration of analytic discourse, one may legitimately apply the psychoanalytic method to the collectivity that embodies it.

Indeed, to speak of a loss of the meaning of psychoanalytic action is as true and as pointless as to explain the symptom by its meaning so long as that meaning is not recognized. We know that in the absence of such a recognition, the action of the analyst will be experienced only as an aggressive action at the level at which it occurs, and that in the absence of the social 'resistances' in which the psychoanalytic group used to find reassurance, the limits of its tolerance towards its own activity – now 'acknowledged', if not actually approved of – no longer depend upon anything more than the numerical strength by which its presence is measured on the social scale.

These principles are adequate in the distribution of the symbolic, imaginary, and real conditions that will determine the defence mechanisms we can recognize in the doctrine – isolation, undoing what has been done, negation and, in general, *méconnaissance*.

Thus, if the importance of the American group in relation to the psychoanalytic movement as a whole is measured by its mass, it will be easy enough to weigh accurately the conditions to be met with there.

In the symbolic order first of all, one cannot neglect the importance of the *c* factor, which I noted at the Congress of Psychiatry in 1950 as being the constant characteristic of any given cultural milieu: the condition here of the ahistoricism, which, by common accord, is recognized as being the principal feature of 'communication' in the United States, and which, in my opinion, is at the antipodes of the psychoanalytic

experience. To this must be added a native mental form, known as be-
haviourism, which so dominates the notion of psychology in America
that it has now completely obscured the inspiration of Freud in psychoanalysis itself.

As for the other two orders, we leave to those concerned the task of
assessing what the mechanisms that manifest themselves in the life of the
psychoanalytic societies owe, respectively, to the relative eminence of
those within the group, and to the experienced effects of their free enterprise on the whole of the social body – as well as the value to be placed
on a notion emphasized by one of their most lucid representatives, namely,
the convergence that can be observed between the foreignness of a group
dominated by the immigrant, and the distancing into which it is drawn
by the function demanded by the cultural conditions indicated above.

In any case it appears incontestable that the conception of psychoanalysis in the United States has inclined towards the adaptation of the
individual to the social environment, towards the quest for behaviour
patterns, and towards all the objectification implied in the notion of
'human relations'.[2] And the indigenous term 'human engineering'[2]
strongly implies a privileged position of exclusion in relation to the human
object.

Indeed, the eclipse in psychoanalysis of the most living terms of its
experience – the unconscious and sexuality, which apparently will cease
before long even to be mentioned – may be attributed to the distance
from the human object without which such a position could not be held.

We do not have to take sides over the doctrinaire and commercial
mentalities, both of which have been noted and denounced in the official
writings of the analytic group itself. The Pharisee and the shopkeeper
interest us only because of their common essence, the source of the
difficulties that both have with speech, particularly when it comes to
'talking shop'.[2]

The fact is that although the incommunicability of motives may sustain a master, it is not on a par with true mastery – that at least which the
teaching of psychoanalysis requires. This became all the more obvious
when, not long ago, in order to sustain his primacy, a master felt impelled,
if only for the sake of appearances, to give at least one lesson.

This is why the attachment to the traditional technique, unshakably re-
affirmed from the same quarters, after a consideration of the results of
the work on the frontier lines enumerated above, is not without equivocation; this equivocation is to be measured by the substitution of the term

'classic' for 'orthodox' in describing this technique. One remains loyal to tradition because one has nothing to say about the doctrine itself.

As far as I am concerned, I would assert that the technique cannot be understood, nor therefore correctly applied, if the concepts on which it is based are ignored. It is our task to demonstrate that these concepts take on their full meaning only when orientated in a field of language, only when ordered in relation to the function of speech.

At this point I must note that in order to handle any Freudian concept, reading Freud cannot be considered superfluous, even for those concepts that are homonyms of current notions. This has been well demonstrated, I am opportunely reminded, by the misadventure that befell a theory of the instincts in a revision of Freud's position by an author somewhat less than alert to its explicitly stated mythical content. Obviously he could hardly be aware of it, since he tackles the theory through the work of Marie Bonaparte, which he repeatedly cites as an equivalent of the text of Freud – without the reader being in any way advised of the fact – relying no doubt on the good taste of the reader, not without reason, not to confuse the two, but proving no less that he has not the remotest understanding of the true level of the secondary text. As a result, from reductions to deductions, and from inductions to hypotheses, the author comes to his conclusion by way of the strict tautology of his false premises: namely, that the instincts in question are reducible to the reflex arc. Like the pile of plates whose collapse is the main attraction of the classic music hall turn – leaving nothing in the hands of the performer but a couple of ill-assorted fragments – the complex construction that moves from the discovery of the migrations of the libido in the erogenous zones to the metapsychological passage from a generalized pleasure principle to the death instinct becomes the binomial dualism of a passive erotic instinct, modelled on the activity of the lice seekers so dear to the poet,[3] and a destructive instinct, identified simply with motility. A result that merits an honourable mention for the art, intentional or otherwise, of carrying a misunderstanding to its ultimate logical conclusions.

I *Empty speech and full speech in the psychoanalytic realization of the subject*

Donne en ma bouche parole vraie et estable et fay de moy langue caulte.
(*L'Internele Consolacion*, XLVᵉ Chapitre:
'qu'on ne doit pas chascun croire et du legier
trebuchement de paroles.'[4]

Cause toujours.
(Motto of causalist thought)[5]

Whether it sees itself as an instrument of healing, of training, or of exploration in depth, psychoanalysis has only a single medium: the patient's speech. That this is self-evident is no excuse for our neglecting it. And all speech calls for a reply.

I shall show that there is no speech without a reply, even if it is met only with silence, provided that it has an auditor: this is the heart of its function in analysis.

But if the psychoanalyst is not aware that this is how the function of speech operates, he will simply experience its appeal all the more strongly, and if the first thing to make itself heard is the void, it is within himself that he will experience it, and it is beyond speech that he will seek a reality to fill this void.

Thus it is that he will come to analyse the subject's behaviour in order to find in it what the subject is not saying. Yet in order to obtain an avowal of what he finds, he must nevertheless talk about it. He then resorts once again to speech, but that speech is now rendered suspect by having replied only to the failure of his silence, in the fact of the echo perceived from his own nothingness.

But what in fact was this appeal from the subject beyond the void of his speech? It was an appeal to the very principle of truth, through which other appeals resulting from humbler needs will vacillate. But first and foremost it was the appeal of the void, in the ambiguous gap of an attempted seduction of the other by the means on which the subject has come compliantly to rely, and to which he will commit the monumental construct of his narcissism.

'That's it all right, introspection!' exclaims the *prud'homme* who knows its dangers only too well. He is certainly not the last, he admits, to have tasted its charms, if he has exhausted its profit. Too bad that he hasn't more time to waste. For you would hear some fine profundities from him were he to arrive on your couch.

It is strange that an analyst, for whom this sort of person is one of the first encounters in his experience, should still take introspection into account in psychoanalysis. For from the moment that the wager is taken up, all those fine things that one thought one had in reserve disappear from view. If he does engage in it, they will appear of little account, but others present themselves sufficiently unexpected by our friend to seem ridiculous to him and to silence him for a while. The common lot.[6]

He then grasps the difference between the mirage of the monologue whose accommodating fancies once animated his outpourings, and the forced labour of this discourse without escape, on which the psychologist (not without humour) and the therapist (not without cunning) have bestowed the name of 'free association'.

For free association really is a labour – so much so that some have gone so far as to say that it requires an apprenticeship, even to the point of seeing in such an apprenticeship its true formative value. But if viewed in this way, what does it form but a skilled craftsman?

Well, then, what of this labour? Let us consider its conditions and its fruit, in the hope of throwing more light on its aim and profit.

The aptness of the German word *durcharbeiten* – equivalent to the English 'working through' – has been recognized in passing. It has been the despair of French translators, in spite of what the immortal words of a master of French style offered them by way of an exercise in exhausting every last drop of sense: '*Cent fois sur le métier, remettez . . .*'[7] – but how does the work (*l'ouvrage*) make any progress here?

The theory reminds us of the triad: frustration, aggressivity, regression. This is an explanation so apparently comprehensible that we may well be spared the need to understand it. Intuition is prompt, but we should be all the more suspicious of the self-evident that has become an *idée reçue*. If analysis should come round to exposing its weakness, it will be advisable not to rest content with recourse to affectivity – that taboo-word of dialectical incapacity which, with the verb to *intellectualize* (whose pejorative acceptation makes a merit of this incapacity), will go down in the history of the language as the stigmata of our obtuseness regarding the subject.[8]

Shall we ask instead where the subject's frustration comes from? Does it come from the silence of the analyst? A reply to the subject's empty speech, even – or especially – an approving one, often shows by its effects that it is much more frustrating than silence. Is it not rather a matter of a frustration inherent in the very discourse of the subject?

Does the subject not become engaged in an ever-growing dispossession of that being of his, concerning which – by dint of sincere portraits which leave its idea no less incoherent, of rectifications that do not succeed in freeing its essence, of stays and defences that do not prevent his statue from tottering, of narcissistic embraces that become like a puff of air in animating it – he ends up by recognizing that this being has never been anything more than his construct in the imaginary and that this construct disappoints all his certainties? For in this labour which he undertakes to reconstruct *for another*, he rediscovers the fundamental alienation that made him construct it *like another*, and which has always destined it to be taken from him *by another*.[9]

This ego, whose strength our theorists now define by its capacity to bear frustration, is frustration in its essence.[10] Not frustration of a desire of the subject, but frustration by an object in which his desire is alienated and which the more it is elaborated, the more profound the alienation from his *jouissance* becomes for the subject. Frustration at a second remove, therefore, and such that even if the subject were to reintroduce its form into his discourse to the point of reconstituting the passifying image through which the subject makes himself an object by displaying himself before the mirror, he could not be satisfied with it, since even if he achieved his most perfect likeness in that image, it would still be the *jouissance* of the other that he would cause to be recognized in it. This is why there is no adequate reply to this discourse, for the subject will regard as contempt anything that is said about his misapprehension.

The aggressivity experienced by the subject at this point has nothing to do with the animal aggressivity of frustrated desire. This assumption, which seems to satisfy most people, actually masks another that is less agreeable for each and every one of us: the aggressivity of the slave whose response to the frustration of his labour is a desire for death.

It is therefore readily conceivable how this aggressivity may respond to any intervention which, by denouncing the imaginary intentions of the discourse, dismantles the object constructed by the subject to satisfy them. This is in effect what is called the analysis of resistances, the dangerous aspect of which is immediately apparent. It is already indicated by the existence of the simple-minded analyst who has never seen revealed anything but the aggressive signification of his subjects' phantasies.[11]

Such an individual who, not hestitating to plead for a 'causalist' analysis that would aim to transform the subject in his present by learned explanations of his past, betrays well enough by his very intonation the anxiety that he wishes to spare himself – the anxiety of having to think that his patient's freedom may be dependent upon that of his own intervention. Whether or not the expedient into which he plunges may possibly be beneficial at some moment or other to the subject, this has no more importance than a stimulating pleasantry and will not detain me any longer.

Rather let us focus on this hic et nunc to which some analysts feel we should confine the handling of the analysis. It may indeed be useful, provided the imaginary intention that the analyst uncovers in it is not detached by him from the symbolic relation in which it is expressed. Nothing must be read into it concerning the ego of the subject that cannot be reassumed by him in the form of the 'I', that is, in the first person.

'I have been this only in order to become what I can be': if this were not the permanent high point of the subject's assumption of his own mirages, in what sense would this constitute progress?

From this point on, the analyst cannot without peril track the subject down into the intimacy of his gestures, nor even into that of his static state, except by reintegrating them as silent parts into his narcissistic discourse – and this has been noted very sensitively, even by young practitioners.

The danger involved here is not that of the subject's negative reaction, but rather that of his capture in an objectification – no less imaginary than before – of his static state or of his 'statue', in a renewed status of his alienation.

Quite the contrary, the art of the analyst must be to suspend the subject's certainties until their last mirages have been consumed. And it is in the discourse that the progress of their resolution must be marked.

Indeed, however empty this discourse may seem, it is so only if taken at its face value: that which justifies the remark of Mallarmé's, in which he compares the common use of language to the exchange of a coin whose obverse and reverse no longer bear any but effaced figures, and which people pass from hand to hand 'in silence'. This metaphor is enough to remind us that speech, even when almost completely worn out, retains its value as a *tessera*.[12]

Even if it communicates nothing, the discourse represents the existence of communication; even if it denies the evidence, it affirms that speech constitutes truth; even if it is intended to deceive, the discourse speculates on faith in testimony.

Moreover, it is the psychoanalyst who knows better than anyone else that the question is to understand which 'part' of this discourse carries the significative term, and this is, ideally, just how he proceeds: he takes the description of an everyday event for a fable addressed to whoever hath ears to hear, a long tirade for a direct interjection, or on the other hand a simple *lapsus* for a highly complex statement, or even the sigh of a momentary silence for the whole lyrical development it replaces.

It is, therefore, a beneficent punctuation, one which confers its meaning on the subject's discourse. This is why the adjournment of a session – which according to present-day technique is simply a chronometric break and, as such, a matter of indifference to the thread of the discourse – plays the part of a metric beat which has the full value of an actual intervention by the analyst for hastening the concluding moments. This fact should lead us to free this act of termination from its routine usage and to employ it for the purposes of the technique in every useful way possible.

It is in this way that regression is able to operate. Regression is simply the actualization in the discourse of the phantasy relations reconstituted by an *ego* at each stage in the decomposition of its structure. After all, this regression is not real; even in language it manifests itself only by inflections, by turns of phrase, by '*trébuchements si légiers*' that in the extreme case they cannot go beyond the artifice of 'baby talk' in the adult. To impute to regression the reality of an actual relation to the object amounts to projecting the subject into an alienating illusion that does no more than echo an alibi of the psychoanalyst.

It is for this reason that nothing could be more misleading for the analyst than to seek to guide himself by some supposed 'contact' experienced with the reality of the subject. This cream puff of intuitionist and even phenomenological psychology has become extended in contemporary usage in a way that is thoroughly symptomatic of the rarefaction of the effects of speech in the present social context. But its obsessional power becomes flagrantly obvious when put forward in a relation which, by its very rules, excludes all real contact.

Young analysts, who might nevertheless allow themselves to be taken in by the impenetrable gifts that such a recourse implies, will find no better way of retracing their steps than to consider the successful outcome of the actual supervision they themselves undergo. From the point of view of contact with the real, the very possibility of such supervision would become a problem. In fact the contrary is the case: here the supervisor manifests a second sight, make no mistake about it, which makes the experience at least as instructive for him as for the person supervised. And this is almost all the more so because the person under his supervision demonstrates in the process fewer of these gifts, which are held by some people to be all the less communicable in proportion as they themselves draw attention to their technical secrets.

The reason for this enigma is that the supervised person acts as a filter, or even as a refractor, of the subject's discourse, and in this way there is presented to the supervisor a ready-made stereograph, making clear from the start the three or four registers on which the muscial score constituted by the subject's discourse can be read.

If the supervised person could be put by the supervisor into a subjective position different from that implied by the sinister term *contrôle* (advantageously replaced, but only in English, by 'supervision'), the greatest profit he would derive from this exercise would be to learn to maintain himself in the position of second subjectivity into which the situation automatically puts the supervisor.

There he would find the authentic way to reach what the classic formula of the analyst's vague, even absent-minded, attention expresses only very approximately. For it is essential to know towards what that attention is directed; and, as all our labours show, it is certainly not directed towards an object beyond the subject's speech in the way it is for certain analysts who make it a strict rule never to lose sight of that object. If this were to be the way of analysis, then it would surely have recourse to other means – otherwise it would be the only example of a method that forbade itself the means necessary to its own ends.

The only object that is within the analyst's reach is the imaginary relation that links him to the subject *qua* ego. And although he cannot eliminate it, he can use it to regulate the yield of his ears, which is normal practice, according to both physiology and the Gospels: having ears *in order not to hear*, in other words, in order to pick up what is to be heard. For he has no other ears, no third or fourth ear to serve as what some have tried to describe as a direct transaudition of the unconscious by the unconscious.[13] I shall deal with the question of this supposed mode of communication later.

I have tackled the function of speech in analysis from its least rewarding angle, that of 'empty' speech, where the subject seems to be talking in vain about someone who, even if he were his spitting image, can never become one with the assumption of his desire. I have pointed out the source of the growing devaluation of which speech has been the object in both theory and technique. I have had to raise by slow degrees, as if they were a heavy millstone that had fallen on speech, what can serve only as a sort of steering-wheel for the movement of analysis: that is to say, the individual psycho-physiological factors that, in reality, are excluded from its dialectic. To regard the goal of psychoanalysis to be to modify the individual inertia of these factors is to be condemned to a fiction of movement with which a certain trend in psychoanalytic technique seems in fact to be satisfied.

If we now turn to the other extreme of the psychoanalytic experience – its history, its argumentation, the process of the treatment – we shall find that to the analysis of the here and now is to be opposed the value of anamnesis as the index and source of therapeutic progesss; that to obsessional intrasubjectivity is to be opposed hysterical intersubjectivity; and that to the analysis of resistance is to be opposed symbolic interpretation. The realization of full speech begins here.

Let us examine the relation constituted by this realization.

It will be recalled that shortly after its birth the method introduced by Breuer and Freud was baptized by one of Breuer's patients, Anna O., the 'talking cure'. It was the experience inaugurated with this hysterical patient that led them to the discovery of the pathogenic event dubbed the traumatic experience.

If this event was recognized as being the cause of the symptom, it was because the putting into words of the event (in the patient's 'stories') determined the lifting of the symptom. Here the term *'prise de conscience'*, borrowed from the psychological theory that was constructed on this fact, retains a prestige that merits a healthy distrust of explanations that do office as self-evident truths. The psychological prejudices of Freud's day were opposed to acknowledging in verbalization as such any reality other than its own *flatus vocis*. The fact remains that in the hypnotic state verbalization is dissociated from the *prise de conscience*, and this fact alone is enough to require a revision of that conception of its effects.

But why is it that the doughty advocates of the behaviourist *Aufhebung* do not use this as their example to show that they do not have to know whether the subject has remembered anything whatever from the past? He has simply recounted the event. But I would say that he has verbalized it – or, to develop a term whose echoes in French call to mind a Pandora figure other than the one with the box (in which the term should probably be locked up for good),[14] that he has made it pass into the *verbe*,[15] or, more precisely, into the *epos*[16] by which he brings back into present time the origins of his own person. And he does this in a language that allows his discourse to be understood by his contemporaries, and which furthermore presupposes their present discourse. Thus it happens that the recitation of the *epos* may include a discourse of earlier days in its own archaic, even foreign language, or may even pursue its course in present time with all the animation of the actor; but it is like an indirect discourse, isolated in quotation marks within the thread of the narration, and, if the discourse is played out, it is on a stage implying the presence not only of the chorus, but also of spectators.

Hypnotic recollection is, no doubt, a reproduction of the past, but it is above all a spoken representation – and as such implies all sorts of presences. It stands in the same relation to the waking recollection of what is curiously called in analysis 'the material', as the drama in which the original myths of the City State are produced before its assembled citizens stands in relation to a history that may well be made up of materials, but in which a nation today learns to read the symbols of a destiny on the march. In Heideggerian language one could say that both types of re-collection constitute the subject as *gewesend* – that is to say, as being the one who thus has been. But in the internal unity of this temporalization, the existent marks the convergence of the having-beens. That is to say, other encounters being assumed to have taken place since any one of these moments having been, there would have issued from it another existent that would cause him to have been quite otherwise.

The ambiguity of the hysterical revelation of the past is due not so much to the vacillation of its content between the imaginary and the real, for it is situated in both. Nor is it because it is made up of lies. The reason is that it presents us with the birth of truth in speech, and thereby brings us up against the reality of what is neither true nor false. At any rate, that is the most disquieting aspect of the problem.

For it is present speech that bears witness to the truth of this revelation in present reality, and which grounds it in the name of that reality. Yet in that reality, only speech bears witness to that portion of the powers of the past that has been thrust aside at each crossroads where the event has made its choice.

This is why the condition of continuity in anamnesis, by which Freud measures the completeness of the cure, has nothing to do with the Berg-sonian myth of a restoration of duration in which the authenticity of each instant would be destroyed if it did not sum up the modulation of all the preceding ones. The point is that for Freud it is not a question of biological memory, nor of its intuitionist mystification, nor of the paramnesis of the symptom, but a question of recollection, that is, of history, balancing the scales, in which conjectures about the past are balanced against promises of the future, upon the single knife-edge or fulcrum of chronological certainties. I might as well be categorical: in psychoanalytic anamnesis, it is not a question of reality, but of truth, because the effect of full speech is to reorder past contingences by conferring on them the sense of necessities to come, such as they are constituted by the little freedom through which the subject makes them present.

The meanders of the research pursued by Freud into the case of the Wolf Man confirm these remarks by deriving their full meaning from them.

Freud demands a total objectification of proof so long as it is a question of dating the primal scene, but he no more than presupposes all the resubjectifications of the event that seem to him to be necessary to explain its effects at each turning-point where the subject restructures himself – that is, as many restructurings of the event as take place, as he puts it, *nachträglich*, at a later date.[17] What is more, with an audacity bordering on offhandedness, he asserts that he holds it legitimate in the analysis of processes to elide the time intervals in which the event remains latent in the subject.[18] That is to say, he annuls the *times for understanding* in favour of the *moments of concluding* which precipitate the meditation of the subject towards deciding the meaning to attach to the original event.

Let it be noted that *time for understanding* and *moment of concluding* are functions that I have defined in a purely logical theorem and which are familiar to my students as having proved extremely favourable to the dialectical analysis through which we guide their steps in the process of a psychoanalysis.

It is certainly this assumption of his history by the subject, in so far as it is constituted by the speech addressed to the other, that constitutes the ground of the new method that Freud called psychoanalysis, not in 1904 – as was taught until recently by an authority who, when he finally threw off the cloak of prudent silence, appeared on that day to know nothing of Freud except the titles of his works – but in 1895.[19]

In this analysis of the meaning of his method, I do not deny, any more than Freud himself did, the psycho-physiological discontinuity manifested by the states in which the hysterical symptom appears, nor do I deny that this symptom may be treated by methods – hypnosis or even narcosis –

that reproduce the discontinuity of these states. I simply repudiate any reliance on these states – and as deliberately as Freud forbade himself recourse to them after a certain time – whether to explain the symptom or to cure it.

For if the originality of the analytic method depends on means that it must forego, it is because the means that it reserves to itself are enough to constitute a domain whose limits define the relativity of its operations.

Its means are those of speech, in so far as speech confers a meaning on the functions of the individual; its domain is that of concrete discourse, in so far as this is the field of the transindividual reality of the subject; its operations are those of history, in so far as history constitutes the emergence of truth in the real.

To begin with, in fact, when the subject begins analysis he accepts a position more constituting in itself than all the duties by which he allows himself to be more or less enticed: that of interlocution, and I see no objection in the fact that this remark may leave the listener nonplussed.[20] For I shall take this opportunity of stressing that the allocution of the subject entails an allocutor[21] – in other words, that the locutor[22] is constituted in it as intersubjectivity.

Secondly, it is on the basis of this interlocution, in so far as it includes the response of the interlocutor, that the meaning of what Freud insists on as the restoration of continuity in the subject's motivations becomes clear. An operational examination of this objective shows us in effect that it can be satisfied only in the intersubjective continuity of the discourse in which the subject's history is constituted.

In this way, the subject may vaticinate on his history under the influence of one or other of those drugs that anaesthetize the consciousness and which have been christened in our day 'truth serums' – an unwitting *contresens* that reveals all the irony inherent in language. But precisely because it comes to him through an alienated form, even a retransmission of his own recorded discourse, be it from the mouth of his own doctor, cannot have the same effects as psychoanalytic interlocution.

It is therefore in the position of a third term that the Freudian discovery of the unconscious becomes clear as to its true grounding. This discovery may be simply formulated in the following terms:

The unconscious is that part of the concrete discourse, in so far as it is transindividual, that is not at the disposal of the subject in re-establishing the continuity of his conscious discourse.

This disposes of the paradox presented by the concept of the un-conscious if it is related to an individual reality. For to reduce this con-cept to unconscious tendencies is to resolve the paradox only by ignoring the experience that shows clearly that the unconscious participates in the functions of the idea, and even of thought – as Freud plainly insisted when, unable to avoid a conjunction of contrary terms in the term 'un-conscious thought', he bestowed on it the sacramental invocation: *sit venia verbo*.[23] In any case we obey him by throwing the blame, in effect, on the *verbum*, but on that *verbum* that is realized in the discourse that runs from mouth to mouth – like the hidden object in hunt-the-slipper – so as to confer on the act of the subject who receives its message the sense that makes of this act an act of his history, and which confers on him his truth.

Hence the objection that is raised against the notion of unconscious thought as a contradiction in terms by a psychology inadequately grounded in its logic, collapses when confronted by the very distinction of the psychoanalytic domain, in so far as this domain reveals the reality of the discourse in its autonomy. And the psychoanalyst's *eppur si muove*! has the same effect as Galileo's; an effect that is not that of factual experience, but that of the *experimentum mentis*.

The unconscious is that chapter of my history that is marked by a blank or occupied by a falsehood: it is the censored chapter. But the truth can be rediscovered; usually it has already been written down elsewhere. Namely:

— in monuments: this is my body. That is to say, the hysterical nucleus of the neurosis in which the hysterical symptom reveals the structure of a language, and is deciphered like an inscription which, once recovered, can without serious loss be destroyed;
— in archival documents: these are my childhood memories, just as impenetrable as are such documents when I do not know their provenance;
— in semantic evolution: this corresponds to the stock of words and acceptations of my own particular vocabulary, as it does to my style of life and to my character;
— in traditions, too, and even in the legends which, in a heroicized form, bear my history;
— and, lastly, in the traces that are inevitably preserved by the distortions necessitated by the linking of the adulterated chapter to the chapters surrounding it, and whose meaning will be re-established by my exegesis.

The student who has the idea that reading Freud in order to understand Freud is preferable to reading Mr. Fenichel – an idea rare enough, it is true, for my teaching to have to go about recommending it – will realize, once he sets about it, that what I have just said has so little originality, even in its verve, that there appears in it not a single metaphor that Freud's works do not repeat with the frequency of a *leitmotif* in which the very fabric of the work is revealed.

At every instant of his practice from then on, he will be more easily able to grasp the fact that these metaphors, like the negation whose doubling undoes it, lose their metaphorical dimension, and he will recognize that this is so because he is operating in the proper domain of the metaphor, which is simply the synonym for the symbolic displacement brought into play in the symptom.

After that it will be easier for him to form an opinion of the imaginary displacement that motivates the works of Mr Fenichel, by measuring the difference in consistency and technical efficacy between reference to the supposedly organic stages of individual development and research into the particular events of a subject's history. The difference is precisely that which separates authentic historical research from the so-called laws of history, of which it can be said that every age finds its own philosopher to diffuse them according to the values then prevailing.

This is not to say that there is nothing to be gained from the different meanings uncovered in the general march of history along the path which runs from Bossuet (Jacques-Bénigne) to Toynbee (Arnold), and which is punctuated by the edifices of Auguste Comte and Karl Marx. Everyone knows very well that they are worth as little for directing research into the recent past as they are for making any reasonable presumptions about the events of tomorrow. Besides, they are modest enough to postpone their certainties until the day after tomorrow, and not too prudish either to admit the retouching that permits predictions about what happened yesterday.

If, therefore, their role is somewhat too slender for scientific progress, their interest lies elsewhere: in their very considerable role as ideals. It is this which prompts me to make a distinction between what might be called the primary and the secondary functions of historization.

For to say of psychoanalysis or of history that, considered as sciences, they are both sciences of the particular, does not mean that the facts they deal with are purely accidental, or simply factitious, and that their ultimate value is reducible to the brute aspect of the trauma.

Events are engendered in a primary historization. In other words, history is already producing itself on the stage where it will be played out, once it has been written down, both within the subject and outside him.

At such and such a period, some riot or other in the Faubourg Saint-Antoine is experienced by its actors as a victory or defeat of the Parlement or the Court; at another, as a victory or defeat of the proletariat or the bourgeoisie. And although it is 'the peoples' (as Cardinal de Retz would have said) who always foot its bill, it is not at all the same historical event – I mean that the two events do not leave the same sort of memory behind in men's minds.

This is to say that, with the disappearance of the reality of the Parlement and the Court, the first event will return to its traumatic value, admitting a progressive and authentic effacement, unless its meaning is deliberately revived. Whereas the memory of the second event will remain very much alive even under censorship – in the same way that the amnesia of repression is one of the most lively forms of memory – as long as there are men to place their revolt under the command of the struggle for the coming to political power of the proletariat, that is to say, men for whom the key-words of dialectical materialism will have a meaning.

At this point it would be too much to say that I was about to carry these remarks over into the field of psychoanalysis, since they are there already, and since the disentanglement that they bring about in psychoanalysis between the technique of deciphering the unconscious and the theory of instincts – to say nothing of the theory of drives – goes without saying.

What we teach the subject to recognize as his unconscious is his history – that is to say, we help him to perfect the present historization of the facts that have already determined a certain number of the historical 'turning-points' in his existence. But if they have played this role, it is already as facts of history, that is to say, in so far as they have been recognized in one particular sense or censored in a certain order.

Thus, every fixation at a so-called instinctual stage is above all a historical scar: a page of shame that is forgotten or undone, or a page of glory that compels. But what is forgotten is recalled in acts, and undoing what has been done is opposed to what is said elsewhere, just as compulsion perpetuates in the symbol the very mirage in which the subject found himself trapped.

To put it briefly, the instinctual stages, when they are being lived, are already organized in subjectivity. And to put it clearly, the subjectivity of the child who registers as victories and defeats the heroic chronicle of the training of his sphincters, enjoying (*jouissant*) the imaginary sexualization of his cloacal orifices, turning his excremental expulsions into aggressions, his retentions into seductions, and his movements of release into symbols – this subjectivity *is not fundamentally different* from the subjectivity of the psychoanalyst who, in order to understand them, tries to reconstitute the forms of love that he calls pregenital.

In other words, the anal stage is no less purely historical when it is actually experienced than when it is reconstituted in thought, nor is it less purely grounded in intersubjectivity. On the other hand, seeing it as a mere stage in some instinctual maturation leads even the best minds straight off the track, to the point that there is seen in it the reproduction in ontogenesis of a stage of the animal phylum that is to be looked for among threadworms, even jellyfish – a speculation which, ingenious as it may be when penned by Balint, leads elsewhere to the most nebulous daydreams, or even to the folly that goes looking in the *protistum* for the imaginary blueprint of breaking and entering the body, fear of which is supposed to control female sexuality. Why, then, not look for the image of the ego in the shrimp, under the pretext that both acquire a new carapace after shedding the old?

In the years 1910–20, a certain Jaworski constructed a very fine system in which the 'biological plan' could be found right up to the confines of culture, and which actually provided the crustacea with a historical counterpart at some period or other of the later Middle Ages, if I remember rightly, in the form of a widespread flowering of armour – and, indeed, left no animal form without a human respondent, not excepting molluscs and bedbugs.

Analogy is not metaphor, and the use that philosophers of nature have made of it calls for the genius of a Goethe, but even his example is not encouraging. Nothing is more repugnant to the spirit of our discipline, and it was by deliberately avoiding analogy that Freud opened up the right way to the interpretation of dreams, and so to the notion of analytic symbolism. Analytic symbolism, I insist, is strictly opposed to analogical thinking, whose dubious tradition results in the fact that some people, even in our own ranks, still consider it to be part and parcel of our method.

This is why excessive excursions into the ridiculous must be used for their eye-opening value, since, by opening our eyes to the absurdity of a theory, they will bring our attention to bear on dangers that have nothing theoretical about them.

This mythology of instinctual maturation, built out of selections from the works of Freud, actually engenders spiritual problems whose vapour, condensing into nebulous ideals, returns to inundate the original myth with its showers. The best writers set their wits to postulating formulae that will satisfy the demands of the mysterious 'genital love'[23] (there are some notions whose strangeness adapts itself better to the parenthesis of a borrowed term, and they initial their attempt with the avowal of a *non liquet*). However, nobody appears to be disturbed by the *malaise* that results; and it can be seen rather as matter fit to encourage all the Münchhausens of psychoanalytic normalization to pull themselves up by the hair in the hope of attaining the paradise of the full realization of the genital object, indeed of the object, period.

If we, as psychoanalysts, are well placed to appreciate the power of words, this is no reason to display it in the interests of the insoluble, nor for 'binding heavy burdens and grievous to be borne, and laying them on men's shoulders', as Christ's malediction is expressed to the Pharisees in the text of St Matthew.

In this way the poverty of the terms in which we try to enclose a subjective problem may leave a great deal to be desired for particularly exacting spirits, should they ever compare these terms to those that structured in their very confusion the ancient quarrels centred around Nature and Grace.[24] Thus this poverty may well leave them apprehensive concerning the quality of the psychological and sociological results that one may expect from their use. And it is to be hoped that a better appreci-action of the functions of the *logos* will dissipate the mysteries of our phantastic charismata.

To confine ourselves to a more lucid tradition, perhaps we shall understand the celebrated maxim in which La Rochefoucauld tells us that '*il y a des gens qui n'auraient jamais été amoureux, s'ils n'avaient jamais entendu parler de l'amour*',[25] not in the Romantic sense of an entirely imaginary 'realization' of love, which would make of this remark a bitter objection on his part, but as an authentic recognition of what love owes to the symbol and of what speech entails of love.

In any case, one has only to go back to the works of Freud to realize to what a secondary and hypothetical place he relegates the theory of instincts. The theory cannot in his eyes stand for a single instant against the least important particular fact of a history, he insists, and the *genital narcissism* he invokes when summing up the case of the Wolf Man shows us well enough the disdain in which he holds the constituted order of the libidinal stages. Furthermore, he evokes the instinctual conflict in his summing up only to move away from it immediately and to recognize in the symbolic isolation of the 'I am not castrated', in which the subject asserts himself, the compulsive form in which his heterosexual choice remains riveted, in opposition to the effect of homosexualizing capture undergone by the ego when brought back to the imaginary matrix of the primal scene. This is in truth the subjective conflict, in which it is only a question of the vicissitudes of subjectivity, in so far as the 'I' wins and loses against the 'ego' at the whim of religious catechizing or of the indoctrinating *Aufklärung* – a conflict whose effects Freud made the subject bring to realization through his help before explaining them to us in the dialectic of the Oedipus complex.

It is in the analysis of such a case that one sees clearly that the realization of perfect love is a fruit not of nature but of grace – that is to say, the fruit of an intersubjective agreement imposing its harmony on the divided nature that supports it.

'But what, then, is this subject that you keep dinning into our ears?' some impatient listener finally protests. 'Haven't we already learned the lesson from Monsieur de la Palice[26] that everything experienced by the individual is subjective?'

Naïve lips, whose praise will occupy my final days, open yourselves again to hear me. No need to close your eyes. The subject goes well beyond what is experienced 'subjectively' by the individual, exactly as far as the truth he is able to attain, and which perhaps will fall from those lips you have already closed again. Yes, this truth of his history is not all contained in his script, and yet the place is marked there by the painful shocks he feels from knowing only his own lines, and not simply there, but also in pages whose disorder gives him little comfort.

That the unconscious of the subject is the discourse of the other appears even more clearly than anywhere else in the studies that Freud devoted to what he called telepathy, as manifested in the context of an analytic experience. This is the coincidence of the subject's remarks with facts about which he cannot have information, but which are still at work in the connexions of another experience in which the same psychoanalyst is the interlocutor – a coincidence moreover constituted most often by an entirely verbal, even homonymic, convergence, or which, if it involves an act, is concerned with an 'acting out'[27] by one of the analyst's other patients or by a child of the person being analysed who is also in analysis. It is a case of resonance in the communicating networks of discourse, an exhaustive study of which would throw light on similar facts presented by everyday life.

The omnipresence of human discourse will perhaps one day be embraced under the open sky of an omnicommunication of its text. This is not to say that human discourse will be any more harmonious than now. But this is the field that our experience polarizes in a relation that is only apparently two-way, for any positing of its structure in merely dual terms is as inadequate to it in theory as it is ruinous for its technique.

❧❧❦❦

II *Symbol and language as structure and limit
of the psychoanalytic field*

Τὴν ἀρχὴν ὅ τι καὶ λαλῶ ὑμιν

(Gospel according to St John, VIII, 25)

'Do crossword puzzles.'
(Advice to a young psychoanalyst)

To take up the thread of my argument again, let me repeat that it is by a reduction of the history of the particular subject that psychoanalysis touches on relational *Gestalten*, which analysis then extrapolates into a regular process of development. But I also repeat that neither genetic psychology nor differential psychology, on both of which analysis may throw light, is within its compass, because both require experimental and observational conditions that are related to those of analysis only by homonymy.

To go even further: what stands out from common experience (which is confused with sense experience only by the professional of ideas) as crude psychology – namely, the wonder that wells up during some momentary suspension of daily care at whatever it is that pairs off human beings in a disparity that goes beyond that of the grotesques of a Leonardo or of a Goya, or the surprise that the thickness proper to a person's skin opposes to the caress of a hand still animated by the thrill of discovery without yet being blunted by desire – all this, it may well be said, is done away with in an experience that is averse to such caprices and resistant to such mysteries.

A psychoanalysis normally proceeds to its termination without revealing to us very much of what our patient derives in his own right from his particular sensitivity to events or colours, from his readiness to grasp things or to accede to his weaknesses of the flesh, from his ability to retain or to invent, and even from the vivacity of his tastes.

This paradox is only an apparent one and is not due to any personal deficiency, and if it is possible to base it on the negative conditions of our experience, it simply presses us a little harder to examine that experience for what there is in it that is positive.

For this paradox does not become resolved in the efforts of certain people – like the philosophers mocked by Plato for being so driven by their appetite for reality that they went about embracing trees[28] – who go so far as to take every episode in which this fleeting reality appears for the lived reaction of which they show themselves so fond. For these are the very people who, making their objective what lies beyond language, react to our rule of 'Don't touch' by a sort of obsession. Keep going in that direction, and I dare say the last word in the transference reaction will be a reciprocal sniffing. I am not exaggerating: nowadays a young analyst-in-training, after two or three years of fruitless analysis, can actually hail the long-awaited arrival of the object relation in such a sniffing of his subject, and can reap as a result of it the *dignus est intrare*[29] of our approval, the guarantee of his abilities.

If psychoanalysis can become a science (for it is not yet one) and if it is not to degenerate in its technique (and perhaps that has already happened), we must rediscover the sense of its experience.

To this end, we can do no better than to return to the work of Freud. For an analyst to point out that he is a practitioner of the technique does not give him sufficient authority, from the fact that he does not understand Freud III, to challenge the latter in the name of a Freud II whom he thinks he understands. And his very ignorance of Freud I is no excuse for considering the five great psychoanalyses as a series of case studies as badly chosen as they are badly expressed, however marvellous he thinks it that the grain of truth hidden within them ever managed to escape.[30]

Take up the work of Freud again at the *Traumdeutung* to remind yourself that the dream has the structure of a sentence or, rather, to stick to the letter of the work, of a rebus; that is to say, it has the structure of a form of writing, of which the child's dream represents the primordial ideography, and which, in the adult, reproduces the simultaneously phonetic and symbolic use of signifying elements, which can also be found both in the hieroglyphs of ancient Egypt and in the characters still used in China.

But even this is no more than the deciphering of the instrument. The important part begins with the translation of the text, the important part that Freud tells us is given in the elaboration of the dream – that is to say, in its rhetoric. Ellipsis and pleonasm, hyperbaton or syllepsis, regression, repetition, apposition – these are the syntactical displacements; metaphor, catachresis, autonomasis, allegory, metonymy, and synecdoche – these are the semantic condensations in which Freud teaches us to read the intentions – ostentatious or demonstrative, dissimulating or persuasive, retaliatory or seductive – out of which the subject modulates his oneiric discourse.

We know that he laid it down as a rule that the expression of a desire must always be sought in the dream. But let us be sure what he meant by this. If Freud admits, as the motive of a dream apparently contrary to his thesis, the very desire to contradict him on the part of the subject whom he had tried to convince of his theory,[31] how could he fail to admit the same motive for himself from the moment that, having arrived at this point, it was from another that his own law came back to him?

In short, nowhere does it appear more clearly than that man's desire finds its meaning in the desire of the other, not so much because the other holds the key to the object desired, as because the first object of desire is to be recognized by the other.

Indeed, we all know from experience that from the moment the analysis becomes engaged in the path of transference – and for us it is the index that this has taken place – each of the patient's dreams is to be interpreted as a provocation, a masked avowal, or a diversion, by its relation to the analytic discourse, and that in proportion to the progress of the analysis, his dreams become more and more reduced to the function of elements in the dialogue being realized in the analysis.

In the case of the psychopathology of everyday life,[32] another field to which Freud turned his attention, it is clear that every unsuccessful act is a successful, not to say 'well turned', discourse, and that in the *lapsus* it is the gag that hinges on speech, and exactly in the right quarter for its word to be sufficient to the wise.

But let us go straight to the part where the book deals with chance and the beliefs it gives rise to, and especially to the facts in which Freud applies himself to showing the subjective efficacy of number associations left to the fate of a random choice, or to the luck of the draw. Nowhere do the dominant structures of the psychoanalytic field reveal themselves better than in such a success, and the appeal made in passing to unknown intellectual mechanisms is no more in this case than his distressed excuse for the total confidence he placed in the symbols, a confidence that wavers as the result of being justified beyond all limits.

If for a symptom, whether neurotic or not, to be admitted in psycho-analytic psychopathology, Freud insists on the minimum of over-determination constituted by a double meaning (symbol of a conflict long dead over and above its function in a *no less symbolic* present conflict), and if he has taught us to follow the ascending ramification of the sym-bolic lineage in the text of the patient's free associations, in order to map it out at the points where its verbal forms intersect with the nodal points of its structure, then it is already quite clear that the symptom resolves itself entirely in an analysis of language, because the symptom is itself structured like a language, because it is from language that speech must be delivered.

To those who have not studied the nature of language in any depth, the experience of number association will show immediately what must be grasped here, namely, the combinatory power that orders its ambi-guities, and they will recognize in this the very mainspring of the un-conscious.

Indeed, if from the numbers obtained by breaking up the series of digits in the chosen number, from their combination by all the operations of arithmetic, even from the repeated division of the original number by one of the numbers split off from it, if the resulting numbers[33] prove among all the numbers in the actual history of the subject, to possess a symbolizing function, it is because they were already latent in the choice from which they began. And if the idea that it was the figures themselves that determined the destiny of the subject is then refuted as superstitious, we are forced to admit that it is in the order of existence of their combina-tions, that is to say, in the concrete language that they represent that everything that analysis reveals to the subject as his unconscious resides.

We shall see that philologists and ethnographers reveal enough to us about the combinatory certainty that is established in the completely un-conscious systems with which they deal for them to find nothing sur-prising in the proposition advanced here.

But if anyone should still be in doubt about the validity of what I am saying, I would appeal once more to the testimony of the man who since he discovered the unconscious, is not entirely without credentials to designate its place; he will not fail us.

For, however little interest has been taken in it – and with good reason

– *Jokes and their relation to the Unconscious*[34] remains the most un-challengeable of his works because it is the most transparent, a work in which the effect of the unconscious is demonstrated to us to its most subtle confines; and the face it reveals to us is that of the spirit in the ambiguity conferred on it by language, where the other side of its re-galian power is the witticism or 'conceit' (*'pointe'*), by which the whole of its order is annihilated in an instant – the 'conceit', in fact, where its domination over the real is expressed in the challenge of non-sense, where humour, in the malicious grace of the 'mind free from care' (*esprit libre*), symbolizes a truth that has not said its last word.

We must accompany Freud along the admirably compelling detours of this book on his walk through this chosen garden of bitterest love.

Here all is substance, all is pearl. The spirit that lives as an exile in the creation whose invisible support it is, knows that it is at every instant the master capable of annihilating it. Not even the most despised of all the forms of this hidden royalty – haughty or perfidious, dandylike or easy-going – but Freud can make their secret lustre gleam. Stories of that derided Eros figure, like him born of penury and pain: the marriage broker on his rounds of the ghettos of Moravia, discreetly guiding the avidity of the apprentices, and suddenly discomfiting his client with the illuminating non-sense of his reply. 'He who lets the truth escape like that,' comments Freud, 'is in reality happy to throw off the mask.'[35]

It is truth in fact that throws off the mask in his words, but only so that the spirit might take on another and more deceiving one: the sophistry that is merely a stratagem, the logic that is merely a lure, even the comic that tends merely to dazzle. The spirit (*esprit*) is always elsewhere. 'Wit [*esprit*] in fact entails such a subjective conditionality . . .: wit is only what I accept as such,'[36] continues Freud, who knows what he is talking about.[37]

Nowhere is the intention of the individual more evidently surpassed by what the subject finds – nowhere does the distinction that I make between the individual and the subject make itself better understood – since not only must there have been something foreign to me in what I found for me to take pleasure in it, but it must also remain this way for this find to hit its mark. This takes its place from the necessity, so clearly marked by Freud, of the third listener, always presupposed, and from the fact that the witticism does not lose its power in its transmission into in-direct speech. In short, pointing the amboceptor – illuminated by the pyrotechnics of the word exploding with supreme alacrity – towards the locus of the Other.

There is only one reason for wit to fall flat: the platitude of the truth that is explained.

Now this concerns our problem directly. The present disdain for research into the language of symbols – which can be seen by a glance at the summaries of our publications before and after the 1920s – corresponds in our discipline to nothing less than a change of object, whose tendency to align itself at the most commonplace level of communication, in order to accommodate the new objectives proposed for the psychoanalytic technique, is perhaps responsible for the rather gloomy balance sheet that the most lucid writers have drawn up of its results.[38]

How, indeed, could speech exhaust the meaning of speech, or, to put it better, with the Oxford logical positivists, the meaning of meaning – except in the act that engenders it? Thus Goethe's reversal of its presence at the origin of things, 'In the beginning was the act', is itself reversed in its turn: it was certainly the Word (*verbe*) that was in the beginning, and we live in its creation, but it is the action of our spirit that continues this creation by constantly renewing it. And we can only turn back on that action by allowing ourselves to be driven ever further ahead by it.

I shall try it myself only in the knowledge that *that* is its way . . .

No one is supposed to be ignorant of the law; this somewhat humorous formula taken direct from our Code of Justice nevertheless expresses the truth in which our experience is grounded, and which our experience confirms. No man is actually ignorant of it, since the law of man has been the law of language since the first words of recognition presided over the first gifts – although it took the detestable *Danaoi* who came and fled over the sea for men to learn to fear deceiving words accompanying faithless gifts. Until that time, for the pacific Argonauts[39] – uniting the islets of the community with the bonds of a symbolic commerce – these gifts, their act and their objects, their erection into signs, and even their fabrication, were so much a part of speech that they were designated by its name.[40]

Is it with these gifts or with the passwords that give them their salutary non-sense that language, with the law, begins? For these gifts are already symbols, in the sense that symbol means pact and that they are first and foremost signifiers of the pact that they constitute as signified, as is plainly seen in the fact that the objects of symbolic exchange – pots made to remain empty, shields too heavy to be carried, sheaves of wheat that wither, lances stuck into the ground – all are destined to be useless, if not simply superfluous by their very abundance.

Is this neutralization of the signifier the whole of the nature of language? On this assessment, one could see the beginning of it among sea swallows, for instance, during the mating parade, materialized in the fish they pass between each other from beak to beak. And if the ethologists are right in seeing in this the instrument of an activation of the group that might be called the equivalent of a festival, they would be completely justified in recognizing it as a symbol.

It can be seen that I do not shrink from seeking the origins of symbolic behaviour outside the human sphere. But this is certainly not to be done by way of an elaboration of the sign. It is on this path that Mr Jules H. Massermann,[41] after so many others, has set off, and I shall stop here for an instant, not only because of the knowing tone with which he makes his approach, but also because of the welcome that his work has found among the editors of our official journal. Following a tradition borrowed from employment agencies, they never neglect anything that might provide our discipline with 'good references'.

Think of it – here we have a man who has reproduced neurosis ex-pe-ri-men-tal-ly in a dog tied down to a table, and by what ingenious methods: a bell, the plate of meat that it announces, and the plate of potatoes that arrives instead; you can imagine the rest. He will certainly not be one, at least so he assures us, to let himself be taken in by the 'ample ruminations', as he puts it, that philosophers have devoted to the problem of language. Not him, he's going to grab it from your throat.

We are told that a raccoon can be taught by a judicious conditioning of his reflexes to go to his feeding trough when he is presented with a card on which his menu is listed. We are not told whether it shows the various prices, but the convincing detail is added that if the service disappoints him, he comes back and tears up the card that promised too much, just as an irritated woman might do with the letters of an unfaithful lover (*sic*).

This is one of the supporting arches of the bridge over which the author carries the road that leads from the signal to the symbol. It is a two-way road, and the return journey from the symbol to the signal is illustrated by no less imposing works of art.

For if you associate the projection of a bright light into the eyes of a human subject with the ringing of a bell, and then the ringing alone to the command 'Contract',[42] you will succeed in getting the subject to make his pupils contract just by giving the order himself, then by muttering it, and eventually just by thinking it – in other words you will obtain a reaction of the nervous system that is called autonomous because it is usually inaccessible to intentional effects. Thus, if we are to believe this writer, Mr Hudgins 'has created in a group of subjects a highly individualized configuration of related and visceral reactions from the "idea-symbol"[43], "Contract", a response that could be referred back through their individual experiences to an apparently distant source, but in reality basically physiological – in this example, simply the protection of the retina against an excessively bright light'. And the author concludes: 'The significance of such experiments for psychosomatic and linguistic research does not even need further elaboration.'

For my part, I would have been curious to learn whether subjects trained in this way also react to the enunciation of the same syllables in the expressions: 'marriage contract', 'contract bridge', 'breach of contract',[44] or even to the word 'contract' progressively reduced to the articulation of its first syllable: contract, contrac, contra, contr . . . The control experiment required by strict scientific method would then be offered all by itself as the French reader murmured this syllable between his teeth, even though he would have been subjected to no conditioning other than that of the bright light projected on the problem by Mr Jules H. Massermann. I would then ask this author whether the effects observed in this way among conditioned subjects still appeared to dispose so easily of further elaboration. For either the effects would no longer be produced, thus revealing that they do not depend even conditionally on the semanteme, or they would continue to be produced, posing the question of its limits.

In other words, they would cause the distinction of signifier and signified, so blithely confused by the author in the English term 'idea-symbol', to appear in the very instrument of the word. And without needing to examine the reactions of subjects conditioned by the command 'Don't contract', or even by the entire conjugation of the verb 'to contract', I could draw the author's attention to the fact that what defines any element whatever of a language (*langue*) as belonging to language, is that, for all the users of this language (*langue*), this element is distinguished as such in the ensemble supposedly constituted of homologous elements.

The result is that the particular effects of this element of language are bound up with the existence of this ensemble, anterior to any possible link with any particular experience of the subject. And to consider this last link independently of any reference to the first is simply to deny in this element the function proper to language.

This reminder of first principles might perhaps have saved our author, in his unequalled naïveté, from discovering the textual correspondence of the grammatical categories of his childhood in the relations of reality.

This monument of naïveté, in any case of a kind common enough in these matters, would not be worth so much attention if it were not the achievement of a psychoanalyst, or rather of someone who, as chance will have it, represents everything produced by a certain tendency in psychoanalysis – in the name of the theory of the *ego* or of the technique of the analysis of defences – everything, that is, most contrary to the Freudian experience. In this way the coherence of a sound conception of language along with the maintenance of this conception is revealed *a contrario*. For Freud's discovery was that of the field of the effects in the nature of man of his relations to the symbolic order and the tracing of their meaning right back to the most radical agencies of symbolization in being. To ignore this symbolic order is to condemn the discovery to oblivion, and the experience to ruin.

And I affirm – an affirmation that cannot be divorced from the serious intent of my present remarks – that it would seem to me preferable to have the raccoon I mentioned sitting in the armchair where, according to to our author, Freud's timidity confined the analyst by putting him behind the couch, rather than a 'scientist' who discourses on language and speech as he does.

For the raccoon, at least, thanks to Jacques Prévert (*'une pierre, deux maisons, trois ruines, quatre fossoyeurs, un jardin, des fleurs, un raton-laveur'*),[45] has entered the poetic bestiary once and for all and participates as such, in its essence, in the high function of the symbol. But that being resembling us who professes, as he has done, a systematic *méconnaissance* of that function, banishes himself from everything that can be called into existence by it. This being so, the question of the place to be assigned to our friend in the classification of nature would seem to me to be simply that of an irrelevant humanism, if his discourse, crossed with a technique of speech of which we are the custodians, were not in fact too fruitful, even in engendering sterile monstrosities within it. Let it be known therefore, since he also prides himself on braving the reproach of anthropomorphism, that it is this last term that I would employ in saying that he makes his own being the measure of all things.

Let us return to our symbolic object, which is itself extremely consistent in its matter, even if it has lost the weight of its use, but whose imponderable meaning will produce displacements of some weight. Is it there, then, that the law and language are to be found? Perhaps not yet.

For even if there appeared among the sea swallows some kaid of the colony who, by gulping down the symbolic fish before the gaping beaks of the others, were to inaugurate that exploitation of swallow by swallow – a phantasy I once took pleasure in developing – this would not be in any way sufficient to reproduce among them that fabulous history, the image of our own, whose winged epic kept us captive on Anatole France's *Penguin Island*; and there would still be something else needed to create a 'hirundinized' universe.

This something completes the symbol, thus making language of it. In order for the symbolic object freed from its usage to become the word freed from the *hic et nunc*, the difference resides not in its material quality as sound, but in its evanescent being in which the symbol finds the permanence of the concept.

Through the word – already a presence made of absence – absence itself gives itself a name in that moment of origin whose perpetual re-creation Freud's genius detected in the play of the child. And from this pair of sounds modulated on presence and absence[46] – a coupling that the tracing in the sand of the single and the broken line of the mantic *kwa* of China would also serve to constitute – there is born the world of meaning of a particular language in which the world of things will come to be arranged.

Through that which becomes embodied only by being the trace of a nothingness and whose support cannot thereafter be impaired, the concept, saving the duration of what passes by, engenders the thing.

For it is still not enough to say that the concept is the thing itself, as any child can demonstrate against the pedant. It is the world of words that creates the world of things – the things originally confused in the *hic et nunc* of the all in the process of coming-into-being – by giving its concrete being to their essence, and its ubiquity to what has always been:[47] χτῆμα ἐς ἀεί.

Man speaks, then, but it is because the symbol has made him man. Even if in fact overabundant gifts welcome the stranger who has introduced himself to the group, the life of the natural groups that constitute the community is subjected to the rules of matrimonial alliance governing the exchange of women, and to the exchange of gifts determined by the marriage: as the Sironga proverb says, a relative by marriage is an elephant's thigh.[48] The marriage tie is governed by an order of preference whose law concerning the kinship names is, like language, imperative for the group in its forms, but unconscious in its structure. In this structure, whose harmony or conflicts govern the restricted or generalized exchange discerned in it by the social anthropologist, the startled theoretician finds the whole of the logic of combinations: thus the laws of number – that is to say, the laws of the most refined of all symbols – prove to be immanent in the original symbolism. At least, it is the richness of the forms in which are developed what are known as the elementary structures of kinship that makes it possible to read those laws in the original symbolism. And this would suggest that it is perhaps only our unconsciousness of their permanence that allows us to believe in the freedom of choice in the so-called complex structures of marriage ties under whose law we live. If statistics have already allowed us to glimpse that this freedom is not exercised in a random manner, it is because a subjective logic orients this freedom in its effects.

This is precisely where the Oedipus complex – in so far as we continue to recognize it as covering the whole field of our experience with its signification – may be said, in this connexion, to mark the limits that our discipline assigns to subjectivity: namely, what the subject can know of his unconscious participation in the movement of the complex structures of marriage ties, by verifying the symbolic effects in his individual existence of the tangential movement towards incest that has manifested itself ever since the coming of a universal community.

The primordial Law is therefore that which in regulating marriage ties superimposes the kingdom of culture on that of a nature abandoned to the law of mating. The prohibition of incest is merely its subjective pivot, revealed by the modern tendency to reduce to the mother and the sister the objects forbidden to the subject's choice, although full licence outside of these is not yet entirely open.

This law, then, is revealed clearly enough as identical with an order of language. For without kinship nominations, no power is capable of instituting the order of preferences and taboos that bind and weave the yarn of lineage through succeeding generations. And it is indeed the confusion of generations which, in the Bible as in all traditional laws, is accused as being the abomination of the Word (*verbe*) and the desolation of the sinner.

We know in fact what ravages a falsified filiation can produce, going as far as the dissociation of the subject's personality, when the constraint of his entourage is used to sustain the lie. They may be no less when, as a result of a man having married the mother of the woman of whom he has had a son, the son will have for a brother a child who is his mother's brother. But if he is later adopted – and the case is not invented – by the sympathetic couple formed by a daughter of his father's previous marriage and her husband, he will find himself once again the half-brother of his foster mother, and one can imagine the complex feelings with which he will await the birth of a child who will be in this recurring situation his brother and his nephew at the same time.

As a matter of fact the mere 'time-lag' (*décalage*) produced in the order of generations by a late-born child of a second marriage, in which the young mother finds herself the contemporary of an older brother, can produce similar effects, as we know was the case of Freud himself.

This same function of symbolic identification through which primitive man believes he reincarnates an ancestor with the same name – and which even determines an alternating recurrence of characters in modern man – therefore introduces in subjects exposed to these discordances in the father relation a dissociation of the Oedipus relation in which the constant source of its pathogenic effects must be seen. Even when in fact it is represented by a single person, the paternal function concentrates in itself both imaginary and real relations, always more or less inadequate to the symbolic relation that essentially constitutes it.

It is in the *name of the father* that we must recognize the support of the symbolic function which, from the dawn of history, has identified his person with the figure of the law. This conception enables us to distinguish clearly, in the analysis of a case, the unconscious effects of this function from the narcissistic relations, or even from the real relations that the subject sustains with the image and the action of the person who embodies it; and there results from this a mode of comprehension that will tend to have repercussions on the very way in which the interventions of the analyst are conducted. Practice has confirmed its fecundity for me, as well as for the students whom I have introduced to this method. And, both in supervising analyses and in commenting on cases being demonstrated, I have often had the opportunity of emphasizing the harmful confusion produced by ignoring it.

Thus it is the virtue of the Word that perpetuates the movement of the Great Debt whose economy Rabelais, in a famous metaphor, extended to the stars themselves. And we shall not be surprised that the chapter in which, with the macaronic inversion of kinship names, he presents us with an anticipation of the discoveries of the anthropologists, should reveal in him the substantific divination of the human mystery that I am trying to elucidate here.[49]

Identified with the sacred *hau* or with the omnipresent *mana*, the inviolable Debt is the guarantee that the voyage on which wives and goods are embarked will bring back to their point of departure in a never-failing cycle other women and other goods, all carrying an identical entity: what Lévi-Strauss calls a 'zero-symbol' (*symbole zéro*), thus reducing the power of Speech to the form of an algebraic sign.[50]

Symbols in fact envelop the life of man in a network so total that they join together, before he comes into the world, those who are going to engender him 'by flesh and blood';[51] so total that they bring to his birth, along with the gifts of the stars, if not with the gifts of the fairies, the shape of his destiny; so total that they give the words that will make him faithful or renegade, the law of the acts that will follow him right to the very place where he *is* not yet and even beyond his death; and so total that through them his end finds its meaning in the last judgement, where the Word absolves his being or condemns it – unless he attain the subjective bringing to realization of being-for-death.

Servitude and grandeur in which the living being would be annihilated, if desire did not preserve its part in the interferences and pulsations that the cycles of language cause to converge on him, when the confusion of tongues takes a hand and when the orders contradict one another in the tearing apart of the universal work.

But for this desire itself to be satisfied in man requires that it be recognized, through the agreement of speech or through the struggle for prestige, in the symbol or in the imaginary.

What is at stake in an analysis is the advent in the subject of that little reality that this desire sustains in him with respect to the symbolic conflicts and imaginary fixations as the means of their agreement, and our path is the intersubjective experience where this desire makes itself recognized.

From this point on it will be seen that the problem is that of the relations between speech and language in the subject.

Three paradoxes in these relations present themselves in our domain.

In madness, of whatever nature, we must recognize on the one hand the negative freedom of speech that has given up trying to make itself recognized, or what we call an obstacle to transference, and, on the other hand, we must recognize the singular formation of a delusion which – fabulous, fantastic, or cosmological; interpretative, demanding, or idealist – objectifies the subject in a language without dialectic.[52]

The absence of speech is manifested here by the stereotypes of a discourse in which the subject, one might say, is spoken rather than speaking: here we recognize the symbols of the unconscious in petrified forms that find their place in a natural history of these symbols beside the embalmed forms in which myths are presented in our story-books. But it is an error to say that the subject assumes these symbols: the resistance to their recognition is no less strong in psychosis than in the neuroses when the subject is led into it by an attempt at treatment.

Let it be noted in passing that it would be worthwhile mapping the places in social space that our culture has assigned to these subjects, especially as regards their assignment to the social services relating to language, for it is not unlikely that there is at work here one of the factors that consign such subjects to the effects of the breakdown produced by the symbolic discordances that characterize the complex structures of civilization.

The second case is represented by the privileged domain of psychoanalytic discovery: that is, symptoms, inhibition, and anxiety in the constituent economy of the different neuroses.

Here speech is driven out of the concrete discourse that orders the subject's consciousness, but it finds its support either in the natural functions of the subject, in so far as an organic stimulus sets off that opening (*béance*) of his individual being to his essence, which makes of the illness the introduction of the living being to the existence of the subject[53] – or in the images that organize at the limit of the *Umwelt* and of the *Innenwelt* their relational structuring.

The symptom is here the signifier of a signified repressed from the consciousness of the subject. A symbol written in the sand of the flesh and on the veil of Maia, it participates in language by the semantic ambiguity that I have already emphasized in its constitution.

But it is speech functioning to the full, for it includes the discourse of the other in the secret of its cipher.

It was by deciphering this speech that Freud rediscovered the primary language of symbols,[54] still living on in the suffering of civilized man (*Das Unbehagen in der Kultur*).

Hieroglyphics of hysteria, blazons of phobia, labyrinths of the *Zwangsneurose* – charms of impotence, enigmas of inhibition, oracles of anxiety – talking arms of character,[55] seals of self-punishment, disguises of perversion – these are the hermetic elements that our exegesis resolves, the equivocations that our invocation dissolves, the artifices that our dialectic absolves, in a deliverance of the mprisoned meaning, from the revelation of the palimpsest[56] to the given word of the mystery and to the pardon of speech.

The third paradox of the relation of language to speech is that of the subject who loses his meaning in the objectifications of discourse. However metaphysical its definition may appear, we cannot ignore (*méconnaître*) its presence in the foreground of our experience. For here is the most profound alienation of the subject in our scientific civilization, and it is this alienation that we encounter first of all when the subject begins to talk to us about himself: hence, in order to resolve it entirely, analysis should be conducted to the limits of wisdom.

To give an exemplary formulation of this, I could not find a more pertinent terrain than the usage of common speech – pointing out that the '*ce suis-je*' of the time of Villon has become reversed in the '*c'est moi*' of modern man.

The *moi*, the ego, of modern man, as I have indicated elsewhere, has taken on its form in the dialectical impasse of the *belle âme* who does not recognize his very own *raison d'être* in the disorder that he denounces in the world.

But a way out is offered to the subject for the resolution of that impasse when his discourse is delusional. Communication can be validly established for him in the common task of science and in the posts that it commands in our universal civilization; this communication will be effective within the enormous objectification constituted by that science, and it will enable him to forget his subjectivity. He will make an effective contribution to the common task in his daily work and will be able to furnish his leisure time with all the pleasures of a profuse culture which, from detective novels to historical memoirs, from educational lectures to the orthopaedics of group relations, will give him the wherewithal to forget his own existence and his death, at the same time to misconstrue (*méconnaître*) the particular meaning of his life in false communication.

If the subject did not rediscover in a regression – often pushed right back to the 'mirror stage' – the enclosure of a stage in which his ego contains its imaginary exploits, there would hardly be any assignable limits to the credulity to which he must succumb in that situation. And this is what makes our responsibility so formidable when, along with the mythical manipulations of our doctrine, we bring him one more opportunity to alienate himself, in the decomposed trinity of the ego, the superego, and the id, for example.[57]

Here there is a language-barrier opposed to speech, and the precautions against verbalism that are a theme of the discourse of the 'normal' man in our culture merely serve to reinforce its thickness.

There might be some point in measuring its thickness by the statistically determined total of pounds of printed paper, miles of record grooves, and hours of radio broadcasting that the said culture produces per head of population in the sectors A, B, and C of its domain. This would be a fine research project for our cultural organizations, and it would be seen that the question of language does not remain entirely within the domain of the convolutions in which its use is reflected in the individual.

> *We are the hollow men*
> *We are the stuffed men*
> *Leaning together*
> *Headpiece filled with straw. Alas!*
>   and so on.

The resemblance between this situation and the alienation of madness, in so far as the formula given above is authentic – that is, that here the subject is spoken rather than speaking – obviously derives from the demand, presupposed by psychoanalysis, for 'true' speech. If this consequence, which pushes the constituent paradoxes of what I am saying here to their limit, were to be turned against the good sense of the psychoanalytic perspective, I would readily accept the pertinence of this objection, but only to find my own position confirmed in it – and this by a dialectical return in which there would be no shortage of authorized godfathers, beginning with Hegel's denunciation of 'the philosophy of the cranium', and stopping only at Pascal's warning, at the dawn of the historical era of the 'ego', echoing in these terms: '*Les hommes sont si nécessairement fous, que ce serait être fou par un autre tour de folie, de n'être pas fou.*'[58]

This is not to say, however, that our culture pursues its course in the shadowy regions beyond creative subjectivity. On the contrary, creative subjectivity has not ceased in its struggle to renew the never-exhausted power of symbols in the human exchange that brings them to the light of day.

To take into account how few subjects support this creation would be to accede to a Romantic viewpoint by comparing what is not equivalent. The fact is that this subjectivity, in whatever domain it appears – in mathematics, in politics, in religion, or even in advertising – continues to animate the whole movement of humanity. And another look, probably no less illusory, would make us accentuate this opposing trait: that its symbolic character has never been more manifest. It is the irony of revolutions that they engender a power all the more absolute in its exercise, not because it is more anonymous, as people say, but because it is more reduced to the words that signify it. And more than ever, on the other hand, the strength of the churches resides in the language that they have been able to maintain: an authority, it must be said, that Freud left in the dark in the article where he sketches for us what we would call the collective subjectivities of the Church and the Army.[59]

Psychoanalysis has played a role in the direction[60] of modern subjectivity, and it cannot continue to sustain this role without bringing it into line with the movement in modern science that elucidates it.

This is the problem of the grounding that must assure our discipline its place among the sciences: a problem of formalization, which, it must be admitted, has not got off to a very good start.

For it seems that, caught by the very quirk in the medical mind against which psychoanalysis had to constitute itself, it is with the handicap of being half a century behind the movement of the sciences, like medicine itself, that we are seeking to join up with them again.

It is in the abstract objectification of our experience on fictitious, or even simulated, principles of the experimental method, that we find the effect of prejudices that must first be swept from our field if we wish to cultivate it according to its authentic structure.

Since we are practitioners of the symbolic function, it is astonishing that we should turn away from probing deeper into it, to the extent of failing to recognize (*méconnaître*) that it is this function that situates us at the heart of the movement that is now establishing a new order of the sciences, with a new putting in question of anthropology.

This new order signifies nothing more than a return to a conception of true science whose claims have been inscribed in a tradition beginning with Plato's *Theaetetus*. This conception has become degraded, as we know, in the positivist reversal which, by making the human sciences the crowning glory of the experimental sciences, in actual fact made them subordinate to experimental science. This notion results from an erroneous view of the history of science founded on the prestige of a specialized development of the experiment.

But since today the conjectural sciences are discovering once again the age-old conception of science, they are forcing us to revise the classification of the sciences that we have inherited from the nineteenth century, in a sense indicated clearly by the most lucid spirits.

One has only to follow the concrete evolution of the various disciplines in order to become aware of this.

Linguistics can serve us as a guide here, since that is the role it plays in the vanguard of contemporary anthropology, and we cannot possibly remain indifferent to it.

The mathematicized form in which is inscribed the discovery of the *phoneme* as the function of pairs of oppositions formed by the smallest discriminate elements capable of being distinguished in the semantic structure, leads us to the very grounding in which the last of Freud's doctrines designates the subjective sources of the symbolic function in a vocalic connotation of presence and absence.

And the reduction of every language to the group of a very small number of these phonemic oppositions, by initiating an equally rigorous formalization of its highest morphemes, puts within our reach a precisely defined access to our own field.

It is up to us to make use of these advances to discover their effects in the domain of psychoanalysis, just as ethnography – which is on a line parallel to our own – has already done for its own by deciphering myths according to the synchrony of mythemes.

Isn't it striking that Lévi-Strauss, in suggesting the implication of the structures of language with that part of the social laws that regulate marriage ties and kinship, is already conquering the very terrain in which Freud situates the unconscious?[61]

From now on, it is impossible not to make a general theory of the symbol the axis of a new classification of the sciences where the sciences of man will once more take up their central position as sciences of subjectivity. Let me indicate its basic principle, which, of course, does not preclude further elaboration.

The symbolic function presents itself as a double movement within the subject: man makes an object of his action, but only in order to restore to this action in due time its place as a grounding. In this equivocation, operating at every instant, lies the whole process of a function in which action and knowledge alternate.[62]

Two examples, one borrowed from the classroom, the other from the everyday life of our time:
– the first, mathematical: phase one, man objectifies in two cardinal numbers two collections he has counted; phase two, with these numbers he realizes the act of adding them up (cf. the example cited by Kant in the introduction to the transcendental aesthetic, section IV, in the second edition of the *Critique of Pure Reason*);
– the second, historical: phase one, the man who works at the level of production in our society considers himself as belonging to the proletariat; phase two, in the name of belonging to it, he joins in a general strike.

If these two examples come from areas which, for us, are the most contrasted in the domain of the concrete – the first involving an operation always open to a mathematical law, the second, the brazen face[63] of capitalist exploitation – it is because, although they seem to come from a long way apart, their effects come to constitute our subsistence, and precisely by meeting each other in the concrete in a double reversal: the most subjective of the sciences having forged a new reality, and the shadow of social distribution arming itself with a symbol in action.

Here the opposition that is traced between the exact sciences and those for which there is no reason to decline the appellation of 'conjectural' no longer seems to be acceptable – for lack of any grounds for that opposition.[64]

For exactitude is to be distinguished from truth, and conjecture does not exclude rigour. And even if experimental science derives its exactitude from mathematics, its relation to nature does not remain any less problematic.

Indeed, if our link to nature urges us to wonder poetically whether it is not its very own movement that we rediscover in our science, in

> . . . *cette voix*
> *Qui se connaît quand elle sonne*
> *N'être plus la voix de personne*
> *Tant que des ondes et des bois,*[65]

it is clear that our physics is simply a mental fabrication whose instrument is the mathematical symbol.

For experimental science is not so much defined by the quantity to which it is in fact applied, as by the measurement it introduces into the real.

This can be seen in relation to the measurement of time without which experimental science would be impossible. Huyghens' clock, which alone gave experimental science its precision, is merely the organ embodying Galileo's hypothesis on the equigravity of bodies – that is, the hypothesis on uniform acceleration that confers its law, since it is the same, on any kind of fall.

It is amusing to point out that the instrument was completed before it had been possible to verify the hypothesis by observation, and that by this fact the clock rendered the observation useless at the same time as it offered it the instrument of its rigour.[66]

But mathematics can symbolize another kind of time, notably the intersubjective time that structures human action, whose formulae are beginning to be given us by the theory of games, still called strategy, but which it would be better to call *stochastics*.

The author of these lines has attempted to demonstrate in the logic of a sophism the temporal sources through which human action, in so far as it orders itself according to the action of the other, finds in the scansion of its hesitations the advent of its certainty; and in the decision that concludes it, this action given to that of the other – which it includes from that point on – together with its consequences deriving from the past, its meaning-to-come.

In this article it is demonstrated that it is the certainty anticipated by the subject in the *'time for understanding'* which, by the haste which precipitates the *'moment of concluding'*, determines in the other the decision that makes of the subject's own movement error or truth.

It can be seen by this example how the mathematical formalization that inspired Boolean logic, to say nothing of set theory, can bring to the science of human action the structure of intersubjective time that is needed by psychoanalytic conjecture if it is to ensure its own rigour.

If, on the other hand, the history of the technique of the historian shows that its progress is defined in the ideal of an identification of the subjectivity of the historian with the constituting subjectivity of the primary historization in which the event is humanized, it is clear that psychoanalysis finds its precise bearings here: that is to say, in knowledge, as realizing this ideal, and in curative efficacy, as finding its justification there. The example of history will also dissipate like a mirage that recourse to the experienced reaction that obsesses both our technique and our theory, for the fundamental historicity of the event that we retain suffices to conceive the possibility of a subjective reproduction of the past in the present.

Furthermore, this example makes us realize how psychoanalytic regression implies that progressive dimension of the subject's history that Freud emphasizes as lacking in the Jungian concept of neurotic regression, and we understand how the experience itself renews this progression by assuring its relief.

Finally, the reference to linguistics will introduce us to the method which, by distinguishing synchronic from diachronic structurings in language, will enable us to understand better the different value that our language assumes in the interpretation of the resistances and the transference, or even to differentiate the effects proper to repression and the structure of the individual myth in obsessional neurosis.

The list of the disciplines named by Freud as those that should make up the disciplines accessory to an ideal Faculty of Psychoanalysis is well known. Besides psychiatry and sexology, we find 'the history of civilization, mythology, the psychology of religions, literary history, and literary criticism'.[67]

This whole group of subjects, determining the *cursus* of an instruction in technique, are normally inscribed within the epistemological triangle that I have described, and which would provide with its method an advanced level of instruction in analytic theory and technique.

For my part, I should be inclined to add: rhetoric, dialectic in the technical sense that this term assumes in the *Topics* of Aristotle, grammar, and, that supreme pinnacle of the aesthetics of language, poetics, which would include the neglected technique of the witticism.

And if these subject headings tended to evoke somewhat outmoded echoes for some people, I would not be unwilling to accept them, as constituting a return to our sources.

For psychoanalysis in its early development, intimately linked to the discovery and study of symbols, was on the way to participating in the structure of what was called in the Middle Ages, 'the liberal arts'. Deprived, like them, of a true formalization, psychoanalysis became organized, like them, in a body of privileged problems, each one promoted by some felicitous relation of man to his own measure, and taking on from this particularity a charm and a humanity that in our eyes might well make up for the somewhat recreational aspect of their presentation. But we should not disdain this aspect of the early development of psychoanalysis; it expresses in fact nothing less than the re-creation of human meaning in an arid period of scientism.

These aspects of the early years should be all the less disdained since psychoanalysis has not raised the level by setting off along the false paths of a theorization contrary to its dialectical structure.

Psychoanalysis will provide scientific bases for its theory or for its technique only by formalizing in an adequate fashion the essential dimensions of its experience which, together with the historical theory of the symbol, are: intersubjective logic and the temporality of the subject.

⋙⋘

III *The resonances of interpretation and the time of the*
      subject in psychoanalytic technique

> *Entre l'homme et l'amour,*
>   *Il y a la femme.*
>
> *Entre l'homme et la femme,*
>   *Il y a monde.*
>
> *Entre l'homme et le monde,*
>   *Il y a un mur.*[68]
> (Antoine Tudal, in *Paris en l'an 2000*)

> *Nam Sibyllam quidem Cumis ego ipse oculis meis vidi in ampulla*
> *pendere, et cum illi pueri dicerent: Σιβύλλα τί θέλεις,*
>   *respondebat illa: ἀπο θανεῖν θέλω.*[69]
> (*Satyricon*, XLVIII)

Bringing the psychoanalytic experience back to speech and language as its grounding is of direct concern to its technique. Psychoanalysis is not yet submerged in the ineffable, but there has certainly been a tendency in this direction, always along the way of no return of separating analytic interpretation more and more from the principle on which it depends. Any suspicion that this deviation of psychoanalytic practice is the motive force behind the new aims to which psychoanalytic theory is being opened up is consequently well founded.

If we look at the situation a little more closely, we can see that the problem of symbolic interpretation began by intimidating our little group before becoming embarrassing to it. The successes obtained by Freud, because of the heedlessness about matters of doctrine from which they seem to proceed, are now a matter of astonishment, and the display so evident in the cases of Dora, the Rat Man, and the Wolf Man seems to us to be little short of scandalous. True, our cleverer friends do not shrink from doubting whether the technique employed in these cases was really the right one.

This disaffection in the psychoanalytic movement can in fact be ascribed to a confusion of tongues, and, in a recent conversation with me, the most representative personality of its present hierarchy made no secret about it.

It is worth noting that this confusion increases when each analyst presumes to consider himself the one chosen to discover in our experience the conditions of a completed objectification, and the enthusiasm which greets these theoretical attempts seems to grow more fervent the more dereistic they prove to be.

It is certain that the principles of the analysis of resistances, however well-founded they may be, have in practice been the occasion of an ever greater *méconnaissance* of the subject for want of being understood in their relation to the intersubjectivity of speech.

If we follow the proceedings of the first seven sessions of the case of the Rat Man, and they are reported to us in full, it seems highly improbable that Freud did not recognize the resistances as they came up, and precisely in the places where our modern technicians drill into us that he overlooked them, since it is Freud's own text, after all, that enables them to pinpoint them. Once again the Freudian text manifests that exhaustion of the subject that continues to amaze us, and no interpretation has so far worked out all its resources.

I mean that Freud not only let himself be trapped into encouraging his subject to go beyond his initial reticence, but that he also understood perfectly the seductive power of this exercise in the imaginary order. To be convinced of this, one has only to refer to the description that he gives us of his patient's expression during the painful recital of the represented torture that supplied the theme of his obsession, that of the rat forced into the victim's anus: 'His face', Freud tells us, 'reflected the horror of a pleasure of which he was unaware.'[70] The effect of the repetition of this account at that time did not escape Freud, any more than did the identification of the psychoanalyst with the 'cruel captain' who had forced this story to enter the subject's memory, nor therefore the import of the theoretical clarifications of which the subject required to be guaranteed before pursuing his discourse.

Far from interpreting the resistance at this point, however, Freud astonishes us by acceding to his request, and to such an extent in fact that he seems to be taking part in the subject's gamè.

But the extremely approximative character of the explanations with which Freud gratifies him, so approximative as to appear somewhat crude, is sufficiently instructive: at this point it is clearly not so much a question of doctrine, nor even of indoctrination, but rather of a symbolic gift of speech, pregnant with a secret pact, in the context of the imaginary participation which includes it and whose import will reveal itself later in the symbolic equivalence that the subject establishes in his thought between rats and the florins with which he remunerates the analyst.

We can see therefore that Freud, far from failing to recognize (*méconnaître*) the resistance, uses it as a propitious predisposition for the setting in movement of the resonances of speech, and he conforms, as far as he can, to the first definition he gave of resistance,[71] by making use of it to implicate the subject in his message. In any case he will change tack abruptly from the moment he sees that, as a result of being carefully manipulated, the resistance is turning towards maintaining the dialogue at the level of a conversation in which the subject would from then on be able to perpetuate his seduction while maintaining his evasion.

But we learn that analysis consists in playing in all the many staves of the score that speech constitutes in the registers of language and on which depends the overdetermination of the symptom, which has no meaning except in that order.

And at the same time we discover the source of Freud's success. In order for the analyst's message to respond to the profound interrogation of the subject, the subject must hear and understand it as the response that is particular to him; and the privilege that Freud's patients enjoyed in receiving its 'good news' from the very lips of the man who was its annunciator, satisfied this demand in them.

Let us note in passing that in the case of the Rat Man the subject had had an advance taste of it, since he had glanced at the *Psychopathology of Everyday Life*, which had just then been published.

This is not to say that this book is very much better known today, even by analysts, but the vulgarization of Freudian concepts, which have passed into the common consciousness, their collision with what I call the language barrier, would deaden the effect of our speech, if we were to give it the style of Freud's remarks to the Rat Man.

But it is not a question of imitating him. In order to rediscover the effect of Freud's speech, it is not to its terms that we shall have recourse, but to the principles that govern it.

These principles are simply the dialectic of the consciousness-of-self, as realized from Socrates to Hegel, from the ironic presupposition that all that is rational is real to its culmination in the scientific view that all that is real is rational. But Freud's discovery was to demonstrate that this verifying process authentically attains the subject only by decentring him from the consciousness-of-self, in the axis of which the Hegelian reconstruction of the phenomenology of mind, maintained it: that is, that this discovery renders even more decrepit any pursuit of the *prise de conscience* which, beyond its status as a psychological phenomenon, cannot be inscribed within the conjuncture of the particular moment that alone embodies the universal and in default of which it vanishes into generality.

These remarks define the limits within which it is impossible for our technique to fail to recognize the structuring moments of the Hegelian phenomenology: in the first place the master-slave dialectic, or the dialectic of the *belle âme* and of the law of the heart, and generally whatever enables us to understand how the constitution of the object is subordinated to the realization of the subject.

But if there still remains something prophetic in Hegel's insistence on the fundamental identity of the particular and the universal, an insistence that reveals the measure of his genius, it is certainly psychoanalysis that provides it with its paradigm by revealing the structure in which that identity is realized as disjunctive of the subject, and without appeal to any tomorrow.

Let me simply say that this is what leads me to object to any reference to totality in the individual, since it is the subject who introduces division into the individual, as well as into the collectivity that is his equivalent. Psychoanalysis is properly that which reveals both the one and the other to be no more than mirages.

This would seem to be something that could no longer be forgotten, were it not precisely the teaching of psychoanalysis that it is forgettable – concerning which we find, by a return more legitimate than it is believed to be, that confirmation comes from psychoanalysts themselves, from the fact that their 'new tendencies' represent this forgetting.

For if, on the other hand, Hegel is precisely what we needed to confer a meaning other than that of stupor on our so-called analytic neutrality, this does not mean that we have nothing to learn from the elasticity of the Socratic maieutics, or 'art of midwifery', or even from the fascinating technical procedure by which Plato presents it to us – be it only by our experiencing in Socrates and in his desire the still-intact enigma of the psychoanalyst, and by situating in relation to the Platonic *skopia* our own relation to truth – in this case, however, in a way that would respect the distance separating the reminiscence that Plato came to presuppose as necessary for any advent of the idea, from the exhaustion of being that is consummated in Kierkegaardian repetition.[72]

But there is also a historical difference between Socrates' interlocutor and ours that is worth examining. When Socrates relies on a naïve reason that he can extract equally well from the discourse of the slave, it is in order to give authentic masters access to the necessity of an order that makes justice of their power, and truth of the master words of the city. But we analysts have to deal with slaves who think they are masters, and who find in a language whose mission is universal the support of their servitude, and the bonds of its ambiguity. So much so that, as one might humorously put it, our goal is to restore in them the sovereign freedom displayed by Humpty Dumpty when he reminds Alice that after all he is the master of the signifier, even if he isn't the master of the signified in which his being took on its form.

We always come back, then, to our double reference to speech and to language. In order to free the subject's speech, we introduce him into the language of his desire, that is to say, into the *primary language* in which, beyond what he tells us of himself, he is already talking to us unknown to himself, and, in the first place, in the symbols of the symptom.

In the symbolism brought to light in analysis, it is certainly a question of a language. This language, corresponding to the playful wish to be found in one of Lichtenberg's aphorisms, has the universal character of a language (*langue*) that would be understood in all other languages (*langues*), but, at the same time, since it is the language that seizes desire at the very moment in which it is humanized by making itself recognized, it is absolutely particular to the subject.

Primary Language, I say, by which I do not mean 'primitive language' ('*langue primitive*'), since Freud, whose feat in this total discovery merits comparison with Champollion's, deciphered it in its entirety in the dreams of our contemporaries. Moreover, the essential field of this language was authoritatively defined by one of the earliest pioneers associated with this work, and one of the few to have brought anything new to it: I mean Ernest Jones, the last survivor of those to whom the seven rings of the master were given and who attested by his presence in the highest places of an international association that they were not reserved simply for bearers of relics.

In a fundamental paper on symbolism,[73] Dr Jones points out, some-where around page 15, that although there are thousands of symbols in the sense that the term is understood in analysis, all of them refer to one's own body, to kinship relations, to birth, to life, and to death.

This truth, recognized here as a fact, enables us to understand that although, in psychoanalytic terms, the symbol is repressed in the un-conscious, it carries in itself no index of regression, or even of immaturity. For it to induce its effects in the subject, it is enough that it make itself heard, since these effects operate without his being aware of it – as we admit in our everyday experience, explaining many reactions of normal as well as of neurotic subjects by their response to the symbolic sense of an act, of a relation, or of an object.

There is therefore no doubt that the analyst can play on the power of the symbol by evoking it in a carefully calculated fashion in the semantic resonances of his remarks.

This is surely the way for a return to the use of symbolic effects in a renewed technique of interpretation in analysis.

In this regard, we could take note of what the Hindu tradition teaches about *dhvani*,[74] in the sense that this tradition stresses the property of speech by which it communicates what it does not actually say. Hindu tradition illustrates this by a tale whose ingenuousness, which appears to be the usual thing in these examples, shows itself humorous enough to induce us to penetrate the truth that it conceals.

A girl, it begins, is waiting for her lover on the bank of a stream when she sees a Brahmin coming along towards her. She runs to him and ex-claims in the warmest and most amiable tones: 'What a lucky day this is for you! The dog that used to frighten you by its barking will not be along this river bank again, for it has just been devoured by a lion that is often seen around here . . .'

The absence of the lion may thus have as much effect as his spring would have were he present, for the lion only springs once, says the proverb appreciated by Freud.[75]

The *primary* character of symbols in fact brings them close to those numbers out of which all the others are composed, and if they therefore underlie all the semantemes of a language (*langue*), we shall be able to restore to speech its full value of evocation by a discreet search for their interferences, using as our guide a metaphor whose symbolic displacement will neutralize the secondary meanings of the terms that it associates.

This technique would require for its teaching as well as for its learning a profound assimilation of the resources of a language (*langue*), and especially of those that are concretely realized in its poetic texts. It is well known that Freud was in this position in relation to German literature, which, by virtue of an incomparable translation, can be said to include Shakespeare's plays. Every one of his works bears witness to this, and to the continual recourse he had to it, no less in his technique than in his discovery – this in addition to a knowledge of the ancient classics, a modern initiation into folklore, and an interested participation in the conquests of contemporary humanism in the domain of ethnography.

It might well be demanded of the practitioner of analysis not to denigrate any attempt to follow Freud along this road.

But the tide is against us. It can be measured by the condescending attention paid to the 'wording',[76] as if to some novelty; and the English morphology of the term gives a subtle enough support to a notion still difficult to define, for people to make a point of using it.

What this notion masks, however, is not exactly encouraging when an author[77] is amazed by the fact of having obtained an entirely different result in the interpretation of one and the same resistance by the use, 'without conscious premeditation', he emphasizes, of the term 'need for love'[78] instead and in the place of 'demand for love',[79] which he had first put forward, without seeing anything deeper in it (as he emphasizes himself). If the anecdote is to confirm this reference of the interpretation to the 'ego psychology' in the title of the article, it is rather, it seems, a reference to the 'ego psychology' of the analyst, in so far as this interpretation makes shift with such a weak use of English that this writer can push his practice of analysis to the limits of a nonsensical stuttering.[80]

The fact is that 'need' and 'demand' have a diametrically opposed meaning for the subject, and to hold that their use can be confused even for an instant amounts to a radical *méconnaissance* of the 'intimation' of speech.

For in its symbolizing function speech is moving towards nothing less than a transformation of the subject to whom it is addressed by means of the link that it establishes with the one who emits it – in other words, by introducing the effect of a signifier.

This is why it is necessary for us to return once more to the structure of communication in language and to dissipate once and for all the mistaken notion of 'language as a sign', a source in this domain of confusions in discourse and of malpractices in speech.

If the communication of language is conceived as a signal by which the sender informs the receiver of something by means of a certain code, there is no reason why we should not give as much credence and even more to any other sign when the 'something' in question is of the individual: there is even every reason for us to give preference to any mode of expression that comes close to the natural sign.

It is in this way that the technique of speech has fallen into discredit among us. We can be seen in search of a gesture, a grimace, an attitude, an act of mimicry, a movement, a shudder, nay, an arrest of habitual movement; shrewd as we are, nothing can now stop us from letting our bloodhounds off the leash to follow these tracks.

I shall show the inadequacy of the conception of 'language as a sign' by the very manifestation that best illustrates it in the animal kingdom, a manifestation which, if it had not recently been the object of an authentic discovery, it seems it would have been necessary to invent for this purpose.

It is now generally admitted that when the bee returns to the hive from its honey-gathering it indicates to its companions by two sorts of dance the existence of nectar and its relative distance, near or far, from the hive. The second type of dance is the most remarkable, for the plane in which the bee traces the figure-of-eight curve – which is why it has been called the 'wagging dance',[81] – and the frequency of the figures executed within a given time, designate, on the one hand, exactly the direction to be followed, determined in relation to the inclination of the sun (on which bees are able to orientate themselves in all weathers, thanks to their sensitivity to polarized light), and, on the other hand, the distance, up to several miles, at which the nectar is to be found. And the other bees respond to this message by setting off immediately for the place thus designated.

It took some ten years of patient observation for Karl von Frisch to decode this kind of message, for it is certainly a code, or system of signalling, whose generic character alone forbids us to qualify it as conventional.

But is it necessarily a language? We can say that it is distinguished from language precisely by the fixed correlation of its signs to the reality that they signify. For in a language signs take on their value from their relations to each other in the lexical distribution of semantemes as much as in the positional, or even flectional, use of morphemes, in sharp contrast to the fixity of the coding used by bees. And the diversity of human languages (*langues*) takes on its full value from this enlightening discovery.

Furthermore, while the message of the kind described here determines the action of the *socius*, it is never retransmitted by it. This means that the message remains fixed in its function as a relay of the action, from which no subject detaches it as a symbol of communication itself.[82]

The form in which language is expressed itself defines subjectivity. Language says: 'You will go here, and when you see this, you will turn off there.' In other words, it refers itself to the discourse of the other. As such it is enveloped in the highest function of speech, in as much as speech commits its author by investing the person to whom it is addressed with a new reality, as for example, when by a 'You are my wife', a subject marks himself with the seal of wedlock.

This is in fact the essential form from which all human speech derives rather than the form at which it arrives.

Hence the paradox by which one of my most acute listeners, when I began to make my views known on analysis as dialectic, thought he could oppose my position by a remark that he formulated in the following terms: 'Human Language (according to you) constitutes a communication in which the sender receives his own message back from the receiver in an inverted form.' This was an objection that I had only to reflect on for a moment before recognizing that it carried the stamp of my own thinking – in other words, that speech always subjectively includes its own reply, that Pascal's '*Tu ne me chercherais pas si tu ne m'avais trouvé*'[83] simply confirms the same truth in different words, and that this is the reason why, in the paranoiac refusal of recognition, it is in the form of a negative verbalization that the inavowable feeling finally emerges in the persecutory 'interpretation'.

Furthermore, when you congratulate yourself on having met someone who speaks the same kind of language as you do, you do not mean that you meet with him in the discourse of everybody, but that you are united to him by a special kind of speech.

Thus the antinomy immanent in the relations between speech and language becomes clear. As language becomes more functional, it becomes improper for speech, and as it becomes too particular to us, it loses its function as language.

One is aware of the use made in primitive traditions of secret names in which the subject identifies his own person or his gods, to the point that to reveal these names is to lose himself or to betray these gods; and the confidences of our subjects, as well as our own memories, teach us that it is not at all rare for children to rediscover spontaneously the virtue of such a usage.

Finally, it is by the intersubjectivity of the 'we' that it assumes that the value of a language as speech is measured.

By an inverse antinomy, it can be observed that the more the function of language becomes neutralized as it moves closer to information, the more language is imputed to be laden with *redundancies*. This notion of redundancy in language originated in research that was all the more precise because a vested interest was involved, having been prompted by the economic problem of long-distance communication, and in particular that of the possibility of carrying several conversations at once on a single telephone line. It can be asserted that a substantial portion of the phonetic material is superfluous to the realization of the communication actually sought.

This is highly instructive for us,[84] for what is redundant as far as information is concerned is precisely that which does duty as resonance in speech.

For the function of language is not to inform but to evoke.

What I seek in speech is the response of the other. What constitutes me as subject is my question. In order to be recognized by the other, I utter what was only in view of what will be. In order to find him, I call him by a name that he must assume or refuse in order to reply to me.

I identify myself in language, but only by losing myself in it like an object. What is realized in my history is not the past definite of what was, since it is no more, or even the present perfect of what has been in what I am, but the future anterior of what I shall have been for what I am in the process of becoming.

If I now place myself in front of the other to question him, there is no cybernetic computer imaginable that can make a reaction out of what the response will be. The definition of response as the second term in the 'stimulus response' circuit is simply a metaphor sustained by the subjectivity imputed to the animal, a subjectivity that is then ignored in the physical schema to which the metaphor reduces it. This is what I have called putting the rabbit into the hat so as to be able to pull it out again later. But a reaction is not a reply.

If I press an electric button and a light goes on, there is no response except for *my* desire. If in order to obtain the same result I must try a whole system of relays whose correct position is unknown to me, there is no question except as concerns my anticipation, and there will not be one any longer, once I have learned enough about the system to operate it without mistakes.

But if I call the person to whom I am speaking by whatever name I choose to give him, I intimate to him the subjective function that he will take on again in order to reply to me, even if it is to repudiate this function.

Henceforth the decisive function of my own reply appears, and this function is not, as has been said, simply to be received by the subject as acceptance or rejection of his discourse, but really to recognize him or to abolish him as subject. Such is the nature of the analyst's *responsibility* whenever he intervenes by means of speech.

Moreover, the problem of the therapeutic effects of correct interpretation posed by Mr Edward Glover[85] in a remarkable paper has led him to conclusions where the question of correctness moves into the background. In other words, not only is every spoken intervention received by the subject in terms of his structure, but the intervention takes on a structuring function in him in proportion to its form. It is precisely the scope of nonanalytic psychotherapy, and even of the most ordinary medical 'prescriptions', to be interventions that could be described as obsessional systems of suggestion, as hysterical suggestions of a phobic order, even as persecutory supports, each one taking its particular character from the sanction it gives to the subject's *méconnaissance* of his own reality.

Speech is in fact a gift of language, and language is not immaterial. It is a subtle body, but body it is. Words are trapped in all the corporeal images that captivate the subject; they may make the hysteric 'pregnant', be identified with the object of *penis-neid*, represent the flood of urine of urethral ambition, or the retained faeces of avaricious *jouissance*.

What is more, words themselves can undergo symbolic lesions and accomplish imaginary acts of which the patient is the subject. You will remember the *Wespe* (wasp), castrated of its initial W to become the S.P. of the Wolf Man's initials at the moment when he realizes the symbolic punishment whose object he was on the part of Grusha, the wasp.[86]

You will remember also the S that constitutes the residue of the hermetic formula into which the conjuratory invocations of the Rat Man became condensed after Freud had extracted the anagram of the name of his beloved from its cipher, and which, tacked on to the final 'amen' of his jaculatory prayer, externally floods the lady's name with the symbolic ejection of his impotent desire.[87]

Similarly, an article by Robert Fliess,[88] inspired by Abraham's inaugural remarks, shows us that the discourse as a whole may become the object of an erotization, following the displacements of erogeneity in the body image as they are momentarily determined by the analytic relation.

The discourse then takes on a phallic-urethral, anal-erotic, or even an oral-sadistic function. It is in any case remarkable that the author seizes the effect of this function above all in the silences that mark the inhibition of the satisfaction experienced through it by the subject.

In this way speech may become an imaginary, or even real object in the subject and, as such, swallow up in more than one respect the function of language. We shall then place speech inside the parentheses of the resistance that it manifests.

But this will not be in order to put speech on the index of the analytic relation, for that relation would then lose everything, including its *raison d'être.*

Analysis can have for its goal only the advent of a true speech and the realization by the subject of his history in his relation to a future.

Maintaining this dialectic is in direct opposition to any objectifying orientation of analysis, and emphasizing this necessity is of first importance if we are to see through the aberrations of the new tendencies being manifested in psychoanalysis.

I shall illustrate my remarks on this point again by a return to Freud, and, since I have already made use of it, by the case of the Rat Man.

Freud even goes so far as to take liberties with factual accuracy when it is a question of attaining to the truth of the subject. At one moment he perceives the determining role played by the proposal of marriage brought to the subject by his mother at the origin of the present phase of his neurosis. In any case, as I have shown in my seminar, Freud had had a lightning intuition of it as a result of personal experience. Nevertheless, he does not hesitate to interpret its effect to the subject as that of his dead father's prohibition against his liaison with the lady of his thoughts.

This interpretation is not only factually inaccurate. It is also psychologically inaccurate, for the castrating action of the father, which Freud affirms here with an insistence that might be considered systematic, played only a secondary role in this case. But the apperception of the dialectical relationship is so apt that Freud's act of interpretation at that moment sets off the decisive lifting of the death-bearing symbols that bind the subject narcissistically both to his dead father and to the idealized lady, their two images being sustained, in an equivalence characteristic of the obsessional neurotic, one by the phantasmic aggressivity that perpetuates it, the other by the mortifying cult that transforms it into an idol.

Similarly, it is by recognizing the forced subjectification of the obsessional debt[89] in the scenario of the vain attempts at restitution – a scenario that too perfectly expresses the imaginary terms of this debt for the subject even to try to realize it – a debt whose pressure is exploited by the subject to the point of delusion, that Freud achieves his goal. This is the goal of bringing the subject to rediscover – in the history of his father's lack of delicacy, his marriage with the subject's mother, the 'poor, but pretty' girl, his marred love-life, the distasteful memory of the beneficent friend – to rediscover in this history, together with the fateful constellation[90] that had presided over the subject's very birth, the gap impossible to fill, of the symbolic debt of which his neurosis is the notice of non-payment.

There is no trace here at all of a recourse to the ignoble spectre of some sort of original 'fear', nor even to a masochism that it would be easy enough to brandish, even less to that obsessional counterforcing propagated by some analysts in the name of the analysis of defences. The resistances themselves, as I have shown elsewhere, are used as long as possible in the sense of the progress of the discourse. And when it is time to put an end to them, it is in acceding to them that the end is reached.

For it is in this way that the Rat Man succeeds in introducing into his subjectivity his true mediation in the transferential form of the imaginary daughter that he ascribes to Freud in order to receive through her a marriage tie with him, and who unveils her true face to him in a key dream: that of death gazing at him with her bituminous eyes.

Moreover, if it is with this symbolic pact that the ruses of the subject's servitude came to an end, reality did not fail him, it seems, in consummating these nuptials. And the footnote of 1923 [p. 249], which Freud dedicated by way of epitaph to this young man who had found in the risks of war 'the end that awaited so many young men of value on whom so many hopes could be founded', thus concluding the case with all the rigour of destiny, elevates it to the beauty of tragedy.

In order to know how to reply to the subject in analysis, the procedure is to recognize first of all the place where his *ego* is, the *ego* that Freud himself defined as an *ego* formed of a verbal nucleus; in other words, to know through whom and for whom the subject poses *his question*. So long as this is not known, there will be the risk of a misunderstanding concerning the desire that is there to be recognized and concerning the object to whom this desire is addressed.

The hysterical subject captures this object in an elaborate intrigue and, his *ego* is in the third party by whose mediation the subject enjoys that object in which his question is embodied. The obsessional subject drags into the cage of his narcissism the objects in which his question reverberates back and forth in the multiplied alibi of mortal figures and, subduing their heady acrobatics, addresses its ambiguous homage towards the box in which he himself has his seat, that of the master who cannot be seen or see himself.

Trahit sua quemque voluptas; one identifies himself with the spectacle, and the other puts one on.

For the hysterical subject, for whom the technical term 'acting out' takes on its literal meaning since he is acting outside himself, you have to get him to recognize where his action is situated. For the obsessional neurotic, you have to get him to recognize you in the spectator, invisible from the stage, to whom he is united by the mediation of death.

It is therefore always in the relation between the subject's ego (*moi*) and the 'I' (*je*) of his discourse that you must understand the meaning of the discourse if you are to achieve the dealienation of the subject.

But you cannot possibly achieve this if you cling to the idea that the ego of the subject is identical with the presence that is speaking to you.

This error is fostered by the terminology of the analytic topography, which is all too tempting to an objectifying cast of mind, allowing it to make an almost imperceptible transition from the concept of the ego defined as the perception-consciousness system, that is, as the system of the objectification of the subject – to the concept of the ego as correlative with an absolute reality and thus, in a singular return of the repressed in psychologistic thought, to rediscover in the ego the 'function of the real' in relation to which Pierre Janet, for instance, orders his psychological conceptions.

Such a transition can occur only when it has not been recognized that in the works of Freud the topography of the *ego*, the *id*, and the *superego* is subordinated to the metapsychology whose terms he was propounding at the same period and without which the new topography becomes meaningless. Thus analysts became involved in a sort of psychological orthopaedics that is still having its effect.

Michael Balint has analysed in a thoroughly penetrating way the intricate interaction of theory and technique in the genesis of a new conception of analysis, and he finds no better term to indicate the problem than the catchphrase, borrowed from Rickman, of the advent of a 'two-body psychology'.

It couldn't be better put. Analysis is becoming the relation of two bodies between which is established a phantasmic communication in which the analyst teaches the subject to apprehend himself as an object; subjectivity is admitted into it only within the parentheses of the illusion, and speech is placed on the index of a search for the lived experience that becomes its supreme aim, but the dialectically necessary result appears in the fact that, since the subjectivity of the analyst is free of all restraint, his subjectivity leaves the subject at the mercy of every summons of his speech.

Once the intrasubjective topography has become entified, it is in fact realized in the division of labour between the two subjects involved. And this deformed usage of Freud's formula that all that is of the *id* must become of the *ego* appears under a demystified form; the subject, transformed into a *cela*,[91] has to conform to an *ego* in which the analyst will have little trouble in recognizing his ally, since in actual fact it is to the analyst's *ego* that the subject is expected to conform.

This is precisely that process expressed in many a theoretical formulation of the 'splitting of the *ego*' in analysis. Half of the subject's *ego* passes over to the other side of the wall that separates the analysand from the analyst, then half of that half, and so on, in an asymptotic procession that will never succeed, however far it advances into the opinion that the subject has acquired of himself, in cancelling out the whole of the margin from which he can go back on the aberration of the analysis.

But how could the subject of a type of analysis whose axis is the principle that all his formulations are systems of defence be defended against the total disorientation in which this principle leaves the dialectic of the analyst?

Freud's interpretation, whose dialectical method appears so clearly in the case of Dora,[92] does not present these dangers, for, when the analyst's prejudices (that is to say, his counter-transference, a term whose use in my opinion cannot be extended beyond the dialectical reasons for the error) have misled him in his intervention, he pays the price for it on the spot by a negative transference. For this negative transference manifests itself with a force that is all the greater the further such an analysis has already involved the subject in an authentic recognition, and what usually results is the breaking off of the analysis.

This is exactly what happened in Dora's case, because of Freud's relentless persistence in wanting to make her recognize the hidden object of her desire in the person of Herr K, in whom the constituting presumptions of his counter-transference lured him into seeing the promise of her happiness.

Dora herself was undoubtedly deceived in this relation, but she did not resent any the less the fact that Freud, too, was deceived. But she came back to see him, after a delay of fifteen months in which the fateful cipher of her 'time for understanding' is inscribed, we can sense her embarking on a deception that she had been deceiving, and the convergence of this second-degree deception with the aggressive intention imputed to her by Freud – and not inaccurately, but without his recognizing what it actually sprang from – presents us with the rough outline of the intersubjective complicity that any 'analysis of resistances' sure of its rights might have perpetuated between them. There can be little doubt that with the means now offered us by the progress of our technique, this human error could have been extended beyond the limits of the diabolical.

None of this is of my own invention, for Freud himself later recognized the prejudicial source of his defeat in his own *méconnaissance* at the time of the homosexual position of the object at which the hysterical subject's desire was aimed.[93]

No doubt the whole process that has culminated in this present tendency of psychoanalysis goes back, and from the very first, to the analyst's guilty conscience about the miracle operated by his speech. He interprets the symbol and, lo and behold, the symptom, which inscribes the symbol in letters of suffering in the subject's flesh, disappears. This unseemly thaumaturgy is unbecoming to us, for after all we are scientists, and magic is not a practice we can defend. So we disclaim responsibility by attributing magical thinking to the patient. Before long we'll be preaching the Gospel according to Lévy-Bruhl to him. But in the meantime, lo and behold, we have become thinkers again, and have re-established the proper distance between ourselves and our patients – a traditional distance that was perhaps a little too recklessly abandoned, a distance expressed so nobly in the words of Pierre Janet when he spoke of the feeble abilities of the hysterical subject compared to our own lofty position. The poor little thing, he confides to us, 'she understands nothing about science, and doesn't even imagine how anybody could be interested in it. . . . If we consider the absence of control that characterizes their thinking, instead of allowing ourselves to be scandalized by their lies, which, in any case, are very naïve, we should rather be astonished that there are so many truthful ones', and so on.

Since these words represent the feelings to which many present-day analysts who condescend to talk to the patient 'in his own language' have returned, they may help us to understand what has happened in the meantime. For if Freud had been capable of subscribing to such feelings, how would he have been able to hear as he did the truth enclosed within the little stories of his first patients, or decipher a gloomy delusion like Schreber's to the point of extending it to embrace man eternally bound to his symbols?

Is our reason so weak that it cannot recognize itself on equal terms in the mediation of scientific discourse and in the primary exchange of the symbolic object, and cannot rediscover there the identical measure of its original cunning?

Need I point out what the yardstick of 'thought' is worth to practitioners of an experience that is occupied rather more closely with an intestinal eroticism than with an equivalent of action?

Need I point out that I do not have to resort to 'thought' to understand that if I am talking to you in this moment of speech, it is in so far as we have in common a technique of speech that enables you to understand me when I speak to you, and which disposes me to address myself through you to those who understand nothing of that technique?

Certainly we must be attentive to the 'un-said' that lies in the holes of the discourse, but this does not mean that we are to listen as if to someone knocking on the other side of a wall.

For if we are to concern ourselves from now on with nothing but these sounds, as some analysts pride themselves on doing, it must be admitted that we have not placed ourselves in the most favourable conditions to decipher their meaning. Without first racking our brains to understand this meaning, how can one translate what is not of itself language? Led in this way to appeal to the subject, since it is after all to *his* account that we must transfer this understanding, we shall implicate him with us in the wager, a wager that we understand him and then wait until a return makes us both winners. As a result, in continuing to perform this shuttling back and forth, he will learn quite simply to set the pace himself, a form of suggestion that is no worse than any other – in other words, a form of suggestion in which, as in every other form of suggestion, one does not know who is keeping the score. The procedure is recognized as being sound enough when it is a question of being six feet under.[94]

Half-way to this extreme the question arises: does psychoanalysis remain a dialectical relation in which the non-action of the analyst guides the subject's discourse towards the realization of his truth, or is it to be reduced to a phantasmatic relation in which 'two abysses brush against each other' without touching, while the whole gamut of imaginary regressions is exhausted – like a sort of 'bundling'[95] pushed to its extreme limits as a psychological experience?

In fact, this illusion that impels us to seek the reality of the subject beyond the language barrier is the same as that by which the subject believes that his truth is already given in us and that we know it in advance; and it is moreover as a result of this that he is wide open to our objectifying intervention.

But for his part, no doubt, he does not have to answer for this subjective error which, whether it is avowed or not in his discourse, is immanent in the fact that he has entered analysis, and that he has already concluded the original pact involved in it. And the fact that we find in the subjectivity of this moment the reason for what can be called the constituting effects of the transference – in so far as they are distinguished by an index of reality from the constituted effects that succeed them – is all the more ground for not neglecting this subjectivity.[96]

Freud, let it be recalled, in touching on the feelings involved in the transference, insisted on the need to distinguish in it a factor of reality. He concluded that it would be an abuse of the subject's docility to want to persuade him in every case that these sentiments are a mere transferential repetition of the neurosis.[97] Consequently, since these real feelings manifest themselves as primary and since the charm of our own persons remains a doubtful factor, there would seem to be some mystery here.

But this mystery becomes clarified if it is viewed within the phenomenology of the subject, in so far as the subject constitutes himself in the search for truth. One has only to go back to the traditional givens – which the Buddhists could provide us with, although they are not the only ones who could – to recognize in this form of the transference the normal error of existence, under the three headings of love, hate, and ignorance. It is therefore as a counter-effect of the movement of analysis that we shall understand their equivalence in what is called an originally positive transference – each one being illuminated by the other two under this existential aspect, if one does not except the third, which is usually omitted because of its proximity to the subject.

Here I evoke the invective through which I was called on as a witness to the lack of discretion shown by a certain work (which I have already cited too often) in its senseless objectification of the play of the instincts in analysis, by someone whose debt to me can be recognized by his use of the term 'real' in conformity with mine. It was in these words that, as people say, he 'unburdened his heart': 'It is high time to put an end to the fraud that tends to perpetrate the belief that anything real whatsoever takes place during treatment.' Let us leave aside what has befallen it, for alas, if analysis has not cured the dog's oral vice of which the Gospel speaks, its condition is worse than before: it is other people's vomit that it laps up.

For this sally was not ill directed, since it sought in fact to distinguish between those elementary registers whose grounding I later put forward in these terms: the symbolic, the imaginary, and the real – a distinction never previously made in psychoanalysis.

Reality in the analytic experience does in fact often remain veiled under negative forms, but it is not too difficult to situate it.

Reality is encountered, for instance, in what we usually condemn as active interventions; but it would be an error to define the limit of reality in this way.

For it is clear on the other hand that the analyst's abstention, his refusal to reply, is an element of reality in analysis. More exactly, it is in this negativity in so far as it is a pure negativity – that is, detached from any particular motive – that lies the junction between the symbolic and the real. This naturally follows from the fact that this non-action of the analyst is founded on our firm and stated knowledge of the principle that all that is real is rational, and on the resulting precept that it is up to the subject to show what he is made of.

The fact remains that this abstention is not maintained indefinitely; when the subject's question has taken on the form of true speech, we give it the sanction of our reply, but thereby we have shown that true speech already contains its own reply and that we are simply adding our own lay to its antiphon. What can this mean except that we do no more than to confer on the subject's speech its dialectical punctuation?

The other moment in which the symbolic and the real come together is consequently revealed, and I have already marked it theoretically: that is to say, in the function of time, and this makes it worth pausing for a moment to consider the technical effects of time.

Time plays its role in analytic technique in several ways.

It presents itself first of all in the total duration of the analysis, and involves the meaning to be given to the termination of the analysis, which is the question that must precede that of the signs of its end. I shall touch on the problem of fixing its termination. But it is now clear that this duration can only be anticipated for the subject as indefinite.

This is for two reasons that can only be distinguished in a dialectical perspective:

The first, which is linked to the limits of our field, and which confirms my remarks on the definition of its confines: we cannot predict for the subject what his 'time for understanding' will be, in so far as it includes a psychological factor that escapes us as such.

The second, which is properly of the subject and through which the fixing of a termination is equivalent to a spatializing projection in which he finds himself already alienated from himself at the very beginning: from the moment that the coming-to-term of his truth can be predicted – whatever may come about in the ensuing interval in the intersubjective relation of the subject and the analyst – the fact is that the truth is already there. That is to say that in this way we re-establish in the subject his original mirage in so far as he places his truth in us, and that if we then give him the sanction of our authority, we are setting the analysis off on an aberrant path whose results will be impossible to correct.

This is precisely what happened in the celebrated case of the Wolf Man, and Freud so well understood its exemplary importance that he took support from it again in his article on finite or indefinite analysis.[98]

The fixing in advance of a termination to an analysis, a first form of active intervention, inaugurated (*pro pudor!*) by Freud himself,[99] whatever may be the divinatory sureness (in the proper sense of the term)[100] of which the analyst may give proof in following his example, will invariably leave the subject in the alienation of his truth.

Moreover, we find the confirmation of this point in two facts from Freud's case:

In the first place, in spite of the whole cluster of proofs demonstrating the historicity of the primal scene, in spite of the conviction that he shows concerning it – remaining imperturbable to the doubts that Freud methodically cast on it in order to test him – the Wolf Man never managed in spite of it all to integrate his recollection of the primal scene into his history.

Secondly, the same patient later demonstrated his alienation in the most categorical way, in a paranoid form.

It is true that here there is at work another factor through which reality intervenes in the analysis – namely, the gift of money whose symbolic value I shall save to treat of elsewhere, but whose import is indicated in what I have already said concerning the link between speech and the constituting gift of primitive exchange. In this case the gift of money is reversed by an initiative of Freud's in which, as much as in his insistence

on coming back to the case, we can recognize the unresolved subjectification within him of the problems that this case leaves in suspense. And
nobody doubts that this was a factor in the subsequent onset of the psychosis, however without really being able to say why.

Surely it is understood nevertheless that admitting a subject to be
nurtured in the prytaneum[101] of psychoanalysis in return for services
he renders to science as a case available for study (for it was in fact through
a group collection that the Wolf Man was supported), is also to initiate
and establish him in the alienation of his truth?

The material of the supplementary analysis of the Wolf Man undertaken by Ruth Mack Brunswick[102] illustrates the responsibility of the
previous treatment with Freud by demonstrating my remarks on the
respective places of speech and language in psychoanalytic mediation.

What is more, it is in the perspective of speech and language that one
can grasp how Ruth Mack Brunswick has not at all taken her bearings
incorrectly in her delicate position in relation to the transference. (The
reader will be reminded of the very wall of my metaphor of the lar ʒuage
barrier, in that the wall figures in one of the Wolf Man's dreams, the wolves
of the key-dream showing themselves eager to get around it . . .) Those
who follow my seminar know all this, and the others can try their hand
at it if they like.[103]

What I want to do is to touch on another aspect of analysis that is
particularly ticklish at the moment, that of the function of time in the
technique of analysis. I wish to say something about the duration of the
session.

Once again it is a question of an element that manifestly belongs to
reality, since it represents our working time, and from that angle it falls
under the heading of the prevalent professional rule.

But its subjective effects are no less important – and in the first place
for the analyst. The taboo nature that has recently characterized discussion
of this time limit proves well enough that the subjectivity of the psychoanalytic group is not at all entirely free in this respect, and the scrupulous,
not to say obsessional, character that the observation of a standard time
limit takes on for some if not most analysts – a standard whose historical
and geographical variation seems nevertheless to bother no one – is
certainly the sign of the existence of a problem that they are all the more
reluctant to deal with because they realize to what extent it would entail
a putting into question of the function of the analyst.

On the other hand, nobody can possibly fail to recognize its importance for the subject in analysis. The unconscious, it is said, in a tone that is all the more evident in proportion as the speaker is less capable of justifying what he means – the unconscious needs time to reveal itself. I quite agree. But I ask: how is this time to be measured? Is its measure to be that of what Alexandre Koyré calls 'the universe of precision'? Obviously we live in this universe, but its advent for man is relatively recent, since it goes back precisely to Huyghens' clock – in other words, to 1659 – and the *malaise* of modern man does not exactly indicate that this precision is in itself a liberating factor for him. Are we to say that this time, the time of the fall of heavy bodies, is in some way sacred in the sense that it corresponds to the time of the stars as they were fixed in eternity by God who, as Lichtenberg put it, winds up our sundials? Perhaps we might get a somewhat better idea of time by comparing the time required for the creation of a symbolic object with the moment of inattention when we let it fall.

However this may be, if the labour of our function during this time remains problematic, I believe I have brought out clearly enough the function of labour in what the patient brings to realization during that time.

But the reality of this time, whatever that reality may be, consequently takes on a localized value from it: that of receiving the product of this labour.

We play a recording role by assuming the function, fundamental in any symbolic exchange, of gathering what *do kamo*, man in his authenticity, calls 'the lasting word'.[104]

As a witness called to account for the sincerity of the subject, depositary of the minutes of his discourse, reference as to his exactitude, guarantor of his uprightness, custodian of his testament, scrivener of his codicils, the analyst has something of the scribe about him.

But above all he remains the master of the truth of which this discourse is the progress. As I have said, it is he above all who punctuates its dialectic. And here he is apprehended as the judge of the value of this discourse. This entails two consequences.

The suspension of a session cannot *not* be experienced by the subject as a punctuation in his progress. We know very well how he calculates its coming-to-term in order to articulate it upon his own delays, or even upon the loopholes he leaves himself, how he anticipates its end by weighing it like a weapon, by watching out for it as he would for a place of shelter.

It is a fact, which can be plainly seen in the study of the manuscripts of symbolic writings, whether it is a question of the Bible or of the Chinese canonicals, that the absence of punctuation in them is a source of ambiguity. The punctuation, once inserted, fixes the meaning; changing the punctuation renews or upsets it; and a faulty punctuation amounts to a change for the worse.

The indifference with which the cutting up of the 'timing'[105] interrupts the moments of haste within the subject can be fatal to the conclusion towards which his discourse was being precipitated, or can even fix a misunderstanding or misreading in it, if not furnish a pretext for a retaliatory ruse.

Beginners seem more struck by the effects of this fact than others – which makes one think that for the others it is simply a matter of submitting to routine.

Certainly the neutrality that we manifest in strictly applying the rule concerning the length of the session maintains us in the path of our non-action.

But this non-action has its limits, otherwise there would be no interventions at all – and why make an intervention impossible at this point, which is consequently privileged in this way?

The danger that this point may take on an obsessional value for the analyst rests simply in the fact that it lends itself to the connivance of the subject, a connivance that is not only overt for the obsessional subject, but which takes on a special force for him, precisely from his feelings about his labour. The keynote of forced labour that envelops everything for this subject, even the activities of his leisure time, is only too well known.

This meaning is sustained by his subjective relation to the master in so far as it is the master's death for which he waits.

In fact the obsessional subject manifests one of the attitudes that Hegel did not develop in his dialectic of the master and the slave. The slave has given way in face of the risk of death in which mastery was being offered to him in a struggle of pure prestige. But since he knows that he is mortal, he also knows that the master can die. From this moment on he is able to accept his labouring for the master and his renunciation of pleasure in the meantime; and, in the uncertainty of the moment when the master will die, he waits.

Such is the intersubjective reason, as much for the doubt as for the procrastination that are character traits of the obsessional subject.

In the meantime, all his labour falls under the heading of this intention, and becomes doubly alienating by this fact. For not only is the subject's handiwork taken from him by another – which is the constituting relation of all labour – but the subject's recognition of his own essence in his handiwork, in which this labour finds its justification, also eludes him, for he himself '*is* not in it'. He *is* in the anticipated moment of the master's death, from which moment he will begin to live, but in the meantime he identifies himself with the master as dead, and as a result of this he is himself already dead.

Nevertheless he makes an effort to deceive the master by the demonstration of the good intentions manifested in his labour. This is what the dutiful children of the analytic catechism express in their rough and ready way by saying that the subject's *ego* is trying to seduce his *superego*.

This intrasubjective formulation becomes immediately demystified once it is understood in the analytic relation, where the subject's 'working through' is in fact employed for the seduction of the analyst.

Nor is it by chance that, from the moment that the dialectical progress begins to approach the questioning of the intentions of the *ego* in our subjects, the phantasy of the analyst's death – often felt in the form of fear or even of anxiety – never fails to be produced.

And the subject then sets off again in an even more demonstrative elaboration of his 'good will'.

How, then, can we doubt the effect of any disdain shown by the master towards the product of such labour? The subject's resistance may even become completely disconcerted because of it.

From this moment, his alibi – hitherto unconscious – begins to unveil itself for him, and he can be seen passionately in quest of the justification of so many efforts.

I would not have so much to say about it if I had not been convinced that, in experimenting with what have been called my short sessions, at a stage in my experience that is now concluded, I was able to bring to light in a certain male subject phantasies of anal pregnancy as well as the dream of its resolution by Caesarean section, in a delaying of the end of the session where I would otherwise have had to go on listening to his speculations on the art of Dostoievsky.

However, I am not here to defend this procedure, but to show that it has a precise dialectical meaning in its technical application.[106]

And I am not the only one to have remarked that it ultimately becomes one with the technique known as *Zen*, which is applied as the means of the subject's revelation in the traditional ascesis of certain Far Eastern schools.

Without going to the extremes to which this technique is carried, since they would be contrary to certain of the limitations imposed by ours, a discreet application of its basic principle in analysis seems much more acceptable to me than certain modes of analysis known as the analysis of resistances, in so far as this technique does not in itself entail any danger of the subject's alienation.

For this technique only breaks the discourse in order to deliver speech.

Here we are then, at the foot of the wall, at the foot of the language barrier. We are in our place there, that is to say, on the same side as the patient, and it is on this wall – the same for him as for us – that we shall try to respond to the echo of his speech.

Beyond this wall, there is nothing for us but outer darkness. Does this mean that we are entirely masters of the situation? Certainly not, and on this point Freud has bequeathed us his testament on the negative therapeutic reaction.

The key to this mystery, it is said, is in the agency of a primordial masochism – in other words, in a pure manifestation of that death instinct whose enigma Freud propounded for us at the height of his experience.

We cannot turn up our noses at this problem, any more than I can postpone examination of it here.

For I note that this same refusal to accept this culminating point of Freud's doctrine is shared by those who conduct their analysis on the basis of a conception of the *ego* whose error I have denounced, and by those whom, like Reich, go so far with the principle of seeking the ineffable organic expression beyond speech that, like him, in order to deliver it from its armour, they might symbolize, as he does, the orgasmic induction that, like him, they expect from analysis, in the superimposition of the two vermicular forms whose stupefying schema may be seen in his book on character analysis.

Such a combination will no doubt allow me an optimistic view of the rigour of the formations of the mind, when I have demonstrated the profound relationship uniting the notion of the death instinct to the problems of speech.

As a moment's reflection shows, the notion of the death instinct involves a basic irony, since its meaning has to be sought in the conjunction of two contrary terms: instinct in its most comprehensive acceptation being the law that governs in its succession a cycle of behaviour whose goal is the accomplishment of a vital function; and death appearing first of all as the destruction of life.

Nevertheless, both the definition of life, given by Bichat at the dawn of biology, as being the whole set of forces that resist death; as well as the most modern conception of life – to be found in Cannon's notion of homeostasis – as the function of a system maintaining its own equilibrium, are there to remind us that life and death are compounded in a polar relation at the very heart of phenomena related to life.

So the congruence between the contrasted terms of the death instinct and the phenomena of repetition to which Freud's explanation in fact related them under the term 'automatism'[107] ought not to cause difficulty, if it were simply a question of a biological notion.

But we all know very well that it is not a question of biology, and this is what makes this problem a stumbling block for so many of us. The fact that so many people come to a halt on the apparent incompatibility of these terms might well be worth our attention in that it manifests a dialectical innocence that would probably be somewhat disconcerted by the classical problem posed to semantics in the determinative declaration: a hamlet on the Ganges, by which Hindu aesthetics illustrates the second form of the resonances of language.[108]

This notion must be approached through its resonances in what I shall call the poetics of the Freudian corpus, the first way of access to the penetration of its meaning, and the essential dimension, from the origins of the work to the apogee marked in it by this notion, for an understanding of its dialectical repercussions. It must be remembered, for example, that Freud tells us he found his vocation for medicine in the call heard during a public reading of Goethe's famous 'Hymn to Nature' – in that text brought to light by a friend in which the poet, in the declining years of his life, agreed to recognize a putative child of the most youthful effusions of his pen.

At the other end of Freud's life, we find in the article on analysis considered as finite or indefinite, the express reference of his new conception to the conflict of the two principles to which the alternation of universal life was subjected by Empedocles of Agrigentum in the fifth century B.C. – that is, in the pre-Socratic period where nature and mind were not distinguished.[109]

These two facts are a sufficient indication that here it is a question of a myth of the dyad, whose exposition by Plato is in any case evoked in *Beyond the Pleasure Principle*, a myth that can only be understood in the subjectivity of modern man by its elevation to the negativity of the judgement in which it is inscribed.

This is to say that, in the same was as the repetition compulsion – all the more misunderstood by those who wish to divide the two terms from each other – has in view nothing less than the historizing temporality of the experience of transference,[110] so does the death instinct essentially express the limit of the historical function of the subject. This limit is death – not as an eventual coming-to-term of the life of the individual, nor as the empirical certainty of the subject, but, as Heidegger's formula puts it, as that 'possibility which is one's ownmost, unconditional, unsupersedable, certain and as such indeterminable (*unüberholbare*)',[111] for the subject – 'subject' understood as meaning the subject defined by his historicity.

Indeed, this limit is at every instant present in what this history possesses as achieved. This limit represents the past in its real form, that is to say, not the physical past whose existence is abolished, nor the epic past as it has become perfected in the work of memory, nor the historic past in which man finds the guarantor of his future, but the past which reveals itself reversed in repetition.[112]

This is the dead partner taken by subjectivity in the triad which its mediation institutes in the univeral conflict of *Philia*, 'love', and *Neikos*, 'discord'.

There is therefore no further need to have recourse to the outworn notion of primordial masochism in order to understand the reason for the repetitive games in which subjectivity brings together mastery of its dereliction and the birth of the symbol.

These are the games of occultation[113] which Freud, in a flash of genius, revealed to us so that we might recognize in them that the moment in which desire becomes human is also that in which the child is born into language.

We can now grasp in this the fact that in this moment the subject is not simply mastering his privation by assuming it, but that here he is raising his desire to a second power. For his action destroys the object that it causes to appear and disappear in the anticipating *provocation* of its absence and its presence. His action thus negatives the field of forces of desire in order to become its own object to itelf. And this object, being immediately embodied in the symbolic dyad of two elementary exclamations, announces in the subject the diachronic integration of the dichotomy of the phonemes, whose synchronic structure existing language offers to his assimilation; moreover, the child begins to become engaged in the system of the concrete discourse of the environment, by reproducing more or less approximately in his *Fort!* and in his *Da!* the vocables that he receives from it.

Fort! Da! It is precisely in his solitude that the desire of the little child has already become the desire of another, of an *alter ego* who dominates him and whose object of desire is henceforth his own affliction.

If the child now addresses himself to an imaginary or real partner, he will also see this partner obey the negativity of his discourse, and since his appeal has the effect of making the partner disappear, he will seek in a banishing summons the provocation of the return that brings the partner back to his desire.

Thus the symbol manifests itself first of all as the murder of the thing, and this death constitutes in the subject the eternalization of his desire.

The first symbol in which we recognize humanity in its vestigial traces is the sepulture, and the intermediary of death can be recognized in every relation in which man comes to the life of his history.

This is the only life that endures and is true, since it is transmitted without being lost in the perpetuated tradition of subject to subject. How is it possible not to see how loftily this life transcends that inherited by the animal, in which the individual disappears into the species, since no memorial distinguishes his ephemeral apparition from that which will reproduce it again in the invariability of the type. In fact, apart from those hypothetical mutations of the *phylum* that must be integrated by a subjectivity that man is still only approaching from the outside – nothing, except the experiments to which man associates it, distinguishes a rat from the rat, a horse from the horse, nothing except this inconsistent passage from life to death – whereas Empedocles, by throwing himself into Mount Etna, leaves forever present in the memory of men this symbolic act of his being-for-death.

Man's freedom is entirely inscribed within the constituting triangle of the renunciation that he imposes on the desire of the other by the menace of death for the enjoyment of the fruits of his serfdom – of the consented-to sacrifice of his life for the reasons that give to human life its measure – and of the suicidal renunciation of the vanquished partner, depriving of his victory the master whom he abandons to his inhuman solitude.

Of these figures of death, the third is the supreme detour through which the immediate particularity of desire, reconquering its ineffable form, rediscovers in negation a final triumph. And we must recognize its meaning, for we have to deal with it. This third figure is not in fact a perversion of the instinct, but rather that desperate affirmation of life that is the purest form in which we recognize the death instinct.

The subject says 'No!' to this intersubjective game of hunt-the-slipper in which desire makes itself recognized for a moment, only to become lost in a will that is will of the other. Patiently, the subject withdraws his precarious life from the sheeplike conglomerations of the Eros of the symbol in order to affirm it at the last in an unspoken curse.

So when we wish to attain in the subject what was before the serial articulations of speech, and what is primordial to the birth of symbols, we find it in death, from which his existence takes on all the meaning it has. It is in effect as a desire for death that he affirms himself for others; if he identifies himself with the other, it is by fixing him solidly in the metamorphosis of his essential image, and no being is ever evoked by him except among the shadows of death.

To say that this mortal meaning reveals in speech a centre exterior to language is more than a metaphor; it manifests a structure. This structure is different from the spatialization of the circumference or of the sphere in which some people like to schematize the limits of the living being and his milieu:[114] it corresponds rather to the relational group that symbolic logic designates topologically as an annulus.

If I wished to give an intuitive representation of it, it seems that, rather than have recourse to the surface aspect of a zone, I should call on the three-dimensional form of a torus, in so far as its peripheral exteriority and its central exteriority constitute only one single region.[115]

This schema satisfactorily expresses the endless circularity of the dialectical process that is produced when the subject brings his solitude to realization, be it in the vital ambiguity of immediate desire or in the full assumption of his being-for-death.

But by the same fact it can be grasped that the dialectic is not individual, and that the question of the termination of the analysis is that of the moment when the satisfaction of the subject finds a way to realize himself in the satisfaction of everyone – that is to say, of all those whom this satisfaction associates with itself in a human undertaking. Of all the undertakings that have been proposed in this century, that of the psychoanalyst is perhaps the loftiest, because the undertaking of the psychoanalyst acts in our time as a mediator between the man of care and the subject of absolute knowledge.[116] This is therefore why it requires a long subjective ascesis, and one which can never be interrupted, since the end of the training analysis itself is not separable from the engagement of the subject in its practice.

Let it be renounced, then, by whoever cannot rejoin at its horizon the subjectivity of his time. For how could he possibly make his being the axis of so many lives if he knew nothing of the dialectic that engages him with these lives in a symbolic movement? Let him be well acquainted with the whorl into which his period draws him in the continued enterprise of Babel, and let him be aware of his function as interpreter in the discord of languages. As for the darkness of the *mundus* around which the immense tower is coiled, let him leave to the mystic vision the task of seeing in it the putrescent serpent of life raised on an everlasting rod.[117]

I may be permitted a laugh if these remarks are accused of turning the meaning of Freud's work away from the biological basis he would have wished for it towards the cultural references with which it is shot through. I do not want to preach to you the doctrine of factor *b*, designating the first, nor of factor *c*, designating the second. All I have tried to do is to remind you of the misconstrued *a*, *b*, *c* of the structure of language, and to teach you to spell once again the forgotten *b–a*, *ba*, of speech.[118]

For what recipe would guide you in a technique that is composed of the first and draws its effects from the second, if you did not recognize the field and the function of both?

The psychoanalytic experience has rediscovered in man the imperative of the Word as the law that has formed him in its image. It manipulates the poetic function of language to give to his desire its symbolic mediation. May that experience enable you to understand at last that it is in the gift of speech[119] that all the reality of its effects resides; for it is by way of this gift that all reality has come to man and it is by his continued act that he maintains it.

If the domain defined by this gift of speech is to be sufficient for your action as also for your knowledge, it will also be sufficient for your devotion. For it offers it a privileged field.

When the Devas, the men, and the Asuras were ending their novitiate with Prajapâti, so we read in the second Brâhmana of the fifth lesson of the Bhrad-âranyaka Upanishad, they addressed to him this prayer: 'Speak to us.'

'*Da*', said Prajapâti, god of thunder. 'Did you hear me?' And the Devas answered and said: 'Thou hast said to us: *Damyata*, master yourselves' – the sacred text meaning that the powers above submit to the law of speech.

'*Da*', said Prajapâti, god of thunder. 'Did you hear me?' And the men answered and said: 'Thou hast said to us: *Datta*, give' – the sacred text meaning that men recognize each other by the gift of speech.

'*Da*', said Prajapâti, god of thunder. 'Did you hear me?' And the Asuras answered and said: 'Thou has said to us: *Dayadhyam*, be merciful'

– the sacred text meaning that the powers below resound to the invocation of speech.[120]

That, continues the text, is what the divine voice caused to be heard in the thunder: Submission, gift, grace. *Da da da*.[121]

For Prajapâti replies to all: 'You have heard me.'

〉〉〈〈

Notes

1. Ferenczi, 'Confusion of Tongues between the Adult and the Child', *International Journal of Psycho-Analysis* XXX (1949), iv; 225–30.

2. English in the original [Tr.].

3. The reference is Rimbaud's *The Lice Seekers*. The author in question is the French analyst Bénassy [Tr.].

4. 'Put true and stable speech into my mouth and make of me a cautious tongue' (*The Internal Consolation*, Chapter XLV: That one should not believe everyone and of slight stumbling over words) [Tr.].

5. 'Always a cause' or 'keep talking' [Tr.].

6. Paragraph rewritten in 1966.

7. Boileau, *L'Art Poétique*, I:
Hâtez-vous lentement; et, sans perdre courage,
Vingt fois sur le métier remettez votre ouvrage:
In Pope's translation:
Gently make haste, of labour not afraid
A hundred times consider what you've said: [Tr.].

8. Previously I had written: 'in psychological matters . . .' (1966).

9. Paragraph rewritten in 1966.

10. This is the crux of a deviation as much practical as theoretical. For to identify the *ego* with the discipline of the subject is to confuse imaginary isolation with the mastery of the instincts. This lays one open to errors of judgement in the conduct of the treatment: such as trying to reinforce the *ego* in many neuroses caused by its overforceful structure – and that is a dead end. Hasn't my friend Michael Balint written that a reinforcement of the *ego* should be beneficial to the subject suffering from *ejaculatio praecox* because it would permit him to prolong the suspension of his desire? But this can surely not be so, if it is precisely to the fact that his desire is made dependent upon the imaginary function of the *ego* that the subject owes the short-circuiting of the act – which psychoanalytic clinical experience shows clearly to be intimately linked to narcissistic identification with the partner.

11. This is the same work that I praised at the end of my Introduction. [Added 1966.] It is clear in what follows that aggressivity is only a lateral effect of analytic frustration, even if this effect can be reinforced by a certain type of intervention; as such, this effect is not the reason for the frustration/regression dyad.

12. The allusion is to the function of the *tessera* as a token of recognition, or 'password'. The *tessera* was used in the early mystery religions where fitting together again the two halves of a broken piece of pottery was used as a means of recognition by the initiates – and in Greece the *tessera* was called the *sumbolon*. The central concept involved in the symbol is that of a *link* [Tr.].

The allusion to Mallarmé is to a passage in his preface to René Ghil's *Traité du Verbe* (1866); it can be found in the *Oeuvres complètes* (Paris: Pléiade, 1945, 368 and 857) [Tr.].

13. The reference is to Reik's *Listening with the Third Ear* [Tr.].

14. *Verbaliser*, in its legal sense, is the

equivalent of 'to write a traffic ticket'. *Pandore* is a slang term for a policeman. But *verbaliser* also has the sense of 'to talk too long' [Tr.].

15. '*Le verbe*'. Like 'the Word', *le verbe* translates the Greek 'Logos' [Tr.].

16. The Greek '*epos*' may variously mean 'word', 'speech', 'tale', 'song', 'promise', 'saying', 'message', and, in the plural, 'epic poetry', 'lines of verse' [Tr.].

17. *Gesammelte Werke* henceforth abbreviated *GW*, **XII**: 71; *Cinq psychanalyses*, Presses Universitaires de France henceforth abbreviated PUF, 356, a weak translation of the term.

18. *GW*, **XII**: 72, n.1, last few lines. The concept of *Nachträglichkeit* is to be found once more stressed in the note. *Cinq psychanalyses*, 356, n.1. *Standard Edition*, **XVII**: 45, n.1.

19. An article originally published in French in the *Revue Neurologique* as 'L'Hérédité et l'étiologie des névroses'. See *Standard Edition*, **III**: 143–56. The blunder denounced here illustrates among others how the said authority measured up to his 'leadership'.

20. The word-play is on '*interlocution*' and '*interloqué*' [Tr.].

21. Even if he is speaking 'off', he addresses himself to that Other with a capital 'O' whose theoretical basis I have consolidated since this was written, and which demands a certain *epoché* in the resumption of the term to which I limited myself at that time: that of 'inter-subjectivity' (1966).

22. I borrow these terms from the late Édouard Pichon who, both in the indications he gave for the development of our discipline and in those that guided him in people's dark places, showed a divination that I can attribute only to his practice of semantics.

23. English in the original [Tr.].

24. [Added 1966:] This reference to the aporia of Christianity announced a more precise one in its Jansenist culmen: a reference to Pascal in fact, whose wager, still intact, forced me to take the whole question up again in order to get at what

it conceals, which is inestimable for psychoanalysis – at this date (June 1966) still in reserve. [Pascal's '*pari*' on the '*infini-rien*' is to be found in *Pensée* 233 of the Brunschvicq edition, 451 of the Pléiade edition.]

25. 'There are people who would never have been in love, if they had never heard talk of love' (Maxim CXXXVI, Garnier edition) [Tr.].

26. '*Une vérité de La Palice*' is a self-evident truth, a truism [Tr.].

27. English in the original [Tr.].

28. The reference is to the *Sophist*, 2496.

29. This is the phrase used by the chorus in the macaronic Latin of the burlesqued ceremony with which Molière's *Le Malade Imaginaire* ends.

30. This remark was made by one of the psychoanalysts most interested in this debate (1966).

31. See *Gegenwunschträume* in the *Traumdeutung*, *GW*: 156–7 and 163–4; *Standard Edition*, **IV**: 151 and 157–8.

32. *Standard Edition*, **VI** (1901). See also 'The Psychical Mechanism of Forgetfulness' (1898), *Standard Edition*, **III**: 287, which is reproduced in the *Psychopathology of Everyday Life*, 5. Freud reported the incident to Fliess in Letter 96 of the *Origins of Psycho-analysis* (1954).

33. In order to appreciate the results of these procedures the reader should become thoroughly acquainted with the notes to be found in Émile Borel's book *Le Hasard*, and which I have since circulated, on the actual triviality of the supposedly 'remarkable' results obtained by beginning in this way with a particular number (1966).

34. (*Der Witz und seine Beziehung zum Unbewussten*, 1905), *Standard Edition*, **VIII** [Tr.].

35. *Standard Edition*, **VIII**: 106: 'Anyone who has allowed the truth to slip out in an unguarded moment is in fact glad to be free of pretence' [Tr.].

36. *Standard Edition*, **VIII**: 105: 'Thus jokes can also have a subjective deter-

minant of this kind ... It declares that only what I allow to be a joke *is* a joke' [Tr.].

37. *Esprit* translates 'wit', 'mind', 'spirit', I have chosen to use 'spirit' here, except in the quotation from Freud, in which *Witz* (wit) is used in the German, and in the expression *'esprit libre'* ('mind free from care') [Tr.].

38. Cf. C. I. Oberndorf, 'Unsatisfactory Results of Psychoanalytic Therapy', *Psychoanalytic Quarterly*, XIX: 393–407.

39. The *'Argonautes pacifiques'* suggests the title of Malinowski's book, *Argonauts of the Western Pacific* [Tr.].

40. Cf. among others, *Do Kamo*, by Maurice Leenhardt, Chapters IX and X.

41. Jules H. Massermann, 'Language Behaviour and Dynamic Psychiatry', *IJP* (1944), 1 and 2: 1–8.

42. English in the original.

43. English in the original.

44. English in the original.

45. 'A stone, two houses, three ruins, four ditchdiggers, a garden, some flowers, a raccoon' [Tr.].

46. That is, the *Fort! Da!*, where a child's (phonemic) opposition O/A was related by Freud to the presence and absence of persons and things. See 'Beyond the Pleasure Principle' (1920), *Standard Edition*, XVIII, 14–17 [Tr.].

47. 'An everlasting possession'. Thucydides, I, xxii: 'My history has been composed to be an everlasting possession, not the showpiece of an hour' [Tr.].

48. This proverb is the epigraph to Claude Lévi-Strauss, *Les Structures élémentaires de la parenté*, 1949 (*Elementary Structures of Kinship*, 1971), which is alluded to more directly in the two sentences that follow [Tr.].

49. *Tiers Livre*, iii, iv; *Quart Livre*, ix. Debts, says Panurge, are 'the connecting link between Earth and Heaven, the unique mainstay of the human race; one, I believe, without which all mankind would speedily perish'; they are 'the great soul of the universe' [Tr.].

50. Cf., for example, his 'Introduction à l'oeuvre de Marcel Mauss' (1950), where he compares the notion of mana to the concept of the zero-phoneme introduced into phonology by Roman Jakobson [Tr.].

51. *'Par l'os et par la chair'*, an allusion to an anthropological binary opposition brought out by Lévi-Strauss in *Les Structures élémentaires de la parenté* (1949) [Tr.].

52. Aphorism of Lichtenberg's: 'A madman who imagines himself a prince differs from the prince who is in fact a prince only because the former is a negative prince, while the latter is a negative madman. Considered without their sign, they are alike.'

53. To obtain an immediate subjective confirmation of this remark of Hegel's, it is enough to have seen in the recent myxomatosis epidemic a blinded rabbit in the middle of a road, lifting the emptiness of his vision changed into a *look* towards the setting sun: he was human to the point of the tragic.

54. The lines before and after this term will show what I mean by it.

55. Reich's error, to which I shall return, caused him to take armorial bearings for an armour.

56. The palimpsest is a piece of parchment or other writing material from which the writing has been erased to make way for a new text. Cf. Freud's discussion of recollection and memory in 'A Note on the Mystic Writing Pad' (1925), *Standard Edition*, XIX: 227–32 [Tr.].

57. Cf. 'The Mirror Stage', pp. 1–7. Lacan here uses the English translations for all three terms of the Freudian topography [Tr.].

58. 'Men are not so necessarily mad that it would be being mad by another kind of madness *not* to be mad' (*Pensées*, Brunschvicq ed. 414, Pléiade ed. 184) [Tr.].

59. Cf., in particular, Chapter V. of *Group Psychology and the Analysis of the Ego* (1921), *Standard Edition*, XVIII.

60. That is, 'guidance', as in the religious sense of '*direction de consciences*' [Tr.].

61. Cf. Claude Lévi-Strauss, 'Language and the Analysis of Social Laws', *American Anthropologist*, **53**, No. 2 (April–June, 1951): 155–63. (An English translation of a later version of the article is to be found in Claude Lévi-Strauss, *Structural Anthropology*, trans. C. Jacobson and B. G. Schoepf, New York, London, 1963 [Tr.].

62. The last four paragraphs have been rewritten (1966).

63. '*Front d'airain*' – an allusion to Lassalle's *loi d'airain*, the 'iron law of wages' [Tr.].

64. These two paragraphs have been rewritten (1966).

65. '. . . that [*august*] voice
Who knows herself when she sings
To be no longer the voice of anyone
As much as the voice of the waves
and woods.'
(Valéry: *La Pythie*.)

66. On the Galilean hypothesis and Huyghens' chronometer, cf. Alexandre Koyré, 'An Experiment in Measurement', *Proceedings of the American Philosophical Society*, 97 (April, 1953). (The last two paragraphs of my text were rewritten in 1966.)

67. In 'The Question of Lay Analysis' (1926), *Standard Edition*, **XX**: 246.

68. 'Between man and love, there is woman. Between man and woman, there is a world. Between man and the world, there is a wall' [Tr.].

69. 'For I have seen with my own eyes the Cumean Sibyll hanging inside a jar, and whenever boys ask her: "What do you wish, O Sibyll", she would reply: "I wish to die." ' This is the epitaph to *The Waste Land* (1922); Lacan has already quoted from *The Hollow Men* (1925) [Tr.].

70. *Standard Edition*, **X**: 167–8.

71. In 'The psychotherapy of Hysteria' (1895), *Standard Edition*, **II**: 288–292.

72. I have fully developed these in-dications as the opportunity presented itself (1966). Four paragraphs rewritten.

73. 'The Theory of Symbolism', *British Journal of Psychology*, **IX** (2). Reprinted in his *Papers on Psycho-Analysis*, London, 5th ed., 1948. Cf. the article: 'À la mémoire d'Ernest Jones: Sur sa theorie du symbolisme', *La Psychanalyse*, **V** (1960): 1–20; *Écrits*, 697–717.

74. The reference is to the teaching of Abhinavagupta (tenth century). Cf. Dr Kanti Chandra Pandey, 'Indian Aesthetics', *Chowkamba Sanskrit Series*, Studies, **II**, Benares, 1950.

75. In his 'Analysis Terminable and Interminable' (1937), *Standard Edition*, **XXIII**: 219.

76. English in the original.

77. Ernst Kris, 'Ego Psychology and Interpretation', *Psychoanalytic Quarterly*, **XX**, No. 1 (January, 1951): 15–29, in particular the passage quoted on pp. 27–8.

78. English in the original.

79. English in the original.

80. Paragraph rewritten (1966).

81. English in the original.

82. This for the use of whoever can still understand it after going to Littré to look for the justification of a theory that makes of speech an 'action beside', by the translation that Littré does in fact give of the Greek *parabole* (but why not 'action towards'?) without having noticed at the same time that if this word always designates what it means, it is because of ecclesiastical usage that since the tenth century has reserved the word 'Word' for the Logos incarnate.

83. 'You would not be looking for me if you had not already found me', the words of Christ in *Le mystère de Jesus*, *Pensées* (Brunschvicq ed. 553, Pléiade ed. 736) [Tr.].

84. Each language has its own taste in transmission, and since the legitimacy of such research is founded on its success, nothing forbids us to draw a moral from it. Consider, for example, the maxim pinned to the prefatory note as an epigraph. [En particulier, il ne faudra pas

oublier que la séparation en embryologie, sociologie, clinique n'existe pas dans la nature et qu'il n'y a qu'une discipline: la *neurobiologie* à laquelle l'observation nous oblige d'ajouter l'épithète d'humaine en ce qui nous concerne.] Since it is so laden with redundancies, its style may possibly appear a little flat to you. But lighten it of them, and its audacity will get the enthusiasm it deserves: 'Parfaupe ouclaspa nannanbryle anaphi ologi psysocline ixispad anlana – égnia kune n'rbiol' ô blijouter têtumaine ennouconç. . . .' There we have the purity of its message finally laid bare. There meaning raises its head, there the avowal of being emerges, and our victorious wit bequeaths to the future its immortal imprint.

85. 'The Therapeutic Effect of Inexact Interpretation; a Contribution to the Theory of Suggestion', *IJP*, **XII**: 4.

86. Cf. *Standard Edition*, **XVII**: 89–97, 107–8, 112–13 (and note). The *Wespe* incident is reported on p. 94 [Tr.].

87. *Standard Edition*, **X**: 225, 260, 280–81, 294–5. The original formula is decondensed on pp. 280–81, where the condensation of 'Gisela' into 'S' is also demonstrated [Tr.].

88. 'Silence and Verbalization. A Supplement to the Theory of the "Analytic Rule" ', *IJP*, **XXX**: 1.

89. Here equivalent for me to the term *Zwangsbefürchtung* 'obsessional or compulsive (transitive) fearing', 'apprehension', which needs to be rendered into its component elements without losing any of the semantic resources of the German language.

90. This is the subject's *'constellation familiale'*, the history and the internal relationships of the subject's family – and 'history' in the precise sense of both a lived experience as well as of what the subject is told by his parents about their lives [Tr.].

91. Literally 'that (thing)'. The French for the *id* is *le ça*, but this *cela* – the 'phenomenological' object – is precisely not the *ça* [Tr.].

92. 'Fragment of an Analysis of a Case of Hysteria' (1905), *Standard Edition*, **VII**: 7. It is here (pp. 117–18) that Freud for the first time indicates the importance of transference in the progress of psychoanalytic theory [Tr.].

93. *Standard Edition*, **VII**: 120. The account itself was published four years after the breaking off of the analysis in 1901 [Tr.].

94. Two paragraphs rewritten (1966).

95. This term refers to the custom, of Celtic origin and still employed among certain American Biblical sects, of allowing a couple engaged to be married, or even a passing guest and the daughter of the house, to pass the night together in the same bed, provided that they keep their outdoor clothes on. The word takes its meaning from the fact that the girl is usually wrapped up tightly in several sheets. (Quincey speaks of it. See also the book by Aurand le Jeune on this practice amongst the Amish people.)

In this way the myth of Tristan and Iseult, and even the complex that it represents, would henceforth act as a sponsor for the analyst in his quest for the soul betrothed to mystifying nuptials via the extenuation of its instinctual phantasies.

96. Thus what I have designated in what follows as the support of transference, namely, *le sujet-supposé-savoir*, is to be found defined here (1966).

97. Cf. 'Observations on Transference-Love' (1915), *Standard Edition*, **XII**: 159 and, especially, 168 ff.

98. For this is the correct translation of the two terms that have been rendered, with that unfailing *contresens* already noted, by 'terminated and interminable analysis'.

The usual French translation of the title 'Die endliche und die unendliche Analyse' (1937), *Standard Edition*, **XXIII**, is 'Analyse terminée et analyse interminable'; the English: 'Analysis Terminable and Interminable'. Lacan renders the title by 'analyse finie ou indéfinie' [Tr.].

99. In the case of the Wolf Man, *op. cit.*: 10–11.

100. Cf. Aulus-Gellius, *Attic Nights*, II, 4:

'In a trial, when it is a question of knowing who shall be given the task of presenting the accusation, and when two or more people volunteer for this office, the judgement by which the tribunal names the accuser is called divination.... This word comes from the fact that since accuser and accused are two correlative terms that cannot continue to exist without each other, and since the type of judgement in question here presents an accused without accuser, it is necessary to have recourse to divination in order to find what the trial does not provide, what it leaves still unknown – that is to say, the accuser.'

101. In France, a type of boarding school [Tr.].

102. 'A supplement to Freud's "History of an Infantile Neurosis"' (1928), republished in *The Psycho-Analytic Reader* (1950). See the further details and references in Ernest Jones, *Sigmund Freud*, II: 306–12. Dr Mack Brunswick notes that she was simply the mediator between the Wolf Man and the absent Freud [Tr.].

103. Two paragraphs rewritten (1966).

104. '*La parole qui dure*'. Cf. Leenhardt, 'La parole qui dure' (Tradition, mythe, statut), *Do Kamo* (1947): 173 ff. [Tr.].

105. English in the original.

106. Whether a damaged stone or a cornerstone, my strong point is that I have never yielded over this (1966).

107. Notably in *Beyond the Pleasure Principle* [Tr.].

108. This is the form called *Laksana-laksana*.

109. Cf. 'Analysis Terminable and Interminable' (1937), *Standard Edition*, XXIII: 245 ff.; and *An Outline of Psychoanalysis* (1940), *ibid.*: 248 f.

110. Cf. 'Remembering, Repeating and Working-Through' (1914), *Standard Edition*, XII: 145.

111. *Being and Time* (1962): 294.

112. The four words '*renversé dans la répétition*' in which is inscribed my latest formulation of repetition (1966) are substituted for an improper recourse to the 'eternal return' ['*toujours présent dans l'éternel retour*'], which was all that I could convey at that time.

113. '*Jeux d'occultation*'. The child would associate the appearance and disappearance of a toy that he alternately threw away and drew back again with the vowel sounds 'o' and 'a', which Freud interpreted as those of the German words for 'gone!' (*Fort!*) and 'here!' (*Da!*). The repetition of this game was apparently evidence of the child's beginning to master his environment actively through speech, for the active repetition seemed clearly to replace the passivity of the situation where the child's mother was alternately present and absent. Freud notes the eventual detachment of the game from the figure of the mother, and he notes the importance of the antithesis of disappearance and return rather than the content of the opposition: by means of his image in a mirror, the child soon discovered how to make himself disappear. Cf. *Beyond the Pleasure Principle* (1920), *Standard Edition*, XVIII: 14 ff. [Tr.].

114. Leenhardt, for example, uses this spatial representation in his *Do Kamo* to represent the native's existence as a locus of relationships with others [Tr.].

115. Premises of the topology that I have been putting into practice over the past five years (1966).

116. '. . . *comme médiatrice entre l'homme du souci et le sujet du savoir absolu*'. *Souci* is the usual French rendering of the Heideggerian *Sorge*, and *savoir* of the Hegelian *Wissen* [Tr.]

117. The serpent is Moses's brazen serpent, god of healing (*Numbers*, xxi, 9) [Tr.].

118. Cf. Freud's analysis of Dora, *Standard Edition*, VII: 39:

'It is a rule of psycho-analytic technique that an internal connection which is still undisclosed will announce its presence by means of a contiguity – a temporal proximity – of associations; just as in writing, if "a" and "b" are put side by side, it means that the syllable "ab" is to be formed out of them.'

Freud's first use of this metaphor occurs in 'The Interpretation of Dreams', *Standard Edition*, **IV**: 247 and 314 [Tr.].

119. Let it be understood that it is not a question of those 'gifts' that are always supposed to be lacking in novices, but of a gift that is in fact lacking to them more often than they lack it.

120. Ponge writes it: *réson* (1966). [In his *Pour un Malherbe*. 'Resound' is *'résonner'* in French; *réson* is a homonym of *raison*.]

121. *'Soumission, don, grâce'*. The three Sanskrit nouns (*damah, dânam, dayâ*) are also rendered 'self-control'; 'giving', 'compassion' (Rhadhakrishnan), the three verbs, 'control', 'give', 'sympathize' (T. S. Eliot, *The Waste Land*, Part V; 'What the thunder said').

FOUR

The Freudian thing, or the meaning of the return to Freud in psychoanalysis

An expanded version of a lecture given at the
Neuro-psychiatric Clinic, Vienna 7 November 1955[1]

❯❯❮❮

To Sylvia

❯❯❮❮

Situation in time and place of this exercise

At a time when Vienna is making itself heard once again through the voice of its Opera, thus, in a most moving way, resuming what had always been its mission, namely, to create harmony at this point of cultural convergence as only it knew how, I have come here, not, I think, out of season, to evoke the election by which this city will remain, this time for ever, linked to a revolution in knowledge worthy of the name of Copernicus, the eternal city of Freud's discovery, if it can be said that as a result of that discovery the very centre of the human being was no longer to be found at the place assigned to it by a whole humanist tradition.

Even, perhaps, for prophets whose own countries were not entirely deaf to them, the moment of eclipse must come, if only after their deaths. It is only right that an outsider should exercise restraint in assessing the forces at work in such apparent phases.

In any case, the return to Freud for which I am assuming here the role of herald is situated elsewhere: one has only to remember the symbolic scandal to which Dr Alfred Winterstein, then president of the Vienna Psychoanalytic Association, who is with us here today, rightly drew attention on the occasion of the inauguration of the commemorative plaque marking the house in which Freud pursued his heroic work – the scandal being not that this monument was not dedicated to Freud by his fellow citizens, but that it was not commissioned by the international association of those who live from his sponsorship.

Such a failure is symptomatic, for it reveals a betrayal that comes not from the land in which Freud, by virtue of his tradition, was merely a temporary guest, but from the very field that he has left in our care, and from those in whom that care was entrusted, from the psychoanalytical movement itself, where things have not reached the point when a return to Freud is seen as a reversal.

From the moment when the first sound of the Freudian message echoed across the world from the great bell of Vienna, many incidental factors have been involved in the story. Those first reverberations seemed, with the first world conflict, to be drowned by the heavy thud of a collapsing structure. They resumed, with renewed power, after the immense human laceration that fomented the second, and which was their most powerful vehicle. It was on the waves set up by the tocsin of hate, the tumult of discord, the panic-stricken breath of war, that Freud's voice reached us, as we witnessed the diaspora of those who were its bearers and a persecution that did not strike blindly. The shock waves were to reverberate beyond the confines of our world, in a continent where it would be untrue to say that history loses its meaning since it is there that it finds its limit – it would even be wrong to think that history was absent there, since, having been already formed over several centuries, it weighs all the more heavily there by virtue of the gulf that represents its all too limited horizon – but it is denied with a categorical will that gives the industrial corporations their style, a cultural ahistoricism peculiar to the United States of America.

It is this ahistoricism that defines the assimilation required if one is to be recognized in the society constituted by that culture. It was to its summons that a group of emigrants had to respond – men who, in order to be recognized, could only stress their difference, but whose function presupposed history in its very principle, their discipline being that which had re-established the bridge linking modern man to the ancient myths. The combination of circumstances was too strong, the opportunity too tempting for them to resist: they abandoned the principle and based function upon difference. Let us be clear as to the nature of this temptation. It involved neither facility nor profit. It is certainly easier to efface the principles of a doctrine than the stigmata of one's origins, more profitable to make one's function serve demand; but, here, to reduce one's function to one's difference is to give in to a mirage internal to the function itself, a mirage that bases function upon that difference. It is to return to the reactionary principle operant in the duality of the sick and the healer, the opposition between someone who knows and someone who does not.

How can one avoid regarding this opposition as true when it is real, how can one avoid becoming a manager of souls in a social context that demands such an office? The most corrupting of comforts is intellectual comfort, and the worst corruption that of the best.

Thus Freud's words to Jung – I have it from Jung's own mouth – when, on an invitation from Clark University, they arrived in New York harbour and caught their first glimpse of the famous statue illuminating the universe, 'They don't realize we're bringing them the plague', are attributed to him as confirmation of a hubris whose antiphrasis and gloom do not extinguish their troubled brightness. To catch their author in its trap, Nemesis had only to take him at his word. We would be justified in fearing that Nemesis had added a first-class return ticket.

Indeed, if something of the sort has taken place, we have only ourselves to thank. For Europe seems rather to have been effaced from the concerns, the style, not to say the memory, of those who left, together with the repression of their bad memories.

I will not grudge you this act of forgetting, if it leaves me freer to present to you the project of a return to Freud, as some of us in the *Société Française de Psychanalyse* conceive it. What such a return involves for me is not a return of the repressed, but rather taking the antithesis constituted by the phase in the history of the psychoanalytic movement since the death of Freud, showing what psychoanalysis is not, and seeking with you the means of revitalizing that which has continued to sustain it, even in deviation, namely, the primary meaning that Freud preserved in it by his very presence, and which I should like to explicitate here.

How could this meaning elude us when it is so clearly apparent in a body of written work of the most lucid, most coherent kind? And how could it leave us hesitant when a study of this *oeuvre* shows us that its different stages and changes in direction are governed by Freud's inflexibly effective concern to maintain it in its primary rigour?

Such texts may even be compared with those that, in other times, human veneration has invested with the highest qualities, in that they endure the test of that discipline of commentary, the virtue of which one rediscovers in making use of it, in the time-honoured way, not only to situate what Freud said in the context of its time, but to determine whether the answer that it brings to the questions it poses is or is not superseded by the answer that one finds in it to the questions of the real.

It will no doubt come as no surprise to you if I tell you that these texts, to which for the past four years I have devoted a two-hour seminar every Wednesday from November to July, without having covered more-than a quarter of the total, if indeed my commentary presupposes their totality at all, have given me, and those who have attended my seminars, the surprise afforded only by genuine discoveries. These discoveries range from concepts that have remained unused to clinical details un-covered by our exploration that demonstrate how far the field investigated by Freud extended beyond the avenues that he left us to tend, and how little his observation, which sometimes gives an impression of exhaustive-ness, was the slave of what he had to demonstrate. Who, among the tech-nicians of disciplines other than analysis whom I have persuaded to read these texts, has not been moved by this research in action, whether in 'The Interpretation of Dreams', 'The Wolf Man', or 'Beyond the Pleasure Principle'? What an exercise for the training of minds, and what a message to lend one's voice to! And what control of the methodological value of this training and of the effect of truth that this message produces when the students to whom you transmit them bring you evidence of a transform-ation, occurring sometimes from one day to the next, in their practice, which becomes simpler or more effective even before it becomes more transparent to themselves. I cannot provide you with an extensive account of this work in the talk that I am now giving in this place of noble memory – an opportunity that I owe to the kindness of Professor Hoff, to Dr Arnold, to whom I owe the suggestion, and to my excellent and long-standing relations with Igor Caruso, who assured me of the welcome that I would receive in Vienna.

But I must not forget that I owe part of this audience to the kindness of M. Susini, the director of our French Institute in Vienna. And this is why, when coming to the meaning of this return to Freud that I am proposing here, I must ask myself whether, because they are less prepared than specialists may be to understand me, I am not running the risk of dis-appointing them.

❧❧❧

The adversary

I am sure what my answer would be: Certainly not, if what I am going to say is as it must be. The meaning of a return to Freud is a return to the meaning of Freud. And the meaning of what Freud said may be conveyed to anyone because, addressed as it is to all, it concerns each individual: to make this clear, one has only to remember that Freud's discovery puts truth into question, and there is no one who is not personally concerned by the truth.

It must seem rather odd that I should be flinging this word in your faces – a word almost of ill repute, a word banished from polite society. Yet is it not inscribed at the very heart of analytic practice, since this practice is constantly re-making the discovery of the power of the truth in ourselves, in our very flesh?

In what could the unconscious be better recognized, in fact, than in the defences that are set up in the subject against it, with such success that they appear no less real? I am not reviving here the shoddy Nietzschean notion of the lie of life, nor am I astonished that one should believe oneself capable of belief, nor do I accept that it is enough to wish for something sufficiently to will it. But I am asking where the peace that follows the recognition of an unconscious tendency comes from if it is not more true than that which constrains it in the conflict? Indeed, for some time now, this peace has proved to be an illusory one, for, not content with recognizing as unconscious the defences attributable to the ego, psycho-analysts have more and more identified their mechanisms – displacement from the object, the turning against the subject, regression of the form – with the very dynamic that Freud had analysed in the tendency, which thus seems to continue in them with little more than a change of sign. Have we not overstepped the limit when we admit that the drive itself may be led to consciousness by the defence in order to prevent the subject from recognizing it?

In order to translate the exposition of these mysteries into a coherent discourse, I must once again use words that, in spite of myself, re-establish in that discourse the duality that sustains them. But what I deplore is not simply that one cannot see the wood of the theory for the trees of the technical process, but rather that it takes so little to believe that one is in the forest of Bondy, no more than the shape lurking behind every tree, the notion that some trees must be more real than others, or, if you prefer, that all the trees are not bandits.[2] Failing which, one might ask where the bandits are that are not trees. Perhaps this little, then, which can become everything on occasion, deserves an explanation? What is this truth without which there is no way of discerning the face from the mask, and outside of which there appears to be no other monster than the labyrinth itself? In other words, in what way are they to be distinguished, in fact, if they are all of equal reality?

Here the big clogs move forward to cover the dove's feet, on which, as we know, the truth is borne, and on occasion to swallow up the bird as well: what an ideologist you are, someone cries; our criterion is simply economic. All arrangements of reality are not equally economic. But at the point at which the truth has already been brought to bear, the bird flies off unscathed with our question: Economic for whom?

This time the business has gone too far. The adversary laughs: 'It's clear what's happening. Monsieur is about to launch into philosophy. We'll be meeting Plato and Hegel before long. These signatures are enough. What they represent is much the same, and, anyway, as you say, this concerns everybody, it's of no interest to specialists like us. It can't even be classified in our files.'

You think I'm joking. I assure you this is not the case. I really believe what I am saying.

If Freud had brought to man's knowledge nothing more than the truth that there is such a thing as the true, there would be no Freudian discovery. Freud would belong to the line of moralists in whom a whole tradition of humanist analysis is embodied, a milky way to the heavens of European culture in which Balthazar Gracian and La Rochefoucauld shine as stars of the first order, and in which Nietzsche features as a nova as dazzling as it is short-lived. The latest to join them, and, like them, stimulated no doubt by a properly Christian concern for the authenticity of the movement of the soul, Freud was able to precipitate a whole casuistics into a map of Tendre,[3] which has only to be set in accordance with the offices for which it was intended. Its objectivity, in fact, is strictly bound up with the analytic situation, which, between the four walls that limit its field, can work perfectly well without one knowing where the north is since it lies along the axis of the couch, which is supposed to point in the direction of the analyst. Psychoanalysis is the science of the mirages that appear within this field. A unique experience, a rather abject one after all, but one that cannot be recommended too highly to those who wish to be introduced to the principle of man's follies, for, by revealing itself as akin to a whole gamut of disorders, it throws light upon them.

This language is moderate enough – I did not invent it. We have lived to hear a zealot of a supposedly classical psychoanalysis define psycho-analysis as an experience whose privilege is strictly bound up with the forms that govern its practice, forms that cannot be altered a jot, because they were obtained by means of a miracle of chance; these forms provide access to a transcendent reality possessing the characteristics of history, a reality in which a taste for order and a love of the beautiful, for example, have their permanent foundation – namely, the objects of the pre-Oedipal relation, shit and nappy-rash.

This position cannot be refuted since the rules are justified by their outcome, which is regarded as proof that the rules are well founded. And yet our questions proliferate. How did this prodigious operation of chance occur? What is the origin of this contradiction between the pre-Oedipal intrigue, to which, in the opinon of certain of our modern analysts, the analytic relation can be reduced, and the fact that Freud was satisfied with having situated it in the position of the Oedipus complex? How can the sort of hot-house osculation to which this 'new look' of experience is limited be the ultimate in a progress that first appeared to open up innumerable links between all the fields of creation – or the same question presented the other way round? If the objects discerned in this elective fermentation were thus discovered through some method other than experimental psychology, is experimental psychology able to find them again through its own methods?

The replies that we will receive from the interested parties leave no room for doubt. The motive force of the experience, even when motivated in their terms, cannot simply be this illusory truth that can be reduced to the illusion of truth. It all began with a particular truth, a disclosure, the effect of which is that reality is no longer the same for us as it was before, and it is there that the senseless cacophony of theory continues to catch human things alive, as if to prevent practice from declining to the level of the unfortunates who never succeed in escaping from it (I use the term to exclude the cynics).

A truth, it must be admitted, is not easy to recognize, once it has become accepted. Not that there are established truths, but they then become so easily confused with the reality that surrounds them that no other artifice has yet been found to distinguish them from it than to mark them with the sign of the spirit, to pay them homage, to regard them as coming from another world. It is not to attribute everything to a sort of blindness on man's part to point out the fact that truth is never for him more beautiful than at the moment when the light, which he holds aloft as in the proverbial emblem, surprises her naked. And one must feign stupidity to some extent to pretend that one knows nothing of what happens afterwards. But the stupidity of bovine frankness remains if one wonders where one could have been looking for her before, since the emblem scarcely indicated the well, an unseemly, not to say malodorous place, rather than the casket in which any precious form should be preserved intact.

>>+<<

The thing speaks of itself

But the truth in Freud's mouth takes the said beast by the horns: 'So for you I am the enigma of her who vanishes as soon as she appears, men who try so hard to hide me under the tawdry finery of your proprieties! But I am prepared to believe that your embarrassment is sincere, for even when you take it upon yourselves to serve as my heralds, you place no greater value on wearing my colours than your own, which are like you yourselves, phantoms that you are. Where, then, will I pass into you? Where was I before I entered you? Perhaps one day I will tell you? But so that you will find me where I am, I will teach you by what sign you will recognize me. Men, listen, I am giving you the secret. I, truth, will speak.

'Must I remind you that you did not yet know this? Certainly some of you who claim to be my lovers, no doubt by virtue of the principle that in this kind of braggadocio one is never better served than by oneself, had posited, in an ambiguous manner, and not without somewhat clumsily revealing the self-love that really concerned them, that the errors of philosophy, that is to say, their own, could subsist only on my subsidies. Yet by embracing these girls with their thought, they found them in the end insipid and vain, and set to once again to contend with vulgar opinions in the manner of the sages of old who knew how to put them in their place, whether they appeared in the form of tales, law-suits, guile, or, quite simply, lies, but also to seek them out in their places, in the home and in the forum, in the forge or in the market-place. They then realized that by not being my parasites these vulgar opinions seemed to be serving me much more, and, who knows?, acting as my militia, as the secret agents of my power. Several cases observed in the game of forfeits, of sudden transformations of errors into truths, which seemed to be due to nothing more than perseverance, set them on the path of this discovery. The discourse of error, its articulation in acts, could bear witness to the truth against evidence itself. It was at this point that one of them tried to get the cunning of reason accepted into the rank of objects worthy of study. Unfortunately, he was a professor, and you were too happy to turn against his teachings the ass's ears that you were made to wear at school and which have since served as ear-trumpets for those of you who are a little hard of hearing. So keep your vague sense of history and leave it to those cleverer than yourselves to found on the guarantee of my future firm the world market in lies, the trade in total war and the new law of self-criticism. If reason is as cunning as Hegel said, it will do its job without your help.

'But for all that you have made your debts to me neither outdated nor in perpetuity. They are dated after yesterday and before tomorrow. And it hardly matters whether you rush ahead to honour them or to evade them, since they will seize you from behind in either case. Whether you flee me in fraud or think to entrap me in error, I will reach you in the mistake against which you have no refuge. In that place where the most caustic speech reveals a slight hesitation, it is lacking in perfidy, I am now publicly announcing the fact, and it would be rather more subtle to pretend that nothing had happened, in good, or for that matter, bad company. But there is no need to give yourselves the trouble to keep a closer watch on yourselves. All the same the conjoint jurisdictions of politeness and politics would declare as unacceptable whatever is associated with me by presenting itself in so illicit a way, you will not get off so lightly, for the most innocent intention is disconcerted at being unable to conceal the fact that one's unsuccessful acts are the most successful and that one's failure fulfills one's most secret wish. In any case, is it not enough to judge of your defeat to see me escape first from the dungeon of the fortress in which you are so sure you have me secured by situating me not in you yourselves, but in being itself? I wander about in what you regard as being the least true in essence: in the dream, in the way the most far-fetched conceit, the most grotesque nonsense of the joke defies sense, in chance, not in its law, but in its contingence, and I never do more to change the face of the world than when I give it the profile of Cleopatra's nose.

'So you can reduce the traffic on the roads that you strive so hard to radiate from the consciousness, and which constitute the pride of the ego, crowned by Fichte with the emblems of transcendence. The trade route of truth no longer passes through thought: strange to say, it now seems to pass through things: *riddle*, it is through you that I communicate, as Freud formulates it at the end of the first paragraph of the sixth chapter, devoted to the work of the dream, of his work on dreams and what dreams mean.

'But you will take care: all the trouble this individual put into becoming a professor may spare him your neglect, if not your errors, the tirade continues. Listen carefully to what he says, and, as he said of me, the truth that speaks, the better to grasp its meaning and to take it literally. Here, no doubt, things are my signs, but, I repeat, signs of my speech. If Cleopatra's nose changed the course of the world, it was because it entered the world's discourse, for to change it in the long or short term, it was enough, indeed, it was necessary, for it to be a speaking nose.

'But it is your own that you must now avail yourself of, but to more natural ends. Let a sharper scent than all your categories guide you in the chase to which I incite you: for it the cunning of reason, however disdainful she may be of you, remained open to your faith, beside you, I, the truth, would be Deceit itself, since my ways pass not only through a crack too narrow to find for want of pretence and through the inaccessible cloud of the dream, through the motiveless fascination of the mediocre and the seductive impasse of absurdity. Seek, dogs that you become on hearing me, blood-hounds that Sophocles preferred to unleash upon the hermetic traces of the thief of Apollo than on the bleeding sockets of Oedipus, certain as he was of finding with him at the sinister meeting at Colonus the hour of truth. Enter the lists to my call and howl at my voice. There you are lost already, I contradict myself, I defy you, I take cover: you say that I am defending myself.'

⊁⊁⊰⊰

Parade

The return to the shades, which we believe is to be expected at this moment, is the signal for a 'murder party'[4] initiated by the order forbidding anyone to leave, since anyone may now be hiding the truth, under her dress, for example, or even, as in the amorous fiction of the 'indiscreet jewels', in her belly. The general question is: Who is speaking? And the question is not an irrelevant one. Unfortunately, the answers are a little hasty. First the libido is accused, which takes us in the direction of the jewels, but we must realize that the ego itself, although it places fetters on the libido, which is so desperate for satisfaction, is sometimes the object of its activities. One feels, in fact, that it is about to collapse from one minute to the next, when the sound of broken glass informs everyone that it is the large drawing-room mirror that has sustained the accident, the golem of narcissism, hastily called in to assist, having made his entrance through it. The ego is then generally regarded as the murderer, or, if not, the victim, in which case the divine rays of the good Judge Schreber begin to spread their net over the world, and the sabbath of the instincts really does become complicated.

The comedy, which I shall interrupt here at the beginning of its second act, is gentler than is usually believed, since, bringing to bear upon a drama of knowledge a buffoonery that belongs only to those who act this drama without understanding it, it restores to such people the authenticity from which they were moving farther and farther away.

But if a more serious metaphor befits the protagonist, it is that which shows us in Freud an Actaeon perpetually slipped by dogs that have been tracked down from the beginning, and which he strives to draw back into pursuit, without being able to slacken the chase in which only his passion for the goddess leads him on. Leads him on so far that he cannot stop until he reaches the grottoes in which the chtonian Diana in the damp shade, which makes them appear as the emblematic seat of truth, offers to his thirst, with the smooth surface of death, the quasi-mystical limit of the most rational discourse in the world, so that we might recognize the place in which the symbol is substituted for death in order to take possession of the first swelling of life.

As we know, this limit and this place are still well outside the reach of his disciples, if indeed they make any attempt at all to seek it, and so the Actaeon who is dismembered here is not Freud, but every analyst who can measure up to the passion that consumed him and which has made him, according to the signification that Giordano Bruno gave this myth in his *Furori eroici*, the prey of the dogs of his thoughts.

In order to appreciate the scope of this split we must hear the irrepressible cries that arise from the best as well as the worst, attempting to bring them back to the beginning of the chase, with the words that truth has given us as viaticum: 'I speak', adding: 'There is no other speech but language.' The rest is drowned in their tumult.

'Logomachia!' goes the strophe on one side. 'What are you doing with the preverbal, gesture and mime, tone, the tune of a song, mood and af-fec-tive con-tact?' To which others no less animated give the antistrophe: 'Everything is language: language when my heart beats faster when I'm in a funk, and if my patient flinches at the throbbing of an aeroplane at its zenith it is a way of *saying* how she remembers the last bomb attack.' – Yes, eagle of thought, and when the plane's shape cuts out your likeness in the night-piercing brush of the searchlight, it is the sky's answer.

Yet one did not challenge, in dealing with these premises, the use of any form of communication to which anyone might have recourse in his exploits, whether signals or images, content or form, if this content is a content of sympathy, and virtue is not discussed by good form.

One began only to repeat after Freud the word of his discovery: *it speaks*, and, no doubt, where it is least expected, namely, where there is pain. If there ever was a time when simply listening to what it said was sufficient reply (for hearing it is already a reply), let us suppose therefore that the great ones of the early days, the arm-chair giants, were struck by the curse destined to titanic acts of daring, or that their seats ceased to be conductors of the good speech before which they were expected to sit. However, since then, the meetings between the psychoanalyst and psychoanalysis have increased in the hope that the Athenian could be reached with Athene having emerged fully armed from the head of Freud. Shall I tell you of the jealous fate, ever the same, that thwarted these meetings: beneath the mask in which everyone was to meet his promised, alas! thrice alas! and a cry of horror at the thought of it, another having taken her place, he who was there was not he either.

Let us return, then, quite deliberately, and with the truth spell out what it has said of itself. The truth has said: 'I speak'. To recognize this 'I' by what he speaks, perhaps we should not have turned to the 'I', but paused at the angle of intersection of the speech. 'There is no speech that is not language' reminds us that language is an order constituted by laws, of which we might at least learn what they exclude. For example, that language is different from natural expression and that it is not a code either; that it is not to be confused with information – and don't forget it when you are dealing with cybernetics; and that it is so irreducible to a superstructure that materialism itself is seen to be alarmed by this heresy – see Stalin's bull on the question.

If you want to know more, read Saussure, and since a clock-tower can hide even the sun, I would add that I am not referring to the signature to be found in psychoanalysis, but to Ferdinand, who can truly be said to be the founder of modern linguistics.

≫≫≪≪

Order of the thing

A psychoanalyst should find it easy enough to grasp the fundamental distinction between signifier and signified, and to begin to use the two non-overlapping networks of relations that they organize.

The first network, that of the signifier, is the synchronic structure of the language material in so far as in that structure each element assumes its precise function by being different from the others; this is the principle of distribution that alone governs the function of the elements of the language (*langue*) at its different levels, from the phonematic pair of oppositions to the compound expressions to disengage the stable forms of which is the task of the most modern research.

The second network, that of the signified, is the diachronic set of the concretely pronounced discourses, which reacts historically on the first, just as the structure of the first governs the pathways of the second. The dominant factor here is the unity of signification, which proves never to be resolved into a pure indication of the real, but always refers back to another signification. That is to say, the signification is realized only on the basis of a grasp of things in their totality.

Its origin cannot be grasped at the level at which it usually assures itself of the redundancy proper to it, for it always proves to be in excess over the things that it leaves floating within it.

The signifier alone guarantees the theoretical coherence of the whole as a whole. This adequacy is confirmed by the latest development of the science, as, on reflexion, it is found to be implicit in primary linguistic experience.

Such are the bases that distinguish language from the sign. From them the dialectic has derived a new trenchancy.

For the remark on which Hegel bases his critique of the *belle âme*, and in accordance with which it is said to live (in every sense, even the economic sense of making a living) precisely on the disorder that it denounces, escapes tautology only to maintain the tauto-ontic of the *belle âme* as mediation, unrecognized by itself, of that disorder as primary in being.

Whatever dialectic it is, this remark cannot shake the delusion of the presumption to which Hegel applied it, remaining caught in the trap offered by the mirage of consciousness to the *I* infatuated with its feelings, which he erects into a law of the heart.

This '*I*' in Hegel is defined, no doubt, as a legal being, in which respect it is more concrete than the real being from which it was earlier thought it could be abstracted – as appears from the fact that it possesses both a civil status (*état civil*) and a statement of account (*état-comptable*).

But it was left to Freud to make this legal being responsible for the manifest disorder to be found in the most enclosed field of the real being, namely, in the organism's pseudo-totality.

I would explain the possibility of this by the congenital gap presented by man's real being in his natural relations, and by the resumption, for a sometimes ideographical, but also a phonetic, not to say grammatical, usage, of imaginary elements that appear fragmented in this gap.

But there is no need of this genesis for the signifying structure of the symptom to be demonstrated. When deciphered, it appears as self-evident, imprinted upon the flesh, the omnipresence for the human being of the symbolic function.

It is this that distinguishes a society founded in language from an animal society, and even what enables ethnology to stand back and perceive such a distribution: that is, the exchange that characterizes such a society has other foundations than the needs even to satisfy them, what has been called the gift 'as total social fact'. All this is then carried much farther, to the point where this society may no longer be defined as a collection of individuals, when the immixture of subjects makes it a group with a quite different structure.

This is to introduce the effects of truth as cause at a quite different point, and to impose a revision of the process of causality – the first stage of which would seem to be to recognize the inherent nature of the heterogeneity of these effects.[5] It is strange that materialist thought seems to forget that it was from this recourse to the heterogeneous that it derived its initial momentum. More interest might then be shown in a much more striking feature than the resistance to Freud displayed by the pedants, namely, the connivence that this resistance has encountered in the common consciousness.

If all causality evidences an implication of the subject, there can be no doubt that every conflict of order can be attributed to it.

The terms of psychoanalytic intervention – the problem of which I am posing here – make it sufficiently clear, I think, that its ethic is not an individualist one.

But its practice in the American sphere has been so summarily reduced to a means of obtaining 'success' and to a mode of demanding 'happiness' that it should be pointed out that this constitutes a repudiation of psycho-analysis, a repudiation that occurs among too many of its adherents from the simple, basic fact, that they have never wished to know anything about the Freudian discovery, and that they will never know anything about it, even by way of repression: for it is a question here of the mechanism of systematic *méconnaissance* in so far as it simulates delusion, even in its group forms.

A more rigorous reference from analytic experience to the general structure of the semantics in which it has its roots should nevertheless have made it possible to convince them before having to conquer them.

For the subject of which I was speaking just now as the legatee of recognized truth is definitely *not* the ego perceptible in the more or less immediate data of conscious pleasure or alienation in labour. This *de facto* distinction is the same that is to be found between the α of the Freudian unconscious, in so far as it is separated by an abyss of preconscious functions, and the ω of Freud's will in the 31st of his *Neue Vorlesungen*: 'Wo Es war, soll Ich werden.'

A formula in which the dominance of the signifying structuration is made sufficiently clear.

Let us analyse it. Contrary to the form that the English translation – 'Where the id was, there the ego shall be' – cannot avoid, Freud did not say '*das Es*', nor '*das Ich*', as was his custom when designating the agencies by which for the previous ten years he had ordered his new topography, and this fact, in view of the inflexible rigour of his style, gives special accent to their use in this sentence. In any case – even without having to confirm by internal criticism of Freud's work that he in fact wrote *Das Ich und das Es* in order to maintain this fundamental distinction between the true subject of the unconscious and the ego as constituted in its nucleus by a series of alienating identifications – the true meaning would seem to be the following: *Wo* (Where) *Es* (the subject – devoid of any *das* or other objectivating article) *war* (was – it is a locus of being that is referred to here, and that in this locus) *soll* (must – that is, a duty in the moral sense, as is confirmed by the single sentence that follows and brings the chapter to a close)[6] *Ich* (I, there must I – just as one declared, 'this am I', before saying, 'it is I'), *werden* (become – that is to say, not occur (*survenir*), or even happen (*advenir*), but emerge (*venir au jour*) from this very locus in so far as it is a locus of being).

Thus I would agree, against the principles of the economy of signification that must dominate a translation, to force a little in French the forms of the signifier in order to bring them into line with the weight of a still rebellious signification, which the German carries better here, and therefore to employ the homophony of the German *es* with the initial of the word '*sujet*' (subject). By the same token, I might feel more indulgence, for a time at least, to the first translation that was given of the word *es*, namely, '*le soi*' (the self). The '*ça*' (id), which not without very good reason, was eventually preferred, does not seem to me to be much more adequate, since it corresponds rather to the German *das*, as in the question, '*Was ist das?*', and the answer '*das ist*' ('*c'est*'). Thus the elided '*c*' that will appear if we hold to the accepted equivalence, suggests to me the production of a verb, '*s'être*', in which would be expressed the mode of absolute subjectivity, in the sense that Freud properly discovered it in its radical eccentricity: 'There where it was' ('*Là où c'était*'), I would like it to be understood, 'it is my duty that I should come to being'.[7]

You see, it is not in a grammatical conception of the functions in which they appear that one should analyse if and how the *I* (*le je*) and the ego (*le moi*) may be distinguished or overlap in each particular subject.

What the linguistic conception, which must guide the worker in his basic initiation, will teach him is to expect the symptom to prove its function as a signifier, that is to say, as that by which it is to be distinguished from the natural index that the same term currently designates in medicine. And in order to satisfy this methodological requirement, he will force himself to recognize its conventional use in the significations raised by the analytic dialogue. (A dialogue whose structure I will try to describe.) But he will insist that these same significations can be grasped with certainty only in their context, that is, in the sequence that is constituted for each by the signification that refers back to it and the signification to which it refers back in analytic discourse.

These basic principles are applied easily enough in analytic technique, and in illuminating it, they dissipate many of the ambiguities which, in order to maintain themselves even in the major concepts of transference and resistance, make the use that is made of them in practice quite ruinous.

❧❧❦❦

Resistance to the resisters

To consider only resistance, whose use is increasingly confused with that of defence, and all that this implies in terms of reductive manoeuvres – and we can no longer remain blind to the coercion that such manoeuvres exert – it is as well to remember that the first resistance with which analysis has to deal is that of the discourse itself in that it is first a discourse of opinion, and that all psychological objectification will prove to be bound up with this discourse. This, in effect, is what motivated the remarkable simultaneity with which the psychoanalytic practice of the burgraves of analysis came to a standstill in the 1920s: by that time they knew both too much and not enough to get their patients, who scarcely knew less about it, to recognize the fact.

But the principle adopted at that time of the primacy to be accorded to the analysis of resistance hardly led to a favourable development. For the simple reason that it is not enough to carry out an operation with extreme urgency for it to achieve its aim if one is unclear as to what it consists of.

And it was precisely towards a reinforcement of the objectifying position in the subject that the analysis of resistance was orientated, to such an extent, indeed, that this directive now permeates the principles to be applied in the conduct of a standard analysis.

Far from having to maintain the subject in a state of observation, therefore, one must know that by engaging him there one enters a circle of misunderstanding that nothing in analysis, or in criticism, will be able to break. Any intervention in this direction could only be justified, therefore, by a dialectical aim, namely, to demonstrate its value as an impasse.

But I will go further and say: you cannot at the same time proceed yourself to this objectification of the subject and speak to him as you should. And for a very good reason, which is not only that one cannot, as the English proverb has it, have one's cake and eat it: that is to say, have towards the same objects two approaches whose consequences are mutually exclusive. But for the deeper reason that is expressed in the saying 'one cannot serve two masters', that is, one's being cannnot conform to two actions that lead in opposite directions.

For, in psychology, objectification is subjected in its very principle to a law of *méconnaissance* that governs the subject not only as observed, but also as observer. That is to say, it is not about him that you have to speak to him, for he can do this himself, and therefore, it is not even to you that he speaks. If it is to him that you have to speak, it is literally of something else, that is, of something other than that which is in question when he speaks of himself, and which is the thing that speaks to you, a thing which, whatever he says, would remain forever inaccessible to him, if in being speech addressed to you it could not elicit its response in you and if, from having heard its message in this inverted form, you could not, by returning it to him, give him the double satisfaction of having recognized it and of making him recognize its truth.

Can we therefore know this truth that we know in this way? *Adoequatio rei et intellectus*, thus has the concept of truth been defined since there were thinkers, and this definition leads us into the ways of their thought. Intellects like ours will certainly be adequate to this thing that speaks to us, which speaks within us, and even in escaping behind the discourse that says nothing but to make us speak, it would be strange indeed if it did not find to whom it might speak.

This is certainly the grace that I wish you, and what we must now do is speak about it, and it is up to those who put the thing into practice to speak.

❧❧

Interlude

However, don't expect too much here, for since the psychoanalytic thing has become an accepted thing and its servants have their hands manicured, the arrangement they have come to can accommodate sacrifices to good form, which, as far as ideas, which psychoanalysts have never had enough of, are concerned, is certainly convenient: cut-price ideas for all will make up the balance of what everyone needs. We are sufficiently *au fait* with things to know that *chosisme* is hardly the latest thing; and there we have found our pirouette.

'What are you going to look for if not this ego that you distinguish, at the same time forbidding us to see it?' it may be objected. 'All right, we objectify it. So what's wrong with that?' Here the delicate shoes move stealthily forward to deliver the following kick in the shins: do you think, then, that the ego can be taken as a thing – I'd rather starve first!

From thirty-five years of cohabitation with the ego under the roof of the second Freudian topography, including ten years of a stormier liaison, regularized at last through the good offices of Miss Anna Freud in a marriage whose social credit has been on the up and up ever since, to the point that I am assured that it will soon request the blessing of the Church, in short, from the most sustained work of psychoanalysts, you will draw nothing more than this drawer.

It is true that it is filled to overflowing with old novelties and new junk the sheer mass of which is certainly entertaining. The ego is a function, the ego is a synthesis, a synthesis of functions, a function of synthesis.

It is autonomous! That's a good one! It's the latest fetish introduced into the holy of holies of a practice that derives its authority from the superiority of the superiors. It's worth another of the same kind, since everyone knows that for this function, which is entirely real, it is always the most outmoded, dirty, repulsive object that serves the purpose best. That it should gain for its inventor the veneration that it does where it is in operation is understandable enough, but the most amazing thing is that in enlightened circles it has earned for him the prestige of introducing psychoanalysis into the laws of general psychology. It is as if His Excellency the Aga Khan, not content with receiving his weight in gold, a fact that does nothing to damage the esteem in which he is held in cosmopolitan society, was then awarded the Nobel Prize for having given away in exchange to his followers the precise rules for betting on horses.

But the last find is the best: the ego, like everything else we've been dealing with of late in the human sciences, is an o-pe-ra-tion-al notion.

At this point I will have recourse, with the kind permission of my listeners, to that naïve *chosime* that rivets them so respectfully in those seats to listen to me despite the ballet of calls to work, so that they might, with me, wish to put a stop to this operation.

How does this operation distinguish rationally what one makes of the notion of the ego in analysis from the current usage of any other thing, of this desk to take the first thing to hand? Of so little use is it that I undertake to show that the discourses concerning the ego and the desk (and that is what is at stake) coincide point by point.

For this desk, no less than the ego, is dependent on the signifier, namely on the word, which, bearing its function to the general, to the lectern of quarrelsome memory and to the Tronchin piece of noble pedigree, is responsible for the fact that it is not merely a piece of wood, worked in turn by the woodcutter, the joiner and the cabinet-maker, for reasons of commerce, combined with fashion, itself productive of needs that sustain its exchange value, providing it is not led too quickly to satisfy the least superfluous of those needs by the last use to which it will eventually be put, namely, as firewood.

Furthermore, the significations to which the desk refers are in no way less dignified than those of the ego, and the proof is that on occasion they envelop the ego itself, if it is by the functions that Mr Heinz Hartmann accords it that one of our fellow men may become our desk: namely, to maintain a position involving consent. An operational function no doubt that will enable the said fellow man to dispose within him all the possible values of the thing constituted by the desk: from the burdensome renting that maintained and still maintains the reputation of the little hunchback of the rue Quincampoix above the vicissitudes and memory itself of the first great speculative crash of modern times, through all the offices of domestic use, of space-filling, of market transfer or usufruct, till it is used as firewood, and why not? It wouldn't be the first time.

But that isn't all, for I am prepared to lend my voice to the real desk so that it might speak of its existence, which, though utilitarian, is individual, of its history, which, however radically alienated it may seem, has left all the evidence that a historian might need: documents, texts, bills detailing its fate, which, though inert, is dramatic, since a desk is a perishable article, engendered in work, a fate subject to chance, to accident, to the ups and downs of fashion, of fatalities even, of which it becomes the intersign, and which is promised to an end of which there is no need to know anything for it to be one's own, since we all know what that end is.

But the whole thing would become banal if, after this prosopopoeia, one of you dreams that he is this desk, possessed or not with the gift of speech, and since the interpretation of dreams has become a well known, if not everyday, practice, it could hardly come as a surprise if, in deciphering the use as a signifier that this desk will have assumed in the riddle in which the dreamer encloses his desire, and in analysing the more or less equivocal reference back that this use involves in the significations that the consciousness of this desk will have aroused in him, with or without its discourse, we touch on what might be called the preconscious of this desk.

At this point I am aware of a protest, which, although ruled like music paper, I am not sure how to name: the thing is, it concerns what has no name in any language, and which, being generally referred to by the white-nigger notion of the total personality, sums up everything that a facile phenomenology-psychiatry, in our society of stationary 'progress', trumpets in our ears. A protest on the part of the *belle âme* no doubt, but in forms suited to the neither-one-thing-nor-the-other being, the half-this-half-that manner, the stealthy tread of the modern intellectual, whether of right or left. Indeed, it is from this direction that the fictional protest of those who cultivate disorder finds its aristocratic connexions. Let us listen rather to the tone of this protest.

The tone is measured, but grave: the preconscious, or for that matter the consciousness, we are told, belongs not to the desk, but to ourselves.

We perceive the desk and give it its meaning, and as much trouble goes into doing so, perhaps, as into the making of the thing. But even if it had been a question of a more natural being, we should never inconsiderately swallow into the consciousness the high form which, however weak we may be in the universe, guarantees us an imprescriptible dignity in it – look up 'reed' in the dictionary of spiritualist thought.

I must admit that Freud arouses my irreverence here by the way in which, in a passing remark somewhere, as if without touching on it, he speaks of the modes of spontaneous provocation that operate when the universal consciousness goes into action. And this relieves me of any embarrassment I may have felt in pursuing my paradox.

Is the difference between the desk and us, as far as consciousness is concerned, so very great, then, if the desk can so easily come to resemble us, and be brought into play between you and me, that my words should have made any mistake possible? Thus by being placed with one of us between two parallel mirrors, it would be seen to be reflected to infinity, which means that it will be much more like the observer than one might think, since in seeing one's image repeated in the same way, it too is seen by the eyes of another when it looks at itself, since without this other that is its image, it would not see itself seeing itself.

In other words, the privilege of the ego in relation to things is to be sought elsewhere than in this false recurrence to infinity of reflexion that the mirage of consciousness consists of, and which, despite its perfect inanity, still to some extent excites those who work with thought into seeing in it some supposed progress in interiority, whereas it is a topological phenomenon whose distribution in nature is as sporadic as the dispositions of pure exteriority that condition it, if indeed man has helped to spread them with such immoderate frequency.

Furthermore, how can we separate the term 'preconscious' from the affectations of this desk, or those to be found potentially or actually in any other thing, and which, by adjusting itself as exactly to my affections, will enter consciousness with them?

I am quite willing to accept that the ego, and not the desk, is the seat of perceptions but in being so it reflects the essence of the objects it perceives and not its own, in so far as consciousness is its privilege, since these perceptions are very largely unconscious.

It is not for nothing, indeed, that we would locate the origin of the protest with which we are concerned here, in those bastard forms of phenomenology that cloud the technical analyses of human action, and

especially those required in medicine. If their cheap raw material, to use
the term that Herr Jaspers specifically attaches to his estimation of
psychoanalysis, really is what gives his work its style, and its weight to
the cast-iron statue of him as director of conscience and to the tin-plate
statue of him as intellectual master, they have served their turn, which,
indeed, is always the same, namely, to divert.

They are used here, for example, in order to avoid discussing the
fact that the desk does not talk, a fact that the upholders of false protest
would prefer to ignore, because by hearing me grant it them, my desk
would at once begin to speak.

⊁⊁⊰⊰

The discourse of the other

'In what way, then, is this ego that you treat in analysis better than the
desk that I am?' it would ask them.

'For if its health is defined by its adaptation to a reality that is regarded quite simply as being suited to it, and if you need the co-operation
of "the healthy part of the ego" in order to reduce, in the other part no
doubt, incompatibilities with reality, which appear as such only in accordance with your principle of regarding the analytical situation as simple
and anodyne, and will not rest until you make the subject see them as
you see them, is it not clear that there is no other way of distinguishing
the healthy part of the subject's ego than by its agreement with your point
of view, which, in order to be regarded as healthy, becomes the measure
of things, just as there is no other criterion of cure than the complete
adoption by the subject of this measure of yours – all of which confirms
the current admission to be found in certain very serious authors that
the purpose of analysis is achieved with identification with the analyst's
ego?'

'Certainly, the fact that such a view can become so widespread and be
received as it is leads one to think that, contrary to the commonly held
view that we hoodwink the naïve, it is much easier for the naïve to hoodwink us. And the hypocrisy that is revealed in the declaration – regret
for which appears with such curious regularity in this discourse – that we
should speak to the subject in "his own language", leads one to reflect
still further on the depth of this naïvety. Do we still have to overcome
the nausea that rises at the suggestion of talking *babyish*,[8] without which
well informed parents would believe themselves incapable of inducting

into their high reasons the poor little beggars that have to be kept quiet! This is the least one might expect in view of the fact that analytical imbecility projects neuroses into the notion of the weakness of the ego.

'But we are not here to dream between nausea and vertigo. The fact remains that I who am speaking to you, mere desk though I be, am the ideal patient since with me not so much trouble has to be taken, the results are acquired at once, I am cured in advance. Since it is simply a question of substituting your discourse for mine, I am a perfect ego, since I have never had any other, and I leave it to you to inform me of the things to which my regulating devices do not allow you to adapt me directly, namely, all those things that are not your diopters, your size and the dimension of your papers.'

Well, that's a pretty good speech for a desk, it seems to me. I am joking, of course. In what it said under my command, it did not have its say. For the simple reason that it was itself a word; it was *I* as grammatical subject. Well, that's one rank attained, one to be picked up by the occasional soldier in the ditch of an entirely eristic claim, but it also provides us with an illustration of the Freudian motto, which, expressed as '*Là où était ça, le* je *doit être*' ('*Wo es war, soll Ich werden*'), would confirm to our advantage the feeble character of a translation that substantifies the *Ich* by giving a 't' to the '*doit*' of *soll* [i.e. making it third person singular – Tr.] and fixes the price of the *Es* at the rate of the 'c' cedilla. Nevertheless, the desk is not an ego, eloquent though it has been, but a means that I have employed in my discourse.

But, after all, if one takes into account its virtue, in analysis, the ego, too, is a means, and so they can be compared.

As the desk remarked so pertinently, it has the advantage over the ego of not being a means of resistance, and that's precisely why I chose it to support my discourse and so reduce as much as possible the resistance that would have been aroused in you by too great an interference on the part of my ego in the words of Freud: satisfied as I should already be, if what must be left to you despite this effacement allows you to find what I am saying 'interesting'. And it is no accident that this expression designates in its euphemism what interests us only moderately, and which manages to loop the loop in its antithesis, by which speculations of universal interest are called 'disinterested'.

But let's look and see (*voyons voir*) whether what I am saying happens to interest you, as one says, thus piling a pleonasm on to an antonomasis: personally, the desk will soon be torn to pieces for use as ammunition.

Oh, well! The same applies to the ego, apart from the fact that its uses seem to be reversed in their relation to its states. A means of the speech addressed to you from the subject's unconscious, a weapon to resist its recognition, it is fragmented in that it bears speech, and whole in that it helps in not hearing it.

In effect, it is in the disintegration of the imaginary unity constituted by the ego that the subject finds the signifying material of his symptoms. And it is from the sort of interest aroused in him by the ego that the significations that turn his discourse away from those symptoms proceed.

><<

Imaginary passion

This interest in the ego is a passion whose nature was already glimpsed by the traditional moralists, who called it *amour-propre*, but whose dynamics in its relation to one's own body image only psychoanalytic investigation has succeeded in analysing. This passion brings to every relation with this image, constantly represented by my fellow-man, a signification that interests me so much, that is to say, which places me in such a dependence on this image that it links all the objects of my desires more closely to the desire of the other than to the desire that they arouse in me.

The objects in question here are those whose appearance we expect in a space structured by vision, that is to say, objects characteristic of the human world. As to the knowledge on which the desire of these objects depends, men are far from confirming the expression that wishes that they should see further than the ends of their noses, for, on the contrary, their misfortune wishes that the world should begin at the ends of their noses, and that they should be able to apprehend their desire only by the same trick that enables them to see their own noses, that is to say, in a mirror. But scarcely has this nose been discerned than they fall in love with it, and this is the first signification by which narcissism envelops the forms of desire. It is not the only one, and the progressive rise of aggressivity in the firmament of analytic preoccupations would remain obscure if it kept to this one alone.

This is a point that I think I have myself helped to elucidate by conceiving the dynamics of the so-called *mirror stage* as a consequence of a prematuration at birth, generic to man, from which results at the time indicated the jubilant identification of the as yet *infans* individual with the total form in which this reflexion of the nose is integrated, namely, the image of his body: an operation which by being performed at a glance (*à vue de nez*), is of much the same kind as the 'aha!' that reveals to us the intelligence of the chimpanzee (we never fail to be amazed when confronted by the miracle of intelligence on the faces of our peers), does not fail to bring with it deplorable consequences.

As a witty poet remarks so rightly, the mirror would do well to reflect a little more before returning our image to us. For at this moment the subject has not yet seen anything. But as soon as the same capture is reproduced before the nose of one of one's fellow-men, the nose of a notory, for example, God knows where the subject will be led by the nose, in view of the places where these ministerial officers are in the habit of sticking theirs. So that whatever else we have – hands, feet, heart, mouth, even the eyes, so reluctant to follow – is threatened by dislocation (*une rupture d'attelage*), whose announcement in anxiety could only involve severe measures. Fall in! That is, an appeal to the power of the image in which the honeymoon of the mirror so delighted, to that sacred union of right and left that is affirmed in it, interverted as it may seem if the subject proves to be a little more observant.

But what finer model of this union could be found than the very image of the other, that is to say, of the notory in his function? It is thus that the functions of mastery, which we incorrectly call the synthesizing functions of the ego, establish on the basis of a libidinal alienation the development that follows from it, namely, what I once called the paranoiac principle of human knowledge, according to which its objects are subjected to a law of imaginary reduplication, evoking the homologation of an endless series of notaries, who owe nothing to their professional body.

But for me the decisive signification of the alienation that constitutes the *Urbild* of the ego appears in the relation of exclusion that then structures the dual relation of ego to ego. For if the imaginary coadaptation of each by the other should result in the roles being distributed in a complementary manner between the notary and his client, for example, the identification precipitated from the ego to the other in the subject has the effect that this apportionment of functions never constitutes even a kinetic harmony, but is established on the permanent 'you or I' of a war involving the existence of one or other of the two notaries in each of the subjects. A situation that is symbolized in the 'Yah-boo, so are you' of the transitivist quarrel, the original form of aggressive communication.

One can see to what the language of the ego is reduced: intuitive illumination, recollective command, the retorsive aggressivity of the verbal echo. Let us add what comes back to it from the automatic detritus of common discourse: the educative cramming and delusional *ritornello*, modes of communication that perfectly reproduce objects scarcely more complicated than this desk, a feed-back construction for the first, for the second a gramophone record, preferably scratched in the right place.

Yet it is in that register that the systematic analysis of defence is offered. It is corroborated by what looks like regression. The object relation provides its appearances and this forcing has no other outcome than one of the three admitted in the technique in operation. Either the impulsive leap into the real through the paper hoop of phantasy: acting out in a sense usually signifying the opposite of suggestion. Or transitory hypomania by ejection of the object itself, which is properly described in the megalomaniac ebriety which my friend Michael Balint, in an account so veracious as to make him the more my friend, recognizes as the index of the termination of the analysis in present practice. Or in the sort of somatization represented by hypochondria *a minima*, modestly theorized under the heading of the doctor/patient relationship.

The dimension of 'two body psychology'[9], as suggested by Rickman, is the fantasy from which a 'two ego analysis',[9] which is as untenable as it is coherent in its results, shelters.

꙯꙯

Analytic action

That is why we teach that there are not only two subjects present in the analytic situation, but two subjects each provided with two objects, the ego and the other (*autre*), this other being indicated by a small *o* (*a*). Now by virtue of the singularities of a dialectical mathematics with which we must familiarize ourselves, their meeting in the pair of sub-subjects S and O comprises in all only four terms, because the relation of exclusion that operates between o and o' reduces the two couples thus indicated to a single couple in the confrontation of the subjects.

In this game for four players, the analyst will act on the significative resistances that weigh down, impede and divert speech, while himself introducing into the quartet the primordial sign of the exclusion that connotes the either/or of presence or absence that formally releases the death included in the narcissistic *Bildung*. A sign that is lacking, let us note in passing, in the algorithmic apparatus of a modern logic that calls itself symbolic, and thus demonstrates the dialectical inadequacy that still renders it unsuited to the formalization of the human sciences.

This means that the analyst intervenes concretely in the dialectic of analysis by pretending he is dead, by cadaverizing his position as the Chinese say, either by his silence when he is the Other with a capital *O*, or by annulling his own resistance when he is the other with a small *o*. In either case, and under the respective effects of the symbolic and the imaginary, he makes death present.

It is important, moreover, that he recognizes and therefore distinguishes his action in each of these two registers if he is to know why he intervenes, at what moment the opportunity presents itself and how to seize it.

The prime condition for this is that he should be thoroughly imbued with the radical difference between the Other to which his speech must be addressed, and that second other who is the individual that he sees before him, and from whom and by means of whom the first speaks to him in the discourse that he holds before him. For, in this way, he will be able to be he to whom this discourse is addressed.

The fable of my desk and the current practice of the discourse of conviction will show him sufficiently, if he thinks about it, that no discourse, whatever inertia it may be based on or to whatever passion it may appeal, is ever addressed to anyone but the good listener to whom it brings its salvation. What is called the argument *ad hominem* itself is regarded by him who practises it only as a seduction destined to obtain from the other in his authenticity the acceptance of what he says, which constitutes a pact, whether admitted or not, between the two subjects, a pact that is situated in each case beyond the reasons of the argument.

As a rule everyone knows that others will remain, like himself, inaccessible to the constraints of reason, outside an acceptance in principle of a rule of debate that does not come into force without an explicit or implicit agreement as to what is called its basis, which is almost always tantamount to an anticipated agreement as to what is at stake. What is called logic or law is never more than a body of rules that were laboriously drawn up at a moment of history duly certificated as to time and place, by agora or forum, church, even party. I shall expect nothing therefore of those rules except the good faith of the Other, and, as a last resort, will make use of them, if I think fit or if I am forced to, only to amuse bad faith.

The locus of speech

The Other is, therefore, the locus in which is constituted the I who speaks to him who hears, that which is said by the one being already the reply, the other deciding to hear it whether the one has or has not spoken.

But this locus also extends as far into the subject as the laws of speech, that is to say, well beyond the discourse that takes its orders from the ego, as we have known ever since Freud discovered its unconscious field and the laws that structure it.

It is not because of some mystery concerning the indestructibility of certain infantile desires that these laws of the unconscious determine the analysable symptoms. The imaginary shaping of the subject by desires more or less fixed or regressed in their relation to the object is too inadequate and partial to provide the key to it.

The repetitive insistence of these desires in the transference and their permanent recollection in a signifier that has been taken possession of by repression, that is to say, in which the repressed element returns, find their necessary and sufficient reason, if one admits that the desire of recognition dominates in these determinations the desire that is to be recognized, by preserving it as such until it is recognized.

The laws of recollection and symbolic recognition are, in effect, different in essence and manifestation from the laws of imaginary reminiscence, that is to say, from the echo of feeling or instinctual imprint (*Prägung*), even if the elements ordered by the first as signifiers are taken from the material to which the second give signification.

To touch on the nature of symbolic memory, it is enough to have studied once, as we have done in my seminar, the simplest symbolic sequence, that of a linear series of signs connoting the alternative of presence or absence, each being chosen at random by whatever pure or impure mode adopted. One then elaborates this sequence in the simplest way, that is, by noting in it the ternary sequences in a new series, and one will see the appearance of the syntactical laws that impose on each term of this series certain exclusions of possibility until the compensations demanded by its antecedents have been lifted.

With his discovery of the unconscious – which, he insisted, was a quite different matter from everything that had previously been designated by that term – Freud was taken at once to the heart of this determination of the symbolic law. For, in establishing, in 'The Interpretation of Dreams', the Oedipus Complex as the central motivation of the unconscious, he recognized this unconscious as the agency of the laws on which marriage alliance and kinship are based. This is why I can say to you now that the motives of the unconscious are limited – a point on which Freud was quite clear from the outset and never altered his view – to sexual desire. Indeed, it is essentially on sexual relations – by ordering them according to the law of preferential marriage alliances and forbidden relations – that the first combinatory for the exchanges of women between nominal lineages is based, in order to develop in an exchange of gifts and in an exchange of master-words the fundamental commerce and concrete discourse on which human societies are based.

The concrete field of individual preservation, on the other hand, through its links with the division not of labour, but of desire and labour, already manifested from the first transformation introducing into food its human signification to the most developed forms of the production of consumer goods, shows that it is structured in this dialectic of master and slave, in which we can recognize the symbolic emergence of the imaginary struggle to the death in which we earlier defined the essential structure of the ego: it is hardly surprising, then, if this field is reflected exclusively in this structure. In other words, this explains why the other great generic desire, that of hunger, is not represented, as Freud always maintained, in what the unconscious preserves in order to gain recognition for it.

Thus Freud's intention, which is so legible to anyone who is not content simply to stumble through his text, becomes increasingly clear when he promulgated the topography of the ego, which involved restoring in all its rigour the separation, even in their unconscious interference, between the field of the ego and that of the unconscious first discovered by him, by showing the 'transverse' position of the first in relation to the second, to the recognition of which it resists by the effect of its own significations in speech.

It is certainly there that the contrast is to be found between the significations of guilt, the discovery of which in the subject's action dominated the first phase in the history of psychoanalysis, and the significations of the subject's affective frustration, instinctual deprivation, and imaginary dependence that dominate its present phase.

To say that the prevalence of the latter, as it is now being consolidated in a neglect of the former, should lead to a propedeutics of general infantilization is not to say very much, when psychoanalysis is already allowing its principles to authorize large-scale practices of social mystification.

Symbolic debt

Will our action go as far, then, as to repress the very truth that it bears in its exercise? Will it send this truth back to sleep, a truth that Freud in the passion of the Rat Man would maintain presented for ever to our recognition, even if we must increasingly divert our vigilance away from it: namely, that it is out of the forfeits and vain oaths, lapses in speech and unconsidered words, the constellation of which presided at the putting into the world of a man, that is moulded the stone guest who comes, in symptoms, to disturb the banquet of one's desires?

For the unripe grape of speech by which the child receives too early from a father the authentification of the nothingness of existence, and the bunch of wrath that replies to the words of false hope with which the mother has baited him in feeding him with the milk of her true despair, set his teeth on edge more than having been weaned on an imaginary *jouissance* or even having been deprived of such real attentions.

Will we manage to escape unscathed from the symbolic game in which the real misdeed pays the price of imaginary temptation? Will we divert our study from what will become of the law when, from having been intolerable to a fidelity of the subject, it was already misunderstood by him when still unknown, and of the imperative if, from having been presented to him in imposture, it is challenged within itself before being discerned: that is to say, springs which, in the broken link of the symbolic chain, raise from the imaginary that obscene, ferocious figure in which we must see the true signification of the superego?

It should be made clear that our critique of an analysis that claims to be an analysis of resistance and is reduced more and more to the mobilization of defences is directed solely at the fact that it is as disorientated in its practice as in its principles, and in order to recall it to the order of its legitimate ends.

The manœuvres of dual complicity in which it strives for effects of happiness and success can have value in our eyes only by reducing the resistance of the effects of prestige in which the ego is affirmed to the speech that is avowed at that moment of the analysis that is the analytic moment.

I believe that it is in the avowal of this speech, of which the transference is the enigmatic actualization, that the analysis must rediscover its centre and its gravity, and let no one imagine from what I said earlier that I conceive of this speech in some mystical mode reminiscent of *karma*. For what strikes one in the moving drama of neurosis are the absurd aspects of a disconcerted symbolization of which the *quid pro quo* appears more derisory the more one penetrates it.

Adoequatio rei et intellectus: the homonymic enigma that we can extract from the genitive *rei*, which without even a change of accent can be that of the word *reus*, which means the party to a suit in a trial, in particular, the defendant, and metaphorically he who is in debt for something, surprises us by giving at the end its formula with the strange adequation with which we posed the question for our intellect and which finds its response in the symbolic debt for which the subject as subject of speech is responsible.

≫≪

The training of the analysts of the future

So it is to the structures of language so manifestly recognizable in the earliest discovered mechanisms of the unconscious that we will return in taking up once more our analysis of the modes in which speech is able to recover the debt that it engenders.

One has only to turn the pages of his works for it to become abundantly clear that Freud regarded a study of languages and institutions, of the resonances, whether attested or not in memory, of literature and of the significations involved in works of art as necessary to an understanding of the text of our experience. Indeed, Freud himself is a striking instance of his own belief: he derived his inspiration, his ways of thinking and his technical weapons from just such a study. But he also regarded it as a necessary condition in any teaching of psychoanalysis.

That this condition should have been neglected, even in the selection of analysts, cannot be unconnected with the present state of analysis: only by articulating the requirements of this condition in technique will we be able to satisfy it. It is with an initiation into the methods of the linguist, the historian and, I would say, the mathematician that we should now be concerned if a new generation of practitioners and researchers is to recover the meaning and the motive force of the Freudian experience. These younger analysts will also find in these methods a means of preserving themselves from the psycho-sociological objectification, in which the psychoanalyst will seek, in his uncertainty, the substance of what he does, whereas it can bring him no more than an inadequate abstraction in which his practice is engulfed and dissolved.

This reform will be an institutional operation, for it can be sustained only by means of a constant communication with disciplines that would define themselves as sciences of intersubjectivity, or by the term 'conjectural sciences', a term by which I indicate the order of the researches that are diverting the implication of the term 'human sciences'.

But such a direction will be maintained only by a true teaching, that is to say, one that will constantly be subject to what is known as innovation. For the pact instituting the analytic experience must take account of the fact that this experience establishes the very effects that capture it in order to separate it from the subject.

Thus, in exposing magical thinking, one does not see that it is magical thinking, and in fact the alibi of thoughts of power, ever ready to produce their offspring in an action that is sustained only by its connexion with truth.

It is to this connexion with truth that Freud refers when he declares that it is impossible to keep to three undertakings: to educate, to govern, and to psychoanalyse. Why, indeed, should this be so, if not that the subject can only be lacking there, be pushed out to the edge that Freud reserves for truth?

For truth proves to be complex in essence, humble in its offices and alien to reality, stubborn to the choice of sex, akin to death and, all in all, rather inhuman, Diana perhaps . . . Actaeon, too guilty to hunt the goddess, the prey in which is caught, O huntsman, the shadow that you become, let the pack pass by without hastening your step, Diana will recognize the hounds for what they are . . .

✦✦✦✦
Notes

1. First appeared in *L'Évolution psychiatrique*, 1956, no. 1.

2. A pun on 'Bondy' and 'bandits'. The Forest of Bondy, to the north of Paris, was long famous as a haunt of robbers. [Tr.].

3. The *Pays du Tendre* was an allegorical country in which love was the sole preoccupation. It was the creation of Mlle de Scudéry and other novelists of the seventeenth century [Tr.].

4. English in the original [Tr.].

5. This rewritten paragraph antedates a line of thought that I have since explored further (1966).

6. Namely: '*Es ist Kulturarbeit etwa die Trockenlegung der Zuydersee*' (It is a civilizing task rather like the drying out of the Zuydersee).

7. One can but wonder what devil inspired the French translator, whoever he was, to render it as '*Le moi doit déloger le ça*'. It is true that one can savour there the tone in the sense in which one understands the sort of operation referred to here.

8. English in the original [Tr.].

9. English in the original [Tr.].

FIVE

The agency of the letter in the unconscious or reason since Freud

❧❧❧

'Of Children in Swaddling Clothes
*O cities of the sea, I behold in you your citizens, women
as well as men tightly bound with stout bonds around
their arms and legs by folk who will not understand
your language; and you will only be able to give
vent to your griefs and sense of loss of liberty
by making tearful complaints, and sighs, and
lamentations one to another; for those who
bind you will not understand your
language nor will you
understand them.'*
LEONARDO DA VINCI[1]

❧❧❧

Although the nature of this contribution was determined by the theme of the third volume of *La Psychanalyse*,[2] I owe to what will be found there to insert it at a point somewhere between writing (*l'écrit*) and speech – it will be half-way between the two.

Writing is distinguished by a prevalence of the *text* in the sense that this factor of discourse will assume in this essay a factor that makes possible the kind of tightening up that I like in order to leave the reader no other way out than the way in, which I prefer to be difficult. In that sense, then, this will not be writing.

Because I always try to provide my seminars each time with something new, I have refrained so far from giving such a text, with one exception, which is not particularly outstanding in the context of the series, and which I refer to at all only for the general level of its argument.

For the urgency that I now take as a pretext for leaving aside such an aim only masks the difficulty that, in trying to maintain it at the level at which I ought to present my teaching here, I might push it too far from speech, whose very different techniques are essential to the formative effect I seek.

That is why I have taken the expedient offered me by the invitation to lecture to the philosophy group of the Fédération des étudiants ès lettres[3] to produce an adaptation suitable to what I have to say: its necessary generality matches the exceptional character of the audience, but its sole object encounters the collusion of their common training, a literary one, to which my title pays homage.

Indeed, how could we forget that to the end of his days Freud constantly maintained that such a training was the prime requisite in the formation of analysts, and that he designated the eternal *universitas litterarum* as the ideal place for its institution.[4]

Thus my recourse (in rewriting) to the movement of the (spoken) discourse, restored to its vitality, by showing whom I meant it for, marks even more clearly those for whom it is not intended.

I mean that it is not intended for those who, for any reason whatever, in psychoanalysis, allow their discipline to avail itself of some false identity – a fault of habit, but its effect on the mind is such that the true identity may appear as simply one alibi among others, a sort of refined reduplication whose implications will not be lost on the most subtle minds.

So one observes with a certain curiosity the beginnings of a new direction concerning symbolization and language in the *International Journal of Psychoanalysis*, with a great many sticky fingers leafing through the pages of Sapir and Jespersen. These exercises are still somewhat unpractised, but it is above all the tone that is lacking. A certain 'seriousness' as one enters the domain of veracity cannot fail to raise a smile.

And how could a psychoanalyst of today not realize that speech is the key to that truth, when his whole experience must find in speech alone its instrument, its context, its material, and even the background noise of its uncertainties.

❦❦❦

I *The Meaning of the Letter*

As my title suggests, beyond this 'speech', what the psychoanalytic experience discovers in the unconscious is the whole structure of language. Thus from the outset I have alerted informed minds to the extent to which the notion that the unconscious is merely the seat of the instincts will have to be rethought.

But how are we to take this 'letter' here? Quite simply, literally.[5]

By 'letter' I designate that material support that concrete discourse borrows from language.

This simple definition assumes that language is not to be confused with the various psychical and somatic functions that serve it in the speaking subject – primarily because language and its structure exist prior to the moment at which each subject at a certain point in his mental development makes his entry into it.

Let us note, then, that aphasias, although caused by purely anatomical lesions in the cerebral apparatus that supplies the mental centre for these functions, prove, on the whole, to distribute their deficits between the two sides of the signifying effect of what we call here 'the letter' in the creation of signification.[6] A point that will be clarified later.

Thus the subject, too, if he can appear to be the slave of language is all the more so of a discourse in the universal movement in which his place is already inscribed at birth, if only by virtue of his proper name.

Reference to the experience of the community, or to the substance of this discourse, settles nothing. For this experience assumes its essential dimension in the tradition that this discourse itself establishes. This tradition, long before the drama of history is inscribed in it, lays down the elementary structures of culture. And these very structures reveal an ordering of possible exchanges which, even if unconscious, is inconceivable outside the permutations authorized by language.

With the result that the ethnographic duality of nature and culture is giving way to a ternary conception of the human condition – nature, society, and culture – the last term of which could well be reduced to language, or that which essentially distinguishes human society from natural societies.

But I shall not make of this distinction either a point or a point of departure, leaving to its own obscurity the question of the original relations between the signifier and labour. I shall be content, for my little jab at the general function of *praxis* in the genesis of history, to point out that the very society that wished to restore, along with the privileges of the producer, the causal hierarchy of the relations between production and the ideological superstructure to their full political rights, has none the less failed to give birth to an esperanto in which the relations of language to socialist realities would have rendered any literary formalism radically impossible.[7]

For my part, I shall trust only those assumptions that have already proven their value by virtue of the fact that language through them has attained the status of an object of scientific investigation.

For it is by virtue of this fact that linguistics[8] is seen to occupy the key position in this domain, and the reclassification of the sciences and a regrouping of them around it signals, as is usually the case, a revolution in knowledge; only the necessities of communication made me inscribe it at the head of this volume under the title 'the sciences of man' – despite the confusion that is thereby covered over.[9]

To pinpoint the emergence of linguistic science we may say that, as in the case of all sciences in the modern sense, it is contained in the constitutive moment of an algorithm that is its foundation. This algorithm is the following:

$$\frac{S}{s}$$

which is read as: the signifier over the signified, 'over' corresponding to the bar separating the two stages.

This sign should be attributed to Ferdinand de Saussure although it is not found in exactly this form in any of the numerous schemas, which none the less express it, to be found in the printed version of his lectures of the years 1906–7, 1908–9, and 1910–11, which the piety of a group of his disciples caused to be published under the title, *Cours de linguistique générale*, a work of prime importance for the transmission of a teaching worthy of the name, that is, that one can come to terms with only in its own terms.

That is why it is legitimate for us to give him credit for the formulation S/s by which, in spite of the differences among schools, the beginning of modern linguistics can be recognized.

The thematics of this science is henceforth suspended, in effect, at the primordial position of the signifier and the signified as being distinct orders separated initially by a barrier resisting signification. And that is what was to make possible an exact study of the connections proper to the signifier, and of the extent of their function in the genesis of the signified.

For this primordial distinction goes well beyond the discussion concerning the arbitrariness of the sign, as it has been elaborated since the earliest reflections of the ancients, and even beyond the impasse which, through the same period, has been encountered in every discussion of the bi-univocal correspondence between the word and the thing, if only in the mere act of naming. All this, of course, is quite contrary to the appearances suggested by the importance often imputed to the role of the index finger pointing to an object in the learning process of the *infans* subject learning his mother tongue, or the use in foreign language teaching of so-called 'concrete' methods.

One cannot go further along this line of thought than to demonstrate that no signification can be sustained other than by reference to another signification[10]: in its extreme form this amounts to the proposition that there is no language (*langue*) in existence for which there is any question of its inability to cover the whole field of the signified, it being an effect of its existence as a language (*langue*) that it necessarily answers all needs. If we try to grasp in language the constitution of the object, we cannot fail to notice that this constitution is to be found only at the level of concept, a very different thing from a simple nominative, and that the *thing*, when reduced to the noun, breaks up into the double, divergent beam of the 'cause' (*causa*) in which it has taken shelter in the French word *chose*, and the nothing (*rien*) to which it has abandoned its Latin dress (*rem*).

These considerations, important as their existence is for the philosopher, turn us away from the locus in which language questions us as to its very nature. And we will fail to pursue the question further as long as we cling to the illusion that the signifier answers to the function of representing the signified, or better, that the signifier has to answer for its existence in the name of any signification whatever.

For even reduced to this latter formulation, the heresy is the same – the heresy that leads logical positivism in search of the 'meaning of meaning',[11] as its objective is called in the language of its devotees. As a result, we can observe that even a text highly charged with meaning can be reduced, through this sort of analysis, to insignificant bagatelles, all that survives being mathematical algorithms that are, of course, without any meaning.[12]

To return to our formula S/s: if we could infer nothing from it but the notion of the parallelism of its upper and lower terms, each one taken in its globality, it would remain the enigmatic sign of a total mystery. Which of course is not the case.

In order to grasp its function I shall begin by reproducing the classic, yet faulty illustration (see top of facing page) by which its usage is normally introduced, and one can see how it opens the way to the kind of error referred to above.

In my lecture, I replaced this illustration with another, which has no greater claim to correctness than that it has been transplanted into that

TREE

incongruous dimension that the psychoanalyst has not yet altogether renounced because of his quite justified feeling that his conformism takes its value entirely from it. Here is the other diagram:

LADIES   GENTLEMEN

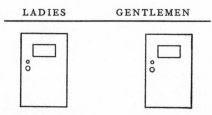

where we see that, without greatly extending the scope of the signifier concerned in the experiment, that is, by doubling a noun through the mere juxtaposition of two terms whose complementary meanings ought apparently to reinforce each other, a surprise is produced by an unexpected precipitation of an unexpected meaning: the image of twin doors symbolizing, through the solitary confinement offered Western Man for the satisfaction of his natural needs away from home, the imperative that he seems to share with the great majority of primitive communities by which his public life is subjected to the laws of urinary segregation.

It is not only with the idea of silencing the nominalist debate with a low blow that I use this example, but rather to show how in fact the signifier enters the signified, namely, in a form which, not being immaterial, raises the question of its place in reality. For the blinking gaze of a short sighted person might be justified in wondering whether this was indeed the signifier as he peered closely at the little enamel signs that bore it, a signifier whose signified would in this call receive its final honours from the double and solemn procession from the upper nave.

But no contrived example can be as telling as the actual experience of truth. So I am happy to have invented the above, since it awoke in the person whose word I most trust a memory of childhood, which having thus happily come to my attention is best placed here.

A train arrives at a station. A little boy and a little girl, brother and sister, are seated in a compartment face to face next to the window through which the buildings along the station platform can be seen passing as the train pulls to a stop. 'Look', says the brother, 'we're at Ladies!'; 'Idiot!' replies his sister, 'Can't you see we're at Gentlemen'.

Besides the fact that the rails in this story materialize the bar in the Saussurian algorithm (and in a form designed to suggest that its resistance may be other than dialectical), we should add that only someone who didn't have his eyes in front of the holes (it's the appropriate image here) could possibly confuse the place of the signifier and the signified in this story, or not see from what radiating centre the signifier sends forth its light into the shadow of incomplete significations.

For this signifier will now carry a purely animal Dissension, destined for the usual oblivion of natural mists, to the unbridled power of ideological warfare, relentless for families, a torment to the Gods. For these children, Ladies and Gentlemen will be henceforth two countries towards which each of their souls will strive on divergent wings, and between which a truce will be the more impossible since they are actually the same country and neither can compromise on its own superiority without detracting from the glory of the other.

But enough. It is beginning to sound like the history of France. Which it is more human, as it ought to be, to evoke here than that of England, destined to tumble from the Large to the Small End of Dean Swift's egg.

It remains to be conceived what steps, what corridor, the S of the signifier, visible here in the plurals[13] in which it focuses its welcome beyond the window, must take in order to rest its elbows on the ventilators through which, like warm and cold air, indignation and scorn come hissing out below.

One thing is certain: if the algorithm S/s with its bar is appropriate, access from one to the other cannot in any case have a signification. For in so far as it is itself only pure function of the signifier, the algorithm can reveal only the structure of a signifier in this transfer.

Now the structure of the signifier is, as it is commonly said of language itself, that it should be articulated.

This means that no matter where one starts to designate their reciprocal encroachments and increasing inclusions, these units are subjected to the double condition of being reducible to ultimate differential elements and of combining them according to the laws of a closed order.

These elements, one of the decisive discoveries of linguistics, are *phonemes*; but we must not expect to find any *phonetic* constancy in the modulatory variability to which this term applies, but rather the synchronic system of differential couplings necessary for the discernment of sounds in a given language. Through this, one sees that an essential element of the spoken word itself was predestined to flow into the mobile characters which, in a jumble of lower-case Didots or Garamonds,[14] render validly present what we call the 'letter', namely, the essentially localized structure of the signifier.

With the second property of the signifier, that of combining according to the laws of a closed order, is affirmed the necessity of the topological substratum of which the term I ordinarily use, namely, the signifying chain, gives an approximate idea: rings of a necklace that is a ring in another necklace made of rings.

Such are the structural conditions that define grammar as the order of constitutive encroachments of the signifier up to the level of the unit immediately superior to the sentence, and lexicology as the order of constitutive inclusions of the signifier to the level of the verbal locution.

In examining the limits by which these two exercises in the understanding of linguistic usage are determined, it is easy to see that only the correlations between signifier and signifier provide the standard for all research into signification, as is indicated by the notion of 'usage' of a taxeme or semanteme which in fact refers to the context just above that of the units concerned.

But it is not because the undertakings of grammar and lexicology are exhausted within certain limits that we must think that beyond those limits signification reigns supreme. That would be an error.

For the signifier, by its very nature, always anticipates meaning by unfolding its dimension before it. As is seen at the level of the sentence when it is interrupted before the significant term: 'I shall never . . .', 'All the same it is . . .', 'And yet there may be . . .'. Such sentences are not without meaning, a meaning all the more oppressive in that it is content to make us wait for it.[15]

But the phenomenon is no different which by the mere recoil of a 'but' brings to the light, comely as the Shulamite, honest as the dew, the negress adorned for the wedding and the poor woman ready for the auction-block.[16]

From which we can say that it is in the chain of the signifier that the meaning 'insists' but that none of its elements 'consists' in the signification of which it is at the moment capable.

We are forced, then, to accept the notion of an incessant sliding of the signified under the signifier – which Ferdinand de Saussure illustrates with an image resembling the wavy lines of the upper and lower Waters in miniatures from manuscripts of *Genesis*; a double flux marked by fine streaks of rain, vertical dotted lines supposedly confining segments of correspondence.

All our experience runs counter to this linearity, which made me speak once, in one of my seminars on psychosis, of something more like 'anchoring points' ('*points de capiton*') as a schema for taking into account the dominance of the letter in the dramatic transformation that dialogue can effect in the subject.[17]

The linearity that Saussure holds to be constitutive of the chain of discourse, in conformity with its emission by a single voice and with its horizontal position in our writing – if this linearity is necessary, in fact, it is not sufficient. It applies to the chain of discourse only in the direction in which it is orientated in time, being taken as a signifying factor in all languages in which 'Peter hits Paul' reverses its time when the terms are inverted.

But one has only to listen to poetry, which Saussure was no doubt in the habit of doing,[18] for a polyphony to be heard, for it to become clear that all discourse is aligned along the several staves of a score.

There is in effect no signifying chain that does not have, as if attached to the punctuation of each of its units, a whole articulation of relevant contexts suspended 'vertically', as it were, from that point.

Let us take our word 'tree' again, this time not as an isolated noun, but at the point of one of these punctuations, and see how it crosses the bar of the Saussurian algorithm. (The anagram of '*arbre*' and '*barre*' should be noted.)

For even broken down into the double spectre of its vowels and consonants, it can still call up with the robur and the plane tree the significations it takes on, in the context of our flora, of strength and majesty. Drawing on all the symbolic contexts suggested in the Hebrew of the Bible, it erects on a barren hill the shadow of the cross. Then reduces to the capital Y, the sign of dichotomy which, except for the illustration used by heraldry, would owe nothing to the tree however genealogical we may think it. Circulatory tree, tree of life of the cerebellum, tree of Saturn, tree of Diana, crystals formed in a tree struck by lightning, is it your figure that traces our destiny for us in the tortoise-shell cracked by the fire, or your lightning that causes that slow shift in the axis of being to surge up from an unnamable night into the "Ἐνπάντα of language:

> *No! says the Tree, it says No! in the shower of sparks*
> *Of its superb head*

lines that require the harmonics of the tree just as much as their continuation:

> *Which the storm treats as universally*
> *As it does a blade of grass.*[19]

For this modern verse is ordered according to the same law of the parallelism of the signifier that creates the harmony governing the primitive Slavic epic or the most refined Chinese poetry.

As is seen in the fact that the tree and the blade of grass are chosen from the same mode of the existent in order for the signs of contradiction – saying 'No!' and 'treat as' – to affect them, and also so as to bring about, through the categorical contrast of the particularity of 'superb' with the 'universally' that reduces it, in the condensation of the 'head' (*tête*) and the 'storm' (*tempête*), the indiscernible shower of sparks of the eternal instant.

But this whole signifier can only operate, it may be said, if it is present in the subject. It is this objection that I answer by supposing that it has passed over to the level of the signified.

For what is important is not that the subject know anything whatsoever. (If LADIES and GENTLEMEN were written in a language unknown to the little boy and girl, their quarrel would simply be the more exclusively a quarrel over words, but no less ready to take on signification.)

What this structure of the signifying chain discloses is the possibility I have, precisely in so far as I have this language in common with other subjects, that is to say, in so far as it exists as a language, to use it in order to signify *something quite other* than what it says. This function of speech is more worth pointing out than that of 'disguising the thought' (more often than not indefinable) of the subject; it is no less than the function of indicating the place of this subject in the search for the true.

I have only to plant my tree in a locution; climb the tree, even project on to it the cunning illumination a descriptive context gives to a word; raise it (*arborer*) so as not to let myself be imprisoned in some sort of *communiqué* of the facts, however official, and if I know the truth, make it heard, in spite of all the *between-the-lines* censures by the only signifier my acrobatics through the branches of the tree can constitute, provocative to the point of burlesque, or perceptible only to the practised eye, according to whether I wish to be heard by the mob or by the few.

The properly signifying function thus depicted in language has a name. We learned this name in some grammar of our childhood, on the last page, where the shade of Quintilian, relegated to some phantom chapter concerning 'final considerations on style', seemed suddenly to speed up his voice in an attempt to get in all he had to say before the end.

It is among the figures of style, or tropes – from which the verb 'to find' (*trouver*) comes to us – that this name is found. This name is *metonymy*.

I shall refer only to the example given there: 'thirty sails'. For the disquietude I felt over the fact that the word 'ship', concealed in this expression, seemed, by taking on its figurative sense, through the endless repetition of the same old example, only to increase its presence, obsured (*voilait*) not so much those illustrious sails (*voiles*) as the definition they were supposed to illustrate.

The part taken for the whole, we said to ourselves, and if the thing is to be taken seriously, we are left with very little idea of the importance of this fleet, which 'thirty sails' is precisely supposed to give us: for each ship to have just one sail is in fact the least likely possibility.

By which we see that the connexion between ship and sail is nowhere but in the signifier, and that it is in the *word-to-word* connexion that metonymy is based.[20]

I shall designate as metonymy, then, the one side (*versant*) of the effective field constituted by the signifier, so that meaning can emerge there.

The other side is *metaphor*. Let us immediately find an illustration; Quillet's dictionary seemed an appropriate place to find a sample that would not seem to be chosen for my own purposes, and I didn't have to go any further than the well known line of Victor Hugo:

His sheaf was neither miserly nor spiteful . . .[21]

under which aspect I presented metaphor in my seminar on the psychoses.

It should be said that modern poetry and especially the Surrealist school have taken us a long way in this direction by showing that any conjunction of two signifiers would be equally sufficient to constitute a metaphor, except for the additional requirement of the greatest possible disparity of the images signified, needed for the production of the poetic spark, or in other words for metaphoric creation to take place.

It is true this radical position is based on the experiment known as automatic writing, which would not have been attempted if its pioneers had not been reassured by the Freudian discovery. But it remains a confused position because the doctrine behind it is false.

The creative spark of the metaphor does not spring from the presentation of two images, that is, of two signifiers equally actualized. It flashes between two signifiers one of which has taken the place of the other in the signifying chain, the occulted signifier remaining present through its (metonymic) connexion with the rest of the chain.

One word for another: that is the formula for the metaphor and if you are a poet you will produce for your own delight a continuous stream, a dazzling tissue of metaphors. If the result is the sort of intoxication of the dialogue that Jean Tardieu wrote under this title, that is only because he was giving us a demonstration of the radical superfluousness of all signification in a perfectly convincing representation of a bourgeois comedy.

It is obvious that in the line of Hugo cited above, not the slightest spark of light springs from the proposition that the sheaf was neither miserly nor spiteful, for the reason that there is no question of the sheaf's having either the merit or demerit of these attributes, since the attributes, like the sheaf, belong to Booz, who exercises the former in disposing of the latter and without informing the latter of his sentiments in the case.

If, however, his sheaf does refer us to Booz, and this is indeed the case, it is because it has replaced him in the signifying chain at the very place where he was to be exalted by the sweeping away of greed and spite. But now Booz himself has been swept away by the sheaf, and hurled into the outer darkness where greed and spite harbour him in the hollow of their negation.

But once *his* sheaf has thus usurped his place, Booz can no longer return there; the slender thread of the little word *his* that binds him to it is only one more obstacle to his return in that it links him to the notion of possession that retains him at the heart of greed and spite. So *his* generosity, affirmed in the passage, is yet reduced to *less than nothing* by the munificence of the sheaf which, coming from nature, knows neither our reserve nor our rejections, and even in its accumulation remains prodigal by our standards.

But if in this profusion the giver has disappeared along with his gift, it is only in order to rise again in what surrounds the figure of speech in which he was annihilated. For it is the figure of the burgeoning of fecundity, and it is this that announces the surprise that the poem celebrates, namely, the promise that the old man will receive in the sacred context of his accession to paternity.

So, it is between the signifier in the form of the proper name of a man and the signifier that metaphorically abolishes him that the poetic spark is produced, and it is in this case all the more effective in realizing the signification of paternity in that it reproduces the mythical event in terms of which Freud reconstructed the progress, in the unconscious of all men, of the paternal mystery.

Modern metaphor has the same structure. So the line *Love is a pebble laughing in the sunlight,* recreates love in a dimension that seems to me most tenable in the face of its imminent lapse into the mirage of narcissistic altruism.

We see, then that, metaphor occurs at the precise point at which sense emerges from non-sense, that is, at that frontier which, as Freud discovered, when crossed the other way produces the word that in French is *the* word *par excellence*, the word that is simply the signifier *'esprit'*;[22] it is at this frontier that we realize that man defies his very destiny when he derides the signifier.

But to come back to our subject, what does man find in metonymy if not the power to circumvent the obstacles of social censure? Does not this form, which gives its field to truth in its very oppression, manifest a certain servitude inherent in its presentation?

One may read with profit a book by Leo Strauss, from the land that traditionally offers asylum to those who choose freedom, in which the author reflects on the relation between the art of writing and persecution.[23] By pushing to its limits the sort of connaturality that links this art to that condition, he lets us glimpse a certain something which in this matter imposes its form, in the effect of truth on desire.

But haven't we felt for some time now that, having followed the ways of the letter in search of Freudian truth, we are getting very warm indeed, that it is burning all about us?

Of course, as it is said, the letter killeth while the spirit giveth life. We can't help but agree, having had to pay homage elsewhere to a noble victim of the error of seeking the spirit in the letter; but we should also like to know how the spirit could live without the letter. Even so, the pretentions of the spirit would remain unassailable if the letter had not shown us that it produces all the effects of truth in man without involving the spirit at all.

It is none other than Freud who had this revelation, and he called his discovery the unconscious.

♦♦♦♦

II *The letter in the unconscious*

In the complete works of Freud, one out of every three pages is devoted to philological references, one out of every two pages to logical inferences, everywhere a dialectical apprehension of experience, the proportion of analysis of language increasing to the extent that the unconscious is directly concerned.

Thus in 'The Interpretation of Dreams' every page deals with what I call the letter of the discourse, in its texture, its usage, its immanence in the matter in question. For it is with this work that the work of Freud begins to open the royal road to the unconscious. And Freud gave us notice of this; his confidence at the time of launching this book in the early days of this century[24] only confirms what he continued to proclaim to the end: that he had staked the whole of his discovery on this essential expression of his message.

The first sentence of the opening chapter announces what for the sake of the exposition could not be postponed: that the dream is a rebus. And Freud goes on to stipulate what I have said from the start, that it must be understood quite literally. This derives from the agency in the dream of that same literal (or phonematic) structure in which the signifier is articulated and analysed in discourse. So the unnatural images of the boat on the roof, or the man with a comma for a head, which are specifically mentioned by Freud, are examples of dream-images that are to be taken only for their value as signifiers, that is to say, in so far as they allow us to spell out the 'proverb' presented by the rebus of the dream. The linguistic structure that enables us to read dreams is the very principle of the 'significance of the dream', the *Traumdeutung*.

Freud shows us in every possible way that the value of the image as signifier has nothing whatever to do with its signification, giving as an example Egyptian hieroglyphics in which it would be sheer buffoonery to pretend that in a given text the frequency of a vulture, which is an *aleph*, or of a chick, which is a *vau*, indicating a form of the verb 'to be' or a plural, prove that the text has anything at all to do with these ornithological specimens. Freud finds in this writing certain uses of the signifier that are lost in ours, such as the use of determinatives, where a categorical figure is added to the literal figuration of a verbal term; but this is only to show us that even in this writing, the so-called 'ideogram' is a letter.

But it does not require the current confusion on this last term for there to prevail in the minds of psychoanalysts lacking linguistic training the prejudice in favour of a symbolism deriving from natural analogy, or even of the image as appropriate to the instinct. And to such an extent that, outside the French school, which has been alerted, a distinction must be drawn between reading coffee grounds and reading hieroglyphics, by recalling to its own principles a technique that could not be justified were it not directed towards the unconscious.

It must be said that this is admitted only with difficulty and that the mental vice denounced above enjoys such favour that today's psychoanalyst can be expected to say that he decodes before he will come around to taking the necessary tour with Freud (turn at the statute of Champollion,[25] says the guide) that will make him understand that what he does is decipher; the distinction is that a cryptogram takes on its full dimension only when it is in a lost language.

Taking the tour is simply continuing in the *Traumdeutung*.

Entstellung, translated as 'distortion' or 'transposition', is what Freud shows to be the general precondition for the functioning of the dream, and it is what I designated above, following Saussure, as the sliding of the signified under the signifier, which is always active in discourse (its action, let us note, is unconscious).

But what we call the two 'sides' of the effect of the signifier on the signified are also found here.

Verdichtung, or 'condensation', is the structure of the superimposition of the signifiers, which metaphor takes as its field, and whose name, condensing in itself the word *Dichtung*, shows how the mechanism is connatural with poetry to the point that it envelops the traditional function proper to poetry.

In the case of *Verschiebung*, 'displacement', the German term is closer to the idea of that veering off of signification that we see in metonymy, and which from its first appearance in Freud is represented as the most appropriate means used by the unconscious to foil censorship.

What distinguishes these two mechanisms, which play such a privileged role in the dream-work (*Traumarbeit*), from their homologous function in discourse? Nothing, except a condition imposed upon the signifying material, called *Rücksicht auf Darstellbarkeit*, which must be translated by 'consideration of the means of representation'. (The translation by 'role of the possibility of figurative expression' being too approximative here.) But this condition constitutes a limitation operating *within* the system of writing; this is a long way from dissolving the system into a figurative semiology on a level with phenomena of natural expression. This fact could perhaps shed light on the problems involved in certain modes of pictography which, simply because they have been abandoned in writing as imperfect, are not therefore to be regarded as mere evolutionary stages. Let us say, then, that the dream is like the parlour-game in which one is supposed to get the spectators to guess some well known saying or variant of it solely by dumb-show. That the dream uses speech makes no difference since for the unconscious it is only one among several elements of the representation. It is precisely the fact that both the game and the dream run up against a lack of taxematic material for the representation of such logical articulations as causality, contradiction, hypothesis, etc., that proves they are a form of writing rather than of mime. The subtle processes that the dream is seen to use to rep resent these logical articulations, in a much less artificial way than games usually employ, are the object of a special study in Freud in which we see once more confirmed that the dream-work follows the laws of the signifier.

The rest of the dream-elaboration is designated as secondary by Freud, the nature of which indicates its value: they are phantasies or daydreams (*Tagtraum*) to use the term Freud prefers in order to emphasize their function of wish-fulfillment (*Wunscherfüllung*). Given the fact that these phantasies may remain unconscious, their distinctive feature is in this case their signification. Now, concerning these phantasies, Freud tells us that their place in the dream is either to be taken up and used as signifying elements for the statement of the unconscious thoughts (*Traumgedanke*), or to be used in the secondary elaboration just mentioned, that is to say, in a function not to be distinguished from our waking thought (*von unserem wachen Denken nicht zu unterschieden*), No better idea of the effects of this function can be given than by comparing it to areas of colour which, when applied here and there to a stencil-plate, can make the stencilled figures, rather forbidding in themselves, more reminiscent of hieroglyphics or of a rebus, look like a figurative painting.

Forgive me if I seem to have to spell out Freud's text; I do so not only to show how much is to be gained by not cutting it about, but also in order to situate the development of psychoanalysis according to its first guide-lines, which were fundamental and never revoked.

Yet from the beginning there was a general *méconnaissance* of the constitutive role of the signifier in the status that Freud from the first assigned to the unconscious and in the most precise formal manner.

There are two reasons for this, of which the least obvious, of course, is that this formalization was not sufficient in itself to bring about a recognition of the agency of the signifier because the *Traumdeutung* appeared long before the formalizations of linguistics for which one could no doubt show that it paved the way by the sheer weight of its truth.

The second reason, which is after all only the reverse side of the first, is that if psychoanalysts were fascinated exclusively by the significations revealed in the unconscious, it is because these significations derived their secret attraction from the dialectic that seemed to be immanent in them.

I have shown in my seminars that it is the need to counteract the continuously accelerating effects of this bias that alone explains the apparent changes of direction or rather changes of tack, which Freud, through his primary concern to preserve for posterity both his discovery and the fundamental revisions it effected in our knowledge, felt it necessary to apply to his doctrine.

For, I repeat, in the situation in which he found himself, having nothing that corresponded to the object of his discovery that was at the same level of scientific development – in this situation, at least he never failed to maintain this object on the level of its ontological dignity.

The rest was the work of the gods and took such a course that analysis today takes its bearings in those imaginary forms that I have just shown to be drawn 'resist-style' (*en reserve*) on the text they mutilate – and the analyst tries to accommodate his direction to them, confusing them, in the interpretation of the dream, with the visionary liberation of the hieroglyphic aviary, and seeking generally the control of the exhaustion of the analysis in a sort of 'scanning'[26] of these forms whenever they appear, in the idea that they are witnesses of the exhaustion of the regressions and of the remodelling of the object relation from which the subject is supposed to derive his 'character-type'.[27]

The technique that is based on such positions can be fertile in its various effects, and under the aegis of therapy, difficult to criticize. But an internal criticism must none the less arise from the flagrant disparity between the mode of operation by which the technique is justified – namely the analytic rule, all the instruments of which, beginning with 'free association', depend on the conception of the unconscious of its inventor – and, on the other hand, the general *méconnaissance* that reigns regarding this conception of the unconscious. The most ardent adherents of this technique believe themselves to be freed of any need to reconcile the two by the merest pirouette: the analytic rule (they say) must be all the more religiously observed since it is only the result of a lucky accident. In other words, Freud never knew what he was doing.

A return to Freud's text shows on the contrary the absolute coherence between his technique and his discovery, and at the same time this coherence allows us to put all his procedures in their proper place.

That is why any rectification of psychoanalysis must inevitably involve a return to the truth of that discovery, which, taken in its original moment, is impossible to obscure.

For in the analysis of dreams, Freud intends only to give us the laws of the unconscious in their most general extension. One of the reasons why dreams were most propitious for this demonstration is exactly, Freud tells us, that they reveal the same laws whether in the normal person or in the neurotic.

But in either case, the efficacy of the unconscious does not cease in the waking state. The psychoanalytic experience does nothing other than establish that the unconscious leaves none of our actions outside its field. The presence of the unconscious in the psychological order, in other words in the relation-functions of the individual, should, however, be more precisely defined: it is not coextensive with that order, for we know that if unconscious motivation is manifest in conscious psychical effects, as well as in unconscious ones, conversely it is only elementary to recall to mind that a large number of psychical effects that are quite legitimately designated as unconscious, in the sense of excluding the characteristic of consciousness, are nonetheless without any relation whatever to the unconscious in the Freudian sense. So it is only by an abuse of the term that unconscious in that sense is confused with psychical, and that one may thus designate as psychical what is in fact an effect of the unconscious, as on the somatic for instance.

It is a matter, therefore, of defining the topography of this unconscious. I say that it is the very topography defined by the algorithm:

$$\frac{S}{s}$$

What we have been able to develop concerning the effects of the signifier on the signified suggests its transformation into:

$$f(S)\frac{I}{s}$$

We have shown the effects not only of the elements of the horizontal signifying chain, but also of its vertical dependencies in the signified, divided into two fundamental structures called metonymy and metaphor. We can symbolize them by, first:

$$f(S \ldots S')S \cong S(-)s$$

that is to say, the metonymic structure, indicating that it is the connexion between signifier and signifier that permits the elision in which the signifier installs the lack-of-being in the object relation, using the value of 'reference back' possessed by signification in order to invest it with the desire aimed at the very lack it supports. The sign — placed between ( ) represents here the maintenance of the bar — which, in the original algorithm, marked the irreducibility in which, in the relations between signifier and signified, the resistance of signification is constituted.[28]

Secondly,

$$f\left(\frac{S'}{S}\right) S \cong S(+)s$$

the metaphoric structure indicating that it is in the substitution of signifier for signifier that an effect of signification is produced that is creative or poetic, in other words, which is the advent of the signification in question.[29] The sign + between ( ) represents here the crossing of the bar — and the constitutive value of this crossing for the emergence of signification.

This crossing expresses the condition of passage of the signifier into the signified that I pointed out above, although provisionally confusing it with the place of the subject.

It is the function of the subject, thus introduced, that we must now turn to since it lies at the crucial point of our problem.

'I think, therefore I am' (*cogito ergo sum*) is not merely the formula in which is constituted, with the historical high point of reflection on the conditions of science, the link between the transparency of the transcendental subject and his existential affirmation.

Perhaps I am only object and mechanism (and so nothing more than phenomenon), but assuredly in so far as I think so, I am – absolutely. No doubt philosophers have brought important corrections to this formulation, notably that in that which thinks (*cogitans*), I can never constitute myself as anything but object (*cogitatum*). Nonetheless it remains true that by way of this extreme purification of the transcendental subject, my existential link to its project seems irrefutable, at least in its present form, and that: '*cogito ergo sum' ubi cogito, ibi sum*, overcomes this objection.

Of course, this limits me to being there in my being only in so far as I think that I am in my thought; just how far I actually think this concerns only myself and if I say it, interests no one.[30]

Yet to elude this problem on the pretext of its philosophical pretensions is simply to admit one's inhibition. For the notion of subject is indispensable even to the operation of a science such as strategy (in the modern sense) whose calculations exclude all 'subjectivism'.

It is also to deny oneself access to what might be called the Freudian universe – in the way that we speak of the Copernican universe. It was in fact the so-called Copernican revolution to which Freud himself compared his discovery, emphasizing that it was once again a question of the place man assigns to himself at the centre of a universe.

Is the place that I occupy as the subject of a signifier concentric or ex-centric, in relation to the place I occupy as subject of the signified? – that is the question.

It is not a question of knowing whether I speak of myself in a way that conforms to what I am, but rather of knowing whether I am the same as that of which I speak. And it is not at all inappropriate to use the word 'thought' here. For Freud uses the term to designate the elements involved in the unconscious, that is the signifying mechanisms that we now recognize as being there.

It is nonetheless true that the philosophical *cogito* is at the centre of the mirage that renders modern man so sure of being himself even in his uncertainties about himself, and even in the mistrust he has learned to practise against the traps of self-love.

Furthermore, if, turning the weapon of metonymy against the nostalgia that it serves, I refuse to seek any meaning beyond tautology, if in the name of 'war is war' and 'a penny's a penny' I decide to be only what I am, how even here can I elude the obvious fact that I am in that very act?

And it is no less true if I take myself to the other, metaphoric pole of the signifying quest, and if I dedicate myself to becoming what I am, to coming into being, I cannot doubt that even if I lose myself in the process, I am in that process.

Now it is on these very points, where evidence will be subverted by the empirical, that the trick of the Freudian conversion lies.

This signifying game between metonymy and metaphor, up to and including the active edge that splits my desire between a refusal of the signifier and a lack of being, and links my fate to the question of my destiny, this game, in all its inexorable subtlety, is played until the match is called, there where I am not, because I cannot situate myself there.

That is to say, what is needed is more than these words with which, for a brief moment I disconcerted my audience: I think where I am not, therefore I am where I do not think. Words that render sensible to an ear properly attuned with what elusive ambiguity[31] the ring of meaning flees from our grasp along the verbal thread.

What one ought to say is: I am not wherever I am the plaything of my thought; I think of what I am where I do not think to think.

This two-sided mystery is linked to the fact that the truth can be evoked only in that dimension of alibi in which all 'realism' in creative works takes its virtue from metonymy; it is likewise linked to this other fact that we accede to meaning only through the double twist of metaphor when we have the one and only key: the S and the *s* of the Saussurian algorithm are not on the same level, and man only deludes himself when he believes his true place is at their axis, which is nowhere.

Was nowhere, that is, until Freud discovered it; for if what Freud discovered isn't that, it isn't anything.

The contents of the unconscious with all their disappointing ambiguities give us no reality in the subject more consistent than the immediate; their virtue derives from the truth and in the dimension of being: *Kern unseres Wesen*[32] are Freud's own terms.

The double-triggered mechanism of metaphor is the very mechanism by which the symptom, in the analytic sense, is determined. Between the enigmatic signifier of the sexual trauma and the term that is substituted for it in an actual signifying chain there passes the spark that fixes in a symptom the signification inaccessible to the conscious subject in which that symptom may be resolved – a symptom being a metaphor in which flesh or function is taken as a signifying element.

And the enigmas that desire seems to pose for a 'natural philosophy' – its frenzy mocking the abyss of the infinite, the secret collusion with which it envelops the pleasure of knowing and of dominating with *jouissance,* these amount to no other derangement of instinct than that of being caught in the rails – eternally stretching forth towards the *desire for something else* – of metonymy. Hence its 'perverse' fixation at the very suspension-point of the signifying chain where the memory-screen is immobilized and the fascinating image of the fetish is petrified.

There is no other way of conceiving the indestructibility of unconscious desire – in the absence of a need which, when forbidden satisfaction, does not sicken and die, even if it means the destruction of the organism itself. It is in a memory, comparable to what is called by that name in our modern thinking-machines (which are in turn based on an electronic realization of the composition of signification), it is in this sort of memory that is found the chain that *insists* on reproducing itself in the transference, and which is the chain of dead desire.

It is the truth of what this desire has been in his history that the patient cries out through his symptom, as Christ said that the stones themselves would have cried out if the children of Israel had not lent them their voice.

And that is why only psychoanalysis allows us to differentiate within memory the function of recollection. Rooted in the signifier, it resolves the Platonic aporias of reminiscence through the ascendancy of history in man.

One has only to read the 'Three Essays on Sexuality' to observe, in spite of the pseudo-biological glosses with which it is decked out for popular consumption, that Freud there derives all accession to the object from a dialectic of return.

Starting from Hölderlin's νοστος, Freud arrives less than twenty years later at Kierkegaard's repetition; that is, in submitting his thought solely to the humble but inflexible consequences of the 'talking cure',[33] he was unable ever to escape the living servitudes that led him from the sovereign principle of the Logos to re-thinking the Empedoclean antinomies of death.

And how else are we to conceive the recourse of a man of science to a *Deus ex machina* than on that 'other scene' he speaks of as the locus of the dream, a *Deus ex machina* only less derisory for the fact that it is revealed to the spectator that the machine directs the director? How else can we imagine that a scientist of the nineteenth century, unless we realize that he had to bow before the force of evidence that went well beyond his prejudices, valued more highly than all his other works his *Totem and Taboo,* with its obscene, ferocious figure of the primordial father, not to be exhausted in the expiation of Oedipus' blindness, and before which the ethnologists of today bow as before the growth of an authentic myth?

So that imperious proliferation of particular symbolic creations, such as what are called the sexual theories of the child, which supply the motivation down to the smallest detail of neurotic compulsions, these reply to the same necessities as do myths.

Thus, to speak of the precise point we are treating in my seminars on Freud, little Hans, left in the lurch at the age of five by his symbolic environment, and suddenly forced to face the enigma of his sex and his existence, developed, under the direction of Freud and of his father, Freud's disciple, in mythic form, around the signifying crystal of his phobia, all the permutations possible on a limited number of signifiers.

The operation shows that even on the individual level the solution of the impossible is brought within man's reach by the exhaustion of all possible forms of the impossibilities encountered in solution by recourse to the signifying equation. It is a striking demonstration that illuminates the labyrinth of a case which so far has only been used as a source of demolished fragments. We should be struck, too, by the fact that it is in the coextensivity of the development of the symptom and of its curative resolution that the nature of the neurosis is revealed: whether phobic, hysterical, or obsessive, the neurosis is a question that being poses for the subject 'from where it was before the subject came into the world' (Freud's phrase, which he used in explaining the Oedipal complex to little Hans).

The 'being' referred to is that which appears in a lightning moment in the void of the verb 'to be' and I said that it poses its question for the subject. What does that mean? It does not pose it *before* the subject, since the subject cannot come to the place where it is posed, but it poses it *in place* of the subject, that is to say, in that place it poses the question *with* the subject, as one poses a problem *with* a pen, or as Aristotle's man thought *with* his soul.

Thus Freud introduced the ego into his doctrine,[34] by defining it according to the resistances that are proper to it. What I have tried to convey is that these resistances are of an imaginary nature much in the same sense as those coaptative lures that the ethology of animal behaviour shows us in display or combat, and that these lures are reduced in man to the narcissistic relation introduced by Freud, which I have elaborated in my essay on the mirror stage. I have tried to show that by situating in this ego the synthesis of the perceptual functions in which the sensorimotor selections are integrated, Freud seems to abound in that delegation that is traditionally supposed to represent reality for the ego, and that this reality is all the more included in the suspension of the ego.

For this ego, which is notable in the first instance for the imaginary inertias that it concentrates against the message of the unconscious, operates solely with a view to covering the displacement constituted by the subject with a resistance that is essential to the discourse as such.

That is why an exhaustion of the mechanisms of defence, which Fenichel the practitioner shows us so well in his studies of analytic technique (while his whole reduction on the theoretical level of neuroses and psychoses to genetic anomalies in libidinal development is pure platitude), manifests itself, without Fenichel's accounting for it or realizing it himself, as simply the reverse side of the mechanisms of the unconscious. Periphrasis, hyperbaton, ellipsis, suspension, anticipation, retraction, negation, digression, irony, these are the figures of style (Quintilian's *figurae sententiarum*); as catachresis, litotes, antonomasia, hypotyposis are the tropes, whose terms suggest themselves as the most proper for the labelling of these mechanisms. Can one really see these as mere figures of speech when it is the figures themselves that are the active principle of the rhetoric of the discourse that the analysand in fact utters?

By persisting in describing the nature of resistance as a permanent emotional state, thus making it alien to the discourse, today's psychoanalysts have simply shown that they have fallen under the blow of one of the fundamental truths that Freud rediscovered through psychoanalysis. One is never happy making way for a new truth, for it always means making our way into it: the truth is always disturbing. We cannot even manage to get used to it. We are used to the real. The truth we repress.

Now it is quite specially necessary to the scientist, to the seer, even to the quack, that he should be the only one to *know*. The idea that deep in the simplest (and even sickest) of souls there is something ready to blossom is bad enough! But if someone seems to know as much as they about what we ought to make of it . . . then the categories of primitive, prelogical, archaic, or even magical thought, so easy to impute to others, rush to our aid! It is not right that these nonentities keep us breathless with enigmas that prove to be only too unreliable.

To interpret the unconscious as Freud did, one would have to be as he was, an encyclopedia of the arts and muses, as well as an assiduous reader of the *Fliegende Blätter*.[35] And the task is made no easier by the fact that we are at the mercy of a thread woven with allusions, quotations, puns, and equivocations. And is that our profession, to be antidotes to trifles?

Yet that is what we must resign ourselves to. The unconscious is neither primordial nor instinctual; what it knows about the elementary is no more than the elements of the signifier.

The three books that one might call canonical with regard to the unconscious – 'The Interpretation of Dreams', 'The Psychopathology of Everyday Life', and 'Jokes and their Relation to the Unconscious' – are simply a web of examples whose development is inscribed in the formulas of connexion and substitution (though carried to the tenth degree by their particular complexity – diagrams of them are sometimes provided by Freud by way of illustration); these are the formulas we give to the signifier in its *transference*-function. For in 'The Interpretation of Dreams' it is in the sense of such a function that the term *Übertragung*, or transference, is introduced, which later gave its name to the mainspring of the intersubjective link between analyst and analysand.

Such diagrams are not only constitutive of each of the symptoms in a neurosis, but they alone make possible the understanding of the thematic of its course and resolution. The great case-histories provided by Freud demonstrate this admirably.

To fall back on a more limited incident, but one more likely to provide us with the final seal on our proposition, let me cite the article on fetishism of 1927,[36] and the case Freud reports there of a patient who, to achieve sexual satisfaction, needed a certain shine on the nose (*Glanz auf der Nase*); analysis showed that his early, English-speaking years had seen the displacement of the burning curiosity that he felt for the phallus of his mother, that is to say, for that eminent *manque-à-être*, for that want-to-be, whose privileged signifier Freud revealed to us, into a *glance at the nose*[37] in the forgotten language of his childhood, rather than a *shine on the nose*.[37]

It is the abyss opened up at the thought that a thought should make itself heard in the abyss that provoked resistance to psychoanalysis from the outset. And not, as is commonly said, the emphasis on man's sexuality. This latter has after all been the dominant object in literature throughout the ages. And in fact the more recent evolution of psychoanalysis has succeeded by a bit of comical legerdemain in turning it into a quite moral affair, the cradle and trysting-place of oblativity and attraction. The Platonic setting of the soul, blessed and illuminated, rises straight to paradise.

The intolerable scandal in the time before Freudian sexuality was sanctified was that it was so 'intellectual'. It was precisely in that that it showed itself to be the worthy ally of all those terrorists whose plottings were going to ruin society.

At a time when psychoanalysts are busy remodelling psychoanalysis into a right-thinking movement whose crowning expression is the sociological poem of the *autonomous ego*, I would like to say, to all those who are listening to me, how they can recognize bad psychoanalysts; this is by the word they use to deprecate all technical or theoretical research that carries forward the Freudian experience along its authentic lines. That word is *'intellectualization'* – execrable to all those who, living in fear of being tried and found wanting by the wine of truth, spit on the bread of men, although their slaver can no longer have any effect other than that of leavening.

❧❧❧

III *The letter, being and the other*[38]

Is what thinks in my place, then, another I? Does Freud's discovery represent the confirmation, on the level of psychological experience, of Manicheism?[39]

In fact, there is no confusion on this point: what Freud's researches led us to is not a few more or less curious cases of split personality. Even at the heroic epoch I have been describing, when, like the animals in fairy stories, sexuality talked, the demonic atmosphere that such an orientation might have given rise to never materialized.[40]

The end that Freud's discovery proposes for man was defined by him at the apex of his thought in these moving terms: *Wo es war, soll Ich werden.* I must come to the place where that was.

This is one of reintegration and harmony, I could even say of reconciliation (*Versöhnung*).

But if we ignore the self's radical ex-centricity to itself with which man is confronted, in other words, the truth discovered by Freud, we shall falsify both the order and methods of psychoanalytic mediation; we shall make of it nothing more than the compromise operation that it has, in effect, become, namely, just what the letter as well as the spirit of Freud's work most repudiates. For since he constantly invoked the notion of compromise as supporting all the miseries that his analysis is supposed to assuage, we can say that any recourse to compromise, explicit or implicit, will necessarily disorient psychoanalytic action and plunge it into darkness.

But neither does it suffice to associate oneself with the moralistic tartufferies of our time or to be forever spouting something about the 'total personality' in order to have said anything articulate about the possibility of mediation.

The radical heteronomy that Freud's discovery shows gaping within man can never again be covered over without whatever is used to hide it being profoundly dishonest.

Who, then, is this other to whom I am more attached than to myself, since, at the heart of my assent to my own identity it is still he who agitates me?

His presence can be understood only at a second degree of otherness, which already places him in the position of mediating between me and the double of myself, as it were with my counterpart.

If I have said that the unconscious is the discourse of the Other (with a capital O), it is in order to indicate the beyond in which the recognition of desire is bound up with the desire for recognition.

In other words this other is the Other that even my lie invokes as a guarantor of the truth in which it subsists.

By which we can also see that it is with the appearance of language the dimension of truth emerges.

Prior to this point, we can recognize in the psychological relation, which can be easily isolated in the observation of animal behaviour, the existence of subjects, not by means of some projective mirage, the phantom of which a certain type of psychologist delights in hacking to pieces, but simply on account of the manifested presence of intersubjectivity. In the animal hidden in his lookout, in the well-laid trap of certain others, in the feint by which an apparent straggler leads a predator away from the flock, something more emerges than in the fascinating display of mating or combat ritual. Yet there is nothing even there that transcends the function of lure in the service of a need, or which affirms a presence in that beyond-the-veil where the whole of Nature can be questioned about its design.

For there even to be a question (and we know that it is one Freud himself posed in 'Beyond the Pleasure Principle'), there must be language.

For I can lure my adversary by means of a movement contrary to my actual plan of battle, and this movement will have its deceiving effect only in so far as I produce it in reality and for my adversary.

But in the propositions with which I open peace negotiations with him, what my negotiations propose to him is situated in a third locus which is neither my speech nor my interlocutor.

This locus is none other than the locus of signifying convention, of the sort revealed in the comedy of the sad plaint of the Jew to his crony: 'Why do you tell me you are going to Cracow so I'll believe you are going to Lvov, when you really are going to Cracow?'

Of course the flock-movement I just spoke of could be understood in the conventional context of game-strategy, where it is a rule that I deceive my adversary, but in that case my success is evaluated within the connotation of betrayal, that is to say, in relation to the Other who is the guarantor of Good Faith.

Here the problems are of an order the heteronomy of which is completely misconstrued (*méconnue*) if reduced to an 'awareness of others', or whatever we choose to call it. For the 'existence of the other' having once upon a time reached the ears of the Midas of psychoanalysis through the partition that separates him from the secret meetings of the phenomenologists, the news is now being whispered through the reeds: 'Midas, King Midas, is the other of his patient. He himself has said it.'

What sort of breakthrough is that? The other, what other?

The young André Gide, defying the landlady to whom his mother had confided him to treat him as a responsible person, opening with a key (false only in that it opened all locks of the same make) the lock that this lady took to be a worthy signifier of her educational intentions, and doing it quite obviously for her benefit – what 'other' was he aiming at? She who was supposed to intervene and to whom he would then say: 'Do you think my obedience can be secured with a ridiculous lock?'. But by remaining out of sight and holding her peace until that evening in order, after primly greeting his return, to lecture him like a child, she showed him not just another with the face of anger, but another André Gide who is no longer sure, either then or later in thinking back on it, of just what he really meant to do – whose own truth has been changed by the doubt thrown on his good faith.

Perhaps it would be worth our while pausing a moment over this empire of confusion which is none other than that in which the whole human opera-buffa plays itself out, in order to understand the ways in which analysis can proceed not just to restore an order but to found the conditions for the possibility of its restoration.

Kern unseres Wesen, the nucleus of our being, but it is not so much

that Freud commands us to seek it as so many others before him have
with the empty adage 'Know thyself' – as to reconsider the ways that
lead to it, and which he shows us.

Or rather that which he proposes for us to attain is not that which can
be the object of knowledge, but that (doesn't he tell us as much?) which
creates our being and about which he teaches us that we bear witness to
it as much and more in our whims, our aberrations, our phobias and
fetishes, as in our more or less civilized personalities.

Madness, you are no longer the object of the ambiguous praise with
which the sage decorated the impregnable burrow of his fear; and if after
all he finds himself tolerably at home there, it is only because the supreme
agent forever at work digging its tunnels is none other than reason, the
very Logos that he serves.

So how do you imagine that a scholar with so little talent for the
'commitments' that solicited him in his age (as they do in all ages), that
a scholar such as Erasmus held such an eminent place in the revolution of
a Reformation in which man has as much of a stake in each man as in all
men?

The answer is that the slightest alteration in the relation between man
and the signifier, in this case in the procedures of exegesis, changes the
whole course of history by modifying the moorings that anchor his
being.

It is precisely in this that Freudianism, however misunderstood it has
been, and however confused its consequences have been, to anyone
capable of perceiving the changes we have lived through in our own
lives, is seen to have founded an intangible but radical revolution. There
is no point in collecting witnesses to the fact:[41] everything involving not
just the human sciences, but the destiny of man, politics, metaphysics,
literature, the arts, advertising, propaganda, and through these even
economics, everything has been affected.

Is all this anything more than the discordant effects of an immense
truth in which Freud traced for us a clear path? What must be said, however, is that any technique that bases its claim on the mere psychological
categorization of its object is not following this path, and this is the case
of psychoanalysis today except in so far as we return to the Freudian
discovery.

Furthermore, the vulgarity of the concepts by which it recommends
itself to us, the embroidery of pseudo-Freudianism (*frofreudisme*) which
is no longer anything but decoration, as well as the bad repute in which

it seems to prosper, all bear witness to its fundamental betrayal of its founder.

By his discovery, Freud brought within the circle of science the boundary between the object and being that seemed to mark its outer limit.

That this is the symptom and the prelude of a re-examination of the situation of man in the existent such as has been assumed up to the present by all our postulates of knowledge – don't be content, I beg of you, to write this off as another case of Heideggerianism, even prefixed by a neo- that adds nothing to the dustbin style in which currently, by the use of his ready-made mental jetsam, one excuses oneself from any real thought.

When I speak of Heidegger, or rather when I translate him, I at least make the effort to leave the speech he proffers us its sovereign significance.

If I speak of being and the letter, if I distinguish the other and the Other, it is because Freud shows me that they are the terms to which must be referred the effects of resistance and transference against which, in the twenty years I have engaged in what we all call after him the impossible practice of psychoanalysis, I have done unequal battle. And it is also because I must help others not to lose their way there.

It is to prevent the field of which they are the inheritors from becoming barren, and for that reason to make it understood that if the symptom is a metaphor, it is not a metaphor to say so, any more than to say that man's desire is a metonymy. For the symptom *is* a metaphor whether one likes it or not, as desire *is* a metonymy, however funny people may find the idea.

Finally, if I am to rouse you to indignation over the fact that, after so many centuries of religious hypocrisy and philosophical bravado, nothing has yet been validly articulated as to what links metaphor to the question of being and metonymy to its lack, there must be an object there to answer to that indignation both as its instigator and its victim: that object is humanistic man and the credit, hopelessly affirmed, which he has drawn over his intentions.

14–26 May, 1957

Notes

1. *Codice Atlantico* 145.

2. *Psychanalyse et sciences de l'homme.*

3. The lecture took place on 9 May, 1957, in the Amphithéâtre Descartes of the Sorbonne, and the discussion was continued afterwards over drinks.

4. *Die Frage der Laienanalyse, G.W.,* XIV: 281–3.

5. '*A la lettre*' [Tr.].

6. This aspect of aphasia, so useful in overthrowing the concept of 'psychological function', which only obscures every aspect of the question, becomes quite clear in the purely linguistic analysis of the two major forms of aphasia worked out by one of the leaders of modern linguistics, Roman Jakobson. See the most accessible of his works, the *Fundamentals of Language* (with Morris Halle), Mouton, 's Gravenhage, part II, Chapters 1 to 4.

7. We may recall that the discussion of the need for a new language in communist society did in fact take place, and Stalin, much to the relief of those who adhered to his philosophy, put an end to it with the following formulation: language is not a superstructure.

8. By 'linguistics' I mean the study of existing languages (*langues*) in their structure and in the laws revealed therein; this excludes any theory of abstract codes sometimes included under the heading of communication theory, as well as the theory, originating in the physical sciences, called information theory, or any semiology more or less hypothetically generalized.

9. *Psychanalyse et sciences de l'homme.*

10. Cf. the *De Magistro* of St Augustine, especially the chapter 'De significatione locutionis' which I analysed in my seminar of 23 June, 1954.

11. English in the original [Tr.].

12. So, Mr I. A. Richards, author of a work precisely in accord with such an objective, has in another work shown us its application. He took for his purposes a page from Mong-tse (Mencius, to the Jesuits) and called the piece, *Mencius on the Mind.* The guarantees of the purity of the experiment are nothing to the luxury of the approaches. And our expert on the traditional Canon that contains the text is found right on the spot in Peking where our demonstration-model mangle has been transported regardless of cost.

But we shall be no less transported, if less expensively, to see a bronze that gives out bell-tones at the slightest contact with thought, transformed into a rag to wipe the blackboard of the most dismaying British psychologism. And not without eventually being identified with the meninx of the author himself – all that remains of him or his object after having exhausted the meaning of the latter and the good sense of the former.

13. Not, unfortunately, the case in the English here – the plural of 'gentleman' being indicated other than by the addition of an 's' [Tr.].

14. Names of different type-faces [Tr.].

15. To which verbal hallucination, when it takes this form, opens a communicating door with the Freudian structure of psychosis – a door until now unnoticed (cf. 'On a Question Preliminary to any Possible Treatment of Psychosis', pp. 179–225).

16. The allusions are to the 'I am black, but comely . . .' of the *Song of Solomon*, and to the nineteenth-century cliché of the 'poor, but honest' woman [Tr.].

17. I spoke in my seminar of 6 June, 1956, of the first scene of *Athalie*, incited by an allusion – tossed off by a high-brow critic in the *New Statesman and Nation* – to the 'high whoredom' of Racine's heroines, to renounce reference to the savage dramas of Shakespeare, which have become compulsional in analytic circles where they play the role of status-symbol for the Philistines.

18. The publication by Jean Staro-binski, in *Le Mercure de France* (February 1964) of Saussure's notes on anagrams and their hypogrammatical use, from the Saturnine verses to the writings of Cicero, provide the corroboration that I then lacked (note 1966).

19.
'*Non! dit l'Arbre, il dit: Non! dans l'étincellement*
De sa tête superbe
Que la tempête traite universellement
Comme elle fait une herbe.'
(Paul Valéry, 'Au Platane', *Les Charmes*)

20. I pay homage here to the works of Roman Jakobson – to which I owe much of this formulation; works to which a psychoanalyst can constantly refer in order to structure his own experience, and which render superfluous the 'personal communications' of which I could boast as much as the next fellow.

Indeed, one recognizes in this oblique form of allegiance the style of that immortal couple, Rosencrantz and Guildenstern, who are virtually indistinguishable, even in the imperfection of their destiny, for it survives by the same method as Jeannot's knife, and for the same reason for which Goethe praised Shakespeare for presenting the character in double form: they represent, in themselves alone, the whole *Gesellschaft*, the Association itself (*Wilhelm Meisters Lehrjahre*, ed. Trunz, Christian Wegner Verlag, Hamburg, **V** (5): 299) – I mean the International Psychoanalytical Association.

We should savour the passage from Goethe as a whole: '*Dieses leise Auftreten dieses Schmiegen und Biegen, dies Jasagen, Streicheln und Schmeicheln, dieses Behendigkeit, dies Schwänzein, diese Allheit und Leerheit, diese rechtliche Schurkerei, diese Unfähigkeit, wie kann sie durch einen Menschen ausgedruckt werden? Es sollten ihrer wenigstens ein Dutzend sein, wenn man sie haben könnte; denn sie bloss in Gesellschaft etwas, sie sind die Gesellschaft . . .*'

Let us thank also, in this context, the author R. M. Loewenstein of 'Some Remarks on the Role of Speech in Psychoanalytic Technique' (*I.J.P.*, Nov.–Dec., 1956, **XXXVII** (6): 467) for taking the trouble to point out that his remarks are 'based on' work dating from 1952. This is no doubt the explanation for the fact that he has learned nothing from work done since then, yet which he is not ignorant of, as he cites me as their 'editor' (sic).

21. 'Sa gerbe n'était pas avare ni haineuse', a line from 'Booz endormi' [Tr.].

22. '*Mot*', in the broad sense, means 'word'. In the narrower sense, however, it means 'a witticism'. The French '*esprit*' is translated, in this context, as 'wit', the equivalent of Freud's *Witz* [Tr.].

'*Esprit*' is certainly the equivalent of the German *Witz* with which Freud marked the approach of his third fundamental work on the unconscious. The much greater difficulty of finding this equivalent in English is instructive: 'wit', burdened with all the discussion of which it was the object from Davenant and Hobbes to Pope and Addison, abandoned its essential virtues to 'humour', which is something else. There only remains the 'pun', but this word is too narrow in its connotation.

23. Leo Strauss, *Persecution and the Art of Writing*, The Free Press, Glencoe, Illinois.

24. Cf. the correspondence, namely letters 107 and 109.

25. Jean-François Champollion (1790–1832), the first scholar to decipher Ancient Egyptian hieroglyphics [Tr.].

26. That is the process by which the results of a piece of research are assured through a mechanical exploration of the entire extent of the field of its object.

27. By referring only to the development of the organism, the typology fails to recognize (*méconnaît*) the structure in which the subject is caught up respectively in phantasy, in drive, in sublimation. I am at present developing the theory of this structure (note 1966).

28. The sign $\cong$ here designates congruence.

29. S' designating here the term productive of the signifying effect (or significance); one can see that the term is latent in metonymy, patent in metaphor.

30. It is quite otherwise if by posing a question such as 'Why philosophers?' I become more candid than nature, for then I am asking not only the question that philosophers have been asking themselves for all time, but also the one in which they are perhaps most interested.

31. '*Ambiguité de furet*' – literally, 'ferret-like ambiguity'. This is one of a number of references in Lacan to the game 'hunt-the-slipper' (*jeu du furet*) [Tr.].

32. 'The nucleus of our being' [Tr.].

33. English in the original [Tr.].

34. This and the next paragraph were rewritten solely with a view to greater clarity of expression (note 1968).

35. A German comic newspaper of the late nineteenth and early twentieth centuries [Tr.].

36. *Fetischismus*, *G.W.* **XIV**: 311; "Fetishism', *Collected Papers*, **V**: 198; *Standard Edition* **XXI**: 149.

37. English in the original [Tr.].

38. *La lettre l'être et l'autre.*

39. One of my colleagues went so far in this direction as to wonder if the id (*Es*) of the last phase wasn't in fact the 'bad ego'. (It should now be obvious whom I am referring to – 1966.)

40. Note, nonetheless, the tone with which one spoke in that period of the 'elfin pranks' of the unconscious; a work of Silberer's is called *Der Zufall und die Koboldstreiche des Unbewussten* (Chance and the Elfin Tricks of the Unconscious) – completely anachronistic in the context of our present soul-managers.

41. To pick the most recent in date, François Mauriac, in the *Figaro littéraire* of 25 May, apologizes for refusing 'to tell the story of his life'. If no one these days can undertake to do that with the old enthusiasm, the reason is that, 'a half century since, Freud, whatever we think of him' has already passed that way. And after being briefly tempted by the old saw that this is only the 'history of our body', Mauriac returns to the truth that his sensitivity as a writer makes him face: to write the history of oneself is to write the confession of the deepest part of our neighbours' souls as well.

SIX

On a question preliminary to any possible treatment of psychosis

This article contains the most important parts of the seminar
given during the first two terms of the academic year
1955–6, at the École Normale Supérieure. It first
appeared in *La Psychanalyse*, vol. 4.

❧❧❧❧

Hoc quod triginta tres per annos in ipso loco studui,
et Sanctae Annae Genio loci, et dilectae
juventuti, quae eo me sectata est,
diligenter dedico.

❧❧❧❧

I *Towards Freud*

1. Half a century of Freudianism applied to psychosis leaves its problem still to be rethought, in other words, at the *status quo ante*.

It might be said that before Freud discussion of psychosis did not detach itself from a theoretical background that presented itself as psychology, but which was merely a 'laicized' remainder of what we shall call the long metaphysical coction of science in the School (with the capital 'S' that it deserves).

Now if our science, which concerns the *physis*, in its ever purer mathematization, retains from this cooking no more than a whiff so subtle that one may legitimately wonder whether there has not been a substitution of person, the same cannot be said of the *antiphysis* (that is, the living apparatus that one hopes is capable of measuring the said physis), whose smell of burnt fat betrays without the slightest doubt the age-old practice in the said cooking of the preparation of brains.

Thus the theory of abstraction, necessary in accounting for knowledge, has become fixed in an abstract theory of the faculties of the subject, which the most radical sensualist petitions could not render more functional with regard to subjective effects.

The constantly renewed attempts to correct its results by the varied counterweights of the affect are doomed to failure as long as one omits to ask if it is indeed the same subject that is affected.

2. It is the question that one learns on the school bench (with a small 's') to avoid once and for all: for even if the alternations of identity of the *percipiens* are admitted, its function in the constitution of the unity of the *perceptum* is not discussed. The diversity of structure of the *perceptum* affects in the *percipiens* only a diversity of register, in the final analysis, that of the *sensoriums*. In law, this diversity is always surmountable if the *percipiens* is capable of apprehending reality.

That is why those whose task it is to answer the question posed by the existence of the madman could not prevent themselves from interposing between it and them those same school benches, which provided such a convenient shelter.

Indeed, I would dare to lump together, if I may say so, all the positions, whether they are mechanist or dynamist, whether they see genesis as deriving from the organism or from the psyche, and structure from disintegration or from conflict. All of them, ingenious as they are in declaring, in the name of a manifest fact that a hallucination is a *perceptum* without an object end up asking the *percipiens* the reason for this *perceptum*, without anyone realizing that in this request, a step has been skipped, the step of asking oneself whether the *perceptum* itself bequeathed a univocal sense to the *percipiens* here required to explain it.

This step, however, ought to appear legitimate in any unbiased examination of verbal hallucination, because it is not reducible to a specific *sensorium*, still less to a *percipiens* in the sense that the latter would give it its unity.

In effect, it is an error to hold it as essentially auditive when it is conceivable that it be not so at all (for a deaf-mute, for example, or in some non-auditive register of hallucinatory spelling). It is an error moreover because we realise that the act of hearing is not the same, according to whether it aims at the coherence of the verbal chain, namely, its overdetermination at each instant by the deferred action (*après-coup*) of its sequence, as, too, the suspension at each instant of its value at the advent of a meaning, ever ready for return – or according to whether it accommodates itself in speech to sound modulation, to this or that end of acoustic analysis: tonal or phonetic, even of musical power.

These very brief remarks were enough to bring out the difference of the subjectivities concerned in the perspective of the *perceptum* (and the extent to which it is misunderstood in the questioning of patients and the nosology of 'voices').

But one might claim to reduce this difference to a level of objectification in the *percipiens*.

This, however, is not the case. For it is at the level at which subjective 'synthesis' confers its full meaning on speech that the subject reveals all the paradoxes of which he is the patient in this singular perception. These paradoxes already appear when it is the other who offers speech: this is sufficiently evidenced in the subject by the possibility of his obeying this speech in so far as it governs his hearing and his being-on-his-guard, for simply by entering the other's auditory field, the subject falls under the sway of a suggestion from which he can escape only by reducing the other to being no more than the spokesman of a discourse that is not his own or of an intention that he is holding in reserve.

But still more striking is the subject's relation to his own speech, in which the important factor is rather masked by the purely acoustic fact that he cannot speak without hearing himself. Nor is there anything special about the fact that he cannot listen to himself without being divided as far as the behaviour of the consciousness is concerned. Clinicians did better by discovering verbal motor hallucination by detecting the outline of phonatory movements. Yet they have not articulated where the crucial point resides; it is that the *sensorium* being indifferent in the production of a signifying chain:

(a) this signifying chain imposes itself, by itself, on the subject in its vocal dimension;

(b) it takes as such a reality proportional to the time, perfectly observable in experience, that its subjective attribution involves;

(c) its own structure *qua* signifier is determinant in this attribution, which, as a rule, is distributive, that is to say, possesses several voices, and, therefore, renders equivocal a supposedly unifying *percipiens*.

3. I shall illustrate what I have just said with a phenomenon taken from one of my clinical presentations for the year 1955–6, that is, the year of the seminar referred to here. Let us say that such a discovery can be made only at the cost of complete submission, even if it is intentional, to the properly subjective positions of the patient, positions which all too often one distorts in reducing them to a morbid process, thus reinforcing the difficulty of penetrating them with a not unjustified reticence on the part of the subject.

It was a case in fact of one of those shared delusions, of which I long ago showed the type in the mother/daughter couple, in which a sense of intrusion, developing into a delusion of being spied on, was merely the development of the defence proper to an affective binary relation, open as such to any form of alienation.

It was the daughter who, when interviewed, gave me as proof of the insults to which both of them were subjected by their neighbours a fact concerning the lover of the neighbour who was supposed to be harrassing them with her attacks, after they had had to break off a friendship with her that was at first encouraged. This man, who was no more therefore than an indirect party to the situation, and indeed a somewhat shadowy figure in the patient's allegations, had, apparently, called after her, as he passed her in the corridor of the block of flats in which they lived, the offensive word: 'Sow!'.

Upon which, I, little inclined to see in it a counter-thrust to 'Pig!', which would be too easy to extrapolate in the name of a projection which, in such a case, is never more than the psychiatrist's own projection, went on to ask her what she might have said the moment before. Not without success: for, with a smile, she conceded that, on seeing the man, she had murmured the apparently harmless enough words: 'I've just been to the pork butcher's . . .'

Who were these words directed to? She was hard put to say it, thus giving me the right to help her. For their textual meaning, we cannot ignore the fact, among others, that the patient had suddenly taken leave of her husband and her family-in-law and thus given to a marriage that her mother disapproved of an outcome that has remained unchanged. This departure rested on the conviction she had acquired that these peasants proposed nothing less, in order to put an end to this good-for-nothing city girl, than to cut her into pieces.

What does it matter, however, whether or not one has to resort to the phantasy of the fragmented body in order to understand how the patient, a prisoner of the dual relationship, responds once more here to a situation that is beyond her comprehension.

For our present purposes, it is enough that the patient should have admitted that the phrase was allusive, even though she was unable to be anything other than perplexed as to which of the two present or the one absent person was being alluded to, for it thus appears that the *I*, as subject of the sentence in direct style, left in suspense, in accordance with its function as a 'shifter', as it is called in linguistics,[1] the designation of the speaking subject, for as long as the allusion, in its conjuratory intention no doubt, itself remained in a state of oscillation. After the pause, this uncertainty came to an end with the apposition of the word 'sow', itself too loaded with invective to follow the oscillation isochronically. Thus the discourse came to realize its intention as rejection in hallucination. In the place where the unspeakable object is rejected in the real, a word makes itself heard, so that, coming in the place of that which has no name, it was unable to follow the intention of the subject without detaching itself from it by the dash preceding the reply: opposing its disparaging antistrophe to the cursing of the strophe thus restored to the patient with the index of the I, resembling in its opacity the ejaculations of love, when, lacking a signifier to name the object of its epithalamium, it employs the crudest trickery of the imaginary. 'I'll eat you up . . . Sweetie!' 'You'll love it . . . Rat!'

4. I have referred to this example here only to show in living, concrete detail that the function of irrealization is not everything in the symbol. For, in order that its irruption into the real should be beyond question, it has only to present itself, as it usually does, in the form of a broken chain.[2]

We also touch here upon the effect that every signifier has, once it is perceived, of arousing in the *percipiens* an assent composed of the awakening of the hidden duplicity of the second by the manifest ambiguity of the first.

Of course, all this may be regarded as mirage effects from the classical point of view of the unifying subject.

But it is striking that this point of view, reduced to itself, should offer, on hallucination for example, only views of such poverty that the work of a madman, no doubt as remarkable as Judge Schreber in his *Memoirs of my Nervous Illness*[3] may, after being welcomed most enthusiastically, before Freud, by psychiatrists, be regarded, even after him, as a collection of writings to be offered as an introduction to the phenomenology of psychosis, and not only for the beginner.[4]

He provided me, too, with the basis of a structural analysis, when, in my seminar for the year 1955–6 on Freudian structures in psychosis, I followed Freud's advice and re-examined his case.

The relation between the signifier and the subject that this analysis reveals is to be met – it is apparent in this address – with the very appearance of these phenomena, if, returning from Freud's experience, one is aware of the point to which it is leading.

But this departure from the phenomenon, if properly carried out, would lead us back to that point, as was the case for me when an early study of paranoia led me thirty years ago to the threshold of psycho-analysis.[5]

Nowhere, in fact, is the fallacious conception of a psychical process in Jaspers' conception of this process, in which the symptom is merely the index, more irrelevant than in the approach to psychosis, because nowhere is the symptom, if one can decipher it, more clearly articulated in the structure itself.

Which makes it incumbent on us to define this process by the most radical determinants of the relation of man to the signifier.

5. But we do not have to have reached that stage to be interested in the variety of verbal hallucinations to be found in Schreber's *Memoirs*, or to recognize in them differences quite other than those in which they are 'classically' classified, according to their mode of involvement in the *percipiens* (the degree of his 'belief') or in the reality of the same ('audi-tivation'): or rather, the differences that derive from their speech structure, in so far as this structure is already in the *perceptum*.

Simply by considering the text of the hallucinations, a distinction arises for the linguist between code phenomena and message phenomena.

To the phenomena of code belong, in this approach, the voices that use the *Grundsprache*, which I would translate as 'basic language' (*langue-de-fond*), and which Schreber describes (S. 13-I)[6] as 'a somewhat archaic, but always rigorous German that is particularly marked by its great wealth of euphemisms'. Elsewhere (S. 167-XII) he refers regretfully to 'its form, which is authentic on account of its characteristics of noble distinction and simplicity'.

This part of the phenomena is specified in expressions that are neo-logical in form (new compound words – the process of compounding being governed here by the rules of the patient's language, *langue*) and usage. Hallucinations inform the subject of the forms and usages that constitute the neo-code: the subject owes to them, for example, primarily, the term *Grundsprache* to designate it.

It is something fairly close to these messages that linguists call *autonyms*, even though it is the signifier itself (and not that which it signifies) that is the object of the communication. But this peculiar, but normal relation between the message and itself is reduplicated here by the fact that these messages are regarded as being supported by beings whose relations they themselves state in modes that prove to be very similar to the connexions of the signifier. The term *Nervenanhang*, which I would translate as nerve-annexation (*annexion-de-nerfs*), and which also derives from these messages, illustrates this remark in that passion and action between these beings is reduced to those annexed or disannexed nerves, but also in that these nerves, quite as much as the divine rays (*Gottesstrahlen*) to which they are homogeneous, are simply the joining together of the words (*paroles*) that they support (S. 130-X: what the voices formulate as: 'Do not forget that the nature of the rays is that they must speak').

There is the relation here of the system to its own constitution as signifier, which would seem to be relevant to the question of metalanguage and which, in my opinion, will demonstrate the impropriety of that notion if it is intended to define differentiated elements in language.

It should be noted, furthermore, that we are presented here with phenomena that have been wrongly called intuitive, on account of the fact that the effect of the signification anticipates the development of the signification. What is involved here, in fact is an effect of the signifier, in so far as its degree of certainty (second degree: signification of signi-fication) assumes a weight proportional to the enigmatic void that first presents itself in the place of the signification itself.

The amusing thing in this case is that it is precisely to the extent that for the subject this high voltage of the signifier drops, that is to say, that the hallucinations are reduced to *ritornelli*, to mere repetitions, the inanity of which imputed to beings devoid of intelligence and personality, if not frankly effaced from the register of being, that it is to precisely this extent, as I say, that the voices take account of the *Seelenauffassung*, the con-ception-of-souls (in the basic language), a conception that is manifested in a catalogue of thoughts that is not unworthy of a book of classical psychology. A catalogue bound up in the voices with a pedantesque in-tention, a fact that does not prevent the subject from introducing the most pertinent commentaries. I would note that in these commentaries the source of the terms is always carefully distinguished, for example that although the subject uses the word *Instanz* (S. note of 30-II – lecture notes from 11 to 21-I), he emphasizes in a note: 'that word is mine'.

Thus the fundamental importance of memory-thoughts (*Erinnerungs-gedanken, pensées-de-mémoire*) in the psychical economy does not escape him, and he immediately offers proof of this in the poetic and musical use of modulating repetition.

Our patient, who provides the priceless description of this 'conception of souls' as 'the somewhat idealized representation that souls have formed of life and human thought' (S. 164-XII), thinks that he has 'gained insights into the essence of the process of thought and feeling in man that might be the envy of many psychologists' (S. 167-XII).

I would agree all the more readily in that, unlike them, he does not imagine that this knowledge, the scope of which he appreciates so humorously, proceeds from the nature of things, and that, although he thinks that he must make use of it, it is, as I have shown, on the basis of a semantic analysis![7]

But to take up the thread of our argument, let us turn to the phenomena that I will contrast with the earlier ones as message phenomena.

We are dealing here with interrupted messages, by which a relation is sustained between the subject and his divine interlocutor, a relation to which the messages give the form of a challenge or endurance test.

Indeed, the voice of the partner limits the messages involved to the beginning of a sentence whose complement of sense presents, moreover, no difficulty for the subject, other than its harrassing, offensive side, which is usually of an ineptitude such as to discourage him. The bravery he shows in not faltering in his reply, in even thwarting the traps laid for him, is not the least important aspect for our analysis of the phenomenon.

But he will pause here again at the very text of what might be called hallucinatory provocation (or protasis). The subject gives us the following examples of such a structure (S. 217-XVI): (1) *Nun will ich mich* (now I will . . . myself . . .); (2) *Sie sollen nämlich* . . . (as for you, you ought to . . .); (3) *Das will ich mir* . . . (I will certainly . . .) – to take only these three – to which he must reply with their significant supplement, for him beyond doubt, namely: (1) face the fact that I am an idiot; (2) as for you, you ought to be exposed (a word of the basic language) as the negator of God and as given up to dissolute sensuality, not to mention other things; (3) think about it.

One might note that the sentence is interrupted at the point at which the group of words that one might call index-terms ends, the terms being either those designated by their function in the signifier, according to the term employed above, as shifters, or precisely the terms which, in the code, indicate the position of the subject on the basis of the message itself.

After which, the properly lexical part of the sentence, in other words that which comprises the words that the code defines by their use, whether the common code or the delusional code is involved, remains elided.

Is one not struck by the predominance of the function of the signifier in these two orders of phenomena, not to say urged to seek what lies at the bottom of the association that they constitute; of a code constituted by messages on the code, and of a message reduced to that in the code which indicates the message.

All this had to be transferred with the greatest care to a graph,[8] in which this year I tried to represent the connexions internal to the signifier, in so far as they structure the subject.

For there is a topology here that is quite distinct from what might be imagined given the requirement of an immediate parallel between the form of the phenomena and their pathways in the neuraxis.

But this topology, which follows the lines laid down by Freud when, after opening up the field of the unconscious through his work on dreams, he set out to describe the dynamics of the unconscious, without feeling restricted by any concern with cortical localization, is precisely what may best prepare the way for the questions that will be addressed to the surface of the cortex.

For it is only after the linguistic analysis of the phenomenon of language that one can legitimately establish the relation that it constitutes in the subject, and at the same time delimit the order of the 'machines' (in the purely associative sense that this term possesses in the mathematical theory of networks) that may realize this phenomenon.

It is no less remarkable that it should have been the Freudian experience that led the author of these lines in the direction presented here. Let us examine, then, what this experience introduces into our question.

$$\maltese\maltese$$

II *After Freud*

1. What has Freud contributed here? We began by stating that, so far as the problem of psychosis was concerned, this contribution had led to a falling back.

This is immediately apparent in the simplistic character of the elements invoked in conceptions that all amount to a single fundamental schema, namely, how can the internal be transmitted to the external? It is no use, in effect, for the subject to try and encompass here an opaque id, since it is as ego, after all, in a way fully expressed in the present psychoanalytic orientation, as this same indestructible *percipiens*, that he is invoked in the motivation of psychosis. This *percipiens* is all-powerful over its no less unchanged correlative, reality, and the model of this power is derived from a datum accessible to common experience, that of affective projection.

For present theories are noteworthy for the totally uncritical way in which this mechanism of projection is used. The objections against such a use are overwhelming, yet this seems to deter no one, and this despite all the clinical evidence that there is nothing in common between affective projection and its supposed delusional effects, between the jealousy of the unfaithful spouse and that of the alcoholic, for example.

That Freud, in his essay of interpretation of the Schreber case, which is read so badly that it is usually reduced to the rehashings that followed, uses the form of a grammatical deduction in order to present the switching of the relation to the other in psychosis, namely, the different ways of denying the proposition, 'I love him', from which it follows that this negative judgement is structured in two stages: the first, the reversal of the value of the verb ('I hate him'), or inversion of the gender of the agent or object ('It is not I' or 'It is not him, but her' – or inversely); the second, an interversion of subjects ('He hates me', 'It is she he loves', 'It is she who loves me') – the logical problems formally involved in this deduction have retained no one's interest.

Expecially as Freud in this text expressly dismisses the mechanism of projection as insufficient to account for the problem, and enters at that point on a very long, detailed and subtle discussion of repression, providing us at the same time with some toothing stones for our problem – let us say simply that these toothing stones continue to stand out inviolate above the clouds of dust produced in the psychoanalytic construction site.

2. Freud has since provided the article 'On Narcissism'. This text has been put to the same use, namely, a sort of pumping in and out of the libido by the *percipiens*, according to every twist and turn of the psychoanalytic party line. The *percipiens* is thus entitled to inflate and deflate a dummy reality.

Freud provided the first theory of the way in which the ego is constituted according to the other in the new subjective economy, determined by the unconscious: one responded to it by acclaiming in this ego the rediscovery of the good old fool-proof *percipiens* and the synthesizing function.

Is it surprising that no other benefit should have been derived from it for psychosis than the definitive promotion of the notion of *loss of reality*?

This is not all. In 1924, Freud wrote an incisive article, 'The Loss of Reality in Neurosis and Psychosis', in which he draws attention to the fact that the problem lies not in the reality that is lost, but in that which takes its place. It is like talking to the deaf, since the problem has been resolved; the store of accessories is inside, and they are taken out as required.

In fact, such is the schema with which even M. Katan, in the studies in which he follows so attentively the different stages of Schreber's psychosis, guided by his concern to penetrate the prepsychotic phase, satisfies himself, when he uses the defence against instinctual temptation, against masturbation and homosexuality in this case, to justify the upsurge of the hallucinatory phantasmagoria, a curtain interposed by the operation of the *percipiens* between the tendency and its real stimulant.

To think that this simplicity should have comforted us for a time, if we had considered that it should suffice to explain the problem of literary creation in psychosis!

3. After all, what problem would he still erect as an obstacle to the discourse of psychoanalysis, when the implication of a tendency in reality is a response from the regression of their couple? What might tire minds who accept that one should talk to them of regression, without distinguishing between regression in structure, regression in history, and regression in development (which Freud always differentiates as topographical, temporal, or genetic)?

I shall refrain from spending more time here drawing up an inventory of the confusion. It is quite familiar to those whom we train and would be of no interest to others. I shall be content to propose for their common meditation the effect of bewilderment (*dépaysement*) produced, at the sight of a speculation that is doomed to go round in circles between development and entourage, simply by features that are nevertheless the armature of the Freudian edifice: namely, the equivalence maintained by Freud of the imaginary function of the phallus in both sexes (for long the despair of lovers of false 'biological' windows, that is to say, the naturalists), the castration complex found as a normative phase of the assumption by the subject of his own sex, the myth of the murder of the father rendered necessary by the constituent presence of the Oedipus complex in every personal history, and, *last but not* . . .,[9] the effect of duplication introduced into the love life by the very repetitive agency of the object that is always to be rediscovered as unique. Must we recall once more the profoundly dissident character of the notion of drive in Freud, the disjunction of principle between the tendency, its direction, and its object, and not only its original 'perversion', but its implication in a conceptual systematic, a systematic whose place Freud indicated, from the very beginning of his work, under the heading of the sexual theories of childhood?

Is it not clear that we left all that behind long ago in an educative naturism that has no other principle than the notion of gratification and its obverse, frustration, which is nowhere mentioned by Freud.

No doubt the structures revealed by Freud continue to sustain, not only in their plausibility, but also in the way they are manipulated, the would-be dynamic forces with which psychoanalysis today claims to direct its flow. A deserted technique would be even more capable of 'miracles', – were it not for the additional conformism that reduces its effects to those of an ambiguous mixture of social suggestion and psychological superstition.

4. It is even striking that a demand for rigour is manifested only in people whom the course of things maintains by some aspect outside this concert, such as Mrs Ida Macalpine, who gave me cause to marvel and who, as I read her, seemed level-headed enough.

Her critique of the cliché that is confined in the factor of the repression of a homosexual drive, which, in fact, is quite unclear, to explain psychosis, is masterly, and she demonstrates this beautifully in the Schreber case itself. Homosexuality, supposedly a determinant of paranoiac psychosis, is really a symptom articulated in its process.

This process began at an early stage, at the moment when the first sign of it appeared in Schreber in the form of one of those hypnopompic ideas, which in their fragility present us with sorts of tomographies of the ego, an idea whose imaginary function is sufficiently indicated to us in its form: that it would be *beautiful* to be a woman undergoing the act of copulation.

Ida Macalpine, to make one just criticism, seems nonetheless to ignore the fact that although Freud placed considerable stress on the homosexual question, it was first to show that it conditions the idea of grandeur in delusion, but, more essentially, he indicates in it the mode of otherness in accordance with which the metamorphosis of the subject operates, in other words, the place in which his delusional 'transferences' succeed one another. She would have done better to trust the reason to which Freud once again clings here in a reference to the Oedipus complex, which she does not accept.

This difficulty should have led her to discoveries that would certainly have been illuminating for us, for nothing has yet been said about the function of what is known as the inverted Oedipus complex. Mrs Macalpine prefers to reject here any recourse to the Oedipus complex, replacing it by a phantasy of procreation, which is observed in children of both sexes, even in the form of phantasies involving pregnancy, which, indeed, she regards as being linked to the structure of hypochondria.[10]

This phantasy is, indeed, essential, and I would add that in the first case in which I obtained this phantasy in a man, it was by a means that marked an important stage in my career, and the man in question was neither a hypochondriac nor a hysteric.

She feels, with some subtlety, even – *mirabile* the way things are today – the need to link this phantasy to a symbolic structure. But in order to find this outside the Oedipus complex, she goes off in search of ethnographical references which, on the evidence of her writing, she does not appear to have fully assimilated. This involves the 'heliolithic' theme, which has been championed by one of the most eminent adherents of the English diffusionist school. I am aware of the merits of these conceptions, but they do not appear to me to support in the least the idea that Mrs Macalpine tries to give of asexual procreation as a 'primitive' conception.[11]

Mrs Macalpine's error is revealed, however, in the fact that she arrives at a result that is the opposite of the one she is looking for.

By isolating a phantasy in a dynamic that she describes as intrapsychical, according to a perspective that she opens up on the notion of the transference, she ends up by designating in the psychotic's uncertainty about his own sex, the weak spot on which the analyst must bring his intervention to bear, contrasting the happy effects of this intervention with the catastrophic effect, which, in fact, is constantly to be observed among psychotics, of any suggestion that he should recognize a latent homosexuality.

Now, uncertainty about one's sex is precisely a common feature in hysteria, whose encroachments in diagnosis Mrs Macalpine denounces.

This is because no imaginary formation is specific,[12] none is determinant either in the structure, or in the dynamics of a process. And that is why one is condemned to lacking both when, in the hope of reaching them more easily, one wishes to ignore the symbolic articulation that Freud discovered at the same time as the unconscious, and which, for him, is, in effect, consubstantial with it: it is the need for this articulation that he signifies for us in his methodical reference to the Oedipus complex.

5. How can one impute responsibility for this *méconnaissance* to Mrs Macalpine, when, far from disappearing, it has continued to grow and flourish in psychoanalysis?

This is why, in order to define the minimal split, which is certainly justifiable between neurosis and psychosis, psychoanalysts are reduced to leaving responsibility for reality to the ego: which is what I would call leaving the problem of psychosis at the *statu quo ante*.

One point, however, was very specifically designated as the bridge across the frontier of the two domains.

They have even made use of it, in the most excessive way, on the question of the transference in psychosis. It would be uncharitable to assemble here what has been said on this subject. I shall simply take the opportunity of paying homage to Ida Macalpine's intelligence, when she sums up a position typical of the genius to be found in psychoanalysis today in these terms: in short, psychoanalysts claim to be able to cure psychosis in all cases where a psychosis is not involved.[13]

It is on this point that Midas, laying down the law one day on what psychoanalysis could do, expressed himself thus: 'It is clear that psychoanalysis is possible only with a subject for whom there is another!' And Midas crossed the two-way bridge thinking it to be a piece of waste land. How could it have been otherwise, since he was unaware that the river was there?

The term 'other', hitherto unheard among the psychoanalyst population, had no more meaning for it than the murmur of the reeds.

〰〰

III *With Freud*

1. It is somewhat striking that a dimension that is felt as that of Something-else in so many of the experiences that men undergo, not at all without thinking about them, rather while thinking about them, but without thinking that they are thinking, and like Telemachus thinking of the expense (*pensant à la dépense*), should never have been thought to the extent of being congruently said by those whom the idea of thought assures of thinking.

Desire, boredom, confinement, revolt, prayer, sleeplessness (I would like to stop there, since Freud refers specifically to it by quoting in the middle of his Schreber a passage from Nietzsche's *Zarathustra*[14]), and panic are there as evidence of the dimension of that Elsewhere, and to draw our attention to it, not so much, as I would say, as mere states of mind that thinking-without-laughing[15] can put back into place, but much more as permanent principles of collective organizations, outside which human life does not appear capable of maintaining itself for long.

No doubt it is not impossible that the most thinkable thinking-to-think, thinking itself to be that Other-thing, should always have been unable to tolerate this possible competition.

But this aversion becomes quite clear once the conceptual juncture, which nobody had yet thought of, was made, between this Elsewhere and the place, present for all and closed to each, in which Freud discovered that, without thinking about it, and without anyone being able to think he thinks about it better than anyone else therefore, it thinks (*ça pense*). It thinks rather badly, but it does think. For it is in these terms that it announces the unconscious to us: thoughts which, if their laws are not quite the same as those of our everyday thoughts, however noble or vulgar they may be, are perfectly articulated.

There is no longer any way, therefore, of reducing this Elsewhere to the imaginary form of a nostalgia, a lost or future Paradise; what one finds is the paradise of the child's loves, where, *baudelaire de Dieu!*,[16] something's going on, I can tell you.

Moreover, if any doubt still remained in our minds, Freud named the locus of the unconscious by a term that had struck him in Fechner (who, incidentally, is an experimentalist, and not at all the realist that our literary reference books suggest), namely, *ein anderer Schauplatz*, another scene; he makes use of it some twenty times in his early works.

This sprinkling of cold water having, let us hope, refreshed our minds, let us move on to the scientific formulation of the subject's relation to this Other.

2. By way of 'fixing our ideas' and the souls suffering here, I will apply the said relation to schema L, already produced and here simplified:

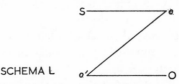

SCHEMA L

This schema signifies that the condition of the subject S (neurosis or psychosis) is dependent on what is being unfolded in the Other O. What is being unfolded there is articulated like a discourse (the unconscious is the discourse of the Other), whose syntax Freud first sought to define for those bits that come to us in certain privileged moments, in dreams, in slips of the tongue or pen, in flashes of wit.

Why would the subject be interested in this discourse, if he were not taking part in it? He is, indeed, a participator, in that he is stretched over the four corners of the schema: namely, S, his ineffable, stupid existence, *o*, his objects, *o'*, his ego, that is, that which is reflected of his form in his objects, and O, the locus from which the question of his existence may be presented to him.

For it is a truth of experience for analysis that the subject is presented with the question of his existence, not in terms of the anxiety that it arouses at the level of the ego, and which is only one element in the series, but as an articulated question: 'What am I there?', concerning his sex and his contingency in being, namely, that, on the one hand, he is a man or a woman, and, on the other, that he might not be, the two conjugating their mystery, and binding it in the symbols of procreation and death. That the question of his existence bathes the subject, supports him, invades him, tears him apart even, is shown in the tensions, the lapses, the phantasies that the analyst encounters; and, it should be added, by means of elements of the particular discourse in which this question is articulated in the Other. It is because these phenomena are ordered in the figures of this discourse that they have the fixity of symptoms, are legible and can be resolved when deciphered.

3. One must insist, therefore, that this question is not presented in the unconscious as ineffable, that this question is a questioning (*une mise en question*), that is to say, that prior to all analysis it is articulated in it in discrete elements. This is most important, for these elements are those that linguistic analysis forces us to isolate as signifiers, and here they are seen at work in their purest form at the most unlikely, yet most likely point:

– the most unlikely, since their chain is found to survive in an alterity in relation to the subject as radical as that of as yet undecipherable hiero- glyphics in the solitude of the desert;

– the most likely, because there alone their function of inducing the signification into the signified by imposing their structure on it may appear quite unambiguously.

For certainly the furrows opened up by the signifier in the real world will seek, in order to broaden them, the gaps that the real world *qua* existent (*étant*) offers to the signifier, to such an extent that an ambiguity may well survive in our understanding as to whether the signifier does not follow the law of the signified here.

But this is not the case at the level of the questioning not of the place of the subject in the world, but of his existence as subject, a questioning which, beginning with himself, will extend to his in-the-world relation to objects, and to the existence of the world, in so far as it, too, may be questioned beyond its order.

4. It is of the utmost importance to realize in the experience of the unconscious Other in which Freud guides us that the question does not find its lineaments in protomorphic proliferations of the image, in vegetative intumescences, in animic halos irradiating from the palpitations of life.

The whole difference between Freud's orientation and that of the Jungian school, which attaches itself to such forms, is there: *Wandlungen der libido*. These forms may be promoted to the first level of a mantic, for they can be produced by the appropriate techniques (promoting imaginary creations: reveries, drawings, etc.) in a mappable site: one sees it on our schema stretched between *o* and *o'*, that is, in the veil of the narcissistic mirage, eminently suited to sustaining with its effects of seduction and capture whatever is reflected in it.

If Freud rejected this mantic, it is at the point at which it neglected the directing function of a signifying articulation, which takes effect from its internal law and from a material subjected to the poverty that is essential to it.

Similarly, it is to the extent that this style of articulation has been maintained, by virtue of the Freudian Word (*verbe*), albeit dismembered, in the community that claims to represent orthodoxy, that so deep a difference remains between the two schools, even to the point, as things now are, that neither is in a position to formulate the reason for it. As a result, the level of their practice will soon appear to be reducible to the distance between the modes of dreaming of the Alps and the Atlantic.

To take up Charcot's formula, which so delighted Freud, 'this does not prevent [the Other] from existing' in his place O.

For if he is taken away, man can no longer even sustain himself in the position of Narcissus. As if by elastic, the *anima* springs back on to the *animus* and the *animus* on to the animal, which between S and *o* sustains with its *Umwelt* 'external relations' noticeably closer than ours, without, moreover, one being able to say that its relation with the Other is negligible, but only that it appears otherwise than in the sporadic sketches of neurosis.

5. The L of the questioning of the subject in his existence has a combinatory structure that must not be confused with its spatial aspect. As such, it is the signifier itself that must be articulated in the Other, especially in its position as fourth term in the topology.

As support for this structure, we find in it the three signifiers in which the Other may be identified in the Oedipus complex. They are sufficient to symbolize the significations of sexed reproduction, under the signifiers of relation, 'love' and 'procreation'.

The fourth term is given by the subject in his reality, foreclosed as such in the system, and entering into the play of the signifiers only in the mode of death, but becoming the true subject to the extent that this play of the signifiers will make it signify.

This play of the signifiers is not, in effect, an inert one, since it is animated in each particular part by the whole history of the ancestry of real others that the denomination of signifying Others involves in the contemporaneity of the Subject. Furthermore, in so far as it is set up *qua* rule over and above each part, this play already structures in the subject the three agencies: ego (ideal), reality, superego, the determination of which was to be the task of the second Freudian topography.

Furthermore, the subject enters the game as the dummy (*mort*), but it is as a living being that he plays it; it is in his life that he must take up the suit (*couleur*) that he may bid. He will do so by means of a set[17] of imaginary figures, selected from among the innumerable forms of animic relations, the choice of which involves a certain arbitrariness, since, in order to correspond homologically to the symbolic triads, it must be numerically reduced.

To do this, the polar relation, by which the specular image (of the narcissistic relation) is linked as a unifier to all the imaginary elements of what is called the fragmented body, provides a couple that is prepared not only by a natural conformity of development and structure to serve as a homologue for the Mother/Child symbolic relation. The imaginary couple of the mirror stage, through that counter-nature that it manifests, if it must be related to a specific prematuration of birth in man, is appropriated to provide the imaginary triangle with the base to which the symbolic relation may in a sense correspond (see schema R).

In effect, it is by means of the gap opened up by this prematuration in the imaginary, and in which the effects of the mirror stage proliferate, that the human animal is *capable* of imagining himself as mortal, which does not mean that he would be able to do so without his symbiosis with the symbolic, but rather that without this gap that alienates him from his own image, this symbiosis with the symbolic, in which he constitutes himself as subject to death, could not have occurred.

6. The third term of the imaginary triad, that in which the subject identifies himself, on the contrary, with himself as a living being is simply

the phallic image the unveiling of which in this function is not the least scandalous aspect of the Freudian discovery.

Let us inscribe here at once, under the heading of conceptual visualization of this double triad, what we shall henceforth call schema R, and which represents the lines of conditioning of the *perceptum*, in other words, of the object, in so far as these lines circumscribe the field of reality, rather than merely depending on them.

Thus taking the summits of the symbolic triangle: I as the ego-ideal, M as the signifier of the primordial object, and F as the position in O of the Name-of-the-Father, one can see how the homological fastening of the signification of the subject S under the signifier of the phallus may affect the support of the field of reality delimited by the quadrangle MieI. The other two summits of this quadrangle, *e* and *i*, represent the two imaginary terms of the narcissistic relation, the ego and the specular image.

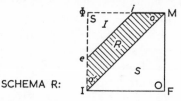

SCHEMA R:

One may thus situate from *i* to M, that is in *o*, the extremities of the segments Si, So^1, So^2, So^n, SM, in which are placed the figures of the imaginary other in the relations of erotic aggression where they are realized – similarly, from *e* to I, that is in *o'*, the extremities of segments Se, So'^1, So'^2, So'^n, SI, in which the ego identifies itself, from its specular *Urbild* to the paternal identification of the ego-ideal.[18]

Those of you who attended my seminar for the year 1956–7 know the use that I made of the imaginary triad presented here, a triad of which the child as the desired object constitutes in reality the summit I – to restore to the notion of the Object Relation,[19] now somewhat discredited by the mass of nonsense that the term has been used in recent years to validate, the capital of experience that legitimately belongs to it.

In effect, this schema enables us to show the relations that refer not to pre-Oedipal stages, which are not of course non-existent, but which cannot be conceived of in analytic terms (as is sufficiently apparent in the hesitant, but controlled work of Melanie Klein), but to the pregenital stages in so far as they are ordered in the retroaction of the Oedipus complex.

The whole problem of the perversions consists in conceiving how the child, in his relation to the mother, a relation constituted in analysis not by his vital dependence on her, but by his dependence on her love, that is to say, by the desire for her desire, identifies himself with the imaginary object of this desire in so far as the mother herself symbolizes it in the phallus.

The phallocentrism produced by this dialectic is all that need concern us here. It is, of course, entirely conditioned by the intrusion of the signifier in man's psyche, and strictly impossible to deduce from any pre-established harmony of this psyche with the nature that it expresses.

This imaginary effect, which can be felt as a discord only from the prejudged vantage point of a normativity proper to instinct, has nevertheless determined the long quarrel, which has now died down, but whose damaging after effects still linger on, concerning the primary or secondary nature of the phallic phase. Even apart from the extreme importance of the question, this quarrel would merit our interest for the dialectical exploits it imposed on Dr Ernest Jones in maintaining that he was in complete agreement with Freud, while affirming a position that was diametrically opposed to his, namely, that which made him, with certain minor reservations no doubt, the champion of the English feminists, with their beloved egalitarian principle: 'to each his own' – for the boys the phallus for the girls the c . . . (*aux boys le phalle, aux girls le c . . .*).

7. Freud revealed this imaginary function of the phallus, then, to be the pivot of the symbolic process that completes *in both sexes* the questioning of the sex by the castration complex.

The present obscuring of this function of the phallus (reduced to the role of partobject) in the psychoanalytic concert is simply the consequence of the profound mystification in which culture maintains the symbol of it, in the sense that paganism itself produced it only at the culmination of its most secret mysteries.

Indeed, in the subjective economy, governed as we see it by the unconscious, it is a signification that is 'evoked only by what we call a metaphor, in particular, the paternal metaphor.

And this leads us, since it is with Mrs Macalpine that we chose to open this dialogue, to her need to refer to a 'heliolithism', by means of which she claims to see the codification of procreation in a pre-Oedipal culture, in which the procreative function of the father would be eluded.

Anything one can advance along these lines, in whatever form, will merely accentuate the signifying function that conditions paternity.

For in another debate dating from the time when psychoanalysts still questioned themselves about doctrine, Dr Ernest Jones, with a remark that was more relevant than his previous one, did not provide a less inappropriate argument.

Concerning, in effect, the state of beliefs in some Australian tribe, he refused to admit that any collectivity of men could fail to recognize the fact of experience that, with certain enigmatic exceptions, no woman gives birth to a child without having undergone coitus, or even be ignorant of the lapse of time between the two events. For the credit that seems to me to be accorded quite legitimately to the human capacities to observe the real is precisely that which has not the slightest importance in the matter.

For, if the symbolic context requires it, paternity will nonetheless be attributed to the fact that the woman met a spirit at some fountain or some rock in which he is supposed to live.

It is certainly this that demonstrates that the attribution of procreation to the father can only be the effect of a pure signifier, of a recognition, not of a real father, but of what religion has taught us to refer to as the Name-of-the-Father.

Of course, there is no need of a signifier to be a father, any more than to be dead, but without a signifier, no one would ever know anything about either state of being.

I would take this opportunity of reminding those who cannot be persuaded to seek in Freud's texts an extension of the enlightenment that their pedagogues dispense to them how insistently Freud stresses the affinity of the two signifying relations that I have just referred to, whenever the neurotic subject (especially the obsessional) manifests this affinity through the conjunction of the themes of the father and death.

How, indeed, could Freud fail to recognize such an affinity, when the necessity of his reflexion led him to link the appearance of the signifier of the Father, as author of the Law, with death, even to the murder of the Father – thus showing that if this murder is the fruitful moment of debt through which the subject binds himself for life to the Law, the symbolic Father is, in so far as he signifies this Law, the dead Father.

≯≯≮≮

IV *Schreber's way*

1. We can now enter the subjectivity of Schreber's delusion.

The signification of the phallus, I have said, must be evoked in the subject's imaginary by the paternal metaphor.

This has a precise meaning in the economy of the signifier, the formalization of which I can do no more than indicate here, but which will be familiar to those of you who are attending the seminar I am giving this year on the formations of the unconscious. Namely: *formula of the metaphor*, or *of signifying substitution*:

$$\frac{S}{S'} \cdot \frac{S'}{x} \rightarrow S\left(\frac{I}{s}\right)$$

in which the capital Ss are signifiers, x the unknown signification and s the signified induced by the metaphor, which consists of the substitution in the signifying chain of S for S'. The elision of S', represented here by the bar through it, is the condition of the success of the metaphor.

This applies equally to the metaphor of the Name-of-the-Father, that is, the metaphor that substitutes this Name in the place first symbolized by the operation of the absence of the mother.

$$\frac{\text{Name-of-the-Father}}{\text{Desire of the Mother}} \cdot \frac{\text{Desire of the Mother}}{\text{Signified to the subject}} \rightarrow$$

$$\text{Name-of-the-Father} \left(\frac{\text{O}}{\text{Phallus}}\right)$$

Let us now try to conceive of a circumstance of the subjective position in which, to the appeal of the Name-of-the-Father responds, not the absence of the real father, for this absence is more than compatible with the presence of the signifier, but the inadequacy of the signifier itself.

This is not a conception that should come as a complete surprise. The presence of the signifier in the Other is, in effect, a presence usually closed to the subject, because it usually persists in a state of repression (*verdrängt*), and because from there it insists on representing itself in the signified by means of its repetition compulsion (*Wiederholungszwang*).

Let us extract from several of Freud's texts a term that is sufficiently articulated in them to render them unjustifiable if this term does not designate in them a function of the unconscious that is distinct from the repressed. Let us take as demonstrated the essence of my seminar on the psychoses, namely, that this term refers to the most necessary implication of his thought on the phenomenon of psychosis: this term is *Verwerfung* (foreclosure).

It is articulated in this register as the absence of that *Bejahung*, or judgement of attribution, that Freud poses as a necessary precedent for any possible application of *Verneinung* (negation), which he opposes to it as a judgement of existence: whereas the whole article from which he detaches this *Verneinung* as an element of analytic experience demonstrates in it the avowal of the signifier itself that it annuls.

It is on the signifier, then, that the primordial *Bejahung* bears, and other texts enable us to recognize this, in particular letter 52 of the Fliess correspondence, in which it is expressly isolated as the term of an original perception under the name of sign, *Zeichen*.

We will take *Verwerfung*, then, to be *foreclosure* of the signifier. To the point at which the Name-of-the-Father is called – we shall see how – may correspond in the Other, then, a mere hole, which, by the inadequacy of the metaphoric effect will provoke a corresponding hole at the place of the phallic signification.

It is the only form in which it is possible for us to conceptualize what Schreber shows us to be the result of the damage that he is in a position to reveal only in part and in which, he says, together with the names of Flechsig and Schreber, the term 'soul-murder' (*Seelenmord*: S. 22-II) plays an essential role.[20]

It is clear that what we are presented with here is a disorder caused at the most personal juncture between the subject and his sense of being alive; the censorship that mutilates the text before the addition mentioned by Schreber to the somewhat distorted explanations that he has offered of his method leaves one to think that he associated with the names of living people facts that could not have been published on account of the conventions of the time. Moreover, the following chapter is missing in its entirety, and Freud had to be content to exercise his perspicacity on the allusion to *Faust*, to *Der Freischütz* and to Byron's *Manfred*, a work (from which he supposes the name of *Ahriman*, one of the apophanies of God in Schreber's delusion, to be borrowed) that seemed to him to derive in that reference all the value of its theme, namely, that the hero dies from the curse borne in him by the death of the object of fraternal incest.

For me, since like Freud I have chosen to trust a text which, apart from these few mutilations, regrettable as they are, remains a document whose guarantees of credibility are unrivalled, it is in the most advanced form of delusion of which the book is an expression, that I will try to show a structure that will prove to be similar to the process of psychosis itself.

2. Following this line of approach, I will observe with the touch of surprise with which Freud sees the subjective connotation of the recognized unconscious, that the delusion deploys all the wealth of its tapestry

around the power of creation attributed to speech, of which the divine rays (*Gottesstrahlen*) are the hypostasis.

This begins as a *leit-motiv* in the first chapter, where the author first pauses at the fact that the act of giving birth to an existence out of nothing offends reason, flies in the face of the evidence that experience provides in the transformations of a matter in which reality finds its substance.

He emphasizes the paradox to be found in his contrast with the most familiar ideas for the man he claims to be, as if there was any need of that: a *gebildet* German of the Wilhelmine period, nourished on Haeckelian metascientism, on the basis of which he provides a list of readings, an occasion for us to complete, by referring to them, what Gavarni calls somewhere a cerebral idea of Man.[21]

It is even in this considered paradox of the intrusion of a thought, for him hitherto unthinkable, that Schreber sees the proof that something must have happened that does not proceed from his own mind: a proof against which, it seems, only the *petitio principii*, outlined above in the position of the psychiatrist, give us the right to resist.

3. Having said this, let us follow a sequence of phenomena that Schreber establishes in his fifteenth chapter (S. 204–15).

We now know that the strength of his hand in the forced game of thought (*Denkzwang*) in which the words of God constrain him (see above, I–5) has a dramatic stake, which is that God, whose powers of misunderstanding, will appear later, considering the subject as annihilated, leaves him in the lurch (*liegen lassen*), a threat to which we will return.

The effort of repost, then, by which the subject is thus suspended, let us say, in his being as subject, eventually fails by a moment of 'thinking-nothing' (*Nichtsdenken*), certainly seems to be the least one can humanly expect by way of rest (Schreber says). This is what, according to him, occurs:

(a) What he calls the miracle of howling (*Brüllenwunder*), a cry torn from his breast that surprises him beyond all expectations, whether he is alone or with others, who are horrified by the spectacle he offers them of his mouth suddenly gaping over the unspeakable void, abandoning the cigar that was stuck there only a moment earlier;

(b) The call for help ('*Hülfe*' *rufen*), emitted by 'divine nerves detached from the mass', the plaintive tone of which is caused by the greater distance into which God withdraws;

(two phenomena in which the subjective tearing is sufficiently indistinguishable enough from its signifying mode for us not to labour the point);

(c) The forthcoming blossoming, that is, in the occult zone of the perceptual field, in the corridor, in the next room, or manifestations which, though not extraordinary, appear to the subject to be intended for him;

(d) The appearance at the next level of the distant, that is, beyond the grasp of the senses, in the park, *in the real*, of miraculous creations, that is, newly created ones, and Mrs Macalpine makes the perceptive observation that they always belong to flying species – birds or insects.

Do not these last meteors of delusion appear as the trace of a furrow, or as a fringe effect, showing both times in which the signifier that remained silent in the subject projects from its darkness a gleam of signification on to the surface of the real, then illuminates the real with a flash projected from below its basement of nothingness?

Thus, at the tip of hallucinatory effects, these creatures which, if one wished to apply with maximum rigour the criterion of the apparition of the phenomenon *in reality*, would alone be worthy of the name of hallucinations, recommend us to reconsider in their symbolic solidarity the trio of Creator, Creature, and Created that emerges here.

4. It is from the position of the Creator, in effect, that we will go back to that of the Created, which subjectively creates it.

Unique in his Multiplicity, Multiple in his Unity (such are the attributes, reminiscent of Heraclitus, with which Schreber defines him), this God, reduced in effect to a hierarchy of realms, which would be worth a study in itself, lowers himself into beings who appropriate disconnected identities.

Immanent in these beings, whose capture by their inclusion in Schreber's being threatens his integrity, God is not without the intuitive support of a hyperspace, in which Schreber even sees significant transmissions conducted along wires (*Fäden*), which materialize the parabolic trajectory in accordance with which they enter his cranium through the occiput (S. 315-P.S. V).

Yet, in the course of time, through his manifestations, God lets the field of non-intelligent beings, beings who do not know what they say, beings of inanity, such as those enchanted birds, those talking birds, those courts of heaven (*Vorhöfe des Himmels*), in which Freud's misogyny detected at first glance the white geese that represented the ideal girls of his time, only to see his view confirmed by the proper names[22] that the subject later gives them. Let me say simply that for me they are much more representative by virtue of the surprise that is brought about in them by the similarity of the vocables and the purely homophonic equivalences on which their use depends (Santiago = Carthago, Chinesenthum = Jesum Christum, etc., S. 210-XV).

Similarly, the being of God in his essence withdraws ever further away into the space that conditions him, a withdrawal that can be intuited from the increasing slowness of his speech, which even goes as far as the beat of a stammered spelling (S. 223-XVI). So much so that simply by following the guide-lines of this process, we would regard this unique Other on which the existence of the subject is articulated as suited above all for emptying the places (S. note on 196-XIV) in which the murmur of the words is deployed, if Schreber did not take care to inform us in addition that this God is foreclosed from any other aspect of the exchange. He does so, while at the same time apologizing for doing so, but whatever regrets he may have about it, he has to state it clearly: God is not only impermeable to experience; he is incapable of understanding the living man; he grasps him only from the outside (which would certainly seem to be his essential mode); all interiority is closed to him. A 'system of notes' (*Aufschreibesystem*) in which acts and thoughts are preserved recalls, of course, in an elusive way, the notebook held by the guardian angel of our catechized childhood, but beyond that let us note the absence of any trace of the sounding of loins or hearts.(S. 20-I).

Thus, after the purification of souls (*Laüterung*) has abolished in them all trace of personal identity, everything will be reduced to the eternal survival of this verbiage, with which only God need know the works that men's ingenuity has constructed (S. 300-P.S. II).

I could hardly fail to remark here that the great-nephew of the author of *Novae species insectorum* (Johann-Christian-Daniel von Schreber) stresses that none of the miraculous creatures is of a new species, or add, in opposition to Mrs Macalpine, who sees in them the Dove that travels from the lap of the Father to bring to the Virgin the fruitful tidings of the Logos, that they remind me rather of the dove that the conjuror pulls out of the opening of his waistcoat or sleeve.

Which will lead us at last to the surprising conclusion that the subject in the grip of these mysteries does not doubt his ability, Created being though he be, either to elude with his words the traps set by the alarming inanity of his Lord, or to maintain himself in the face of the destruction that he believes his Lord capable of launching against him, or anyone else, by virtue of a right to which he is entitled in the name of the order of the World (*Weltordnung*), a right which, for all that it is his motivates this unique example of the victory of a creature that a series of disorders has made the object of his creator's *'perfidie'*. (The word let out, not without reservations, is in French: S. 226-XVI.)

Does not this recalcitrant created being, who prevents his fall only by the support of his Word (*verbe*) and by his faith in speech, form a strange pendant to Malebranche's continuous creation?

Perhaps we should take another look at the authors prescribed for the philosophy paper of the Baccalauréat, among which perhaps we have been too contemptuous of those outside the line leading up to the *homo psychologicus* in which our period finds the measure of a perhaps somewhat pedestrian, don't you think, humanism.

> De Malebranche ou de Locke
> Plus malin le plus loufoque . . .²³

Yes, but which of the two is it? There's the rub, dear colleague. Come on, drop that stiff manner. When will you feel at ease, then, when you are on your own ground?

5. Let us now try and re-situate the position of the subject as it is constituted here in the symbolic order on the triad that maps it in our schema R.

It seems to me, then, that if the Created I assumes in it the place in F, left vacant by the Law, the place of the Creator is designated in it by that *liegen lassen*, that fundamental let-lie, in which the absence that made it possible to construct oneself out of the primordial symbolization M of the mother appears to be denuded, from the foreclosure of the Father.

From one to the other a line, which would end in the Creatures of speech, occupying the place of the child rejected in the hopes of the subject (see the *Post-scriptum*), would thus be conceived as circumventing the hole dug in the field of the signifier by the foreclosure of the Name-of-the-Father (see Schema I, p. 212).

It is around this hole, in which the support of the signifying chain is lacking in the subject, and which has no need, one notes, of being ineffable in order to be awe-inspiring, that the whole struggle in which the subject reconstructed itself took place. In this struggle, he conducted himself with honour, and the vaginas of heaven (another meaning of the word *Vorhöfe*, see above), the cohort of miraculous girls who laid siege to the edges of the hole provided the counterpoint, in the clucks of admiration from their harpies' throats: *'Verfluchter Kerl! What a lad!'* In other words: what a ram! Alas! It was by way of antiphrasis.

6. For already, and not long since, there had opened up for him in the field of the imaginary the gap that corresponded in it to the defect of symbolic metaphor, the gap that could only be resolved in the accomplishment of the *Entmannung* (emasculation).

At first an object of horror for the subject, it was then accepted as a reasonable compromise (*vernünftig*, S. 177-XIII), consequently as an irrevocable choice (S. note to p. 179-XIII), and as a future motive of a redemption of interest to the entire world.

Although we can't leave the term *Entmannung* quite so easily, it will surely embarrass us less than it does Ida Macalpine in the position that I have described as being hers. No doubt she thought she was putting a little order into the matter by substituting the word 'unmanning' for 'emasculation', which the translator of volume III of the *Collected Papers* had innocently believed to suffice, and even going so far as to ensure that the translation was altered in the authorized version then under preparation. Perhaps she detected some imperceptible etymological suggestion that differentiated the two terms, despite their identical usage.[24]

But to what avail? Rejecting as improper the questioning of an organ which Mrs Macalpine, referring to the Memoirs, wishes to be destined to nothing more than a peaceful reabsorption in the subject's entrails – does she mean by this to represent to us the timorous slyboots in which he takes refuge when he shakes with fear, or the conscientious objection to description on which the author of *The Satyricon* lingers so mischievously?

Or does she believe perhaps that it was never a question of real castration in the complex of the same name?

No doubt she has good grounds for noticing the ambiguity there is in regarding as equivalents the transformation of the subject into a woman (*Verweiblichung*) and castration (for that is certainly the meaning of *Entmannung*). But she does not see that this ambiguity is that of the subjective structure itself, which produces it here: which involves only that which is confined at the imaginary level to the transformation of the subject into a woman, namely, precisely that which makes it decline from any heritage from which it may legitimately expect the attribution of a penis to his person. This because if being and having are mutually exclusive in principle, they are confounded, at least as far as the result is concerned, when it is a question of a lack. Which does not prevent the distinction between them being of decisive importance subsequently.

As one realizes in observing that it is not by being foreclosed to the penis, but by having to be the phallus that the patient is doomed to become a woman.

The symbolic parity *Mädchen = Phallus*, or in English the equation *Girl = Phallus*, in the words of M. Fénichel,[25] to whom she gives the theme of an essay of some merit, if somewhat confused, has its root in the imaginary paths by which the child's desire succeeds in identifying itself with the mother's want-to-be, to which of course she was herself introduced by the symbolic law in which this lack is constituted.

It is as a result of the same mechanism that women in the real order serve, if they'll forgive me saying so, as objects for the exchanges required by the elementary structures of kinship and which are sometimes perpetuated in the imaginary order, while what is transmitted in a parallel way in the symbolic order is the phallus.

7. Here the identification, whatever it may be, by which the subject assumed the desire of the mother, triggers off, as a result of being shaken, the dissolution of the imaginary tripod (remarkably enough, it was in his mother's apartment, where he had taken refuge, that the subject had his first attack of anxious confusion with suicidal raptus: S. 39–40-IV).

No doubt the divination of the unconscious very soon warned the subject that, incapable as he is of being the phallus that the mother lacks, he is left with the solution of being the woman that men lack.

This is the meaning of this phantasy, his account of which has often been commented on and which I quoted above as belonging to the incubation period of his second illness, namely the idea 'that it would be beautiful being a woman submitting to copulation'. This *pons asinorum* of the Schreberian literature is here pinned in place.

Yet this solution was a premature one at the time, because for the *Menschenspielerei* ('Men's little games', a term that appeared in the fundamental language) that would normally follow, one can say that the call to the braves was doomed to fall flat, for the good reason that these braves became as improbable as the subject himself, as divested as him of any phallus. This is because there was omitted in the subject's imaginary order, no less for them than for him, that line parallel with the outline of their faces, that can be seen in a drawing by Little Hans, and which is familiar to those who know children's drawing. It is because others were now no more than 'images of men flung together any old how', to combine in this translation of *flüchtig hingemachte Männer* W. G. Niederland's remarks on the uses of *hinmachen* and Édouard Pichon's brilliant stroke in the French translation.[26]

So the affair would have been in danger of marking time in a rather dishonourable way, had not the subject succeeded in saving the day quite brilliantly.

He himself articulated the outcome (in November 1895, that is, two years after the beginning of his illness) under the name of *Versöhnung*: the word has the meaning of expiation, propitiation, and, in view of the characteristics of the fundamental language, must be drawn even more towards the primitive meaning of *Sühne*, that is to say, towards sacrifice, whereas one accentuates it in the direction of compromise (reasonable compromise, which the subject gives as the motivation for accepting his destiny).

Here Freud, going well beyond the rationalization of the subject himself, admits paradoxically that reconciliation (since it is the flat meaning that has been chosen in French), which the subject takes account of, finds its source in the deception of the partner that it involves, namely in the consideration that the spouse of God contracts in any case an alliance of nature to satisfy the most demanding self-love.

I think we can say that in this instance Freud failed his own norms and in the most contradictory way, in that he accepts as a turning-point of the delusion what he rejected in his general conception, namely to make the homosexual theme depend on the idea of grandeur (I will assume that my readers know his text).

The failure is to be found in necessity, that is, in the fact that Freud had not yet formulated what was to become 'On Narcissism: an Introduction'.

8. No doubt had he not three years later (1911–14) failed to grasp the true cause of the reversal of the position of indignation, which was first raised in the person of the subject by the idea of *Entmannung*: it is precisely because in the interval *the subject had died.*

This, at least, was what the voices, always informed by the right sources and always reliable in their information service, made known to him after the event with the date and the name of the newspaper in which the announcement had appeared in the list of recent deaths (S. 81-VII).

Personally, I can content myself with the evidence provided by the medical certificates, which give us at the right moment the picture of the patient plunged in catatonic stupor.

As usual, his memories of this period are plentiful. Thus we know that, modifying the custom by which one departs this life feet first, our patient, so as to cross it only in transit, was pleased to keep his feet out of it, that is to say, stuck out of the window under the tendentious pretext of getting some fresh air (S. 172-XII), thus renewing perhaps (let us leave this to be appreciated by those who will be interested here only by its imaginary manifestation) the presentation of his birth.

But this is not a career that one takes up in one's late fifties without experiencing some feeling of unfamiliarity. Hence the faithful portrait that the voices, the annalists I would say, gave him of himself as a 'leprous corpse leading to another leprous corpse' (S. 92-VII), a very brilliant description, it must be admitted, of an identity reduced to a confrontation with its psychical double, but which moreover renders patent the subject's regression – a topographical, not a genetic, regression – to the mirror stage, even though the relation with the specular other is reduced to its fatal aspect.

It was also the time at which his body was merely a collection of colonies of foreign 'nerves', a sort of sump for fragments detached from the identities of his persecutors (S. XIV).

The relation of all this to homosexuality, which is certainly manifest in the delusion seems to me to necessitate a more advanced regulation of the use that can be made of this reference in theory.

It has great interest, since it is certain that the use of this term in interpretation may produce serious damage, if it is not illuminated with the symbolic relations that I would say were determinant here.

9. I believe that this symbolic determination is demonstrated in the form in which the imaginary structure is restored. At this stage, this imaginary structure presents two aspects that Freud himself distinguished.

The first is that of a trans-sexualist practice, in no way unworthy of being compared with 'perversion', the features of which have emerged in innumerable cases since.[27]

Furthermore, I must indicate in what way the structure outlined here may throw light on the strange insistence shown by the subjects of these cases in obtaining for their more radically rectifying demands the permission, even one might say the co-operation, of their father.

In any case, we see our subject abandon himself to an erotic activity,

which he emphasizes as being strictly reserved for solitude, but the satisfactions of which he nevertheless admits to. They are those given him
by his image in the mirror, when, dressed in the trinkets of female dress,
nothing, he says, in the upper part of his body, seems to him incapable of
convincing any possible lover of the female bust (S. 280-XXI).

To which we must link, I believe, the development, alleged to be an
endosomatic perception, of the so-called nerves of female pleasure in his
own tegument, that is, in those areas in which they are supposed to be
erogenous in women.

One remark, namely, that by concerning oneself unceasingly with the
contemplation of the image of woman, and never detaching one's thoughts
from the support of something feminine, the divine pleasure will be all the
more fulfilled, diverts us into the other aspect of the libidinal phantasies.

This aspect links the feminization of the subject to the co-ordinate of
divine copulation.

Freud saw very clearly the element of mortification in this when he
stressed what linked 'soul-pleasure' (*'volupté d'âme'*) (*Seelenwollust*),
which is included in it, with 'bliss' (*béatitude*) (*Seligkeit*), in the sense in
which it is the state of souls after death (*abschiedenen Wesen*).

That pleasure, regarded henceforth as blessed, should become the
soul's bliss, is, indeed, an essential turning-point, of which Freud, it
should be noted, stresses the linguistic motivation when he suggests that
the history of his language might throw some light on it.[28]

This is simply to make a mistake about the dimension in which the
letter manifests itself in the unconscious, and which, in accordance with
its own agency as letter, is much less etymological (or diachronic, to be
precise) than homophonic (synchronic). Indeed, there is nothing in the
German language that would enable us to link *selig* and *Seele*, or the bliss
that transports the lovers to 'the heavens', even though it is this to which
Freud refers when he quotes from the aria in *Don Giovanni*, and that promised to the 'blessed' souls in heaven. The dead are *selig* in German only
by virtue of a borrowing from Latin, and because the Latin phrase *beatae
memoriae* ('of blessed memory') is translated as *seliger Gedächtnis*. Their
Seelen has more to do with the lakes (*Seen*) in which they resided for a
time than with beatitude. The unconscious, however, is concerned more
with the signifier than with the signified and the phrase *'feu mon père'*
('my late father') may mean, as far as the unconscious is concerned, that
my father was the fire of God (*'le feu de Dieu'*), or even that I am ordering
him to be shot (Fire!)

But this digression apart, it remains that we are here beyond the world, which accommodates itself very well to an endless postponement of the realization of its aim.

Certainly, indeed, when Schreber has completed his transformation into a woman, the act of divine fecundation will take place, in which, of course, God could not commit himself in an obscure passage through the organs (S. 3-Introd.). (We must not forget God's aversion to the living creature.) It is through a spiritual operation, therefore, that Schreber will feel awakening within him the embryonic germ, the stirrings of which he has already experienced in the early stages of his illness.

No doubt the new spiritual humanity of the Schreberian creatures will be entirely engendered through his loins, so that the corrupt, doomed humanity of the present age may be reborn. This is indeed a sort of redemption, since the delusion has been catalogued in this way, but it is a redemption aimed only at the creature of the future, for the creature of the present is struck by a decadence correlative with the capture of the divine rays by the pleasure that rivets them to Schreber (S. 51–2-V).

In this there is adumbrated the dimension of mirage that is even more emphasized by the indefiniteness of the time in which the promise of redemption is suspended, and is profoundly conditioned by the absence of mediation to which the phantasy bears witness. For one can see that it parodies the situation of the couple of ultimate survivors who, following some human catastrophe, would see themselves, with the power to repopulate the earth, confronted by that element of totality that the act of animal reproduction bears within itself.

Here again one can place under the sign of the creature the turning-point at which the line divides into its two branches, that of narcissistic pleasure and that of the ideal identification. But it is in the sense in which its image is the trap of imaginary capture in which each is rooted. And there too the line moves around a hole, more specifically the hole in which 'soul-murder' installed death.

Was this other abyss formed simply by the effect in the imaginary order of the vain appeal made in the symbolic order to the paternal metaphor? Or should we conceive it as produced in a second degree by the elision of the phallus, which the subject seems to re-introduce in order to resolve it in the mortifying gap of the mirror-stage? Certainly the link – this time a genetic one – between this stage and the symbolization of the Mother as primordial could not fail to be referred to in motivating this solution.

Can we map the geometrical points of schema R on to a schema of the structure of the subject at the termination of the psychotic process? This is what I have tried to do in schema I below.

It may well be, of course, that this schema suffers from the excess endemic in any attempt to formalize the intuitive.

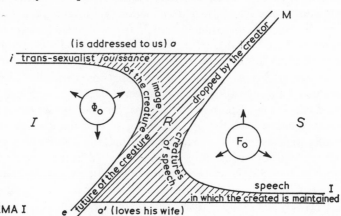

SCHEMA I

That is to say, the distortion that it manifests between the functions identified in it by the letters introduced into it from schema R can be appreciated only in a dialectical way.

Let us point out here simply in the double curve of the hyperbola that it forms, at the closest point of these two curves, along one of the directing lines, the link made apparent, in the double asymptote that unites the delusional ego to the divine other, from their imaginary divergence in space and time to the ideal convergence of their conjunction. But it must not be forgotten that Freud himself had an intuition of such a form, since it was he who introduced the term *asymptotisch* in this regard.[29]

All the density of the real creature, on the other hand, is interposed for the subject between narcissistic *jouissance* of his image and the alienation of speech in which the ego ideal has taken the place of the Other.

The schema shows that the terminal state of the psychosis does not represent the frozen chaos culminating in the débris caused by an earthquake, but rather that bringing to light of lines of efficiency, which causes speech when it is a question of an elegant solution to a problem.

It materializes in a significant way that which lies in the very principle of the effective fruitfulness of Freud's research; for it is a fact that without any other support than a written document, not only evidence, but also the production of this terminal state of the psychosis, Freud first threw light on the evolution itself of the process, thus making it possible to illuminate its own determination, by which I mean the only organicity that is essentially relevant to this process: that which motivates the structure of signification.

Brought together in the form of this schema, the relations emerge by which the induction effects of the signifier, bearing on the imaginary order, determine this overthrow of the subject that clinical experience designates under the aspects of the twilight of the world, necessitating in order to reply to them new signifying effects.

In my seminar I showed that the symbolic succession of the anterior and posterior kingdoms of God, the lower and the higher, Ahriman and Ormuz, and their shifts of 'policy' (a word of the fundamental language) with regard to the subject, give precisely those answers to the different stages of imaginary dissolution, which, indeed, the patient's memories and the medical certificates connote sufficiently, in order to restore to them an order of the subject.

As for the question that I am proposing here concerning the alienating effect of the signifier, I would refer to that nadir of a July night in 1894 when Ahriman, the lower God, revealing himself to Schreber in the most impressive apparel of his power, called him by that simple word, which, according to the subject, is a common word of the fundamental language: *Luder!*[30]

To translate the word we must do more than simply look it up in the Sachs-Villate dictionary, which is what the French translator was content to do. M. Niederland's reference to the English *lewd* does not seem to me to be acceptable as an attempt to convey the sense of 'wretch' or 'slut', which is what it means when used as a term of abuse.

But if we take account of the archaism indicated as characteristic of the fundamental language, we may feel justified in linking this term to the root of the French *leurre*, and of the English *lure*, which is certainly the best address *ad hominem* to be expected from the symbolic order: the Other can be very impertinent.

There remains the disposition of the field *R* in the schema, in that it represents the conditions in which reality was restored for the subject: for him a sort of islet the consistency of which is imposed on him after the trial of his constancy,[31] which for me is linked to that which makes it habitable for him, but also which distorts it, namely, eccentric reshapings of the imaginary *I* and of the symbolic *S*, which reduce it to the field of their staggered shift.

The subordinate conception that we must give ourselves of the function of reality in the process, in its cause as well as in its effects, is important here.

We cannot develop here the admittedly crucial question of knowing what we are for the subject, we, whom he addresses as readers, nor the question of what remains of his relations with his wife, to whom the first draft of his book was dedicated, whose visits during his illness were always welcomed with the most intense emotion, and for whom, he assures us, concurrently with his most decisive avowal of his delusional vocation, he has 'retained his old love' (S. note to p. 179-XIII).

The maintenance in schema I of the trajectory *Soo'*O symbolizes in it the opinion that I have made of the examination of this case, that the relation to the other in so far as it is similar to him, and even a relation as elevated as that of friendship in the sense in which Aristotle sees it as constituting the essence of the conjugal relation, are perfectly compatible with the unbalancing of the relation to the capital Other, and the radical anomaly that it involves, qualified, improperly, but not without some approximation to the truth, in old clinical medicine, as partial delusion.

However, it would be better to confine this schema to the waste-bin, if, like so many others, it was to lead anyone to forget in an intuitive image the analysis on which it is based.

Indeed, one only has to think about it to realize how this would be to the greater credit of the commentator, Mrs Ida Macalpine, whose authentic thinking I should like to praise for the last time, provided one failed to recognize my reasons for introducing this schema.

What I am saying here is that it is the business of reason to recognize the drama of madness, *sua res agitur*, because it is in man's relation to the signifier that this drama is situated.

The notion that one will become as mad as the patient no more intimidates me than it did Freud.

Like Freud, I hold that we must listen to the speaker, when it is a question of a message that does not come from a subject beyond language, but from speech beyond the subject. For only then will one hear that speech, which Schreber captured in the Other, when from Ahriman to Ormuz, from the evil God to the absent God, it brings the seed in which the very law of the signifier is articulated: '*Aller Unsinn hebt sich auf!*' 'All Nonsense is abolished!' (S. 182–3-XIII and 312-P.S. IV).

A point at which I return (leaving to those who will concern themselves with me the trouble of finding out why I have left it in suspense for ten years) to what I said in my dialogue with Henri Ey:[32] 'Not only can man's being not be understood without madness, it would not be man's being if it did not bear madness within itself as the limit of his freedom.'

V *Post-scriptum*

Following Freud I teach that the Other is the locus of that memory that he discovered and called the unconscious, a memory that he regards as the object of a question that has remained open in that it conditions the indestructibility of certain desires. I would reply to this question in terms of the conception of the signifying chain, as inaugurated by the primordial symbolization (made manifest in the game *Fort! Da!*, which Freud revealed as lying at the origin of the repetition compulsion); this chain develops in accordance with logical links whose grasp on that which is to be signified, namely the being (*l'être*) and the existent (*l'étant*) operates through the effects of the signifier, which I describe as metaphor and metonymy.

It is in an accident in this register and in what takes place in it, namely, the foreclosure of the Name-of-the-Father in the place of the Other, and in the failure of the paternal metaphor, that I designate the defect that gives psychosis its essential condition, and the structure that separates it from neurosis.

This thesis, which I introduce here as the question preliminary to any possible treatment of psychosis, pursues its dialectic beyond this point: but I shall stop it here and I will say why.

First, because it is worth indicating what can be discovered from my pause.

A perspective that does not isolate Schreber's relationship with God from its subjective relief, the mark of negative features that make it appear rather as a mixture than a union of being and being, and which, in the voracity that is compounded in it with disgust, in the complicity that supports its exaction, shows nothing, to call things by their real names, of the Presence and Joy that illuminate the mystical experience: an opposition that is not only demonstrated by, but which is based on the astonishing absence in this relationship of the *Du*, in French the *Tu*, which in English (Thou) is reserved for the call from God and the appeal to God, and which is the signifier of the Other in speech.

I know the false modesty that is current in science on this subject; it is a fit companion for the false thought of pedantry, when it argues the ineffable nature of lived experience, even of the 'morbid consciousness', in order to disarm the effort that it expends, namely, that required at precisely the point at which it is not ineffable since it (*ça*) speaks, at which lived experience, far from separating, communicates itself, at which subjectivity yields up its true structure, the structure in which what is analysed is identical with what is articulated.

And from the same dramatic viewpoint to which delusional subjectivity has brought us, we will also turn our attention to scientific subjectivity: I mean that which the scientist at work in science shares with the man of the civilization that supports it. I will not deny that in the part of the world in which we reside, I have seen enough of it to question myself as to the criteria by which man with a discourse on freedom that must certainly be called delusional (I have devoted one of my seminars to it), with a concept of the real in which determinism is no more than an alibi that soon arouses anxiety if one tries to extend its field to chance (I have tried this out on my listeners in an experiment), with a belief that gathers men together, for half the world at least, under the symbol of Father Christmas (which can hardly escape anyone), this man would divert me from situating him, by a legitimate analogy, in the category of social psychosis – in the establishment of which Pascal, if I am not mistaken, preceded me.

That such a psychosis may prove to be compatible with what is called good order is not in question, but neither does it authorize the psychiatrist, even if he is a psychoanalyst, to trust to his own compatibility with that order to the extent of believing that he is in possession of an adequate idea of the *reality* to which his patient appears to be unequal.

Perhaps in these conditions it would be better to abandon this idea of his appreciation of the foundations of psychosis: which brings us back to the aim of his treatment.

To measure the path that separates us, we have only to recall all the delays with which its pilgrims have marked it. Everyone knows that no elaboration of the transference mechanism, however skilful it may be, has succeeded in so arranging things that in practice it is not conceived as a relation that is purely dual in its terms and utterly confused in its substratum.

Let us introduce the question of what, to take the transference only for its fundamental value as a phenomenon of repetition, it should repeat in the persecuting persons in which Freud here designates its effects?

I can just hear the feeble reply: following your approach, paternal inadequacy no doubt. In this style, there has been no shortage of accounts of every kind: and the 'entourage' of the psychotic has been the object of a meticulous enumeration of all the biographical and characterological labels that anamnesis enabled them to extract from the *dramatis personae*, even from their 'interhuman relations'.[33]

But let us proceed according to the structural terms that we have outlined.

For the psychosis to be triggered off, the Name-of-the-Father, *verworfen*, foreclosed, that is to say, never having attained the place of the Other, must be called into symbolic opposition to the subject.

It is the lack of the Name-of-the-Father in that place which, by the hole that it opens up in the signified, sets off the cascade of reshapings of the signifier from which the increasing disaster of the imaginary proceeds, to the point at which the level is reached at which signifier and signified are stabilized in the delusional metaphor.

But how can the Name-of-the-Father be called by the subject to the only place in which it could have reached him and in which it has never been? Simply by a real father, not necessarily by the subject's own father, but by A-father.

Again, this A-father must attain that place to which the subject was unable to call him before. It is enough that this A-father should be situated in a third position in some relation based on the imaginary dyad *o–o'*, that is to say, ego–object or reality–ideal, that interests the subject in the field of eroticized aggression that it induces.

Let us try to find this conjuncture at the beginning of the psychosis. Whether it occurs, for the woman who has just given birth, in her husband's face, for the penitent confessing his sins in the person of his confessor, for the girl in love in her meeting with 'the young man's father', it will always be found, and be found more easily if one allows oneself to be guided by 'situations' in the sense in which the word is used of the novel. It should be said in passing, however, that for the novelist these situations are his true resource, namely, that which makes possible the emergence of 'depth psychology', where no psychological insight would enable him to penetrate.[34]

To move on now to the principle of the foreclosure (*Verwerfung*) of the Name-of-the-Father, it must be admitted that the Name-of-the-Father reduplicates in the place of the Other the signifier itself of the symbolic triad, in that it constitutes the law of the signifier.

The attempt will cost nothing, it seems, for those who in the search for the environmental co-ordinates of psychosis wander like lost souls from the frustrating mother to the smothering mother, feeling nevertheless perhaps that in moving towards the situation of the father of the family, they are getting warmer, as one says in the game of hunt-the-slipper.

Again, in this groping search for a paternal inadequacy, whose cease-less, disquieting hesitation between the dominating father, the easy-going father, the all-powerful father, the humiliated father, the awkward father, the pitiful father, the home-loving father, the father on the loose, would it not be too much to expect some release of tension from the following remark: namely, that the effects of prestige that are involved in all this, and in which (thank heaven!) the ternary relation of the Oedipus complex is not entirely omitted, since the veneration of the mother is regarded as decisive in it, are reduced to the rivalry between the two par-ents in the subject's imaginary order – that is, to that which is articulated in the question that appears to be normal, not to say obligatory, in any self-respecting childhood: 'Who do you love most, mummy or daddy?'

My aim in this parallel is not to reduce anything: quite the contrary, for this question, in which the child never fails to concretize the nausea that he feels at the infantilism of his parents is precisely that with which those children that the parents really are (in this sense, there are no others in the family but them) try to mask the mystery of their union, or dis-union, namely, of that which their offspring knows very well is the whole problem and is posed as such.

It will be said that the accent is placed on precisely the link of love and respect, by which the mother does or does not put the father in his ideal place. Curious, I would reply at first, that one hardly takes account of the same links the other way round, in which it is proved that the theory participates in the veil thrown over the parents' coitus by infantile amnesia.

But what I do wish to insist on is that we should concern ourselves not only with the way in which the mother accommodates herself to the per-son of the father, but also with the way she takes his speech, the word (*mot*), let us say, of his authority, in other words, of the place that she reserves for the Name-of-the-Father in the promulgation of the law.

Further still, the father's relation to this law must be considered in itself, for one will find in it the reason for that paradox, by which the ravaging effects of the paternal figure are to be observed with particular frequency in cases where the father really has the function of a legislator or, at least has the upper hand, whether in fact he is one of those fathers who make the laws or whether he poses as the pillar of the faith, as a paragon of integrity and devotion, as virtuous or as a virtuoso, by serving a work of salvation, of whatever object or lack of object, of nation or of birth, of safeguard or salubrity, of legacy or legality, of the pure, the impure or of empire, all ideals that provide him with all too many opportunities of being in a posture of undeserving, inadequacy, even of fraud, and, in short, of excluding the Name-of-the-Father from its position in the signifier.

So much is not needed to obtain this result, and none of those who practise child analysis will deny that dishonest behaviour is totally transparent to them. But who articulates that the lie thus perceived implies a reference to the constituting function of speech?

It thus proves that a little severity is not too much to give to the most accessible experience its true meaning. The consequences that may be expected in their examination and technique are to be judged elsewhere.

I am giving here only what is needed for an appreciation of the clumsiness with which the most inspired authors handle what they find most valuable in following Freud over the terrain of the pre-eminence that he accords to the transference of the relation to the father in the genesis of psychosis.

Niederland provides a remarkable example of this[35] when he draws attention to Flechsig's delusional genealogy, constructed with the names of Schreber's real ancestors, Gottfried, Gottlieb, Fürchtegott, and, above all, Daniel, which is handed down from father to son and of which he gives the meaning in Hebrew, to show in their convergence on the name of God (*Gott*) an important symbolic chain by which the function of the father can be manifested in the delusion.

But failing to distinguish in it the agency of the Name-of-the-Father, and it is obviously not enough, in order to recognize it, that it should be visible here to the naked eye, he misses the opportunity of grasping it in the chain in which the erotic aggressions experienced by the subject are formed, and thereby of contributing to putting in its place what should properly be termed delusional homosexuality.

How, then, can he stop at what is concealed in the statement of the sentence quoted above from the first lines of Schreber's second chapter:[36] one of those statements so obviously made not to be heard that they must be noted. What, to take it literally, is the meaning of the equal footing on which the author joins the names of Flechsig and Schreber to soul-murder in order to introduce us to the principle of abuse of which he is the victim? We must leave something for future commentators to penetrate.

As uncertain is the attempt made by Niederland in the same article to specify, this time on the basis of the subject, rather than the signifier (the terms, of course, are not his), the role of the paternal function in the triggering off of delusion.

If, indeed, he claims to be able to designate the occasion of the psychosis in the mere assumption of paternity by the subject, which is the theme of his attempt, it is contradictory to regard as equivalent the frustration noted by Schreber of his hopes of paternity and his appointment as a High Court judge, the title of which (*Senätspräsident*) emphasizes the quality of Father (albeit a conscript father) that it accords him: this for the sole motivation of his second crisis, without prejudice to the first, which can be explained in a similar way by the failure of his candidature for the Reichstag.

Whereas the reference to the third position, to which the signifier of paternity is called in all such cases, would be correct and would resolve this contradiction.

But from the point of view of my thesis it is the primordial foreclosure (*Verwerfung*) that dominates everything with its problem, and the preceding considerations leave me here unprepared.

For to refer to the work of Daniel Gottlob Moritz Schreber, founder of an orthopaedic institute at the University of Leipzig, an educator, or, better still, an 'educationalist' as they say in English, a social reformer 'with an apostolic vocation to bring health, well-being and happiness to the masses' (sic. Ida Macalpine, *op. cit.*: 137) through physical culture, initiator of those garden allotments intended to preserve in the employee a kind of cabbage-patch idealism, which in Germany are still known as *Schrebergärten*, not to mention forty editions of the *Indoor Medical Gymnastics*, of which the roughly sketched little fellows that illustrate it are more or less referred to by Schreber (S. 166-XII), we will be able to regard as past the limits at which the native and the natal extend to nature, to the natural, to naturism, even to naturalization, at which virtue becomes vertigo, legacy the league, salvation saltation, at which the pure touches on the 'impure and the empire' (*malempire*), and at which I will not be surprised if the child, like the cabin-boy of Prévert's famous trawler, throws back (*verwerfe*) the whale of imposture, after piercing, according to the line of this immortal piece, the web from one end to the other (*de père en part*).

There can be no doubt that the face of Judge Flechsig, with its scientist's gravity (Mrs Macalpine's book contains a photograph that shows him profiled against a colossal enlargement of a cerebral hemisphere), failed to fill the sudden void perceived in the inaugural *Verwerfung* ('*Kleiner Flechsig!*' 'Little Flechsig!' shout the voices).

At least, that is Freud's conception, in so far as it designates in the transference that the subject operated on the person of Flechsig the factor that precipitated the subject into psychosis.

In consideration of which, some months later, the divine voices will make their concert heard in the subject in order to tell the Name-of-the-Father to fuck himself with the Name of God[38] in his backside and to found the Son in his certainty that at the end of his trials, he could not do better than 'do' on[39] the whole world (S. 226-XVI).

Thus the last word in which 'the internal experience' of our century should have yielded us its computation, is articulated fifty years ahead of its time in the theodicy to which Schreber is exposed: 'God is a tart' (*Dieu est une p . . .*).[40]

The term, in which the process by which the signifier has 'unleashed' itself in the real culminates, after the failure of the Name-of-the-Father was opened up – that is to say, the failure of the signifier in the Other, as locus of the signifier, is the signifier of the Other as locus of the law.

And there for the time being I will leave this question that is preliminary to any possible treatment of the psychoses – a question that introduces, as we see, the conception to be formed of the handling, in this treatment, of the transference.

To say that on this terrain we can do anything would be premature, because it would now be to go 'beyond Freud', and there can be no question of going beyond Freud when post-Freud psychoanalysis has, as I have said, gone back to an earlier stage.

At least that is what separates me from any other object than to restore access to the experience that Freud discovered.

For to use the technique that he established, outside the experience to which it was applied, is as stupid as to toil at the oars when the ship is on sand.

Dec. 1957–Jan. 1958

❧❧❧❧

Notes

1. Roman Jakobson borrows this term from Jesperson to designate those words of the code that take on meaning only from the co-ordinates (attribution, date, place of emission) of the message. In Pierce's classification they are index-symbols. Personal pronouns are the most obvious example: the difficulties involved in their acquisition and their functional deficiencies illustrate the problematic created by these signifiers in the subject. (Roman Jakobson, *Shifters, Verbal Categories and the Russian Verb*, Russian Language Project, Department of Slavic Languages and Literatures, Harvard University, 1957.)

2. Cf. the seminar of 8 February 1956 in which I developed the example of the 'normal' vocalization of *'la paix du soir'*.

3. *Denkwürdigkeiten eines Nervenkranken, von Dr. jur. Daniel-Paul Schreber, Senätspräsident beim kgl. Oberlandesgericht Dresden a-D.*, Oswald Mutze, Leipzig, 1903, the French translation of which I have prepared for the use of my group.

4. This is particularly the opinion expressed by the English translator of these *Memoirs*, which appeared in the same year as this seminar (cf. *Memoirs of my Nervous Illness*, translated by Ida Macalpine and Richard Hunter, London, W. M. Dawson & Sons), in her introduction, p. 25. She also gives an account of the success of the book, pp. 6–10.

5. This was the subject of my thesis for the doctorate in medicine, *De la psychose paranoïaque dans ses rapports avec la personnalité*, which my master Heuyer, in a letter to me, judged very pertinently in these terms: 'One swallow doesn't make a spring', adding in connexion with my bibliography; 'If you've read all that, I'm sorry for you'. In fact I had read it all.

6. The brackets around the letter S followed by figures (Arabic and Roman respectively) will be used here to refer to the corresponding page and chapter of the original edition of the *Denkwürdigkeiten*, the pagination being fortunately retained in the margins of the English translation.

7. It should be noted that my homage here is merely an extension of that of Freud, who was not averse to recognizing in Schreber's delusion itself a foreshadowing of the theory of the Libido (*G.W.*, VIII: 315).

8. Cf. p. 306.

9. English in the original.

10. To attempt to prove too much is to wander from the point. Thus Mrs Macalpine, who otherwise is wise enough to stop at the character, noted by the patient himself as being much too persuasive (S. 39–IV), of the suggestive invigoration in which Judge Flechsig indulges (everything indicates that he was usually more calm) in relation to Schreber on the subject of the promises of a sleep cure that he proposes for him, Mrs Macalpine, I would say, interprets at length the themes of procreation, which she regards as being suggested by this discourse (See *Memoirs . . .*, Discussion, p. 396, lines 12 and 21), basing her case on the use of the verb *to deliver* to designate the effect to be expected from the treatment of his disorders, and on that of the adjective *prolific*, with which she translates, extremely loosely, the German term, *ausgiebig*, applied to the sleep in question.

Now the word *to deliver* is indisputable as a translation, for the simple reason that there is nothing to translate. I looked again and again at the German text. The verb was simply forgotten by either the author or the compositor, and Mrs Macalpine, in an effort to make sense of the translation, has, unknown to herself, restored it. The pleasure that she must later have experienced on rediscovering it so close to her wishes was surely well deserved!

11. Macalpine, *op. cit.*: 361, 379–80.

12. I would ask Mrs Macalpine (see *Memoirs . . .*, pp. 391–2) whether the figure 9, as it is involved in such diverse durations as the delays of 9 hours, 9 days, 9 months, 9 years, which she springs out at us at every point in the patient's anamnesia, only to find it again at the time by the clock at which his anxiety, postponed the beginning of the sleep-cure referred to above, and, again, even in the hesitation between 4 and 5 days that recurs several times in the same period that saw the return of his memory of himself, should be conceived as forming part as such, that is to say, as a symbol of the imaginary relation isolated by it as a procreation phantasy.

The question is of interest to everybody, for it differs from the use Freud, in the Wolf Man Case, makes of the form of the figure V, which is presumed to have been retained from the point of the hand on the clock during a scene witnessed at the age of one and a half, and to reappear in the beating of a butterfly's wings, the open legs of a girl, etc.

13. Cf. her Introduction, pp. 13–19.

14. Before Sunrise, '*Vor Sonnenaufgang*', *Also Sprach Zarathustra*, Dritter Teil. It is the fourth song of this third part.

15. '*Le-pense-sans-rire*' – a pun on the phrase '*pincesans rire*', 'keeping a straight face' [Tr.].

16. A pun on 'Baudelaire' and the oath '*bordel de Dieu*' [Tr.].

17. English in the original [Tr.].

18. The mapping in this schema R of the object (*objet* a) is interesting for the light it sheds on the field of reality (the field that bars it).

I have since laid great stress on the need to develop it – by stating that this field functions only by obturating itself from the screen of phantasy – but this still requires a good deal of attention.

There might be some point in recognizing that, enigmatic as it may then have seemed, but perfectly legible for anyone who knows the outcome, as is the case if one claims to use it as a support, what schema R shows is a projective plan.

In particular the points, and it is not by chance (or by a sense of play) that I chose the letters that correspond to them – *e* M, *i* I – and which are those that frame the only valid cut in this schema $\overrightarrow{ei}, \overrightarrow{MI}$ (the cut *ei*, *MI*), are sufficient indication that this cut isolates a Moebius strip in the field.

To say this is to say all, since this field will now be merely the representative of the phantasy of which this cut provides the entire structure.

I mean that only the cut reveals the structure of the entire surface from being able to detach from it those two heterogeneous elements (represented in my algorithm ($ \$ \Diamond o$) of the phantasy: the $\$$, S barred by the strip to be expected here in fact, that is to say, covering the field *R* of reality, and the *o*, which corresponds to the fields *I* and *S*.

It is as the representative of the representation in phantasy, therefore, that is to say as the originally repressed subject that $\$$, the barred S of desire, here supports the field of reality, and this field is sustained only by the extraction of the object *o*, which, however, gives it its frame.

By measuring in stages, all vectorialized by an intrusion into the field *R* only of the field *I*, which is well articulated in my text only as the effect of narcissism, it is therefore quite out of the question that I would wish to reintroduce, by some back door, the notion that these effects ('system of identifications', as I would say) may, in some way, theoretically ground reality.

Whoever has followed my topological expositions (which are justified by nothing but the structure of the phantasy to be articulated) must know very well that in the Moebius strip there is nothing measurable to be retained in its structure, and that it is reduced, like the real with which we are concerned here, to the cut itself.

This note is indicative for the present stage of my topological elaboration (July 1966).

19. The title of that seminar.

20. Here is the text: *Einleitend habe ich dazu zu bemerken, dass bei der Genesis der betreffenden Entwicklung deren erste Anfänge weit, vielleicht bis zum 18. Jahrhundert zurückreichen, einertheils die Namen Flechsig und Schreber* [my emphasis] *(wahrscheinlich nicht in der Beschränkung auf je ein Individuum der betreffenden Familien) und anderntheils der Begriff des* Seelenmords [in 'Sperrdruck' in the original] *eine Hauptrolle spielen.*

21. In particular Dr Ernst Haeckel's *Natürliche Schöpfungsgeschichte* (Berlin, 1872) and Otto Casari's *Urgeschichte der Menschheit* (Brockhaus, Leipzig, 1877).

22. The relation between the proper name and the voice is to be situated in the structure of language, its two sides sloping in the direction of the message and the code respectively, to which I have already referred. See I. 5. It is this structure that decides the witty character of puns on proper names.

23. 'Between Malebranche and Locke the cleverer is the crazier.'

24. Macalpine, *op. cit.*: 398.

25. '*Die symbolische Gleichung Mächen = Phallus*', *Int. Zeitschrift für Psychoanalyse*, XXII, 1936, since translated into English as 'The Symbolic Equation: Girl = Phallus', and published in *The Psychoanalytic Quarterly*, 1949, XX (3): 303–24. In French, the term can be translated more appropriately as '*pucelle*'. [*Pucelle* lies somewhere between 'maid' and 'virgin' – Tr.]

26. Cf. W. G. Niederland, 'Three Notes on the Schreber Case', *Psychoanalytic Quarterly* XX: 579 (1951).

27. Cf. Jean-Marc Alby's very remarkable thesis, *Contribution à l'étude du transsexualisme*, Paris, 1956.

28. Cf. Freud, *Psychoanalytische Bemerkungen über einen autobiographisch beschriebenen Fall von Paranoia*, G.W., VIII: 264, n. 1. ('Psycho-Analytic Notes on an Autobiographical Account of a Case of Paranoia', *Standard Edition*, XII: 3.)

29. *Ibid.*, 284 and note.

30. S. 136–X.

31. During the acme of imaginary dissolution, the subject displayed in his delusional apperception a strange recourse to this criterion of reality, which is always to return to the same place, and why the stars are the most obvious representation of it: it is the motive designated by his voices as 'tying up lands' (*Anbinden an Erden*, S. 125–IX).

32. *Propos sur la causalité psychique* (Rapport du 28 septembre 1946 pour les Journées de Bonneval).

33. Cf. André Green's thesis, *Le milieu familial des schizophrènes*, Paris, 1957 – a work whose distinct merit would not have suffered if his approach had been more soundly based, in particular in relation to his approach to what he bizarrely terms 'psychotic fracture'.

34. I would wish every success to whichever of my students follows up this remark, in which criticism may be assured of a thread that will not lead it astray.

35. *Op. cit.*

36. Cf. this sentence quoted in note 20 above.

37. In a note on the same page, Ida Macalpine quotes the title of one of this author's books, *Glückseligkeitslehre für das physische Leben des Menschen*, as *How to Achieve Happiness and Bliss by Physical Culture*.

38. S. 194–XIV. *Die Redensart 'Ei verflucht'* . . . *war noch ein Uberbleibsel der Grundsprache, in welcher die Worte 'Ei verflucht, das sagt sich schwer' jedesmal gebraucht werden, wenn irgend ein mit der Weltordnung unerträgliche Erscheinung in das Bewusstsein der Seelen trat, z. B. 'Ei verflucht, das sagt sich schwer, dass der liebe Gott sich f. . . lässt'.*

39. I think I can borrow this euphemism from the register of the *Grundsprache* itself – a euphemism that the voices and Schreber himself, unusually, dispense with here.

I think I can better fulfil my duties to scientific rigour by pointing out the hypocrisy which, in this detour as in others, reduces to the benign, not to say to the inane, what the Freudian experience demonstrates. I mean the indefinable use to which references like the following are put: at this stage in his analysis, the patient regressed to the anal phase. It would be good to see the analyst's face if the patient suddenly defecated, or even slobbered, on his couch.

All this is no more than a concealed return to the sublimation that finds shelter in the *inter urinas et faeces nascimur*, with its implication that this sordid origin is of concern only to our bodies.

What analysis uncovers is something quite other. It is not his rags, but the very being of man that takes up its position among the waste matter in which his first frolics occur, much as the law of symbolization in which his desire must operate catches him in its net by the position of the part-object in which he offers himself on arrival in the world, in a world in which the desire of the Other lays down the law.

This relation, of course, is clearly articulated by Schreber in what he ascribes, to leave no possible ambiguity, to the act of shitting – namely, the fact of feeling the elements of his being, the dispersion of which into the infinity of his delusion constitutes his suffering, gathered together.

40. Under the form: *Die Sonne ist eine Hure* (S. 384–App.). For Schreber, the sun is the central aspect of God. The interior experience referred to here is the title of Georges Bataille's most central work. In *Madame Edwarda*, he describes the strange extremity of this exper_nce.

SEVEN

The direction of the treatment and the principles of its power

Report to the Colloque de Royaumont
10–13 July, 1958[1]

࿓࿓

I *Who analyses today?*

1. It has become a commonplace to say that an analysis is marked by the person of the analysand. But if anyone interests himself in the effects that the person of the analyst may have on the analysis, he is thought to be a very bold man indeed. This, at least, would explain the slight tremor we feel when modish remarks are made about the counter-transference – remarks that serve simply to mask its conceptual inadequacy. What nobility of soul we display when we reveal that we ourselves are made of the same clay as those we mould!

Now that's a naughty thing to say. But it's hardly enough for those at whom it is aimed, when people now go about proclaiming, under the banner of psychoanalysis, that they are striving for 'an emotional re-education of the patient' [22].[2]

Situating the action of the analyst at this level sweeps away a position of principle, with regard to which anything that might be said about the counter-transference, however valid it may be in itself, is merely a diversion. For the imposture that I wish to dislodge here now lies beyond such considerations.[3]

What I am denouncing, however, is not those elements in present-day psychoanalysis that might be termed anti-Freudian. For in that we should be grateful to them for lowering their mask, since they pride themselves on going beyond what, in fact, they are ignorant of, having retained from Freud's teaching just enough to feel to what extent what they have said about their experience is not consonant with that teaching. I hope to show how the inability to sustain a *praxis* in an authentic manner results, as is usually the case with mankind, in the exercise of power.

2. Certainly the psychoanalyst directs the treatment. The first principle of this treatment, the one that is spelt out to him before all else, and which he meets throughout his training, to the extent that he becomes utterly imbued with it, is that he must not direct the patient. The direction of conscience, in the sense of the moral guidance that a Catholic might find in it, is radically excluded here. If psychoanalysis poses problems for moral theology, they are not those of the direction of conscience, speaking of which I would add that the direction of conscience itself poses problems.

The direction of the treatment is something quite different. First of all, it consists in making the subject apply the analytic rule, that is, the directives whose presence cannot be ignored in the principle of what is called 'the analytic situation', on the pretext that the subject would apply them perfectly well without thinking about it.

These directives are initially presented to the patient in the form of instructions which, however little actual comment the analyst makes on them, will reveal, through the way in which they are presented, the analyst's own understanding of them. Which does not mean that the analyst is any the less involved in the mass of prejudices which, depending on the notion that cultural diffusion has allowed him to form of the methods and aim of the psychoanalytic enterprise, beleaguer the patient at this stage.

This is already enough to show us that, from the initial directives on, the problem of direction cannot be formulated in an univocal communication – a fact that forces us to pause at this stage and to throw further light on it in what follows.

Let us simply state that, reducing it to its bare truth, this stage consists in making the patient forget that it is merely a question of words spoken, but that this does not excuse the analyst for forgetting it himself [16].

3. Moreover, I have declared that it is from the angle of the analyst that I intend to approach my subject.

Let us say that in the pooling of resources involved in the common enterprise, the patient is not the only one who finds it difficult to pay his share. The analyst too must pay:
– pay with words no doubt, if the transmutation that they undergo from the analytic operation raises them to the level of interpretation;
– but also pay with his person, in that, whatever happens, he lends it as a support for the singular phenomena that analysis has discovered in the transference;
– can anyone forget that, in order to intervene in an action that goes to

the heart of being (*Kern unseres Wesens*, as Freud put it [6]), he must pay with that which is essential in his most intimate judgement: could he remain alone outside the field of play?

Let those who support our cause not be concerned at the thought that I am offering myself here once again to opponents who are always only too happy to send me back to my metaphysics.

For it is only on the basis of their claim to be satisfied with practical efficacity that a statement like 'the analyst cures not so much by what he says and does than by what he is' [22] can be made. Nobody, apparently, demands an explanation for such a statement, any more than one appeals to their author's sense of modesty when, with a tired smile directed at the derision that he incurs, he falls back on goodness, *his* goodness (we must be good, no transcendence in the context), to put an end to the endless argument about the transference neurosis.[4] But who would be cruel enough to question someone bent double under the weight of his luggage, when his bearing already indicates that it is full of bricks?

Yet being is being, whoever invokes it, and we have a right to ask what it is doing here.

4. So I shall cross-examine the analyst again, in so far as I am myself one, and observe that the less sure he is of his action the more interested he is in his being.

As an interpreter of what is presented to me in words or deeds, I am my own oracle and articulate it as I please, sole master of my ship after God, and of course far from being able to measure the whole effect of my words, but well aware of the fact and striving to guard against it, in other words always free in the timing, frequency and choice of my interventions, to the point that it seems that the rule has been arranged entirely so as not to impede in any way my own freedom of movement, that to which the 'material' aspect is correlative, and under which my action here takes what it produces.

5. In my handling of the transference, on the other hand, my freedom is alienated by the duplication to which my person is subjected in it, and everyone knows that it is there that the secret of analysis is to be sought. This does not prevent people believing that they are really getting somewhere when they discover the learned notion that psychoanalysis must be studied as a situation involving two persons. It is no doubt hedged about by conditions that restrain its movements, but the situation thus conceived serves nevertheless to articulate (and without more artifice than the emotional re-education referred to above) the principles of a

training of the 'weak' ego, by an ego that one pleases to believe is capable, on account of its 'strength', of carrying out such a project. That such a view is not expressed without a certain embarrassment is shown by the strikingly clumsy regrets that are offered, like the one that specifies that there must be no compromise on the need for a 'cure from within' [22].[5] But it is all the more significant to observe that the assent of the subject, referred to in this passage, comes only secondarily, after an effect that was first of all imposed.

It gives me no pleasure to point out these deviations; my aim is rather that these reefs should serve as beacons on our route.

In fact, every analyst (even if he is one of those who wander off course in this way) always experiences the transference in wonder at the least expected effect of a relationship between two people that seems like any other. He tells himself that he has to make his peace with a phenomenon for which he is not responsible, and we know with what insistence Freud stressed the spontaneity of the patient's transference.

For some time now, analysts in the heart-rending revisions that they treat us to have been ready enough to insinuate that this insistence, of which they were for so long the bulwark, expresses in Freud a flight from the commitment that the notion of situation presupposes. We are, you see, up to date.

But it is rather the facile exaltation of their gesture in throwing feelings, which they class under the heading of their counter-transference, in one side of the scales, thus balancing the transference itself with their own weight, which for me is evidence of an unhappy consciousness correlative with a failure to conceive the true nature of the transference.

One cannot regard the phantasies that the analysand imposes on the person of the analyst in the same way as a perfect card player might guess his opponent's intentions. No doubt there is always an element of strategy, but one should not be deceived by the metaphor of the mirror, appropriate as it may be to the smooth surface that the analyst presents to the patient. An impassive face and sealed lips do not have the same purpose here as in a game of bridge. Here the analyst is rather bringing to his aid what in bridge is called the dummy (*le mort*), but he is doing so in order to introduce the fourth player who is to be the partner of the analysand here, and whose hand the analyst, by his tactics, will try to expose: such is the link, let us say the abnegation, that is imposed on the analyst by the stake of the game in the analysis.

One might pursue the metaphor by deducing his game according to whether he places himself 'on the right' or 'on the left' of the patient that, is to say, in a position to play after or before the fourth player, to play, that is to say, before or after the player with the dummy.

But what is certain is that the analyst's feelings have only one possible place in the game, that of the dummy; and that if he is re-animated the game will proceed without anyone knowing who is leading.

That is why the analyst is less free in his strategy than in his tactics.

6. Let us take this further. The analyst is even less free as to that which dominates strategy and tactics, namely, his policy, where he would be better advised to take his bearings from his want-to-be (*manque à être*) rather than from his being.

To put it another way: his action on the patient escapes him through the idea that he forms of it as long as he does not grasp its starting-point in that by which it is possible, as long as he does not retain the paradox of its four-sidedness, in order to revise in principle the structure by which any action intervenes in reality.

For today's psychoanalysts, this relation to reality goes without saying. They measure the patient's defections from that relation on the authoritarian principle that is always employed by educators. Furthermore, they rely on the teaching analysis to ensure its maintenance at a sufficient rate among analysts, who are not allowed to feel that, in confronting the human problems that are presented to them, their views will sometimes be somewhat parochial. This is merely to remove the problem from an individual level.

And it is hardly reassuring, when they trace the procedure of analysis as the reduction in the subject of deviations attributed to his transference and his resistances, but mapped in relation to reality, to hear them declaiming about the 'perfectly simple situation' that is provided by analysis as a means of measuring up to reality. Come now! The educator is not ready to be educated if he can take so lightly an experience that he, too, must have undergone.

One would have expected from such an appreciation that these analysts would have given other twists to this experience if they had had to depend on their sense of reality to invent it themselves: a priority too shameful to be thought of. They suspect as much, and that is why they are so punctilious in preserving its forms.

One understands that in order to prop up so obviously precarious a conception certain individuals on the other side of the Atlantic should have felt the need to introduce into it some stable value, some standard of the measure of the real: this turns out to be the autonomous *ego*.[6] This is the supposedly organized ensemble of the most disparate functions that lend their support to the subject's feeling of innateness. It is regarded as autonomous because it appears to be sheltered from the conflicts of the person (*non-conflictual sphere*) [14].

One recognizes there a down-at-heel mirage that had already been rejected as untenable by the most academic psychology of introspection. Yet this regression is celebrated as a return to the fold of 'general psychology'.

However, it does solve the problem of the analyst's being.[7] A team of *egos* no doubt less equal than autonomous (but by what trade-mark do they recognize in one another the sufficiency of their autonomy?) is offered to the Americans to guide them towards *happiness*,[8] without upsetting the autonomies, egoistical or otherwise, that pave with their non-conflictual spheres the *American way*[8] of getting there.

7. To sum up. If the analyst were dealing only with resistances, he would look twice before hazarding an interpretation, as is in fact the case, but in doing so he would have done all that could be expected of him.

However, this interpretation, if he gives it, will be received as coming from the person that the transference imputes him to be. Will he agree to benefit from this error concerning the person? The ethics of analysis do not contradict this, on condition that the analyst interprets this effect, otherwise the analysis will amount to little more than a crude suggestion.

An incontestable position, except that the analyst's words will still be heard as coming from the Other of the transference, the emergence of the subject from the transference is thus postponed *ad infinitum*.

It is therefore because the subject imputes being (being that is elsewhere) to the analyst that an interpretation can return to the place from which it may bear on the distribution of responses.

But who will say what the analyst is, and what remains of him when it comes to the task of interpreting? Let him dare to say it himself if all he has to say to us by way of an answer is that he is a man. Whether or not he has anything to say would then be all there is to it: yet it is there that he beats a retreat, not only on account of the impudence of the mystery, but because in this *having*, it is *being* that is in question, and how. We shall see later that this 'how' is not an easy matter.

Moreover, he prefers to fall back on his ego, and on the bit of reality he knows. But then he is on terms of I and me (*à je et à moi*) with his patient. How can he manage if it they're at daggers drawn? It is here that one is astute in counting on the intelligences that must be in the place, named, for the purpose of the occasion, the healthy part of the ego, the part that thinks as we do.

Q.E.D., one might conclude, which brings us back to our initial problem, namely, how to reinvent analysis?

Or to recast it – by treating the transference as a particular form of resistance.

Many profess to do just this. It is to them that I would pose the question that forms the title of this chapter: Who is the analyst? He who interprets, profiting from the transference? He who analyses it as resistance? Or he who imposes his idea of reality?

It is a question that may get a tighter grip on those to whom it is addressed, and be less easy to avoid than the question, 'Who is speaking?', which one of my pupils yelled into their ears on behalf of the patient. For the impatient answer: an animal of our species, while it would be more annoyingly tautological to respond dutifully to the changed question with: me.

As bluntly as that.

❧❧❧❧

II *What is the place of interpretation?*

1. The preceding does not amount to a reply to all the questions that occur to a novice. But in gathering together the problems that at present surround the direction of the treatment, in so far as this situation reflects present practice, I think I have kept everything in proportion.

To begin with, there is the less important place occupied by interpretation in present-day psychoanalysis – not that its meaning has been lost, but that the approach to this meaning is always a source of embarrassment. No author confronts it without first distinguishing it from every other form of verbal intervention: explanations, gratifications, responses to demand, etc. The procedure becomes revealing when it gets close to the centre of interest. It means that even something said with the intention of leading the subject to an insight into his behaviour, especially in its signification as resistance, may be given a quite different name, confrontation, for example, if only of the subject with his own words, without meriting the name of interpretation, except in the sense of throwing light on something.

One cannot but be touched by an author's attempts to force the theory of form, in order to find in it the metaphor that allows him to express the resolution that interpretation brings to an intentional ambiguity, and the closure that it brings to a state of incompleteness that is nevertheless realized only after the event [2].

2. One senses that there is concealed some kind of transmutation in the subject that is being avoided here, and that this is all the more painful in that it eludes thought as soon as it becomes fact. Indeed, no index suffices to show where it is that interpretation is operative, unless one accepts in all its radical implications a concept of the function of the signifier, which enables one to grasp where the subject is subordinated, even suborned, by the signifier.

In order to decipher the diachrony of unconscious repetitions, interpretation must introduce into the synchrony of the signifiers that compose it something that suddenly makes translation possible – precisely what is made possible by the function of the Other in the concealment of the code, it being in relation to that Other that the missing element appears.

This importance of the signifier in the localization of analytic truth appears in filigree when an author holds firmly to the connexions of experience in the definition of the aporias. One should read Edward Glover if one wishes to appreciate the price that one pays when one dispenses with this term: when, in articulating the most relevant insights, he finds interpretation everywhere, being unable to stop it anywhere, even in the banality of a medical prescription, and even goes so far as to say quite calmly – I am not sure whether he is aware of what he is saying – that the formation of the symptom is an incorrect interpretation on the subject's part [13].

In this sense, interpretation becomes a sort of phlogiston: manifest in everything that is understood rightly or wrongly, providing it feeds the flame of the imaginary, of that pure display, which, under the name of aggressivity, flourishes in the technique of that period. (1931 – new enough to be still applicable today. Cf. [13].)

It is only in so far as interpretation culminates in the here and now of this play that it will be distinguished from the reading of the *signatura rerum* in which Jung tries to out do Boehme. To follow it there would not suit our analysts at all.

But to keep to Freud's time is a very different matter, and one in which it is useful to know how to take the clock to pieces.

3. My doctrine of the signifier is first of all a discipline in which those I train have to familiarize themselves with the different ways in which the signifier effects the advent of the signified, which is the only conceivable way that interpretation can produce anything new.

For interpretation is based on no assumption of divine archetypes, but on the fact that the unconscious is structured in the most radical way like a language, that a material operates in it according to certain laws, which are the same laws as those discovered in the study of actual languages, languages that are or were actually spoken.

The phlogiston metaphor, which was suggested to me a moment ago by Glover, gets its appropriateness from the error that it suggests: signification no more emanates from life than phlogiston in combustion escapes from bodies. We should speak of it rather as of the combination of life with the atom O of the sign,[9] first and foremost of the sign in so far as it connotes presence *or* absence, by introducing essentially the *and* that links them, since in connoting presence or absence, it establishes presence against a background of absence, just as it constitutes absence in presence.

One will recall that with the sureness of touch that was his in this field, Freud, seeking the model of the repetition compulsion, stopped at the crossroads formed by a game of occultation and an alternate scansion of two phonemes, whose conjugation in a child made a striking impression on him.

At the same time, there also appears in it the value of the object as in itself non-signifying (the object that the child causes to appear and disappear), and the subsidiary character of phonetic perfection in relation to phonematic distinction – and no one would dispute that Freud was right to translate it immediately by the *Fort! Da!* of the German he as an adult spoke [9].

This is the point of insertion of a symbolic order that pre-exists the infantile subject and in accordance with which he will have to structure himself.

4. I will spare myself the task of giving the rules of interpretation. It is not that they cannot be formulated, but their formulae presuppose developments that I cannot presume to be known, and it would be impossible to provide a condensed account of them here.

I will confine myself to remarking that when one reads the classical commentaries on interpretation, one always regrets how little is made of the data offered.

For example, everyone recognizes in his own way that to confirm that an interpretation is well founded, it is not the conviction with which it is received that matters, since the criterion of conviction will be found rather in the material that will emerge as a result of the interpretation.

But the psychologizing superstition is so powerful in people's minds that one will always solicit the phenomenon in terms of the subject's assent, entirely omitting the consequences of what Freud says about *Verneinung* as a form of avowal – to say the least, it cannot be treated as the equivalent of just any old thing.

This is how theory describes the way in which resistance is engendered in practice. It is also what I mean when I say that there is no other resistance to analysis than that of the analyst himself.

5. The serious thing is that with present-day authors the sequence of analytic effects seems to be understood inside out. What they seem to be saying is that interpretation can only be a hesitant and uncertain stammer in comparison with a wider relation in which, at last, true understanding reigns ('from the inside' no doubt).

According to this view, an exigency of the interpretation becomes weakness to which we must offer help. It is also something else, something that is very difficult to swallow without rejecting it. It is both at once, that is to say, a very inconvenient means.

But what we have here is only the effect of the analyst's passions: his fear, which is not error, but ignorance, his taste, which is not to satisfy, but not to disappoint either, his need, which is not to govern, but to keep the upper hand. It has nothing to do with any counter-transference on the part of this or that individual; it is a question of the consequences of the dual relation, if the therapist does not overcome it, and how can he overcome it if he sees it as the ideal of his action?

Primum vivere no doubt: a break must be avoided. That one should regard as technique the practice of puerile, honest civility to be taught to this end is bad enough. But that one should confuse this physical necessity, the patient's presence at the appointment, with the analytic relation, is a mistake that will mislead the novice for a long time to come.

6. From this point of view, the transference becomes the analyst's security, and the relation to the real the terrain on which the combat is decided. The interpretation, which has been postponed until the consolidation of the transference, now becomes subordinated to the reduction of the transference.

As a result, the interpretation is reabsorbed into a 'working through',[10] which serves as an alibi for a sort of revenge taken for the initial timidity, that is to say, for an insistence that opens the door to all kinds of pressure, conveniently dubbed 'strengthening of the ego' [21–22].

7. But has anyone observed, in criticizing Freud's approach, as

presented for example in the case of the Rat Man, that what strikes us as preconceived doctrine is due simply to the fact that he proceeds in inverse order? Namely, that he begins by introducing the patient to an initial mapping of his position in the real, even if the real involves a precipitation – I would even go so far as to say a systematization – of the symptoms [8].

Another famous example: when he reduces Dora to realizing that she has done more than merely contribute to the great disorder of her father's world, the damage to which forms the object of her protest, but that she was in fact the mainspring of it and that he was unable to accept her complacency [7].

I have long stressed the Hegelian procedure at work in this reversal of the positions of the *belle âme* in relation to the reality that it accuses. It is hardly a question of adapting to it, but to show it that it is only too well adapted, since it assists in the construction of that very reality.

But the path to be followed with the other stops here. For the transference has already done its work, showing that it is certainly a question of something other than the relations between the ego and the world.

Freud does not always seem to be quite clear about this in the cases he describes. And that is why they are so valuable.

For he recognized at once that the principle of his power lay there, in the transference – in which respect it was not very different from suggestion – but also that this power gave him a way out of the problem only on condition that he did not use it, for it was then that it took on its whole development as transference.

From that moment it is no longer he whom he holds in proximity that he addresses, and that is why he refuses to meet him face to face.

Freud's conception of interpretation is so bold that a process of popularization has robbed it of its full mantic significance. When he exposes a drive, what he calls *Trieb*, which is quite different from an instinct, the freshness of the discovery prevents us from seeing that the *Trieb* implies in itself the advent of a signifier. But when Freud uncovers what can only be called the subject's lines of fate, it is the face of Tiresias that we question before the ambiguity in which his verdict operates.

For these lines that have been 'read' concern so little the subject's ego, or anything that he may make present here and now in the dual relation, that it is exactly right, in the case of the Rat Man, to seize on the pact that presided over his parents' marriage, on something, therefore, that occurred well before he was born – and that Freud should find the following conditions intermingled in it: honour saved by a hair's breadth, a betrayal in love, social compromise, and prescribed debt, of which the great compulsive scenario that led the patient to him seems to be the cryptographical tracing off – and, finally, motivates at last the impasses in which his moral life and his desire are lost.

But the most striking thing about it is that access to this material was opened up only by an interpretation in which Freud presumed that the Rat Man's father had refused to allow his son to marry the girl to whom he was sublimely devoted, in order to explain the impossibility that seems to have blocked this relationship for him in every way. An interpretation, which, to say the least, is inexact, since it is contradicted by the reality it presumes, but which nevertheless is true in the sense that in it Freud shows an intuition that anticipates my own contribution to the understanding of the function of the Other in obsessional neurosis. I have demonstrated that this function is particularly suited to being held by a dead man (or 'dummy'), and that in this case it could not be better held than by the father, in so far as by his death the Rat Man's father had rejoined the position that Freud recognized as that of the absolute Father.

8. I would ask those who are already familiar with my writings and who have attended my seminars to forgive me if I now cite examples already well known to them.

This is not only because I cannot make use of my own analyses to demonstrate the level to which interpretation reaches, when interpretation, proving to be coextensive with the history, cannot be communicated in the communicating milieu in which many of my analyses take place without risking an infringement of anonymity. For I have succeeded on such occasions in saying enough about a case without saying too much, that is to say to cite my example, without anyone, except the person in question, recognizing it.

Nor is it because I regard the Rat Man as a case that Freud cured – but were I to add that I do not think that the analysis is entirely unconnected with the tragic conclusion of his history by death on the field of battle, what an opportunity for evil thinking I would be offering to those who wish to think evil![11]

What I am saying is that it is in a direction of the treatment, ordered, as I have just shown, according to a process that begins with the rectification of the subject's relations with the real, and proceeds first to the development of the transference, then to interpretation, that Freud made the fundamental discoveries, which we are still living off, concerning the dynamics and structure of obsessional neurosis Nothing more, but nothing less either.

The question now is whether in reversing this order we have lost that horizon.

9. What can be said is that the new paths by which, it has been claimed, the way opened up by the discoverer has been legalized, are proof of terminological confusion that can only be revealed in the particular. I will take an example, therefore, that has already helped me in my teaching; naturally, it has been chosen from a distinguished author, who, by virtue of his background, is particularly sensitive to the dimension of interpretation. I refer to Ernst Kris and a case which – he does not hide the fact – he took over from Melitta Schmideberg [15].

It concerns a subject inhibited in his intellectual life and particularly incapable of bringing his research to a stage at which it might be published – on account of a compulsion to plagiarize, which, it seems, he was unable to master. Such was the subjective drama.

Melitta Schmideberg had seen it as the recurrence of an infantile delinquency; the subject stole sweets and books, and it was from this angle that she had undertaken the analysis of the unconscious conflict.

Ernst Kris is to be credited with taking up the case in accordance with an interpretation more methodical than he says, one that proceeds from the surface to deeper levels. The fact that he accredits this interpretation to 'ego psychology' *à la* Hartmann, whom he believed he was under some obligation to support, is incidental to an appreciation of what takes place. Ernst Kris changes the perspective of the case and claims to give the subject insight into a new departure on the basis of a fact that is merely a repetition of his compulsion, but Kris, to his credit, does not content himself with what the patient says; and when the patient claims to have taken, in spite of himself, the ideas for a piece of work that he has just completed from a book which, on being remembered, enabled him to check his own work after its completion, Kris looks at the evidence and discovers that the patient has apparently done nothing more than is normal practice in the research field. In short, having assured himself that his patient is not a plagiarist when he thinks he is, he sets out to show him that he wants to be one in order to prevent himself from really being one – which is what we call analysing the defence before the drive, which is manifested here in an attraction for others' ideas.

This intervention may be presumed to be erroneous, simply by the fact that it presupposes that defence and drive are concentric, the one being moulded, as it were, on the other.

What proves that it is, in fact, erroneous is the very thing in which Kris is confirmed, namely, that just when he thinks he is able to ask the patient what he thinks of the coat being turned in this way, the patient, day-dreaming for a moment, replies that for some time, on leaving the session, he has wandered along a street full of attractive little restaurants, scrutinizing the menus in search of his favourite dish, cold brains.

An avowal which, rather than sanctioning the benefits of the intervention by virtue of the material that it contributes, seems to me to have the corrective value of *acting out* in the very relation that it makes of it.

This after-the-event air that the patient breathes seems to me rather to tell the hostess that she is failing in her service. Compulsive as he is to inhale it, it is a hint;[12] a transitory symptom no doubt, but it warns the analyst that he is barking up the wrong tree.

You are indeed barking up the wrong tree, I would repeat, addressing the late Ernst Kris, as I remember him at the Marienbad Congress, where the day following my address on the mirror stage, I took a day off, anxious to get a feeling of the spirit of the times, heavy with promises, at the Berlin Olympiad. He gently objected: '*Ça ne se fait pas!*' (in French),[13] thus showing that he had already acquired that taste for the respectable that perhaps deflects his approach here.

Was it this that misled you, Ernst Kris, or simply that upright as your intentions may have been, for your judgement, too, is beyond question, things themselves were shaky.

It's not that your patient doesn't steal that is important here. It's that he doesn't . . . No, not *doesn't*: it's that he steals *nothing*. And that's what he should have been told.

Contrary to what you believe, it is not his defence against the idea of stealing that makes him believe that he steals. It's his having an idea of his own that never occurs to him, or hardly even crosses his mind.

It is useless, therefore, to engage him in this process of taking into consideration, in which God himself could not recognize himself, what his friend pinches from him that is more or less original when they are talking together.

May not this desire for cold brains refresh your own concepts, and remind you of what Roman Jakobson says of the function of metonymy? I shall return to this later.

You speak of Melitta Schmideberg as if she had confused delinquency with the id. I'm not so sure and, looking up the article in which she cites this case, the wording of her title suggests to me a metaphor.

You treat the patient as an obsessional neurotic, but he holds out a hand to you with his food phantasy: in order to give you the opportunity of being a quarter-of-an-hour in advance of the nosology of your period in diagnosing anorexia mentale. By the same token, you will refresh, by giving them back their true meaning, a couple of terms which, in common usage, have been reduced to the dubious quality of an aetiological indication.

Anorexia, in this case, in relation to the mental, in relation to the desire on which the idea lives, and this brings us to the scurvy that rages on the raft in which I embark him with the thin virgins.

Their symbolically motivated refusal seems to me to have a good deal to do with the patient's aversion for what he thinks. His father, you say, was not blessed with many ideas. Is it not that the grandfather, who was celebrated for his ideas, sickened him of them? How can we know? You are surely right to make the signifier *'grand'*, included in the term of kinship, the origin, no more, of the rivalry played out with the father for catching the biggest fish. But this purely formal challenge suggests to me rather that he means: nothing doing.[14]

There is nothing in common, then, between your progress, supposedly from the surface, and subjective rectification, which we dealt with at length above in relation to Freud's method, where, it must be said, it is motivated by no topographical priority.

It is also that in Freud this rectification is dialectical, and sets out from the subject's own words, which means that an interpretation can be right only by being . . . an interpretation.

To opt for the objective here is surely mistaken, if only because plagiarism is relative to the practices operating in a given situation.[15]

But the idea that the surface is the level of the superficial is itself dangerous. Another topology is necessary if we are not to be misled as to the place of desire.

To efface desire from the map when it is already buried in the patient's landscape is not the best way of following in Freud's footsteps.

Nor is it a way of getting rid of depth, for it is at the surface that it is seen as imperfections on the face on feast days.

⋙⋘

III *Where have we got with the transference?*

1. It is to the work of my colleague Daniel Lagache that we must turn for a true account of the work which, around Freud while he was pursuing his activity and since in what he has left us, has been devoted to the transference, which he discovered. The object of this work goes well beyond this, by introducing into the function of the phenomenon structural distinctions that are essential for its critique. One has only to recall the very relevant alternative that he presents, as to its ultimate nature, between the need for repetition and the repetition of need.

Such work, if I believe I have been able to convey in my teaching the consequences that it brings with it, shows very clearly by means of the ordering that it introduces to what extent the aspects on which discussion is centred are often partial, and particularly to what extent the ordinary use of the term, even in analysis, cannot free itself from its most questionable, not to say most vulgar approach, namely, to review or enumerate the positive or negative feelings that the patient has for his analyst.

In deciding where we have got with the transference in our scientific community, could it be said that neither agreement nor illumination has surrounded the following points on which they would seem nevertheless to be necessary: is it the same effect of the relation with the analyst that is manifested in the initial infatuation to be observed at the beginning of treatment and in the web of satisfactions that make this relation so difficult to break when the transference neurosis seems to go beyond the properly analytic means? Is it, again, the relation with the analyst and its fundamental frustration which, in the second period of analysis, sustains the rhythm of frustration, aggression, and regression in which the most fruitful effects of analysis appear to occur? How must we conceive of the subordination of phenomena when their movement is traversed by phantasies that openly involve the figure of the analyst?

The reason for these persistent obscurities has been formulated in an exceptionally lucid study: at each of the stages at which an attempt has been made to revise the problems of the transference, the technical divergences that made such a revision a matter of urgency have left no place for a true critique of the notion itself [20].

2. It is so central a notion for the analytic action that I wish to take up again here that it may serve as a measure for the partiality of the theories in which one spends so much time thinking about it. That is, one will not

be misled into judging it from the handling of the transference that those theories involve. This pragmatism is justified. For this handling of the transference is at one with the notion, and however little elaborated this notion is in practice, it cannot do otherwise than range itself with the partialities of the theory.

On the other hand, the simultaneous existence of these partialities does nothing to make them complement one another – which confirms that they suffer from a central defect.

In order to introduce a little order into the question, I will reduce these peculiarities of the theory to three, even if it means exposing myself to a certain amount of prejudice, less serious for being only a matter of exposition.

3. I will link geneticism, in the sense that it tends to ground analytic phenomena in the developmental stages that concern them and to be nourished on the so-called direct observation of the child, to a special technique that concentrates on the analysis of the defences.

This link is obvious from a historical point of view. One might even say that it is based on nothing else, since this link is constituted only by the failure of the solidarity that it presupposes.

One can locate its beginnings in the legitimate credence given the notion of an unconscious ego with which Freud reorientated his doctrine. To pass from this to the hypothesis that the mechanisms of defence that are grouped together under its function ought themselves to be able to reveal a comparable law of appearance, one that even corresponds to the succession of stages by which Freud had attempted to link the emergence of the drives to physiology – that was the step that Anna Freud, in her book *The Mechanisms of Defence*, proposed to take in order to put it to the test of experience.

It could have been an opportunity to make a fruitful critique of the relations between development and the obviously more complex structures that Freud introduced into psychology. But the sights were lowered – it was so much more tempting to try and insert into the observable stages of sensoriomotor development and of the developing skills of intelligent behaviour these mechanisms of defence, supposedly independent of their development.

One might say that the hopes that Anna Freud placed in such an exploration were disappointed: nothing emerged from this line of approach that threw any light on problems of technique, though the details of a child analysis have yielded some very interesting suggestions.

The notion of *pattern*,[16] which functions here as an alibi of the abandoned typology, dominates a technique which, in pursuing the detection of a non-contemporaneous pattern, concentrates all too easily, it seems, on its departure from a pattern that finds in its conformism the guarantees of its conformity. One cannot recall without a sense of shame the criteria of success in which this shoddy work culminates: the achievement of a higher income, and the emergency exit provided by the affair with one's secretary, regulating the release of forces strictly bound up in marriage, career and the political community, do not seem to me to be worthy of an appeal (articulated in the analyst's planning,[16] and even in his interpretation) to the Discord of the instincts of life and death – except by way of decorating his words with the pretentious term 'economic', and to pursue it, in complete misunderstanding of Freud's thought, as the play of two forces homologous in their opposition.

4. Less eroded in its analytic relief it seems to me is the other side of the coin, where we find depicted that which eludes the transference, namely, the axis taken from the object relation.

This theory, although it has lost much of its appeal in France in recent years, has, like geneticism, a noble origin. It was Karl Abraham who pulled out the stop on this theory, and the notion of the part-object is his original contribution to it. This is not the place to demonstrate the value of that contribution. I am more concerned to indicate its connexion with the partiality of the aspect that Abraham detaches from the transference, and then proceeds in his opaque way to transform it into the ability to love: as if that were a constitutional given of the patient in which one might read the degree of his amenability to treatment, and, in particular, the only one in which the treatment of psychosis would fail.

We have two equations here in effect. The so-called sexual transference (*Sexualübertragung*) is the basis of the love we call object love (*Objektliebe*). The capacity for transference is a measure of the patient's access to the real. One cannot stress too much that this merely begs the question.

Unlike the presuppositions of geneticism, which is supposed to be based on an order of formal emergences in the subject, Abraham's approach can be explained as a finality that allows itself to be instinctual, in the sense that it is based on the image of the maturation of an ineffable object, the Object with a capital O that governs the phase of objectality (to be distinguished, significantly, from objectivity by virtue of its affective substance).

This ectoplasmic conception of the object soon revealed its dangers when it became degraded into the crude dichotomy expressed in the opposition of the pregenital character and the genital character.

This over-simplified thematization is summarily developed by attributing to the pregenital character the accumulated features of projective unrealism, greater or lesser degrees of autism, restriction of satisfaction by the defences, the conditioning of the object by a doubly protective isolation of the destructive effects that connote it, in other words, an amalgam of all the defects of the object relation with a view to showing the motives of extreme dependence that result from them for the subject. A picture that would be useful despite its inveterate confusion if it did not seem made to serve as a negative to the puerility of 'the passage from the pregenital form to the genital form', in which the drives 'no longer take on that character of a need of uncoercible, unlimited, unconditional possession, involving a destructive aspect. They are truly tender, loving, and even if the subject does not show himself to be oblative, that is to say, disinterested, and even if these objects' (here the author recalls my remarks) 'are as profoundly narcissistic objects as in the previous case, he is capable of comprehension, and adaptation to the other. Indeed, the intimate structure of these object relations shows that the objects' participation in its own pleasure is indispensable to the subject's happiness. The proprieties, the desires, the needs of the object [what a mess!][17] are taken into consideration to the highest degree.'

However, this does not prevent the ego from having 'a stability that runs no risk of being compromised by the loss of a significant Object. It remains independent of its objects.'

'Its organization is such that the mode of thought that it uses is essentially logical. It does not spontaneously present regression to an archaic mode of apprehending reality, affective thinking, magical belief, playing only an absolutely secondary role; symbolization does not grow in extent and importance beyond what it is in normal life.[!!][17] The style of the relations between subject and object is one of the most highly evolved [*sic*].'[17]

This is the promise held out to those who 'at the end of a successful analysis . . . realize the enormous difference between what they once believed sexual pleasure to be and what they now experience'.

One is led to understand that for those who enjoy this pleasure from the outset, 'the genital relation is, in short, untroubled' [21].

Untroubled except for conjugating itself irresistibly in the verb 'to tap the chandelier with one's behind' (*se taper le derrière au lustre*), whose place here seems to me to be marked for the future scholiast to meet his eternal opportunity.

5. If, indeed, we must follow Abraham when he presents us with the object-relation as typically demonstrated in the activity of the collector perhaps the rule is not given in this edifying antinomy, but is to be sought rather in some impasse that is constitutive of desire itself.

This means that the object is presented as broken and decomposed, and is perhaps something other than a pathological factor. And what has this absurd hymn to the harmony of the genital got to do with the real?

Should we erase the Oedipal drama from our experience when it must have been forged by Freud precisely to explain the barriers and snubs (*Erniedrigungen*) that are so common in even the most fulfilled love relation?

Is it our job to disguise the black God in the sheep's clothing of the Good Shepherd Eros?

Sublimation may well be at work in the oblation that radiates from love, but we should try to go a little farther into the structure of the sublime, and not confuse it with the perfect orgasm – which was something Freud, at least, was anxious to disprove.

The worst thing about all this is that souls who overflow with the most natural tenderness are led to wonder if they can cope with the delusional 'normality' of the genital relation – a new burden which, like those cursed by the Evangelist, we have bound on to the shoulders of the innocents.

Yet to read what I have written, if any of it survives into a time when people will no longer know what it was in practice that these excited words were a reply to, one might imagine that our art was employed to revive sexual hunger in those inflicted with a retardation of the sexual gland – that it was applied to physiology, to which we have made no contribution, and of which very little was there to be known.

6. At least three sides are needed to make a pyramid, even a heretical one. The one that closes the dihedron described here in the gap left by the conception of the transference, strives, one might say, to reunite the edges.

If the transference takes on its virtue from being brought back to the reality of which the analyst is the representative, and if it is a question of ripening the Object in the hot house of a confined situation, the analysand is left with only one object, if you will pardon the expression, to get his teeth into, and that's the analyst.

Hence the third mistake on our list: the notion of intersubjective intro-jection establishes itself, unfortunately, in a dual relation.

For we are certainly dealing with a unitive way of which the various theoretical sauces with which it is served up, depending on the topo-graphy to which one is referring, can do no more than retain the metaphor whilst varying it according to the level of the operation regarded as serious: introjection for Ferenczi, identification with the analyst's super-ego for Strachey, a terminal narcissistic trance for Balint.

I am trying to draw attention to the substance of this mystical con-summation, and if once more I must take to task what is happening on my doorstep it is because the analytic experience is known to draw its strength from the particular.

That is why the importance given in analysis to the phantasy of phallic devouring, to which the image of the analyst is subjected, seems to me to be worthy of note, because it tallies so well with a conception of the direction of the treatment that is based entirely upon the arrangement of the distance between patient and analyst as the object of the dual relation.

For, however weak the theory with which an author systematizes his technique, the fact remains that he really does analyse, and the coherence revealed in the error is the guarantor here of the wrong route that has been taken in practice.

It is the privileged function of the signifying phallus in the mode of the subject's presence to desire that is illustrated here, but in an experience that might be called blind – blind in the absence of any sense of direction concerning the true relations of the analytic situation, which, as in any other situation involving speech, can only, by trying to inscribe it in a dual relation, be crushed.

Since the nature of symbolic incorporation is misunderstood, and with good reason, and since it is unthinkable that anything real should be accomplished in the analysis, it will appear, from a cursory study of my teaching, that nothing can be recognized in what occurs that is not im-aginary. For it is not necessary to know the plan of a house to knock one's head against its walls: indeed, to do so, one can do very well without any plan.

I have myself suggested to this author, in discussion, that if one con-fines oneself to an imaginary relation between objects there remains only the dimension of distance to order it. This was not how he saw things at all.

To make distance the sole dimension in which the neurotic's relations with the object are played out produces unsurmountable contradictions that can be read well enough both within the system and in the opposed direction that different authors will derive from the same metaphor to organize their impressions. Too much or too little distance from the object will sometimes appear to become confused to an inextricable degree. And it is not the distance from the object, but rather its too great intimacy with the subject that seemed to Ferenczi to characterize the neurotic.

What decides what each one means is its technical use and the technique of the '*bringing-together*' (*le rapprocher*), however priceless the effect of the untranslated term may be in an exposition in English, reveals in practice a tendency that borders upon obsession.

It is difficult to believe that given the ideal reduction of this distance to zero (*nil* in English) which he prescribes its author can fail to see that its theoretical paradox is concentrated there.

Nevertheless, it cannot be doubted that this distance is taken as a universal parameter, regulating variations in the technique (however double-Dutch the debate on their breadth may seem) for the dismantling of neurosis.

What such a conception owes to the special conditions of obsessional neurosis is not to be ascribed entirely to the object.

It does not seem that any justification can be got from the result obtained by the application of this conception to obsessional neurosis. For if I allow myself, as I did Kris, to cite an analysis, which, like Kris, I had taken over from another analyst, I can provide evidence that such a technique in the hands of an analyst of indisputable talent succeeded in producing in a clinical case of pure obsession in a man the irruption of an infatuation that was no less passionate for being Platonic, and which proved no less irreducible for being directed at the first object of the same sex that happened to be to hand.

To speak of transitory perversion here may satisfy an invincible optimist, but only at the cost of recognizing, in this untypical restoration of the usually all too neglected third party of the relation, that one should not pull too hard on the spring of proximity in the object relation.

7. There is no limit to the erosion of analytic technique through deconceptualization. I have already referred to the discoveries of a 'wild' analysis in which, to my painful astonishment, there had been no supervision. To be able to smell one's analyst seemed in one work to be an aim to be taken literally, as an index of the happy outcome of the transference.

One can perceive here a sort of involuntary humour, which is what makes this example so valuable. It would have delighted Jarry. It is, in fact, no more than one might expect from carrying the development of the analytic situation over into the real: and it is true that, taste apart, the olfactory is the only dimension that enables one to reduce the distance to zero (*nil*), this time in the real. To what extent it provides a clue for the direction of the treatment and the principles of its power is more doubtful.

But that the odour of a cage should find its way into a technique that is conducted largely by 'sniffing out' as they say, is not as ridiculous as it sounds. Students from my seminar will recall the smell of urine that marked the turning-point in a case of transitory perversion, which I used as a criticism of this technique. It cannot be said that it was unconnected with the accident that motivates the observation, since it is in spying, through a crack in the wall of a public lavatory, on a woman pissing that the patient suddenly transposed his *libido*, without anything, it seemed, predetermining it: infantile emotions bound up with the phantasy of the phallic mother having until then taken the form of a phobia [23].

It is not a direct link, however, any more than it would be correct to see in this voyeurism an inversion of the exhibition involved in the atypia of the phobia to the correctly posed diagnosis: under the patient's anxiety at being teased for being too tall.

As I said, the analyst to whom we owe this remarkable publication gives proof of rare perspicacity in coming back, to the point of tormenting the patient, to the interpretation that she gave of a coat of arms, which appeared in a dream, in poursuivant and armed, what's more, with a fly-spray, as a symbol of the phallic mother.

Shouldn't I rather have talked about her father? she wondered. She justified not doing so by the fact that the real father had been missing in the patient's history.

At this point, my pupils will be able to deplore the fact that the teaching of my seminar was unable to help her at the time, since they know by what principles I have taught them to distinguish between the phobic object *qua* all-purpose signifier to fill the lack of the Other and the fundamental fetish of every perversion *qua* object perceived in the cut (*coupure*) of the signifier.

Failing that, shouldn't this gifted novice have remembered the dialogue between the suits of armour in André Breton's *Discours sur le peu de réalité*? That would have put her on the right path.

But how could we hope for such a thing when this analysis was, in supervision, given a direction that involved constant harassment to bring the patient back to the real situation? How can we be surprised that, unlike the queen of Spain, the analyst has legs, when she herself emphasizes the fact in the vigour of her appeals to the order of the present?

Of course, this procedure is far from having nothing to do with the benign outcome of the *acting out*[18] under examination: since the analyst, too, who is of course conscious of the fact, was in a situation of permanent castrating intervention.

But why, then, attribute this role to the mother, when everything in the anamnesis of this case would indicate that she always acted rather as a go-between?

The faltering Oedipus complex was compensated, but always in the form, disarming here in its naïvety, of an entirely forced, not to say arbitrary, reference to the person of the analyst's husband – a situation encouraged here by the fact that it was he, himself a psychiatrist, who provided the analyst with this particular patient.

This is not a very common situation. In any case, it is to be rejected as lying outside the analytic situation.

One's reservations about its outcome are not entirely due to the graceless detours of the analysis, and the no doubt unmischievous humour involving the fees for the last session, as misappropriated for the purpose of debauchery, is no bad sign for the future.

The question that can be raised is that of the boundary between analysis and re-education when its very process is guided by a predominant solicitation of its real effects. As further evidence for which in this case one need only compare the given facts of the biography and the transference formations: any contribution made by the decipherment of the unconscious is truly minimal. So much so that one wonders whether most of it does not remain intact in the encystation of the enigma, which, under the label of transitory perversion, constitutes the object of this instructive communication.

8. But the non-analyst reader should not misunderstand me: I wish in no way to depreciate a work to which Virgil's epithet *improbus* can rightly be applied.

My only purpose is to warn analysts of the decline that threatens their technique if they fail to recognize the true place in which its effects are produced.

They are tireless in their attempts to define that place, and one cannot say that when they back fall on positions of modesty, or even when they are guided by fictions, the experience that they develop is always unfruitful.

Genetic research and direct observation are far from being cut off from properly analytic realities. And in my own treatment of the themes of the object relation in a year's seminar, I showed the value of a conception in which child observation is nourished by the most accurate reconsideration of the function of mothering in the genesis of the object: I mean the notion of the transitional object, introduced by D. W. Winnicott, which is a key-point for the explanation of the genseis of fetichism [27].

Nevertheless, the flagrant uncertainties of the reading of the great Freudian concepts are correlative with the weaknesses that encumber analytic practice.

What I mean is that it is in proportion to the impasses encountered in grasping their action in its authenticity that researchers and groups end up forcing it in the direction of the exercise of power.

They substitute this power for the relation to the being where this action takes place, producing a decline of its resources, especially those of speech, from their veridical eminence. This is why it is a sort of return of the repressed, however strange it may be, which, out of the pretensions least disposed to encumber themselves with the dignity of these means, occasions this blunder of a recourse to being as though it were a given of the real, when the discourse that informs it rejects any interrogation beyond mere platitude.

➤➤◄◄

IV *How to act with one's being*

1. The question of the analyst's being appears very early in the history of analysis. And it should come as no surprise that it should have been introduced by the analyst most tormented by the problem of analytic action. Indeed, it can be said that it was in Ferenczi's article, 'Introjection and Transference', dating from 1909 [3], that the question was first introduced, and that it anticipated by a long way all the themes later developed about this topic.

Although Ferenczi conceived of the transference as the introjection of the person of the doctor into the subjective economy, it was not a question of this person as support for a repetition compulsion, for ill-adapted behaviour, or as a phantasy figure. What he means is the absorption into the economy of the subject of all that the psychoanalyst makes present in the duo as the here and now of an incarnated problematic. Does not

Ferenczi reach the extreme conclusion that the completion of the analysis can be attained only in the avowal made by the doctor to the patient that he, too, can suffer a sense of abandonment?[19]

2. Must one pay this comical price for simply recognizing the subject's want-to-be as the heart of the analytic experience, as the very field in which the neurotic's passion is deployed?

Apart from Ferenczi and the now dispersed Hungarian school, only the English, with their cold objectivity, have been able to articulate this gap, of which the neurotic, in wishing to justify his existence, provides evidence, and hence implicitly to distinguish from the interhuman relation, with its warmth and its allurements (*leurres*), that relation to the Other in which being finds its status.

We have only to cite Ella Sharpe and her very relevant remarks to follow the neurotic's true concerns [24]. The strength of her remarks lies in a sort of naïvety reflected in the justly celebrated brusqueness of her style as both therapist and writer. She is far from ordinary in the extent to which she requires the analyst to be familiar with all branches of human knowledge if he is to read the intentions of the analysand's discourse correctly.

We must be grateful to her for having placed a literary culture in pride of place in the training of practitioners, even if she does not seem to realize that in the minimum reading list that she gives them there is a predominance of works of the imagination in which the signifier of the phallus plays a central role beneath a transparent veil. This simply proves that choice is no less guided by experience for being a felicitous analytic principle.

3. It is again by the British, by birth or by adoption, that the end of the analysis has been most categorically defined by the subject's identification with the analyst. Certainly, opinion varies as to whether it is his ego or superego that is involved. It is not so easy to master the structure that Freud elucidated in the subject, unless one distinguishes between the symbolic, the imaginary, and the real.

It is enough to say that statements made so much with a view to oppose are never forged without some pressure from within those who advance them. The dialectic of phantasy objects promulgated in practice by Melanie Klein tends to be expressed in theory in terms of identification.

For these objects, part- or not, but certainly signifying – the breast, excrement, the phallus – are no doubt won or lost by the subject. He is destroyed by them or he preserves them, but above all he *is* these objects, according to the place where they function in his fundamental phantasy. This mode of identification simply demonstrates the pathology of the slope down which the subject is pushed in a world where his needs are reduced to exchange values – this slope itself finding its radical possibility only in the mortification that the signifier imposes on his life in enumerating it.

4. The psychoanalyst, it would seem, simply in order to help the subject, should be saved from this pathology, which, as we will see, rests on nothing less than an iron law.

This is why people imagine that a psychoanalyst should be a happy man. Indeed, is it not happiness that one is asking of him, and how could he give it, common sense asks, if he did not have it to some extent himself?

It is a fact that we do not disclaim our competence to promise happiness in a period in which the question of its extent has become so complicated: principally because happiness, as Saint-Just said, has become a political factor.

To be fair, the progress of humanism from Aristotle to St Francis (of Sales) did not fill the aporias of happiness either.

It is a waste of time, we know, to look for the shirt of a happy man, and what is called a happy shadow is to be avoided for the ills it brings.

It is certainly in the relation to being that the analyst has to find his operating level, and the opportunities that the training analysis offers him for this purpose are not only to be calculated according to the problem supposedly already resolved for the analyst who is guiding him.

There are unhappinesses of being that the prudence of schools and the false shame that ensures domination dare not cut out of one.

An ethic is yet to be formulated that integrates the Freudian conquests in the realm of desire: one that would place in the forefront the question of the analyst's desire.

5. If one is sensitive to the resonance of earlier work, one cannot fail to be struck by the decline, especially in this order, in analytic speculation.

Because they understand a lot of things, analysts on the whole imagine that to understand is an end in itself, and that it can only be a 'happy end'.[20] The example of the physical sciences may show them, however, that the greatest successes do not require that one knows where one is going.

To think, it is often better not to understand, and one can gallop through miles of understanding without the least thought being produced.

This, indeed, was how the Behaviourists began: they gave up the attempt to understand. But because they lacked any other thought as far as our particular subject, which is *antiphysis*, is concerned they adopted the course of using, without understanding it, what we understand: which, I suppose, could be a source of pride for us.

A sample of what we are capable of producing in fact by way of morality is provided by the notion of oblativity. This is the phantasy of an obsessional neurotic, of itself misunderstood: everything for the other, my fellow man, is offered in it, without recognizing in it the anxiety that the Other (with a capital O) inspires by not being a fellow man.

6. I do not claim to teach psychoanalysts what thinking is. They know. But they did not understand this off their own bat. They learnt their lesson from the psychologists. Thought is an attempt at action, they repeat, like well behaved pupils. (The same can be said of Freud himself, which does not prevent him from being a doughty thinker, whose action culminates in thought.)

The thought of analysts is really an action that undoes itself. This leaves some hope that, if one makes them think about it, take it up again, they will come to think about it again.

7. The analyst is the man to whom one speaks and to whom one speaks freely. That is what he is there for. What does that mean?

All that can be said about the association of ideas is mere psychologistic packaging. Induced puns are far-away; because of their protocol, moreover, nothing could be less free.

The subject invited to speak in analysis does not really reveal a great deal of freedom in what he says. Not that he is bound by the rigour of his associations: no doubt they do oppress him, but it is rather that they open up on to a free speech, a full speech that is painful to him.

Nothing is more to be feared than saying something that might be true. For if it were, it would become entirely so, and God knows what happens when something, by the very fact of its being true, can no longer be doubted.

Is that the method used in analysis – a progress towards truth? I can already hear the apprentices murmuring that I intellectualize analysis: though I am in the very act, I believe, of preserving the unsayable aspect of it.

That it is beyond the discourse accommodated by our listening, I know better than anyone, if only I take the trouble to hear, and not to auscultate. Yes certainly not the way of auscultating the resistance, the tension, the opisthotonos, the pallor, the adrenalinic (*sic*) discharge in which a stronger (*resic*) ego should be re-formed: what I listen to comes from hearing.

Hearing does not force me to understand. What I hear is nonetheless a discourse, even if it is as little discursive as an interjection. For an interjection is of the order of language and not of the expressive cry. It is a part of the discourse that is unrivalled for its syntactical effects in a particular language.

To what I hear, I have nothing more to say if I understand nothing, and if I do understand something I am sure to be mistaken. However, this is not what would stop me from replying. It's what happens outside analysis in such a case. I keep quiet. Everybody agrees that I frustrate the speaker, him first, but me too. Why?

If I frustrate him it is because he asks me for something. To answer him, in fact. But he knows very well that it would be mere words. And he can get those from whomever he likes. It's not even certain that he'd be grateful to me if they were good words, let alone if they were bad ones. It's not these words he's asking for. He is simply asking me . . . , from the very fact that he is speaking: his demand is intransitive, it carries no object with it.

Of course, his demand is deployed on the field of an implicit demand, that for which he is there: the demand to cure him, to reveal him to himself, to introduce him to psychoanalysis, to help him to qualify as an analyst. But, as he knows, this demand can wait. His present demand has nothing to do with this, it is not even his own, for after all it is I who have offered to speak to him. (Only the subject is transitive here.)

In short, I have succeeded in doing what in the field of ordinary commerce one would dearly like to be able to do with such ease: with supply I have created demand.

8. But it is, one might say, a radical demand.

Mrs Macalpine is no doubt right to seek the motive force of the transference in the analytic rule alone. But she errs in attributing to the absence of all object the open door to infantile regression [24]. This would seem to be an obstacle, for, as everyone knows, child analysts more than anyone, it takes a lot of little objects to keep up a relation with children.

Through the mediation of the demand, the whole past opens up right down to early infancy. The subject has never done anything other than demand, he could not have survived otherwise, and we just follow on from there.

It is in this way that analytic regression may take place and present itself in effect. One talks of it as if the subject set out to be a child. That no doubt happens, and such pretence is not a very good omen. It stands out in any case from what is usually observed in what passes for regression. For regression shows nothing other than a return to the present of signifiers used in demands for which there is prescription.

9. To return once more to the beginning, this situation explains the primary transference, and the love that is sometimes declared in it.

For if love is giving what one does not have, it is certainly true that the subject can wait to be given it, since the psychoanalyst has nothing else to give him. But he does not even give him this nothing, and it is just as well: and that is why he is paid for this nothing, preferably well paid, in order to show that it would not otherwise be worth much.

But although the primary transference generally remains little more than a shadow, it is not this that prevents the shadow from dreaming and reproducing his demand when there is nothing left to demand. This demand will be all the purer for being empty.

Nonetheless, it may be objected, the analyst gives his presence, but I believe that this presence is first of all simply the implication of his listening, and that this listening is simply the condition of speech. Furthermore why does the technique require that he should be so discreet if, in fact, this is not the case? It is only later that his presence will be felt.

Anyway, the most acute feeling of his presence is bound up with a moment when the subject can only remain silent, that is to say, when he even recoils before the shadow of demand.

Thus the analyst is he who supports the demand, not, as has been said, to frustrate the subject, but in order to allow the signifiers in which his frustration is bound up to reappear.

10. It is worth recalling that it is in the oldest demand that the primary identification is produced, that which is brought about by the mother's omnipotence, that is to say, the identification that not only suspends the satisfaction of needs from the signifying apparatus, but also that which fragments them, filters them, models them upon the defiles of the structure of the signifier.

Needs become subordinated to the same conventional conditions as those of the signifier in its double register: the synchronic register of opposition between irreducible elements, and the diachronic register of substitution and combination, through which language, even if it does not fulfil all functions, structures everything concerning relations between human beings.

Hence the oscillation that is to be observed in Freud's statements concerning the relations between the superego and reality. The superego is not, of course, the source of reality, as he says somewhere, but it marks out the paths that reality will take, before rediscovering in the unconscious the first ideal marks in which the drives are constituted as repressed in the substitution of the signifier for needs.

11. There is now no need to seek further for the source of the identification with the analyst. That identification may assume very different forms, but it will always be an identification with signifiers.

As an analysis develops, the analyst deals in turn with all the articulations of the subject's demand. But, as I will point out later, he must respond to them only from the position of the transference.

Who, in fact, emphasizes the importance of what might be called the permissive hypothesis of the analysis? But we need no particular political régime for that which is not forbidden to become obligatory.

Those analysts who might be said to be fascinated by the sequellae of frustration hold no more than a position of suggestion that reduces the subject to restate his demand. May be that is what is meant by emotional re-education.

Kindness is no doubt as necessary there as everywhere else, but it would be incapable of curing the evil that it engenders. The analyst who desires the subject's well-being repeats that by which he was formed, and sometimes, even, deformed. The most aberrant education has never had any other motive than the well-being of the subject.

A theory of analysis is conceived which, unlike the delicate articulation of Freud's analysis, reduces the source of symptoms to fear. It engenders a practice in which what I have called elsewhere the obscene, ferocious figure of the superego is imprinted, in which there is no other way out of the transference neurosis than to make the patient sit down by the window and show him all the pleasant aspects of nature, adding: 'Go out there. Now you're a good child [22].'

꠹꠹

V *Desire must be taken literally*

1. After all, a dream is just a dream, one sometimes hears these days [22]. Does it mean nothing that Freud should have recognized in it the workings of desire?

Desire, not the drives. For we must read 'The Interpretation of Dreams' to discover what is meant by what Freud calls in that essay 'desire'.

We must pause at the vocables *Wunsch* and its English translation *wish*, and draw a distinction between them and the French *désir* (desire); the sound of a damp squib in which the German and English words explode suggests nothing less than concupiscence. Their French equivalent is rather *voeu*.

These *voeux* may be pious, nostalgic, thwarting, humorous. A lady may have a dream that is animated by no other desire than to provide Freud, who has explained to her the theory that the dream is an expression of a desire, with proof that they are nothing of the kind. The point to be remembered is that this desire is articulated in an extremely clever discourse. But in order to understand what desire means in his thinking, it is no less important to perceive the consequences of the fact that Freud was satisfied to recognize in that discourse the desire of the dream and the confirmation of its law.

For he extends its eccentricity still further – a dream involving punishment may very well signify the desire for what the punishment is repressing.

But let us not stop at the labels on the drawers, though many people confuse them with the fruits of science. Let us read the texts; let us follow Freud's thinking in the twists and turns that it imposes on us, and not forget that in deploring them himself, when seen from the standpoint of an ideal of scientific discourse, he affirms that he was forced into them by the object of his study.[21]

One then sees that this object is identical with those twists and turns, since at the first turning point of his work, when dealing with the dream of a hysteric, he stumbled on the fact that by a process of displacement, in this case specifically by allusion to the desire of another woman, a desire from the previous day is satisfied – a desire that is maintained in its dominant position by a desire that is of a quite different order, since Freud orders it as the desire for an unsatisfied desire [7].[22]

One should try and count the number of substitutions that operate here to bring desire to a geometrically increasing power. A single index would not be enough to characterize the degree. For it would be necessary to distinguish two dimensions in these substitutions: a desire for desire, in other words, a desire signified by a desire (in the case of the hysteric, the desire to have an unsatisfied desire is signified by her desire for caviar: the desire for caviar is its signifier), is inscribed in the different register of one desire substituted for another (in the dream, the desire for smoked salmon, which belonged to the patient's friend, was substituted for the patient's own desire for caviar, which constitutes the substitution of one signifier for another).[23]

2. What we find, then, is in no way microscopic, any more than there is any need of special instruments to recognize that the leaf has the structural features of the plant from which it has been detached. Even if one had never seen a plant with its leaves on, one would realize at once that a leaf is more likely to be a part of a plant than a piece of skin.

The desire of the hysteric's dream, and indeed any other snippet in this text of Freud summarizes what the whole book explains about the so-called unconscious mechanisms, condensation, sliding (*glissement*), etc., by bearing witness to their common structure: that is, the relation of desire to that mark of language that specifies the Freudian unconscious and decentres our conception of the subject.

I think my pupils will appreciate the access that I provide here to the fundamental opposition between the signifier and the signified, in which, as I show them, the powers of language begin, though in conceiving the exercise of these powers I leave them plenty of rope to twist.

Let me recall to your attention the automatism of the laws by which are articulated in the signifying chain:

(a) the substitution of one term for another to produce the effect of metaphor;
(b) the combination of one term with another to produce the effect of metonymy [17].

If we apply them here, we see that whereas in our patient's dream the smoked salmon, the object of her friend's desire, is all that she has to offer, Freud, by suggesting that the smoked salmon is substituted here for caviar, which, indeed, he considers to be the signifier of the patient's desire, is presenting the dream as a metaphor of desire.

But what is metaphor if not an effect of positive meaning, that is, a certain passage from the subject to the meaning of the desire?

Since the subject's desire is presented here as that which is implied by her (conscious) discourse, that is to say as preconscious – which is obvious enough since her husband is willing to satisfy her desire, but the patient, who persuaded him of the existence of this desire, insists that he should do nothing about it, and it has to be Freud again who articulates it as the desire for an unsatisfied desire – one must go further if one is to learn what such a desire means in the unconscious.

Now the dream is not the unconscious itself, but, as Freud points out, the royal way to it. This confirms me in the belief that it proceeds by means of metaphor. It is this metaphorical effect that the dream uncovers. But for whom? We shall return to this later.

Let us observe for the moment that if the desire is signified as unsatisfied, it does so through the signifier: caviar, *qua* signifier, symbolizes the desire as inaccessible, but, as soon as it slips as desire into the caviar, the desire for caviar becomes its metonymy – rendered necessary by the want-to-be in which it is situated.

Metonymy is, as I have shown you, the effect made possible by the fact that there is no signification that does not refer to another signification, and in which their common denominator is produced, namely the little meaning (frequently confused with the insignificant), the little meaning, I say, that proves to lie at the basis of the desire, and lends it that element of perversion that it would be tempting to find in this case of hysteria.

The truth of this appearance is that the desire is the metonymy of the want-to-be.

3. Let us now return to the book we call *La science des rêves* (*Traumdeutung*) – though perhaps *mantique*, or, better, *signifiance* would be a better translation than *science*.[24]

In this book, Freud certainly does not claim to exhaust the psychological problems of the dream. One has only to read it to realize that Freud does not touch on a number of problems that have still been largely ignored (little work of value has been done on space and time in the dream, on the sensorial raw material of the dream, on whether one dreams in colour or in black and white, on whether smell, taste and touch occur, or the sense of vertigo, of the turgid and the heavy). To say that Freudian doctrine is a psychology is a crude equivocation.

Freud does nothing to encourage such an equivocation. On the contrary, he warns us that he is interested only in the elaboration of the dream. What does that mean? It means exactly what we would now call its linguistic structure. How could Freud be aware of this structure, when it was articulated only at a later date by Ferdinand de Saussure? If the two terms are synonymous, it is all the more striking that Freud should have anticipated Saussure. But where did Freud discover this structure? He discovered it in a signifying flow, the mystery of which lies in the fact that the subject does not even know where to pretend to be its organizer.

To do so, to find oneself as the desirer is the opposite of getting oneself recognized as the subject of it, for it is as a derivation of the signifying chain that the channel of desire flows, and the subject must have the advantage of a cross-over to catch his own *feed-back*.

Desire merely subjects what analysis makes subjective.

4. And this brings us back to the question touched on above: to whom does the dream reveal its meaning before the arrival on the scene of the analyst? This meaning exists prior to being read, just as it exists prior to its decipherment.

Both show that the dream is made for the recognition – I have taken a long time to get to it – of desire. For desire, if what Freud says of the unconscious is right and if analysis is necessary, can be grasped only in interpretation.

But let us continue: the elaboration of the dream is nourished by desire. Why does my voice fail to finish, out of recognition, as if the second word was extinguished which, a little while ago the first, re-absorbed the other in its light. For, in fact, it is not while one is asleep that one is recognized. And the dream, Freud tells us, without appearing to be aware of the slightest contradiction, serves above all the desire to sleep. It is a narcissistic folding back of the *libido* and a disinvestment of reality.

Moreover, we know from experience that if my dream overtakes my demand (not reality, as has incorrectly been said, which may preserve my sleep), or what is shown here to be equivalent to it, the demand of the other, I awake.

5. After all, a dream is only a dream. Those who now disdain it as a tool of analysis have found, as we have seen, safer and more direct ways of bringing the patient back to right thinking and normal desires – those that satisfy true needs. Which needs, though? Well, the needs that we all feel. If that scares you, you'd better go and see your analyst, and go up the Eiffel Tower to see how beautiful Paris is. Too bad that there are some who climb over the railings at the first floor, and precisely those whose needs have been reduced to proper size. A negative therapeutic reaction, I would say.

Thank God, refusal does not go so far in everyone! It's just that the sympton reappears like weeds – repetition compulsion.

But that, of course, is merely a misdeal: one is not cured because one remembers. One remembers because one is cured. Ever since this formula was discovered, the reproduction of symptoms is no longer a problem – only the reproduction of analysts is a problem. The reproduction of patients has been resolved.

6. So a dream is only a dream. One psychoanalyst who dabbles in teaching has even written that the dream is a production of the ego. This proves that one runs no great risk in wishing to waken men from their

dreams: here's one that is going on in broad daylight, and among those who hardly allow themselves to dream.

But even for these people, if they are psychoanalysts, Freud on dreams must be read, because it is not otherwise possible to understand what he means by the neurotic's desire, by repressed, by unconscious, by inter-pretation, by analysis itself, or to approach his technique and his doctrine in any way at all. We will see how important the little dream that I picked out above is for my purpose.

For this desire of our witty hysteric (Freud's own description) – I mean her aroused desire, her desire for caviar – is the desire of a woman who has everything, and who rejects precisely that. For her butcher husband is adept at supplying the satisfactions that everyone needs, he dots the 'i's, and he does not mince his words to a painter who is chatting her up, God knows with what end in view, on the subject of her interesting face: 'Nuts! a slice of the backside of some pretty shit is what you need, and if you think I'm going to supply you with it, you can go and jump in the lake.'

There's a man a woman could have nothing to complain about, a genital character, and one, therefore, who no doubt sees to it that, when he fucks his wife, she has no need to masturbate afterwards. In any case, Freud does not hide the fact that she is very much in love with him, and provokes him constantly.

But there you are, she doesn't want to be satisfied only at the level of her real needs. She wants other, gratuitous needs, and to be sure that they are gratuitous they must be satisfied. This is why to the question, 'What does the witty butcher's wife want?', we can reply, 'Caviar'. But this reply is hopeless, because she also does not want it.

7. But that isn't all there is to say about her mystery. Far from im-prisoning her, this impasse provides her with the key to the fields, the key to the field of the desires of all the witty hysterics, whether butchers' wives or not, in the world.

This is what Freud grasps in one of those sidelong looks with which he surprises the true, shattering on his way the abstractions to which positivist minds so readily lend themselves as an explanation for every-thing: what we have here is the imitation dear to Tarde. In each particular case one must activate the mainspring that he provides there – namely, hysterical identification. If our patient identifies with her friend, it is because she is inimitable in her unsatisfied desire for this goddamned salmon – if God doesn't smoke it himself!

Thus the patient's dream corresponds to her friend's request for her to come and dine at her home. And what would make her want to do so, other than that one dines well there, if not the fact, which our butcher's wife never loses sight of, namely, that her husband always speaks well of her. But thin as she is, she is hardly built to attract him, with his taste for curves.

Has he too, perhaps, not got a desire that is somewhat thwarted, when everything in him is satisfied? It is the same mechanism which, in the dream, will, with the desire of her friend, cause the failure of her demand.

For however precisely symbolized the demand may be by means of the new-born telephone, it goes for nothing. The appeal of the patient does not reach its goal; a fine thing it would be to see the other get fatter so that her husband can feast himself on her.

But how can another woman be loved (isn't it enough, for the patient to think about it, that her husband should consider her?) by a man who cannot be satisfied by her (he, the man of the slice of backside)? That's precisely the question, which is usually that of hysterical identification, brought into focus.

8. Even here this question becomes the subject – the question in which the woman identifies herself with the man, and the slice of smoked salmon takes the place of the desire of the Other.

Since this desire is totally inadequate (how can one receive all these people with only one slice of smoked salmon?), I really must when all (or the dream) is said and done give up my desire to give a dinner (that is, my search for the desire of the Other, which is the secret of my desire). Everything has gone wrong, and you say that the dream is wish-fulfilment. How do you work that one out, professor?

For a long time now psychoanalysts have given up answering when questioned in this way, for they have ceased to question themselves about their patients' desires: they reduce these desires to their demands, which makes the task of converting them into their own that much easier. Isn't that the reasonable way? – it is certainly the one they have adopted.

But sometimes desire is not to be conjured away, but appears as here, at the centre of the stage, all too visibly, on the festive board, in the form of a salmon. It is an attractive-looking fish, and if it is presented, as is the custom in restaurants, under a thin gauze, the raising of this gauze creates a similar effect to that which occurred at the culmination of the ancient mysteries.

To be the phallus, if only a somewhat thin one. Was not that the ultimate identification with the signifier of desire?

That does not look like being self-evident for a woman, and there are those among us who prefer to have nothing more to do with this word-puzzle. Are we going to have to spell out the role of the signifier only to find that we have the castration complex and penis envy – which, God knows, we could be well rid of – on our hands? When Freud reached that particular juncture, he found himself at a loss as to how to extricate himself, seeing ahead of him merely the desert of analysis.

Yes, he led them to that point, and it was a less infested place than the transference neurosis, which reduces you to chasing the patient, while at the same time begging him to go slowly so as to take his flies with him.

9. But let us articulate that which structures desire.

Desire is that which is manifested in the interval that demand hollows within itself, in as much as the subject, in articulating the signifying chain, brings to light the want-to-be, together with the appeal to receive the complement from the Other, if the Other, the locus of speech, is also the locus of this want, or lack.

That which is thus given to the Other to fill, and which is strictly that which it does not have, since it, too, lacks being, is what is called love, but it is also hate and ignorance.

It is also what is evoked by any demand beyond the need that is articulated in it, and it is certainly that of which the subject remains all the more deprived to the extent that the need articulated in the demand is satisfied.

Furthermore, the satisfaction of need appears only as the lure in which the demand for love is crushed, by sending the subject back to sleep, where he haunts the limbo regions of being, by letting it speak in him. For the being of language is the non-being of objects, and the fact that desire was discovered by Freud in its place in the dream, which has always been the stumbling-block of any attempt on the part of thought to situate itself in reality, should be sufficient lesson for us.

To be or not to be, to sleep, perchance to dream, even the so-called simplest dreams of the child (as 'simple' as the analytic situation, no doubt) simply show miraculous or forbidden objects.

10. But the child does not always fall asleep in this way in the bosom of being, especially if the Other, which has its own ideas about his needs, interferes, and in place of that which it does not have, stuffs him with the choking pap of what it has, that is to say, confuses his needs with the gift of its love.

It is the child one feeds with most love who refuses food and plays with his refusal as with a desire (anorexia nervosa).

Confines where one grasps as nowhere else that hate pays the coin of love, but where it is ignorance that is unforgivable.

In the final analysis, by refusing to satisfy the mother's demand, is not the child demanding that the mother should have a desire outside him, because the way towards the desire that he lacks is to be found there?

11. One of the principles that follow from this is that:

– if desire is an effect in the subject of the condition that is imposed on him by the existence of the discourse, to make his need pass through the defiles of the signifier;

– if, on the other hand, as I have intimated above, by opening up the dialectic of the transference, we must establish the notion of the Other with a capital O as being the locus of the deployment of speech (the other scene, *ein andere Schauplatz*, of which Freud speaks in 'The Interpretation of Dreams');

– it must be posited that, produced as it is by an animal at the mercy of language, man's desire is the desire of the Other.

This concerns a quite different function from that of the primary identification referred to above, for it does not involve the assumption by the subject of the insignia of the other, but rather the condition that the subject has to find the constituting structure of his desire in the same gap opened up by the effect of the signifiers in those who come to represent the Other for him, in so far as his demand is subjected to them.

Perhaps one can catch a glimpse in passing of the reason for his effect of occultation that caught our attention in the recognition of the desire of the dream. The desire of the dream is not assumed by the subject who says 'I' in his speech. Articulated, nevertheless, in the locus of the Other, it is discourse – a discourse whose grammar Freud has begun to declare to be such. Thus the wishes that it constitutes have no optative inflexion to alter the indicative of their formula.

Looking at this from a linguistic point of view, we can see that what is called the aspect of the verb is here that of the 'perfect', the fulfilled (in the true sense of *Wunscherfüllung*).

It is this ex-sistence (*Entstellung*)[25] of desire in the dream that explains how the significance of the dream masks the desire that is present in it, whereas its motive vanishes by being simply problematic.

12. Desire is produced in the beyond of the demand, in that, in articulating the life of the subject according to its conditions, demand cuts off the need from that life. But desire is also hollowed within the demand, in that, as an unconditional demand of presence and absence, demand evokes the want-to-be under the three figures of the nothing that constitutes the basis of the demand for love, of the hate that even denies the other's being, and of the unspeakable element in that which is ignored in its request. In this embodied aporia, of which one might say that it borrows, as it were, its heavy soul from the hardy shoots of the wounded drive, and its subtle body from the death actualized in the signifying sequence, desire is affirmed as the absolute condition.

Even less than the nothing that passes into the round of significations that act upon men, desire is the furrow inscribed in the course; it is, as it were, the mark of the iron of the signifier on the shoulder of the speaking subject. It is not so much a pure passion of the signified as a pure action of the signifier that stops at the moment when the living being becomes sign, rendering it insignificant.

This moment of cut is haunted by the form of a bloody scrap – the pound of flesh that life pays in order to turn it into the signifier of the signifiers, which it is impossible to restore, as such, to the imaginary body; it is the lost phallus of the embalmed Osiris.

13. The function of this signifier as such in the quest of desire is, as Freud mapped it out, the key to what we need to know in order to terminate his analyses: and no artifice can take its place if we are to achieve that end.

To give some idea of this function, I will describe an incident that occurred at the end of the analysis of an obsessional neurotic, that is, after a great deal of work in which I was not content 'to analyse the subject's aggressivity' (in other words, to play blind man's buff with his imaginary aggressions), but in which he was made to recognize the place that he had assumed in the play of destruction exerted by one of his parents on the desire of the other. He guessed at his powerlessness to desire without destroying the Other, and hence his desire itself in so far as it is desire of the Other.

To arrive at this stage, he was shown how at every moment he manipulated the situation so as to protect the Other, by exhausting in the working-through (*Durcharbeitung*) all the artifices of a verbalization that distinguishes the other from the Other (with a small o and a capital O), and which, from the box reserved for the boredom of the Other (capital O)

makes it arrange the circus acts between the two others (the *petit* a and
the ego, its shadow).

Certainly, it is not enough to go round in circles in some well-explored
area of obsessional neurosis in order to bring him to this round-about,
or to know this round-about in order to bring him to it by a route that
will never be the shortest. What is needed is not only the plan of a reconstructed labyrinth, or even a batch of plans already drawn up. What is
needed above all is to possess the general combinatory that governs their
variety certainly, but which also, even more usefully, accounts for the
illusions, or rather shifts of perspective to be found in the labyrinth. For
there is no shortage of either in obsessional neurosis, which is an archi-
tecture of contrasts – a fact that has not yet been sufficiently remarked
on – which it is not enough to attribute to forms of façade. In the midst
of so many seductive, insurgent, impassive attitudes, we must grasp the
anxieties that are bound up with the performances, the rancour that does
not impede his generosity (to think that anyone could hold that obsessional neurotics are lacking in oblativity!), the mental inconstancies
that sustain unbreakable loyalties. All this moves together in an analysis,
though not without local blemishes; but the great load remains.

And so our subject has come to the end of his tether, to the point at
which he can play a rather special three-card trick on us, in that it partially
reveals a structure of desire.

Let me say that being as he is of mature years, as the comical phrase
goes, and of a mind shorn of illusions, he would be quite ready to mislead
us with his menopause in order to excuse his own impotence, and to
accuse me of the same.

In fact, the redistributions of the libido are not brought about without
certain objects losing their function, even if they are non-detachable.

In short, he is impotent with his mistress, and, having taken it into his
head to use his discoveries about the function of the potential third person
in the couple, he suggests that she sleep with another man to see.

But if she remains in the place given her by the neurosis and if the
analysis effects her in that position it is because of the agreement that no
doubt she long ago made with the patient's desires, but still more with
the unconscious postulates that were maintained by those desires.

And it will come as no surprise to learn that without stopping, even at
night, she has this dream, which, freshly minted, she brings to our unfortunate patient.

She has a phallus, she feels its shape under her clothes, which does not prevent her from having a vagina as well, nor, of course, from wanting this phallus to enter it.

On hearing this, our patient is immediately restored to his virility and demonstrates this quite brilliantly to his partner.

What interpretation is indicated here?

I guessed from the demand that my patient had addressed to his mistress that he had been trying for a long time to get me to confirm his repressed homosexuality.

This was an effect of his discovery of the unconscious that Freud was very quick to anticipate: among the regressive demands, one of the fables will be based on the truths spread by analysis. Analysis on its return trip from America exceeded his expectations.

But I have remained, it is thought, somewhat difficult to persuade on that point.

Let me observe that the dreamer is no more complaisant, since her scenario excludes any coadjutor. This would guide even a novice to trust only the text, if he is trained according to my principles.

Yet I am analysing not her dream, but its effect on my patient.

It would run counter to my practice if I got him to read in the dream this truth, less widespread for having passed into history, of my own contribution: that the refusal of castration, if anything is like it, is first of all a refusal of the castration of the Other (initially, the mother).

A true opinion is not science, and conscience without science is merely the complicity of ignorance. Our science is transmitted only by articulating what is particular in the situation.

Here the situation is unique in showing the figure that I state in these terms; that unconscious desire is the desire of the Other – since the dream is produced in order to satisfy the patient's desire beyond his demand, as is suggested by the fact that it succeeds in doing so. Though not a dream of the patient's it may be no less precious for the analyst if, while not addressed to the analyst, unlike the patient's report, it addresses the patient as clearly as the analyst is able to do so.

It is an opportunity to get the patient to grasp the signifying function that the phallus has in his desire. For it is as such that the phallus operates in the dream in order to enable him to recover the use of the organ that it represents, as I will show by the place at which the dream is aimed in the structure within which his desire is trapped.

Apart from what the woman dreamt, there is the fact that she talks to him about it. If, in this discourse, she presents herself as having the phallus, is that the only way in which her erotic value is restored to her? Having a phallus, in effect, is not enough to restore her to an object position that appropriates her to a phantasy from which, as an obsessional neurotic, our patient can maintain his desire in an impossibility that preserves its metonymic conditions. The choices left open by these conditions govern a game of escape that analysis has disturbed, but which the woman restores here by a ruse, the crudeness of which conceals a refinement well fitted to illustrate the science included in the unconscious.

For, as far as our patient is concerned, it is no good having this phallus, since his desire is to be it. And the woman's desire cedes it here to his, by showing him that she does not have it.

Undiscriminating observation will always make much of the announcement of a castrating mother, however little importance the anamnesis gives it. She looms large here, which is as it should be.

One then thinks that one has finished. But we have nothing to do with it in the interpretation, where to invoke it would not take us very far, except to bring the patient back to the same point where he slips between a desire and contempt for that desire: certainly the contempt of his ill-tempered mother decrying his father's over keen desire the image of which his father bequeathed him.

But it would be not so much to teach him about it, as what his mistress *said* to him: that having this phallus did not diminish her desire for it. And here it is his own want-to-be that has been touched on.

A want that is the result of an exodus: his being is always elsewhere. He has put it 'on the left', one might say. Do we say this in order to explain the difficulty of the desire? No, rather to say that the desire is constituted by difficulty.

We must not be misled, therefore, by this assurance that the subject receives from the fact that the dreamer has a phallus, that she will not have to take it from him – except to point out, wisely, that such an assurance is too strong not to be fragile.

For that would be precisely to fail to recognize that this assurance would not exert so much weight if it did not have to impress itself in a sign, and that it is by showing this sign as such, by making it appear where it cannot be, that it has its effect.

The condition of desire that confines the obsessional neurotic in particular is the very mark of the origin of his object, which spoils it for him – contraband.

A singular mode of grace: which appears only on the basis of a denial of nature. A favour is hidden there and in our subject it is always made to wait. And it is in dismissing it that one day he will let it enter.

14. The importance of preserving the place of desire in the direction of treatment necessitates that one should orientate this place in relation to the effects of demand, which alone are at present conceived as the principle of the power of the treatment.

The fact that the genital act should, in effect, have found its place in the unconscious articulation of desire is the discovery of analysis, and it is precisely because of this that one has never thought of giving in to the patient's illusion that to facilitate his demand for the satisfaction of need would be of any help to him. (Still less to authorize him with the classic: *coitus normalis dosim repetatur.*)

Why does one think differently in believing it to be more essential for the progress of the treatment to operate in any way on other demands, under the pretext that they are regressive?

Let us set out once again with the notion that, because it is produced in the locus of the Other, it is first of all for the subject that his speech is a message. By virtue of this fact even his demand originates in the locus of the Other, and is signed and dated as such. This is not only because it is subjected to the code of the Other, but also because it is marked by this locus (and even the time) of the Other.

This can be clearly seen in the subject's most spontaneous speech. To his wife or to her master, so that they should receive his profession of faith, it is with a 'you're . . .' (one or other) that he refers to them, without declaring what he is other than by murmuring against himself an order of murder that the equivocation of the French brings to the ear.

Although it always shows through demand, as can be seen here, desire is nonetheless beyond it. It also falls short of another demand in which the subject, reverberating in the locus of the other, not so much effaces his dependence by a return agreement as fixes the very being that he has proposed there.

This means that it is only through a speech that lifted the prohibition that the subject has brought to bear upon himself by his own words that he might obtain the absolution that would give him back his desire.

But desire is simply the impossibility of such speech, which, in replying to the first can merely reduplicate its mark of prohibition by completing the split (*Spaltung*) which the subject undergoes by virtue of being a subject only in so far as he speaks.

(Which is symbolized by the oblique bar of noble bastardy that I attach to the S of the subject in order to indicate that it is that subject, thus \$.)[26]

The regression that is placed in the forefront in analysis (temporal regression no doubt, providing one specifies that it is a question of the time of recollection) concerns only the signifiers (oral, anal, etc.) of demand, and involves the corresponding drive only through them.

Reducing this demand to its place may operate on desire an appearance of reduction by the alleviation of need.

But this is really only the effect of the analyst's heavy approach. For if the signifiers of demand have sustained the frustrations in which desire is fixed (Freud's *Fixierung*), it is only in their place that desire is a source of subjection.

Whether it intends to frustrate or to gratify, any reply to demand in analysis brings the transference back to suggestion.

Between the transference and suggestion, there is, as Freud discovered, a relation. The fact is that the transference is also a suggestion, but one that can operate only on the basis of the demand for love, which is not a demand arising from any need. That this demand is constituted only in so far as the subject is the subject of the signifier is what allows it to be misused by reducing it to the needs from which these signifiers have been borrowed – which is what psychoanalysts, as we know, never fail to do.

But identification with the all-powerful signifier of demand, of which I have already spoken, must not be confused with identification with the object of the demand for love. This demand for love is also a regression, as Freud insists, when it produces the second mode of identification, which he distinguished in his second topography when he wrote *Group Psychology and the Analysis of the Ego*. But it is another kind of regression.

There is the exit that enables one to emerge from suggestion. Identification with the object as regression, because it sets out from the demand for love, opens up the sequence of the transference (opens up, not closes it), that is to say, the way by which the identifications that, in blocking this regression, punctuate it, can be denounced.

But this regression is no more dependent on the need in demand than sadistic desire is explained by anal demand, for to believe that the *scybale* is in itself a noxious object is simply one of the ordinary lures of understanding. ('Understanding' in the pejorative sense given the word by Jaspers. 'You understand . . .' is an introductory phrase by which someone who has nothing to be understood thinks he can impose on someone else who understands nothing.) But the demand to be a turd, that's something that makes it preferable to move a little to one side when the subject becomes aware of it. It's the 'misery of being' (*malheur de l'être*) referred to above.

Whoever cannot carry his training analyses to the turning-point at which it is proved with fear and trembling that all the demands that have been articulated in the analysis, and more than any other the original demand to become an analyst, which is now about to be fulfilled, were merely transferences intended to maintain in place a desire that was unstable or dubious in its problematic – such a person knows nothing of what must be obtained from the subject if he is to be able to assume the direction of an analysis, or merely offer an accurate interpretation of it.

These considerations confirm me in the belief that it is natural to analyse the transference. For the transference is already, in itself, an analysis of suggestion, in so far as it places the subject with regard to his demand in a position that he holds only because of his desire.

It is only in order to maintain this framework of the transference that frustration must prevail over gratification.

When the subject's resistance opposes suggestion, it is only a desire to maintain the subject's desire. As such, it would have to be placed in the ranks of the positive transference, since it is desire that maintains the direction of the analysis, quite apart from the effects of demand.

As we see, these propositions are rather different from the received opinions on this matter. If only they lead people to think that something has gone wrong somewhere, I will have succeeded in my aim.

15. This is the place for a few remarks on the formation of symptoms.

Ever since Freud wrote his study of such subjective phenomena as dreams, slips of the tongue and flashes of wit, which, he says quite categorically, are structurally identical with symptoms (but, of course, as far as our scientists are concerned, all this falls too short of the experimental knowledge that they have acquired – and by what means! – for them even to consider returning to it) – Freud, as I was saying, stressed over and over again that symptoms are overdetermined. For the worker employed in the daily threshing that holds out the promise of a future reduction of analysis to its biological bases, this is obvious enough; it is so easy to say that he does not even hear it. So what?

Let us leave to one side my remarks on the fact that overdetermination is strictly speaking only conceivable within the structure of language. What does this mean, as far as neurotic symptoms are concerned?

It means that interference will occur between the effects that correspond in a subject to a particular demand and the effects of a position in relation to the other (here, his counterpart) that he sustains as subject.

'That he sustains as subject' means that language allows him to regard himself as the scene-shifter, or even the director of the entire imaginary capture of which he would otherwise be nothing more than the living marionette.

Phantasy is the perfect illustration of this original possibility. That is why any temptation to reduce it to the imagination, because one cannot admit its failure, is a permanent misconception, a misconception from which the Kleinian school, which has certainly carried things very far in this field, is not free, largely because it has been incapable of even so much as suspecting the existence of the category of the signifier.

However, once it is defined as an image set to work in the signifying structure, the notion of the unconscious phantasy no longer presents any difficulty.

Let us say that in its fundamental use the phantasy is that by which the subject sustains himself at the level of his vanishing desire, vanishing in so far as the very satisfaction of demand hides his object from him.

Oh, these neurotics are so fussy! What can we do with them? You can't understand a word they say, as one father put it.

But this is precisely what was said long ago, and has always been said, yet the analysts don't seem to have got any further. The simple minded call it the irrational, since they haven't even realized that Freud's discovery is confirmed first by regarding as certain that the real is rational – which, in itself, was enough to knock our exegete off balance – and then by affirming that the rational is real. As a result, Freud can articulate the fact that what presents itself as unreasonable in desire is an effect of the passage of the rational in so far as it is real – that is to say, the passage of language – into the real, in so far as the rational has already traced its circumvallation there.

For the paradox of desire is not the privilege of the neurotic; it is rather that he takes the existence of paradox into account when confronting desire. This does not give him such a bad position in the order of human dignity, and does no honour to mediocre analysts (this is not an assessment, but an ideal formulated in a wish, overtly expressed, of the interested parties), who on this point do not achieve the same dignity: a surprising distance that analysts have always noted somewhat cryptically ... others, though I don't know how they can be distinguished, since they would never have thought of doing it themselves, if they had first had to oppose the errors of the former.

16. It is, then, the position of the neurotic with regard to desire, let us say by way of abbreviating the phantasy, that marks with his presence the subject's response to demand, in other words the signification of his need.

But this phantasy has nothing to do with the signification in which it interferes. Indeed, this signification comes from the Other, in so far as it depends on the Other whether the demand is satisfied. But the phantasy arrives there only to find itself on the return journey of a wider circuit, a circuit that, in carrying demand to the limits of being, makes the subject question himself as to the lack in which he appears to himself as desire.

It is incredible that certain features, which have nevertheless always been obvious enough, of man's action as such should not have been illuminated here by analysis. I wish to speak about that by which this action of man is the *geste* that finds support in his *chanson*.[27] This side of exploit, of performance, of outcome strangled by symbol, that which makes it symbolic therefore (but not in the alienating sense that this term denotes for the layman), that for which one speaks of *passage à l'acte*, that Rubicon whose own desire is always concealed in the history to the benefit of its success, all that to which the experience of what the analyst calls 'acting out',[28] gives it a quasi-experimental access, since he shares in its entire artifice, the analyst reduces it at best to a relapse of the subject, at worst to a fault on the part of the therapist.

One is stupified by this false shame displayed by the analyst in the face of action – shame that no doubt conceals true shame, the shame that he has about an action, his own action, one of the highest, when it descends to abjection.

For what else, in fact, is it, when the analyst interposes in order to degrade the message of the transference that he is there to interpret, in a fallacious signification of the real that is nothing more than mystification.

For the point at which the present-day analyst claims to grasp the transference is the distance he defines between the phantasy and the so-called adapted response. But adapted to what if not to the demand of the Other, and in what would this demand have greater or lesser consistency than the response obtained, if he did not believe that he was authorized to deny all value to the phantasy to the extent that it takes on its own reality?

Here the very path by which he proceeds betrays him, when it is necessary for him to introduce himself into the phantasy by way of that path, and offer himself as an imaginary victim to fictions in which a besotted desire proliferates – an unexpected Ulysses giving himself as food so that Circe's pigs may grow fat.

And let it not be said that I am defaming anyone, for it is the precise point at which those who cannot articulate their practice in any other way are themselves sufficiently concerned to question what they are doing: are not phantasies the means by which we provide the subject with the gratification in which the analysis becomes bogged down? That is the question they repeat to themselves with the hopeless insistence of an unconscious obsession.

17. Thus, at best, the present-day analyst leaves his patient at the point of purely imaginary identification in which the hysteric remains captive, because her phantasy implies its ensnarement.

That is to say, at the very point from which Freud, throughout the first part of his career, wished to extricate himself too quickly by forcing the appeal for love on to the object of identification (for Elisabeth von R. . . ., her brother-in-law [5]; for Dora, M. K. . . .; for the young homosexual woman in the case of female homosexuality, he sees the problem more clearly, but errs when he regards himself as the object aimed at in the real by the negative transference).

It was not until the chapter on 'identification' in 'Group Psychology and the Analysis of the Ego' that Freud clearly distinguished this third mode of identification that is conditioned by its function of sustaining desire, and which is therefore specified by the indifference of its object.

But our psychoanalysts insist: this indifferent object is the substance of the object, eat my body, drink my blood (the profanatory reference is theirs). The mystery of the redemption of the analysand is to be found in this imaginary shedding of blood, of which the analyst is the sacrificial object.

How can the ego on which they claim to call for help here not fall, in effect, under the blow of the reinforced alienation to which they lead the subject? Long before Freud came on the scene, psychologists knew, even if they did not express it in these terms, that if desire is the metonymy of the want-to-be, the ego is the metonymy of desire.

This is how the terminal identification, in which analysts take such pride, operates.

If it is a question of their patient's ego or superego, they hesitate, or rather, and there can be no doubt about it, they don't care, but that with which the patient identifies is their strong ego.

Freud predicted this result very clearly in the article just quoted, when he shows the role of ideal that the most insignificant object may assume in the genesis of the leading partner.

It is not in vain that psychoanalytic psychology is turning increasingly towards group psychology, and even to the psychotherapy of that name.

Let us observe the effects of this tendency in the analytic group itself. It is not true that the so-called training analysands conform to the image of their analyst, at whatever level one wishes to examine it. It is rather among themselves that analysands of the same analyst share a common feature that may be quite secondary in the psychical economy of each of them, but in which the inadequacy of the analyst with regard to his work is clearly marked.

Thus the analyst, for whom the problem of desire can be reduced to the lifting of the veil of fear, leaves wrapped in this shroud all those he has guided.

18. So we have now reached the cunning principle of the power that is ever open to a blind direction. It is the power to do good – no power has any other end – and that is why the power has no end. But it is a question here of something else, it is a question of truth, of the only truth, of the truth about the effects of truth. As soon as Oedipus set foot along this path, he had already renounced power.

Where, then, is the direction of the treatment going? Perhaps one would only have to question its means to define it correctly.

It should therefore be noted:

(1) that speech is all-powerful in the treatment, that it possesses special powers;
(2) that, according to the analytic rule, the analyst is a long way from directing the subject towards 'full' speech, or towards a coherent discourse, but that the analyst leaves the subject free to try it;
(3) that this freedom is what the subject tolerates least easily;
(4) that demand is properly that which is placed in parentheses in the analysis, since the analyst is excluded from satisfying any of the patient's demands;
(5) that since no obstacle is put in the way of the subject's avowal of his desire, it is towards this avowal that he is directed, even shepherded;
(6) that his resistance to this avowal can, in the last analysis, only be the result of the incompatibility between desire and speech.

There may still be a few people, even among my usual listeners, who are surprised to find such propositions in my discourse.

One is aware here of the terrible temptation that must face the analyst to respond however little to demand.

Furthermore, how can the analyst prevent the subject from attributing this response to him, in the form of the demand to cure, and in accordance with the horizon of a discourse that the subject imputes to him with all the more reason in that our authority, for no good reason, assumed it.

Who will now disencumber us of this tunic of Nessus that we have spun for ourselves: does analysis respond to all the desiderata of demand, and by diffused norms? Who will sweep away this pile of dung from the Augean stables of the psychoanalytic literature?

What silence must the analyst now impose upon himself if he is to make out, rising above this bog, the raised finger of Leonardo's St John, if interpretation is to rediscover the disinhabited horizon of being in which its allusive virtue must be deployed?

19. Since it is a question of taking desire, and it can only be taken literally, since it is the nets of the letter that determine, overdetermine, its place as a bird of paradise, how can we fail to demand that the birdcatcher be first of all literate?

Which of us, other than a professor of literature at Zürich who has begun to spell it out, has attempted to articulate the importance of the 'literary' element in Freud's work?

This is merely an indication. Let us go further. Let us question what part it should play for the analyst (in the analyst's being), as far as his own desire is concerned.

Who would be so naïve as to continue to see Freud as the Viennese bourgeois of regular habits who so astonished André Breton by his utter lack of any trace of the Bacchanalian? Now that we have nothing but his works, will we not recognize in him a river of fire, which, incidentally, owes nothing to François Mauriac's artificial river?

Who was more able than he, when avowing his dreams, to spin the thread on which is slipped the ring that binds us to being, and, holding it in his closed hands, which pass it through the game of hunt-the-slipper that human passion constitutes, to make it shine with its brief glow?

Who has inveighed as much as this medical practitioner against the monopolization of *jouissance* by those who load the burdens of need on to others' shoulders?

Who, more fearlessly than this clinician, so firmly tied to mundane suffering, has questioned life as to its meaning, and not to say that it has none, which is a convenient way of washing one's hands of the whole business, but to say that it has only one meaning, that in which desire is borne by death?

A man of desire, of a desire that he followed against his will into ways in which he saw himself reflected in feeling, domination and knowledge, but of which he, unaided, succeeded in unveiling, like an initiate at the defunct mysteries, the unparalleled signifier: that phallus of which the receiving and the giving are equally impossible for the neurotic, whether he knows that the Other does not have it, or knows that he does have it, because in either case his desire is elsewhere; it belongs to being, and man, whether male or female, must accept having it and not having it, on the basis of the discovery that he isn't it.

It is here that is inscribed that final *Spaltung* by which the subject articulates himself in the Logos, and on which Freud was beginning to write [12], giving us, at the ultimate point of an *œuvre* that has the dimensions of being, the solution of the 'infinite' analysis, when his death applied to it the word Nothing.

❧❧❦❦

Notes and References

This report formed part of my teaching seminars. It was later replaced by my speech to the Congress and the replies that it elicited.

In that speech I presented a graph that precisely articulates the directions proposed here for the field of analysis and its direction.

Below, the reader will find, in alphabetical order of authors, the references indicated in my text by numbers in square brackets.

I have used the following abbreviations:

G.W.: *Gesammelte Werke*, by Freud; published by Imago Publishing, London. The Roman numeral that follows refers to the volume.

S.E.: The *Standard Edition* of *The Complete Psychological Works of Sigmund Freud*, the English translation of Freud's works, published by the Hogarth Press, London. Again, the Roman numeral refers to the volume.

I.J.P.: *International Journal of Psychoanalysis.*

The P.Q.: *The Psychoanalytic Quarterly.*

La P.D.A.: a work called *La Psychanalyse d'aujourd'hui*, published by the Presses Universitaires de France, to which I refer only for the naïve simplicity with which it presents the tendency to degrade the direction of the treatment and the principles of its power in psychoanalysis. No doubt it performs a task of communication outside the psychoanalytic community, but within that community it is obstructive in its effects. I do not quote, therefore, authors who have made no properly scientific contribution.

[1] Abraham (Karl), 'Die psychosexuellen Differenzen der Hysterie und der Dementia praecox' (1st International Congress of Psychoanalysis, Salzburg, 26 April, 1908), *Centralblatt für Nervenheilkunde und Psychiatrie*, Neue folge, Bd. 19: 521–33, and in *Klinische Beiträge zur Psychoanalyse* (Int. Psych. Verlag, Leipzig–Wien–Zürich, 1921); 'The Psycho-sexual Differences between Hysteria and Dementia Praecox', *Selected Papers*, Hogarth Press: 64–79.

[2] Devereux (Georges), 'Some Criteria for the Timing of Confrontations and Interpretations', April, 1950, *I.J.P.* XXXII, 1 (January, 1951): 19–24.

[3] Ferenczi (Sandor), 'Introjektion und Übertragung', 1909, *Jahrbuch für psychoanalytische Forschungen* I: 422–57; 'Introjection and Transference', *Sex in Psychoanalysis*, Basic Books, N.Y.: 35–93.

[4] Freud (Anna), *Das Ich und die Abwehrmechanismen*, 1936, Chap. IV, 'Die Abwehrmechanismen'. Cf. *Versuch einer Chronologie*: 60–3 (Intern. psychoanal. Verlag, Wien, 1936); *The Ego and the Mechanisms of Defence*, London, Hogarth Press, 1937; New York, International Universities Press, 1946.

[5] Freud (Sigmund), 'Studien über Hysterie', 1895, *G.W.* I, Fall Elisabeth von R. . . : 196–251: esp. 125–7; 'Studies on Hysteria', *S.E.* II: 158–60.

[6] Freud (Sigmund), 'Die Traumdeutung', *G.W.* II–III. Cf. Chap. IV, 'Die Traumentstellung': 152–6, 157, 163–8, and 'Kern unseres Wesens': 609; 'The Interpretation of Dreams' *S.E.* IV, Chap. IV, 'Distortion in dreams': 146–150, 151, 157–62 and 603.

[7] Freud (Sigmund), 'Bruchstück einer Hysterie-Analyse (Dora)', finished

on 24 January 1901 (cf. letter 140 of *Aus den Anfängen*, the correspondence with Fliess published in London: *G.W.* V: cf. 194–5; 'A case of hysteria', *S.E.* VII: 35–6.

[8] Freud (Sigmund), 'Bemerkungen über einen Fall von Zwangsneurose', 1909, *G.W.* VII. Cf. in I(d) 'Die Einführung ins Verständnis der Kur': 402–4, and the notes to pp. 404–5, then: I(f) 'Die Krankheitsveranlassung', and I(g) 'Der Vaterkomplex und die Lösung der Rattenidee': 417–38; 'Notes upon a Case of Obsessional Neurosis', *S.E.* X. Cf. in I(d) 'Initiation into the Nature of Treatment': 178–81 and the note to p. 181. Then: I(f) 'The Precipitating Cause of the Illness', and (g) 'The Father Complex and the Solution of the Rat Idea': 195–220.

[9] Freud (Sigmund), 'Jenseits des Lustprinzips', 1920, *G.W.* XIII: cf. also pp. 11–14 of Chap II; 'Beyond the Pleasure Principle', *S.E.* XVIII: 14–16.

[10] Freud (Sigmund), 'Massenpsychologie und Ich-Analyse', 1921, *G.W.* XIII, Chap. VII: 'Die Identifizierung', esp. 116–18; 'Group Psychology and the Analysis of the Ego', *S.E.* XVIII: 106–8.

[11] Freud (Sigmund), 'Die endliche und die unendliche Analyse', 1937, *G.W.* XVI: 59–99.

[12] Freud (Sigmund), 'Die Ichspaltung im Abwehrvorgang', *G.W.* XVII, 'Schriften aus dem Nachlass': 58–62. Manuscript dated 2 January, 1938 (unfinished); 'Splitting of the Ego in the Defensive Process', *Collected Papers*, V, 32: 372–5.

[13] Glover (Edward), 'The Therapeutic Effect of Inexact Interpretation: a

contribution to the theory of suggestion', *I.J.P.* XII 4 (Oct. 1931): 399–411.

[14] Hartmann, Kris and Loewenstein, various joint contributions in *The Psychoanalytic Study of the Child*, since 1946.

[15] Kris (Ernst), 'Ego Psychology and Interpretation in Psychoanalytic Therapy', *The P.Q.*, XX 1, January, 1951: 21–5.

[16] Lacan (Jacques), Report to the Rome Congress, 26–27 September, 1953: 'Fonction et champ de la parole et du langage en psychanalyse', *Écrits*, Seuil, Paris, 1966; 237. Cf. p. 30.

[17] Lacan (Jacques), 'L'instance de la lettre dans l'inconscient ou la raison depuis Freud', *Écrits*, Seuil, Paris; 493. Cf. p. 146.

[18] Lagache (Daniel), 'Le probleme du transfert' (Rapport de la XIV* Conférence des Psychanalystes de Langue française, 1 November, 1951), *Rev. franç. Psychan.*, XVI, 1952, 1–2: 5–115.

[19] Leclaire (Serge), 'À la recherche des principes d'une psychothérapie des psychoses' (Congrès de Bonneval, 15 April, 1957), *L'Évolution psychiatrique*, 1958, fasc. 2: 377–419.

[20] Macalpine (Ida), 'The Development of the Transference', *The P.Q.* XIX 4, October 1950: 500–39, in particular 502–8 and 522–8.

[21] *La P.D.A.*: 51–2 (on 'prégénitaux' and 'génitaux', and on 'le renforcement du Moi et sa méthode'),

102 (on 'la distance à l'objet, principe de la méthode d'une cure').

[22] *La P.D.A.* Cf. p. 133 (rééducation émotionnelle), p. 133 (opposition de la *P.D.A.* à Freud sur l'importance primordiale de la relation à deux), p. 132 (la guérison 'par le dedans'), p. 135 (ce qui importe . . . ce n'est pas tant ce que l'analyste dit ou fait que ce qu'il est), p. 136, etc., and p. 162 (sur le congé de la fin du traitement), p. 149 (sur le rêve).

[23] R.L., 'Perversion sexuelle transitoire au cours d'un traitement psychanalytique', *Bulletin d'activités de l'Association des Psychanalystes de Belgique*, no. 25: 1–17, 118, rue Froissart, Bruxelles.

[24] Sharpe (Ella), 'Technique of Psychoanalysis', *Coll. Papers*, London, Hogarth Press. Cf. p. 81 (on the need to justify one's existence); pp. 12–14 (on the skills and techniques required of the analyst).

[25] Schmideberg (Melitta), 'Intellektuelle Hemmung und Ess-störung', *Zeitschrift für psa. Pädagogik* VIII, 1934.

[26] Williams (J. D.), *The Compleat Strategyst*, The Rand Series, McGraw-Hill Book Company, Inc., New York, Toronto, London.

[27] Winnicott (D. W.), 'Transitional Objects and Transitional Phenomena', 15 June 1951, in *I.J.P.* XXXIV, 1953: 11, 29–97.

✦✦✦✦

1. First report of the international symposium that met at this time at the invitation of the Société française de psychanalyse, published in *La Psychanalyse*, 6

2. The figures in square brackets indicate references placed immediately at the end of this report.

3. To turn against the spirit of a society a term at the price of which it can be appreciated, when the sentence in which Freud proved himself the equal of the pre-Socratics – *Wo es war, soll Ich*

werden – is translated, quite simply, as *Le Moi doit déloger le Ça*.

4. 'Comment terminer le traitement analytique', *Revue française de Psychanalyse*, 1954 IV: 519 and *passim*. To appreciate the influence of such a training, read: Ch.-H. Nodet, 'Le psychanalyste', *L'évolution psychiatrique*, 1957, no. IV: 689–91.

5. I promise not to tire my readers any further with such stupid formulae, which really have no other use here than to show the state into which analytic

discourse has declined. I apologized to my foreign listeners who no doubt had as many available in their own language, if not of quite the same platitudinous level.

6. Lacan uses the English translation of *Ich* here, not the French *Moi*. Where this is the case I have left 'ego' italicized [Tr.].

7. In France the doctrinaire of being, quoted above, went straight to the following solution: the being of the psychoanalyst is innate [cf. La *P.D.A.*, I: 136].

8. English in the original [Tr.].

9. O, which rather than being vocalized as the symbolic letter of oxygen, referred to by the metaphor followed, may be read as zero, in so far as this figure symbolizes the essential function of place in the structure of the signifier.

10. English in the original [Tr.].

11. '*Que n'offrirais-je à honnir à ceux qui mal y pense*' [Tr.].

12. English in the original [Tr.].

13. 'It's not done!' [Tr.].

14. '*Rien à frire*', in the original. Literally, 'nothing to fry', preferred to the more usual 'rien à faire', on account of the reference to fish in the previous sentence [Tr.].

15. An example: in the United States, where Kris has achieved success, publication makes news, and teaching like mine should stake its claim to priority each week against the pillage that it cannot fail to attract. In France, my ideas penetrate by means of a kind of infiltration into a group, in which individuals obey orders that prohibit my teaching. In being *maudit*, ideas can serve only as decorations for a few dandies. Never mind: the void in which they echo, whether I am acknowledged or not, makes another voice heard.

16. English in the original [Tr.].

17. My parentheses.

18. English in the original [Tr.].

19. Original text altered in the penultimate sentence of this paragraph and in the first line of the next (1966).

20. English in the original [Tr.].

21. Cf. Letter 118 (**II–IX** – 1899) to Fliess in *Aus den Anfängen*, Imago Publishing, London.

22. Here is the dream as it is presented in the patient's account on p. 152 of the *G.W.*, **II–III**: 'I want to give a dinner. But there's only a little smoked salmon left. I think of going out shopping, then remember that it is Sunday afternoon and all the shops are shut. I tell myself that I'll ring round to a few tradesmen. But the telephone is out of order. So I have to give up my desire to give a dinner.'

23. Which Freud gives as the motive for the hysterical identification, when he specifies that the smoked salmon plays for the friend the same role as the caviar plays for the patient.

24. *The Interpretation of Dreams.*

25. It must not be forgotten that the term is used for the first time in *The Interpretation of Dreams* on the subject of the dream, and that this use gives it its meaning and, by the same token, that of the term 'distortion', which translates it when the English analysts apply it to the ego.

26. Cf. the $(\$\Diamond D)$ and $(\$\Diamond o)$ of my graph, reproduced here in 'The Subversion of the subject', p. 315. The sign $\Diamond$ registers the relations envelopment–development – conjunction – disjunction. The links that it signifies in these two parentheses enables us to read the barred S – the 'S' fading in the cutting of the demand, and S fading before the object of desire, that is to say, drive and phantasy. ['Fading' is in English in the original – Tr.]

27. An allusion to the medieval French epic poems, the *Chansons de Geste* [Tr.].

28. English in the original [Tr.].

EIGHT

The signification of the phallus

The following is the original, unaltered text of a lecture that
I delivered in German on 9 May, 1958, at the Max-Planck
Institute, Munich, where Professor Paul Matussek had
invited me to speak.
If one has any notion of the state of mind then prevalent in
even the least unaware circles, one will appreciate the
effect that my use of such terms as, for example,
'the other scene', which I was the first to extract
from Freud's work, must have had.
If 'deferred action' (*Nachtrag*), to rescue another of these
terms from the facility into which they have since fallen,
renders this effort impracticable, it should be known
that they were unheard of at that time.

꙳꙳

We know that the unconscious castration complex has the function of a
knot:

(1) in the dynamic structuring of symptoms in the analytic sense of the
term, that is to say, in that which is analysable in the neuroses,
perversions, and psychoses;

(2) in a regulation of the development that gives its *ratio* to this first
role: namely, the installation in the subject of an unconscious position
without which he would be unable to identify himself with the ideal
type of his sex, or to respond without grave risk to the needs of
his partner in the sexual relation, or even to accept in a satisfactory
way the needs of the child who may be produced by this relation.

There is an antinomy, here, that is internal to the assumption by man
(*Mensch*) of his sex: why must he assume the attributes of that sex only
through a threat – the threat, indeed, of their privation? In 'Civilization
and its Discontents' Freud, as we know, went so far as to suggest a
disturbance of human sexuality, not of a contingent, but of an essential
kind, and one of his last articles concerns the irreducibility in any finite
(*endliche*) analysis of the sequellae resulting from the castration complex
in the masculine unconscious and from *penisneid* in the unconscious of
women.

This is not the only aporia, but it is the first that the Freudian experience and the metapsychology that resulted from it introduced into our experience of man. It is insoluble by any reduction to biological givens: the very necessity of the myth subjacent to the structuring of the Oedipus complex demonstrates this sufficiently.

It would be mere trickery to invoke in this case some hereditary amnesic trait, not only because such a trait is in itself debatable, but because it leaves the problem unsolved: namely, what is the link between the murder of the father and the pact of the primordial law, if it is included in that law that castration should be the punishment for incest?

It is only on the basis of the clinical facts that any discussion can be fruitful. These facts reveal a relation of the subject to the phallus that is established without regard to the anatomical difference of the sexes, and which, by this very fact, makes any interpretation of this relation especially difficult in the case of women. This problem may be treated under the following four headings:

(1) from this 'why', the little girl considers herself, if only momentarily, as castrated, in the sense of deprived of the phallus, by someone, in the first instance by her mother, an important point, and then by her father, but in such a way that one must recognize in it a transference in the analytic sense of the term;

(2) from this 'why', in a more primordial sense, the mother is considered, by both sexes, as possessing the phallus, as the phallic mother;

(3) from this 'why', correlatively, the signification of castration in fact takes on its (clinically manifest) full weight as far as the formation of symptoms is concerned, only on the basis of its discovery as castration of the mother;

(4) these three problems lead, finally, to the question of the reason, in development, for the phallic stage. We know that in this term Freud specifies the first genital maturation: on the one hand, it would seem to be characterized by the imaginary dominance of the phallic attribute and by masturbatory *jouissance* and, on the other, it localizes this *jouissance* for the woman in the clitoris, which is thus raised to the function of the phallus. It therefore seems to exclude in both sexes, until the end of this stage, that is, to the decline of the Oedipal stage, all instinctual mapping of the vagina as locus of genital penetration.

This ignorance is suspiciously like *méconnaissance* in the technical sense of the term – all the more so in that it is sometimes quite false.

Does this not bear out the fable in which Longus shows us the initiation of Daphnis and Chloe subordinated to the explanations of an old woman? Thus certain authors have been led to regard the phallic stage as the effect of a repression, and the function assumed in it by the phallic object as a symptom. The difficulty begins when one asks, *what* symptom? Phobia, says one, perversion, says another, both says a third. It seems in the last case that nothing more can be said: not that interesting transmutations of the object of a phobia into a fetish do not occur, but if they are interesting it is precisely on account of the difference of their place in the structure. It would be pointless to demand of these authors that they formulate this difference from the perspectives currently in favour, that is to say, in terms of the object relation. Indeed, there is no other reference on the subject than the approximate notion of part-object, which – unfortunately, in view of the convenient uses to which it is being put in our time, has never been subjected to criticism since Karl Abraham introduced it.

The fact remains that the now abandoned discussion of the phallic stage, to be found in the surviving texts of the years 1928–32, is refreshing for the example it sets us of a devotion to doctrine – to which the degradation of psychoanalysis consequent on its American transplantation adds a note of nostalgia.

Merely to summarize the debate would be to distort the authentic diversity of the positions taken up by a Helene Deutsch, a Karen Horney, and an Ernest Jones, to mention only the most eminent.

The series of three articles devoted by Jones to the subject are especially fruitful – if only for the development of the notion of *aphanisis*, a term that he himself had coined.[1] For, in positing so correctly the problem of the relation between castration and desire, he demonstrates his inability to recognize what he nevertheless grasped so clearly that the term that earlier provided us with the key to it seems to emerge from his very failure.

Particularly amusing is the way in which he manages to extract from a letter by Freud himself a position that is strictly contrary to it: an excellent model in a difficult *genre*.

Yet the matter refuses to rest there, Jones appearing to contradict his own case for a re-establishment of the equality of natural rights (does he not win the day with the Biblical 'God created them man and woman' with which his plea concludes?). In fact, what has he gained in normalizing the function of the phallus as a part-object if he has to invoke its presence in the mother's body as an internal object, which term is a function of the phantasies revealed by Melanie Klein, and if he cannot separate himself from Klein's view that these phantasies originate as far back as in early childhood, during Oedipal formation?

It might be a good idea to re-examine the question by asking what could have necessitated for Freud the evident paradox of his position. For one has to admit that he was better guided than anyone in his re-cognition of the order of unconscious phenomena, of which he was the inventor, and that, failing an adequate articulation of the nature of these phenomena, his followers were doomed to lose their way to a greater or lesser degree.

It is on the basis of the following bet – which I lay down as the principle of a commentary of Freud's work that I have pursued during the past seven years – that I have been led to certain results: essentially, to promul-gate as necessary to any articulation of analytic phenomena the notion of the signifier, as opposed to that of the signified, in modern linguistic analysis. Freud could not take this notion, which postdates him, into account, but I would claim that Freud's discovery stands out precisely because, although it set out from a domain in which one could not expect to recognize its reign, it could not fail to anticipate its formulas. Con-versely, it is Freud's discovery that gives to the signifier/signified oppo-sition the full extent of its implications: namely, that the signifier has an active function in determining certain effects in which the signifiable appears as submitting to its mark, by becoming through that passion the signified.

This passion of the signifier now becomes a new dimension of the human condition in that it is not only man who speaks, but that in man and through man *it* speaks (*ça parle*), that his nature is woven by effects in which is to be found the structure of language, of which he becomes the material, and that therefore there resounds in him, beyond what could be conceived of by a psychology of ideas, the relation of speech.

In this sense one can say that the consequences of the discovery of the unconscious have not yet been so much as glimpsed in theory, although its effects have been felt in praxis to a greater degree than perhaps we are aware of, if only in the form of effects of retreat.

It should be made clear that this advocacy of man's relation to the signifier as such has nothing to do with a 'culturalist' position in the ordinary sense of the term, the position in which Karen Horney, for example, was anticipated in the dispute concerning the phallus by a position described by Freud himself as a feminist one. It is not a question of the relation between man and language as a social phenomenon, there being no question even of something resembling the ideological psycho-genesis with which we are familiar, and which is not superseded by peremptory recourse to the quite metaphysical notion, which lurks beneath its question-begging appeal to the concrete, conveyed so pitifully by the term 'affect'.

It is a question of rediscovering in the laws that govern that other scene (*ein andere Schauplatz*), which Freud, on the subject of dreams, designates as being that of the unconscious, the effects that are discovered at the level of the chain of materially unstable elements that constitutes language: effects determined by the double play of combination and substitution in the signifier, according to the two aspects that generate the signified, metonymy and metaphor; determining effects for the institution of the subject. From this test, a topology, in the mathematical sense of the term, appears, without which one soon realizes that is impossible simply to note the structure of a symptom in the analytic sense of the term.

It speaks in the Other, I say, designating by the Other the very locus evoked by the recourse to speech in any relation in which the Other intervenes. If *it* speaks in the Other, whether or not the subject hears it with his ear, it is because it is there that the subject, by means of a logic anterior to any awakening of the signified, finds its signifying place. The discovery of what it articulates in that place, that is to say, in the un-conscious, enables us to grasp at the price of what splitting (*Spaltung*) it has thus been constituted.

The phallus reveals its function here. In Freudian doctrine, the phallus is not a phantasy, if by that we mean an imaginary effect. Nor is it as such an object (part-, internal, good, bad, etc.) in the sense that this term tends to accentuate the reality pertaining in a relation. It is even less the organ, penis or clitoris, that it symbolizes. And it is not without reason that Freud used the reference to the simulacrum that it represented for the Ancients.

For the phallus is a signifier, a signifier whose function, in the intra-subjective economy of the analysis, lifts the veil perhaps from the function it performed in the mysteries. For it is the signifier intended to designate as a whole the effects of the signified, in that the signifier conditions them by its presence as a signifier.

Let us now examine the effects of this presence. In the first instance, they proceed from a deviation of man's needs from the fact that he speaks, in the sense that in so far as his needs are subjected to demand, they return to him alienated. This is not the effect of his real dependence (one should not expect to find here the parasitic conception represented by the notion of dependence in the theory of neurosis), but rather the turning into signifying form as such, from the fact that it is from the locus of the Other that its message is emitted.

That which is thus alienated in needs constitutes an *Urverdrängung* (primal repression), an inability, it is supposed, to be articulated in demand, but it re-appears in something it gives rise to that presents itself in man as desire (*das Begehren*). The phenomenology that emerges from analytic experience is certainly of a kind to demonstrate in desire the paradoxical, deviant, erratic, eccentric, even scandalous character by which it is distinguished from need. This fact has been too often affirmed not to have been always obvious to moralists worthy of the name. The Freudianism of earlier days seemed to owe its status to this fact. Paradoxically, however, psychoanalysis is to be found at the head of an ever-present obscurantism that is still more boring when it denies the fact in an ideal of theoretical and practical reduction of desire to need.

This is why we must articulate this status here, beginning with *demand*, whose proper characteristics are eluded in the notion of frustration (which Freud never used).

Demand in itself bears on something other than the satisfactions it calls for. It is demand of a presence or of an absence – which is what is manifested in the primordial relation to the mother, pregnant with that Other to be situated *within* the needs that it can satisfy. Demand constitutes the Other as already possessing the 'privilege' of satisfying needs, that it is to say, the power of depriving them of that alone by which they are satisfied. This privilege of the Other thus outlines the radical form of the gift of that which the Other does not have, namely, its love.

In this way, demand annuls (*aufhebt*) the particularity of everything that can be granted by transmuting it into a proof of love, and the very satisfactions that it obtains for need are reduced (*sich erniedrigt*) to the level of being no more than the crushing of the demand for love (all of which is perfectly apparent in the psychology of child-rearing, to which our analyst-nurses are so attached).

It is necessary, then, that the particularity thus abolished should reappear *beyond* demand. It does, in fact, reappear there, but preserving the structure contained in the unconditional element of the demand for love. By a reversal that is not simply a negation of the negation, the power of pure loss emerges from the residue of an obliteration. For the unconditional element of demand, desire substitutes the 'absolute' condition: this condition unties the knot of that element in the proof of love that is resistant to the satisfaction of a need. Thus desire is neither the appetite for satisfaction, nor the demand for love, but the difference that results from the subtraction of the first from the second, the phenomenon of their splitting (*Spaltung*).

One can see how the sexual relation occupies this closed field of desire, in which it will play out its fate. This is because it is the field made for the production of the enigma that this relation arouses in the subject by doubly 'signifying' it to him: the return of the demand that it gives rise to, as a demand on the subject of the need – an ambiguity made present on to the Other in question in the proof of love demanded. The gap in this enigma betrays what determines it, namely, to put it in the simplest possible way, that for both partners in the relation, both the subject and the Other, it is not enough to be subjects of need, or objects of love, but that they must stand for the cause of desire.

This truth lies at the heart of all the distortions that have appeared in the field of psychoanalysis on the subject of the sexual life. It also constitutes the condition of the happiness of the subject: and to disguise the gap it creates by leaving it to the virtue of the 'genital' to resolve it through the maturation of tenderness (that is to say, solely by recourse to the Other as reality), however well intentioned, is fraudulent nonetheless. It has to be said here that the French analysts, with their hypocritical notion of genital oblativity, opened the way to the moralizing tendency, which, to the accompaniment of its Salvationist choirs, is now to be found everywhere.

In any case, man cannot aim at being whole (the 'total personality' is another of the deviant premises of modern psychotherapy), while ever the play of displacement and condensation to which he is doomed in the exercise of his functions marks his relation as a subject to the signifier.

The phallus is the privileged signifier of that mark in which the role of the logos is joined with the advent of desire.

It can be said that this signifier is chosen because it is the most tangible element in the real of sexual copulation, and also the most symbolic in the literal (typographical) sense of the term, since it is equivalent there to the (logical) copula. It might also be said that, by virtue of its turgidity, it is the image of the vital flow as it is transmitted in generation.

All these propositions merely conceal the fact that it can play its role only when veiled, that is to say, as itself a sign of the latency with which any signifiable is struck, when it is raised (*aufgehoben*) to the function of signifier.

The phallus is the signifier of this *Aufhebung* itself, which it inaugurates (initiates) by its disappearance. That is why the demon of Αἰδώς (*Scham*, shame) arises at the very moment when, in the ancient mysteries, the phallus is unveiled (cf. the famous painting in the Villa di Pompei).

It then becomes the bar which, at the hands of this demon, strikes the signified, marking it as the bastard offspring of this signifying concatenation.

Thus a condition of complementarity is produced in the establishment of the subject by the signifier – which explains the *Spaltung* in the subject and the movement of intervention in which that 'splitting' is completed. Namely:

(1) that the subject designates his being only by barring everything he signifies, as it appears in the fact that he wants to be loved for himself, a mirage that cannot be dismissed as merely grammatical (since it abolishes discourse);

(2) that the living part of that being in the *urverdrängt* (primally repressed) finds its signifier by receiving the mark of the *Verdrängung* (repression) of the phallus (by virtue of which the unconscious is language).

The phallus as signifier gives the ratio of desire (in the sense in which the term is used in music in the 'mean and extreme ratio' of harmonic division).

I shall also be using the phallus as an algorithm, so if I am to help you to grasp this use of the term I shall have to rely on the echoes of the experience that we share – otherwise, my account of the problem could go on indefinitely.

The fact that the phallus is a signifier means that it is in the place of the Other that the subject has access to it. But since this signifier is only veiled, as ratio of the Other's desire, it is this desire of the Other as such that the subject must recognize, that is to say, the other in so far as he is himself a subject divided by the signifying *Spaltung*.

The emergences that appear in psychological genesis confirm this signifying function of the phallus.

Thus, to begin with, the Kleinian fact that the child apprehends from the outset that the mother 'contains' the phallus may be formulated more correctly.

But it is in the dialectic of the demand for love and the test of desire that development is ordered.

The demand for love can only suffer from a desire whose signifier is alien to it. If the desire of the mother *is* the phallus, the child wishes to be the phallus in order to satisfy that desire. Thus the division immanent in desire is already felt to be experienced in the desire of the Other, in that it is already opposed to the fact that the subject is content to present to the Other what in reality he may *have* that corresponds to this phallus, for what he has is worth no more than what he does not have, as far as his demand for love is concerned because that demand requires that he be the phallus.

Clinical experience has shown us that this test of the desire of the Other is decisive not in the sense that the subject learns by it whether or not he has a real phallus, but in the sense that he learns that the mother does not have it. This is the moment of the experience without whi h no symptomatic consequence (phobia) or structural consequence (*Penisneid*) relating to the castration complex can take effect. Here is signed the conjunction of desire, in that the phallic signifier is its mark, with the threat or nostalgia of lacking it.

Of course, its future depends on the law introduced by the father into this sequence.

But one may, simply by reference to the function of the phallus, indicate the structures that will govern the relations between the sexes.

Let us say that these relations will turn around a 'to be' and a 'to have', which, by referring to a signifier, the phallus, have the opposed effect, on the one hand, of giving reality to the subject in this signifier, and, on the other, of derealizing the relations to be signified.

This is brought about by the intervention of a 'to seem' that replaces the 'to have', in order to protect it on the one side, and to mask its lack in the other, and which has the effect of projecting in their entirety the ideal or typical manifestations of the behaviour of each sex, including the act of copulation itself, into the comedy.

These ideals take on new vigour from the demand that they are capable of satisfying, which is always a demand for love, with its complement of the reduction of desire to demand.

Paradoxical as this formulation may seem, I am saying that it is in order to be the phallus, that is to say, the signifier of the desire of the Other, that a woman will reject an essential part of femininity, namely, all her attributes in the masquerade. It is for that which she is not that she wishes to be desired as well as loved. But she finds the signifier of her own desire in the body of him to whom she addresses her demand for love. Perhaps it should not be forgotten that the organ that assumes this signifying function takes on the value of a fetish. But the result for the woman remains that an experience of love, which, as such (cf. above), deprives her ideally of that which the object gives, and a desire which finds its signifier in this object, converge on the same object. That is why one can observe that a lack in the satisfaction proper to sexual need, in other words, frigidity, is relatively well tolerated in women, whereas the *Verdrängung* (repression) inherent in desire is less present in women than in men.

In the case of men, on the other hand, the dialectic of demand and desire engenders the effects – and one must once more admire the sureness with which Freud situated them at the precise articulations on which they depended – of a specific depreciation (*Erniedrigung*) of love.

If, in effect, the man finds satisfaction for his demand for love in the relation with the woman, in as much as the signifier of the phallus constitutes her as giving in love what she does not have – conversely, his own desire for the phallus will make its signifier emerge in its persistent divergence towards 'another woman' who may signify this phallus in various ways, either as a virgin or as a prostitute. There results from this a centrifugal tendency of the genital drive in love life, which makes impotence much more difficult to bear for him, while the *Verdrängung* inherent in desire is more important.

Yet it should not be thought that the sort of infidelity that would appear to be constitutive of the male function is proper to it. For if one looks more closely, the same redoubling is to be found in the woman, except that the Other of Love as such, that is to say, in so far as he is deprived of what he gives, finds it difficult to see himself in the retreat in which he is substituted for the being of the very man whose attributes she cherishes.

One might add here that male homosexuality, in accordance with the phallic mark that constitutes desire, is constituted on the side of desire, while female homosexuality, on the other hand, as observation shows, is orientated on a disappointment that reinforces the side of the demand for love. These remarks should really be examined in greater detail, from the point of view of a return to the function of the mask in so far as it dominates the identifications in which refusals of demand are resolved.

The fact that femininity finds its refuge in this mask, by virtue of the fact of the *Verdrängung* inherent in the phallic mark of desire, has the curious consequence of making virile display in the human being itself seem feminine.

Correlatively, one can glimpse the reason for a characteristic that had never before been elucidated, and which shows once again the depth of Freud's intuition: namely, why he advances the view that there is only one *libido*, his text showing that he conceives it as masculine in nature. The function of the phallic signifier touches here on its most profound relation: that in which the Ancients embodied the Νοῦς and the Λογὸς.

❧❧❦❦

Note

1. *Aphanisis*, the disappearance of sexual desire. This Greek term was introduced into psychoanalysis by Jones in 'Early Development of Female Sexuality' (1927), in *Papers on Psycho-analysis*, 5th edn., London, 1950. For Jones, the fear of aphanisis exists, in both boys and girls, at a deeper level than the castration complex [Tr.].

NINE

The subversion of the subject and the dialectic of desire in the Freudian unconscious

This text represents my contribution to a conference entitled
'La Dialectique', held at Royaumont 19–23 September,
1960. The conference was organized by the 'Colloques
philosophiques internationaux', and I was invited
to participate by Jean Wahl.
This conference preceded by a month the Congrès de Bonneval,
at which I delivered my text, *Position de l'inconscient*. The later
text was very much a development of this (earlier) one,
and its publication serves to demonstrate that my
teaching has always been ahead of my
published work.
(The graph reproduced here first appeared in my seminar on the
formations of the unconscious. It was worked out with particular relation to the structure of the witticism, which, to the
surprise of my audience, I took as a point of departure. An
account of this seminar, which took place in the first term
of the year 1957–8, appeared, together with the graph,
in a number of the *Bulletin de psychologie*.)

❯❯❮❮

The praxis that we call psychoanalysis is constituted by a structure. An audience like the one here today – an audience that we presume to be aware of philosophical problems – cannot ignore this structure.

The notion that to be a philosopher means being interested in what everyone is interested in without knowing it has the interesting peculiarity that its pertinence does not imply that it can be verified. For it can be put to the test only by everyone becoming a philosopher.

I say its philosophical pertinence, for such, in the last resort, is the schema that Hegel gave us of History in *The Phenomenology of Mind*.

Summarizing it in this way is to provide us with a mediation that facilitates the situating of the subject – namely, in relation to knowledge.

It is also easy to demonstrate the ambiguity of such a relation.

The same ambiguity is manifested in the effects of science in the world today.

The scientist, too, is a subject, and one particularly qualified in his constitution, as is shown by the fact that science did not come into the world of its own accord (its birth was not without its vicissitudes, and it was preceded by a number of failures – by abortion or premature birth).

Now this subject who must know what he is doing, or so one presumes, does not know what, in the effects of science, is already, in fact, of interest to everyone. Or so it would appear in the world of today, where everyone finds himself at the same level as the scientist as far as ignorance on this point is concerned.

This fact alone justifies us in speaking of a subject of science – a notion to which an epistemology that can be said to display more promise than success hopes to be equal.

Hence, let it be noted, my entirely didactic reference to Hegel, by which I wished to say something, for the purposes of the training that I have in mind, about the question of the subject, in so far as that question is properly subverted by psychoanalysis.

What qualifies me to proceed in this direction is obviously my experience of this praxis. What has decided me to do so, those who follow my teaching will bear this out, is a theoretical nullity coupled with abuses in the way in which it is passed on, which, while presenting no danger to the praxis itself, result, in either case, in a total absence of scientific status. To pose the question of the minimum conditions required for such a status was not perhaps a dishonest departure. This departure has taken us a long way.

I am not dealing here with anything so broad in scope as a radical questioning of social bases; I do not intend, in particular, to dwell on the conclusions that I have been forced to draw about the notorious deviations in analytic praxis that are perpetrated in the name of psychoanalysis in Britain and America.

What I will try to define is subversion proper, and I apologize to this gathering, whose quality I have already acknowledged, for being unable to do more in its presence than in its absence, that is, to take it as the very pivot of my demonstration, even though it is up to me to justify this latitude with regard to it.

Yet I shall use it in order to take as given the fact that empiricism cannot constitute the foundations for a science.

At a second stage, we encounter what has already been constituted, by virtue of a scientific label, under the name of psychology.

A label that I would reject – precisely because, as I will show, the function of the subject, as it is established in Freudian experience, disqualifies from the outset what, under cover of the term 'psychology', however one dresses up its premises, merely perpetuates an academic framework.

Its criterion is the unity of the subject, which is one of the presuppositions of this sort of psychology, it being even taken as symptomatic that its theme is always more emphatically isolated, as if it were a question of the return of a certain subject of knowledge (*connaissance*), or as if the psychical had to obtain its credentials as a double of the physical organism.

We must take as our standard here the idea in which a whole body of traditional thought comes together to validate a term, 'state of knowledge' (*état de la connaissance*), that is not without foundation. Whether it is a question of the states of enthusiasm described by Plato, the Buddhist degrees of *samadhi*, or the *Erlebnis*, the experience obtained under the influence of hallucinogenic drugs, it is necessary to know how much of these is authenticated by any theory.

Authenticated in the register of the connaturality implied in knowledge (*connaissance*).

It is clear that Hegelian knowledge (*savoir*), in the logicizing *Aufhebung* on which it is based, sets as little store by these states in themselves as modern science, which can recognize in them an object of experience, in the sense of an opportunity to define certain co-ordinates, but in no way an ascesis that might, let us say, be epistemogenic or noophoric.

It is certainly on this account that reference to them is pertinent to my approach.

For I suppose my listeners are sufficiently informed about Freudian practice to grasp that such states play no part in it – but what is not fully appreciated is the fact that the practitioners of this supposedly depth psychology do not think of using them to obtain illumination, for example, do not even attribute to these states any value in relation to the direction indicated by such a depth psychology.

For that is the meaning, which is not insisted on, of that distance from which Freud proceeds when it comes to hynoid states, even when it is merely a question of explaining the phenomena associated with hysteria. The stupifying fact is that Freud prefers the discourse of the hysteric. What I have called 'fruitful moments' (*moments féconds*) in my mapping of paranoiac knowledge (*connaissance*) is not a Freudian reference.

I have some difficulty in getting a hearing in circles infatuated with the most incredible illogicality for what is involved in questioning the unconscious as I do, that is to say, to the point at which it gives a reply that is not some sort of transport of delight, or flat rejection, but rather that 'it says why'.

If we take the subject anywhere it is to a deciphering that already presupposes this sort of logic in the unconscious: in which, for example, an interrogative voice, even the development of an argument, is recognized.

The whole psychoanalytic tradition supports the view that the analyst's voice can intervene only if it enters at the right place, and that if it enters too early it merely produces a closing up of communication.

In other words, psychoanalysis that is sustained by its allegiance to Freud cannot in any circumstances offer itself as a 'rite of passage' to some archetypal, or in any sense ineffable, experience: the day when anyone expresses a view of this order that is not simply a dead loss will be the day when all limits have been abolished. And we are still a long way from that.[1]

This is merely an approach to our subject. For it is a question of grasping more precisely what Freud in his doctrine himself articulates as constituting a 'Copernican' step.

Is it enough that a privilege should be consigned to it, namely the one that put the earth in the central place? The subsequent dislodging of man from a similar place by the triumph of the idea of evolution gives one the feeling that this would involve a gain that would be confirmed by its consistency.

But can one be sure that this is a gain, that it is real progress? Does nothing make it appear that the other truth, if we may so term revealed truth, is seriously affected as a result? Do we not believe that, by exalting the centre, heliocentrism is no less of a lure than seeing the earth as the centre of the Universe, and that the fact of the ecliptic no doubt provided a more stimulating model of our relations with the true, before it lost much of its interest by being no more than the earth nodding its assent?

In any case, it is not because of Darwin that men believe themselves to be any the less the top dogs in creation, for it is precisely of this that he convinces them.

The linguistically suggestive use of Copernicus' name has more hidden resources that touch specifically on what has just slipped from my pen as the relation to the true, namely, the emergence of the ellipse as being not unworthy of the locus from which the so-called higher truths take their name. The revolution is no less important for concerning only the 'celestial revolutions'.

To stop at this stage no longer means simply revoking some idiotic notion deriving from the religious tradition, which, as can be seen well enough, is none the worse for it, but rather of binding more closely the régime of knowledge to the régime of truth.

For if the work of Copernicus, as others have remarked before, is not as Copernican as is customarily believed, it is in this that the doctrine of double truth continues to offer shelter to a knowledge that until that time, it must be said, had every appearance of being quite content with it.

So here we are at this sensitive frontier between truth and knowledge; and it might be said after all that, at first sight, our science certainly seems to have re-adopted the solution of closing the frontier.

Yet if the historical birth of science is still a sufficiently burning question for us to be aware that at that frontier a shift took place, it is perhaps there that psychoanalysis is marked out to represent an earthquake yet to come.

For let us look again from this angle at the service we expected from Hegel's phenomenology, for it represents an ideal solution – a solution, one might say, involving a permanent revisionism, in which truth is in a state of constant re-absorption in its own disturbing element, being in itself no more than that which is lacking for the realization of knowledge. The antinomy that the Scholastic tradition posed as a matter of principle is here taken to be resolved by virtue of being imaginary. Truth is nothing other than that which knowledge can apprehend as knowledge only by setting its ignorance to work. A real crisis in which the imaginary is resolved, thus engendering a new symbolic form, to use my own categories. This dialectic is convergent and attains the conjuncture defined as absolute knowledge. As such it is deduced, it can only be the conjunction of the symbolic with a real of which there is nothing more to be expected. What is this real, if not a subject fulfilled in his identity to himself? From which, one can conclude that this subject is already perfect in this regard, and is the fundamental hypothesis of this whole process. He is named, in effect, as being the substratum of this process; he is called the *Selbstbewusstsein*, the being conscious of self, the fully conscious self.

I would to heaven it were so, but the history of science itself – I mean our science, from its inception, say, in Greek mathematics – presents itself rather in the form of détours that comply very little with this immanentism. In fact, the theories – and let us not be misled by any re-absorption of the limited theory into the generalized theory – do not, in any way, fit together according to the thesis/antithesis/synthesis dialectic.

Indeed, a number of cracks to be heard confusedly in the great consciousnesses responsible for some of the outstanding changes in physics remind us that, after all, for this knowledge as for others it is elsewhere that the hour of truth must strike.

And why would we not see that the astonishing consideration shown to the din emerging from psychoanalysis in science may be due to the theoretical hope psychoanalysis offers – a hope that is not only the result of confusion?

Of course, I am not referring to that extraordinary lateral transference, by which the categories of a psychology that re-invigorates its menial tasks with social exploitation acquire a new strength in psychoanalysis. For the reason already given, I regard the fate of psychology as signed and sealed.

In any case, my double reference to Hegel's absolute subject and to the abolished subject of science provides the illumination necessary to an accurate formulation of Freud's dramatism: the re-entry of truth into the field of science at the same time as it gains recognition in the field of its praxis: repressed, it reappears.

Who cannot see the distance that separates the unhappy consciousness – of which, however strongly it is engraven in Hegel, it can be said that it is still no more than the suspension of a corpus of knowledge – from the 'discontents of civilization' in Freud, even if it is only in a mere phrase, uttered as if disavowed, that marks for us what, on reading it, cannot be articulated otherwise than the 'skew' relation[2] that separates the subject from sexuality?

There is nothing, then, in our expedient for situating Freud that owes anything to the judicial astrology in which the psychologist dabbles. Nothing that proceeds from quality, or even from the intensive, or from any phenomenology from which idealism may draw reassurance. In the Freudian field, in spite of the words themselves, consciousness is a feature as inadequate to ground the unconscious in its negation (that unconscious dates from St Thomas Aquinas) as the affect is unsuited to play the role of the protopathic subject, since it is a service that has no holder.

Since Freud the unconscious has been a chain of signifiers that somewhere (on another stage, in another scene, he wrote) is repeated, and insists on interfering in the breaks offered it by the effective discourse and the cogitation that it informs.

In this formula, which is mine only in the sense that it conforms as closely to Freud's text as to the experience that it opened up, the crucial term is the signifier, brought back to life from the ancient art of rhetoric by modern linguistics, in a doctrine whose various stages cannot be traced here, but of which the names of Ferdinand de Saussure and Roman Jakobson will stand for the dawn and its present-day culmination, not forgetting that the pilot science of structuralism in the West has its roots in Russia, where formalism first flourished. 'Geneva 1910' and 'Petrograd 1920' suffice to explain why Freud lacked this particular tool. But this defect of history makes all the more instructive the fact that the mechanisms described by Freud as those of 'the primary process', in which the unconscious assumes its rule, correspond exactly to the functions that this school believes determines the most radical aspects of the effects of language, namely metaphor and metonymy – in other words, the signifier's effects of substitution and combination on the respectively synchronic and diachronic dimensions in which they appear in discourse.

Once the structure of language has been recognized in the unconscious, what sort of subject can we conceive for it?

We can try, with methodological rigour, to set out from the strictly linguistic definition of the I as signifier, in which there is nothing but the 'shifter' or indicative, which, in the subject of the statement, designates the subject in the sense that he is now speaking.

That is to say, it designates the subject of the enunciation,[3] but it does not signify it. This is apparent from the fact that every signifier of the subject of the enunciation may be lacking in the statement, not to mention the fact that there are those that differ from the I, and not only what is inadequately called the cases of the first person singular, even if one added its accommodation in the plural invocation, or even in the *Self* (*Soi*) of auto-suggestion.

I think, for example, that I recognized the subject of the enunciation in the signifier '*ne*', which grammarians call the expletive, a term that already prefigures the incredible opinion of those, and they are to be found among the best, who regard its form as being a matter of mere chance. May the weight that I give it persuade them to think again, before it becomes obvious that they have missed the point (*avant qu'il* ne *soit avéré qu'ils n'y comprennent rien*) – take out that *ne* and my enunciation loses its attack, *Je* eliding me into the impersonal. But I fear that in this way they will come to curse me (*je crains ainsi qu'ils* n'*en viennent à me honnir*) – slide over that *n'* and its absence, reducing the alleged fear of a declaration of my repugnance to a timid assertion, reduces the emphasis of my enunciation by situating me in the statement.

But if I say '*tue*' [the 3rd person singular of *tuer*, to kill and the past participle of *se taire*, to fall, or remain, silent], because they bore me to death, where am I situated if not in the '*tu*' [the familiar form of 'you'] from which I eye them?

Don't go into a sulk, I am merely referring obliquely to what I am reluctant to cover with the distorting map of clinical medicine.

Namely, the right way to reply to the question, 'Who is speaking?', when it is the subject of the unconscious that is at issue. For this reply cannot come from that subject if he does not know what he is saying, or even if he is speaking, as the entire experience of analysis has taught us.

It follows that the place of the 'inter-said' (*inter-dit*), which is the 'intra-said' (*intra-dit*) of a between-two-subjects, is the very place in which the transparency of the classical subject is divided and passes through the effects of 'fading'[4] that specify the Freudian subject by its occultation by an ever purer signifier: that these effects lead us to the frontiers at which slips of the tongue and witticisms, in their collusion, become confused, even where elision is so much the more allusive in tracking down presence to its lair, that one is surprised that the *Dasein* hunt hasn't done better out of it.

Lest the hunt be in vain for us analysts, we must bring everything back to the function of the cut in discourse, the strongest being that which acts as a bar between the signifier and the signified. There the subject that interests us is surprised, since by binding himself in signification he is placed under the sign of the pre-conscious. By which we would arrive at the paradox of conceiving that the discourse in an analytic session is valuable only in so far as it stumbles or is interrupted: if the session itself were not instituted as a cut in a false discourse, or rather, to the extent that the discourse succeeds in emptying itself as speech, in being no more than Mallarmé's worn coinage that is passed from hand to hand 'in silence'.

This cut in the signifying chain alone verifies the structure of the subject as discontinuity in the real. If linguistics enables us to see the signifier as the determinant of the signified, analysis reveals the truth of this relation by making 'holes' in the meaning of the determinants of its discourse.

It was along this line of approach that Freud was able to carry out the imperative, which he brought to a level of sublimity worthy of the pre-Socratics in the formulation, '*Wo es war, soll Ich werden*', which I have commented upon several times already, and which I will now try to present in a different light.

To take one step at a time in Freud's grammar: 'there where it was ...' (*là où ce fut* ...), which means what? If it were only that which had been (in an aoristic, indefinite form), how can I come there in order to make myself be there, to state it now?

But the French says: '*Là où c'était* ...' Let us make use of the benefit that French gives us of a distinct imperfect.[5] There where it was just now, there where it was for a while, between an extinction that is still glowing and a birth that is retarded, 'I' can come into being and disappear from what I say.

An enunciation that denounces itself, a statement that renounces itself, ignorance that dissipates itself, an opportunity that loses itself, what remains here if not the trace of what *must* be in order to fall from being?

A dream described by Freud in his article, 'Formulations on the Two Principles of the Mental Functioning',[6] gives us, with all the pathos that the figure of a dead father returning as a ghost would be invested, the sentence: 'He did not know that he was dead.'

I have already taken the pretext of this sentence to illustrate the relation of the subject to the signifier – a relation that is embodied in an enunciation (*énonciation*) whose being trembles with the vacillation that comes back to it from its own statement (*enoncé*).

If the figure of the dead father survives only by virtue of the fact that one does not tell him the truth of which he is unaware, what, then, is to be said of the *I*, on which this survival depends?

He did not know ... A little more and he'd have known. Oh! let's hope that never happens! Rather than have him know, *I*'d die. Yes, that's how *I* get there, there where it was: who knew, then, that *I* was dead?

Being of non-being, that is how *I* as subject comes on the scene, conjugated with the double aporia of a true survival that is abolished by knowledge of itself, and by a discourse in which it is death that sustains existence.

Are we to weigh this being against that, which Hegel as subject has forged, of being the subject who treats of history in the discourse of absolute knowledge? We remember that he admits to having experienced the temptation of madness. And is our way not that which overcomes that temptation, in going as far as the truth of the vanity of this discourse?

Let us not advance our doctrine on madness at this point. For this eschatological excursion is here only to designate the gap that separates those two relations of the subject to knowledge, the Freudian and the Hegelian.

And to show that there is no firmer root than the modes that distinguish the dialectic from desire.

For in Hegel it is desire (*Begierde*) that is given the responsibility for that minimum connexion with ancient knowledge (*connaissance*) that the subject must retain if truth is to be immanent in the realization of knowledge (*savoir*). Hegel's 'cunning of reason' means that, from beginning to end, the subject knows what he wants.

It is here that Freud reopens the junction between truth and knowledge to the mobility out of which revolutions come.

In this respect: that desire becomes bound up with the desire of the Other, but that in this loop lies the desire to know.

Freud's biologism has nothing to do with the moralistic abjection that wafts up from the psychoanalytic kitchen.

And you have to be made to live the death instinct, which is held in such abomination there, if you are to catch the true tone of Freud's biology. For to ignore the death instinct in his doctrine is to misunderstand that doctrine entirely.

From the approach that we have indicated, the reader should recognize in the metaphor of the return to the inanimate (which Freud attaches to every living body) that margin beyond life that language gives to the human being by virtue of the fact that he speaks, and which is precisely that in which such a being places in the position of a signifier, not only those parts of his body that are exchangeable, but this body itself. Thus it becomes apparent that the relation of the object to the body is in no way defined as a partial identification that would have to be totalized in such a relation, since, on the contrary, this object is the prototype of the significance of the body as that which for being is at stake.

At this point, I take up the challenge that is offered to me when what Freud calls *Trieb* is translated as '*instinct*'. 'Drive' would seem to translate the German word quite well in English, but is avoided in the *Standard Edition*. In French, my last resort would be '*dérive*', if I were unable to give the bastard term '*pulsion*' the necessary forcefulness.

And so we insist on promoting instinct, whether grounded or not in biological observation, to a place among the modes of knowledge (*connaissance*) required by nature of the living being so that he may satisfy his needs. Instinct is then defined as knowledge (*connaissance*) that has the astonishing property of being unable to be knowledge (*un savoir*). But in Freud it is a question of something quite different, which is a *savoir*, certainly, but one that involves not the least *connaissance*, in that it is inscribed in a discourse, of which, like the 'messenger-slave' of ancient usage, the subject who carries under his hair the codicil that condemns him to death knows neither the meaning nor the text, nor in what language it is written, nor even that it had been tatooed on his shaven scalp as he slept.

This story hardly exaggerates the little physiology that is of interest to the unconscious.

It will be appreciated by the counter-proof of the contribution made by psychoanalysis to physiology since its inception: this contribution is nil, even where the sexual organs are concerned. No amount of fabulation will alter this balance-sheet.

For, of course, psychoanalysis involves the real of the body and the imaginary of its mental schema. But to recognize their scope in the perspective that is authorized by development, we must first perceive that the more or less departmented integrations that appear to order it, function in it above all like heraldic elements, like the body's coat-of-arms. This is confirmed by the use one makes of it to read children's drawings.

What we have here is the principle – we shall return to it later – of the paradoxical privilege possessed by the phallus in the dialectic of the unconscious, without the theory produced by the part-object being a sufficient explanation of it.

Need I now say that if one understands what sort of support we have sought in Hegel to criticize a degradation of psychoanalysis so inept that it can find no other claim to interest than being the psychoanalysis of today, it is inadmissible that I should be thought of as having been lured by a purely dialectical exhaustion of being. Nor can I regard a particular philosopher[7] as being responsible when he authorizes this misunderstanding.

For far from ceding to a logicizing reduction where it is a question of desire, I find in its irreducibility to demand the very source of that which also prevents it from being reduced to need. To put it elliptically: it is precisely because desire is articulated that it is not articulable, I mean in the discourse best suited to it, an ethical, not a psychological discourse.

I must now develop much further for you the topology that I have elaborated in my teaching over the past five years, that is, introduce a certain diagram, which, I should warn you, also serves purposes other than the use that I am going to make of it here, having been constructed and completed quite openly in order to map in its arrangement the most broadly practical structure of the data of our experience. It will serve here to show where desire, in relation to a subject defined in his articulation by the signifier, is situated.

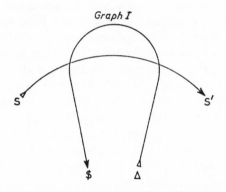

Graph I

This is what might be said to be its elementary cell (cf. *Graph I*). In it is articulated what I have called the 'anchoring point' (*point de capiton*), by which the signifier stops the otherwise endless movement (*glissement*) of the signification. The signifying chain is regarded as being supported by the vector $\overrightarrow{S.S'}$. – even without entering into the subtleties of the retrograde direction in which its double intersection with the vector $\overrightarrow{\triangle.\$}$ occurs. Only in this vector does one see the fish it hooks, a fish less suitable in its free movement to represent what it witholds from our grasp than the intention that tries to bury it in the mass of the pre-text, namely, the reality that is imagined in the ethological schema of the return of need.

The diachronic function of this anchoring point is to be found in the sentence, even if the sentence completes its signification only with its last term, each term being anticipated in the construction of the others, and, inversely, sealing their meaning by its retroactive effect.

But the synchronic structure is more hidden, and it is this structure that takes us to the source. It is metaphor in so far as the first attribution is constituted in it – the attribution that promulgates 'the dog goes miaow, the cat goes woof-woof',[8] by which the child, by disconnecting the animal from its cry, suddenly raises the sign to the function of the signifier, and reality to the sophistics of signification, and by contempt for verisimilitude, opens up the diversity of objectifications of the same thing that have to be verified.

Does this possibility require the topology of a four-cornered game? That is the sort of question that looks innocent enough, but which may give some trouble, if the subsequent construction must be dependent on it.

I will spare you the various stages by giving you at one go the function of the two points of intersection in this simplified graph. The first, connoted O, is the locus of the signifier's treasure, which does not mean the code's treasure, for it is not that the univocal correspondence of a sign with something is preserved in it, but that the signifier is constituted only from a synchronic and enumerable collection of elements in which each is sustained only by the principle of its opposition to each of the others. The second, connoted $s(O)$, is what may be called the punctuation in which the signification is constituted as finished product.

Observe the dyssymetry of the one, which is a locus (a place, rather than a space), to the other, which is a moment (a rhythm, rather than a duration).

Both participate in this offering to the signifier that is constituted by the hole in the real, the one as a hollow for concealment, the other as a boring-hole to escape from.

The subjection of the subject to the signifier, which occurs in the circuit that goes from $s(O)$ to O and back from O to $s(O)$ is really a circle, even though the assertion that is established in it – for lack of being able to end on anything other than its own scansion, in other words, for lack of an act in which it would find its certainty – refers only to its own anticipation in the composition of the signifier, in itself insignificant.

To be possible, the squaring of this circle only requires the completion of the signifying battery set up in O, henceforth symbolizing the locus of the Other. It then becomes apparent that this Other is simply the pure subject of modern games theory, and as such perfectly accessible to the calculation of conjecture, even though the real subject, in order to govern his own calculation, must leave out of account any so-called subjective aberration, in the common, that is, the psychological, acceptation of the term, and concern himself only with the inscription of an exhaustible combinatory.

Yet such a squaring is impossible, but only by virtue of the fact that the subject is constituted only by subtracting himself from it and by decompleting it essentially in order, at one and the same time, to have to depend on it and to make it function as a lack.

The Other as previous site of the pure subject of the signifier holds the master position, even before coming into existence, to use Hegel's term against him, as absolute Master. For what is omitted in the platitude of modern information theory is the fact that one can speak of code only if it is already the code of the Other, and that is something quite different from what is in question in the message, since it is from this code that the subject is constituted, which means that it is from the Other that the subject receives even the message that he emits. And the notations O and s(O) are justified.

Code messages or message codes will be distinguished in pure forms in the subject of psychosis, the subject who is satisfied with that previous Other.

Observe, in parentheses, that this Other, which is distinguished as the locus of Speech, imposes itself no less as witness to the Truth. Without the dimension that it constitutes, the deception practised by Speech would be indistinguishable from the very different pretence to be found in physical combat or sexual display. Pretence of this kind is deployed in imaginary capture, and is integrated into the play of approach and rejection that constituted the original dance, in which these two vital situations find their rhythm, and in accordance with which the partners ordered their movements – what I will dare to call their 'dancity' (*dansité*). Indeed, animals, too, show that they are capable of such behaviour when they are being hunted; they manage to put their pursuers off the scent by making a false start. This can go so far as to suggest on the part of the game animal the nobility of honoring the element of display to be found in the hunt. But an animal does not pretend to pretend. He does not make tracks whose deception lies in the fact that they will be taken as false, while being in fact true ones, ones, that is, that indicate his true trail. Nor does an animal cover up its tracks, which would be tantamount to making itself the subject of the signifier.

All this has been articulated in a confused way even by professional philosophers. But it is clear that Speech begins only with the passage from 'pretence' to the order of the signifier, and that the signifier requires another locus – the locus of the Other, the Other witness, the witness Other than any of the partners – for the Speech that it supports to be capable of lying, that is to say, of presenting itself as Truth.

Thus it is from somewhere other than the Reality that it concerns that

Truth derives its guarantee: it is from Speech. Just as it is from Speech that Truth receives the mark that establishes it in a fictional structure.

The first words spoken (*le dit premier*) stand as a decree, a law, an aphorism, an oracle; they confer their obscure authority upon the real other.

Take just one signifier as an emblem of this omnipotence, that is to say of this wholly potential power (*ce pouvoir tout en puissance*), this birth of possibility, and you have the unbroken line (*trait unaire*) which, by filling in the invisible mark that the subject derives from the signifier, alienates this subject in the primary identification that forms the ego ideal.

This is inscribed in the notation I(O), which, at this stage, I must substitute for the $, the barred S of the retrograde vector, bringing its tip back to its starting point (cf. *Graph II*).

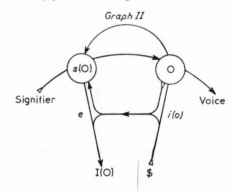

Graph II

This is a retroversion effect by which the subject becomes at each stage what he was before and announces himself – he will have been – only in the future perfect tense.

At this point the ambiguity of a failure to recognize that is essential to knowing myself (*un méconnaître essentiel au me connaître*) is introduced. For, in this 'rear view' (*rétrovisée*), all that the subject can be certain of is the anticipated image coming to meet him that he catches of himself in his mirror. I shall not return here to the function of my 'mirror stage', that first strategic point that I developed in opposition to the favour accorded in psychoanalytic theory to the supposedly *autonomous ego*. The academic restoration of this 'autonomous ego' justified my view that a misunderstanding was involved in any attempt to strengthen the ego in a type of analysis that took as its criterion of 'success' a successful adaptation to society – a phenomenon of mental abdication that was bound up with the ageing of the psychoanalytic group in the diaspora of the war, and the reduction of a distinguished practice to a label suitable to the 'American way of life'.[9]

In any case, what the subject finds in this altered image of his body is the paradigm of all the forms of resemblance that will bring over on to the world of objects a tinge of hostility, by projecting on them the manifestation of the narcissistic image, which, from the pleasure derived from meeting himself in the mirror, becomes when confrontating his fellow man an outlet for his most intimate aggressivity.

It is this image that becomes fixed, the ideal ego, from the point at which the subject stops as ego ideal. From this point on, the ego is a function of mastery, a play of presence, of bearing (*prestance*), and of constituted rivalry. In the capture to which it is subjected by its imaginary nature, the ego masks its duplicity, that is to say, the consciousness in which it assures itself of an incontestable existence (a naivety to be found in the meditation of a Fénelon) is in no way immanent in it, but, on the contrary, is transcendent, since it is supported by the unbroken line of the ego ideal (which the Cartesian *cogito* did not fail to recognize[10]). As a result, the transcendental ego itself is relativized, implicated as it is in the *méconnaissance* in which the ego's identifications take root.

This imaginary process, which begins with the specular image and goes on to the constitution of the ego by way of subjectification by the signifier, is signified in our graph by the vector $\overrightarrow{i(o) \cdot e}$, which is one-way, but which is doubly articulated, once in a short circuit over $\overrightarrow{\$ \cdot I(O)}$, and again in a return direction over $\overrightarrow{s(O) \cdot O}$. This shows that the ego is only completed by being articulated not as the *I* of discourse, but as a metonymy of its signification (what Damourette and Pichon take as the 'alloyed' (*étoffé*) person, as opposed to the 'purified' (*subtile*) person, the latter being no more than the function designated above as the 'shifter').

The promotion of consciousness as being essential to the subject in the historical after-effects of the Cartesian *cogito* is for me the deceptive accentuation of the transparency of the I in action at the expense of the opacity of the signifier that determines the I; and the sliding movement (*glissement*) by which the *Bewusstsein* serves to cover up the confusion of the *Selbst* eventually reveals, with all Hegel's own rigour, the reason for his error in *The Phenomenology of Mind*.

The very movement that shifts the axis of the phenomenon of mind

towards the imaginary relation to the other (that is to say, to the counterpart connoted by the small 'o', the *objet petit* a), reveals its effect: namely,
the aggressivity that becomes the beam of the balance on which will be
centred the decomposition of the equilibrium of counterpart to counterpart in the Master-Slave relationship, a relationship that is pregnant with
all the cunning tricks (*ruses*) by which reason sets its impersonal reign in
motion.

I can now show what is concealed in this initial enslavement – a
mythical, rather than a real genesis, no doubt – of the 'roads to freedom'
precisely because I have revealed it as never before.

The struggle that establishes this initial enslavement is rightly called a
struggle of pure prestige, and the stake, life itself, is well suited to echo
that danger of the generic prematuration of birth, which Hegel was
unaware of, and which I see as the dynamic origin of specular capture.

But precisely because it is drawn into the function of the stakes – a more
honest wager than Pascal's, though it is also a question of poker, since
there is a limit on how high one can raise the bid – death shows by the
same token what is elided from a prior rule, and from the ultimate rule.
For, in the end, the loser must not perish if he is to become a slave. In
other words, the pact is everywhere anterior to the violence before
perpetuating it, and what I call the symbolic dominates the imaginary,
which is why one may ask oneself whether murder is the absolute Master.

For it is not enough to decide on the basis of its effect – Death. It still
remains to be decided which death,[11] that which is brought by life or
that which brings life.

Without detracting from the Hegelian dialectic by an accusation of
inadequacy, which has often been laid against it on the question of what
bound the society of masters together, I simply wish at this point to
stress what, on the basis of my own experience, is self-evidently symptomatic, that is to say, as installation in repression. This is properly the
theme of the Cunning (*Ruse*) practised by reason – and the fact that it is
erroneous, as I pointed out above, in no way diminishes its attraction.
The work to which the slave is subjected and the pleasure that he renounces out of fear of death, we are told, will be precisely the way through
which he will achieve freedom. There can be no more obvious lure
than this, politically or psychologically. *Jouissance* comes easily to the
slave, and it will leave the work in bondage.

The cunning of reason is an attractive notion because it echoes with a
personal myth that is very familiar to the obsessional neurotic, and whose

structure is often found among the *intelligentsia*. But even if the obsessional avoids the bad faith of the professor, he cannot easily deceive himself that it is his work that must make *jouissance* possible for him. Paying very properly unconscious homage to the history written by Hegel, he often finds his alibi in the death of the Master. But what about this death? He quite simply waits for it.

In fact, it is from the locus of the Other where he installs himself that he follows the game, thus rendering any risk inoperant, especially the risk of any contest, in a 'consciousness-of-self' for which death is present only in jest.

So philosophers should not make the mistake of thinking that they can take little account of the irruption that Freud's views on desire represented.

And this under the pretext that demand, together with the effects of frustration, has submerged everything that reaches them from a practice that has declined into educative banality that cannot be revived even by such a sell-out.

Yes, the enigmatic traumas of the Freudian discovery are now merely repressed desires. Psychoanalysis is nourished by the observation of children and by the infantilism of the observations. I will not bore you with case-histories, edifying as they all no doubt are – though they are hardly noted for their humour, their authors being too concerned with their 'responsibilities' to leave any room for the irremediably ridiculous side to the relations that the unconscious maintains with its linguistic roots.

Yet it is impossible, for those who claim that it is through the welcome accorded to demand that incompatibility is introduced into the needs that are supposed to lie at the origin of the subject, to ignore the fact that there is no demand that does not in some sense pass through the defiles of the signifier.

And if the somatic *ananke* of man's powerlessness for some time after birth to move of his own accord, and *a fortiori* to be self-sufficient, en-sures that he will be grounded in a psychology of dependence, how can that *ananke* ignore the fact that this dependence is maintained by a world of language, precisely because by and through language needs are diversi-fied and reduced to a point at which their scope appears to be of a quite different order, whether in relation to the subject or to politics? To sum up: to the point that these needs have passed over into the register of desire, with all that this brings in terms of an obligation to confront our new experience with its paradoxes, which have always interested the moralist, with that mark of the infinite that theologians find in it, even with the precariousness of its status, as expressed in its most extreme form by Sartre: desire, a useless passion.

What psychoanalysis shows us about desire in what might be called its most natural function, since on it depends the propagation of the species, is not only that it is subjected, in its agency, its appropriation, its normality, in short, to the accidents of the subject's history (the notion of trauma as contingency), but also that all this requires the co-operation of structural elements, which, in order to intervene, can do very well without these accidents, whose effects, so unharmonious, so unexpected, so difficult to reduce, certainly seem to leave to experience a remainder that drove Freud to admit that sexuality must bear the mark of some unnatural split (*fêlure*).

It would be wrong to think that the Freudian myth of the Oedipus complex had put an end to theology on the matter. For it is not enough to wave the flag of sexual rivalry. It would be better to read what Freud has to say about its co-ordinates; for they amount to the question with which he himself set out: 'What is a Father?'

'It is the dead Father', Freud replies, but no one listens, and, concerning that part of it that Lacan takes up again under the heading 'Name-of-the-Father', it is regrettable that so unscientific a situation should still deprive him of his normal audience.[12]

Yet analytic reflexion has centred vaguely on the problematic *méconnaissance* on the part of certain primitive peoples of the function of the progenitor, and psychoanalysts have argued, under the contraband banner of 'culturalism', over the forms of an authority of which it cannot even be said that any sector of anthropology has provided a definition of any scope.

Will we have to be overtaken by the practice, which may in the course of time become common practice, of artificially inseminating women who have broken the phallic bounds with the sperm of some great man, before a verdict on the paternal function can be dragged out of us?

Yet the Oedipus complex cannot run indefinitely in forms of society that are more and more losing the sense of tragedy.

Let us set out from the conception of the Other as the locus of the signifier. Any statement of authority has no other guarantee than its very enunciation, and it is pointless for it to seek it in another signifier, which could not appear outside this locus in any way. Which is what I mean when I say that no metalanguage can be spoken, or, more aphoristically, that there is no Other of the Other. And when the Legislator (he who claims to lay down the Law) presents himself to fill the gap, he does so as an imposter.

But there is nothing false about the Law itself, or about him who assumes its authority.

The fact that the Father may be regarded as the original representative of this authority of the Law requires us to specify by what privileged mode of presence he is sustained beyond the subject who is actually led to occupy the place of the Other, namely, the Mother. The question, therefore, is pushed still further back.

It will seem odd, no doubt, that in opening up the immeasurable space that all demand implies, namely, that of being a request for love, I should not leave more play to the question; but should concentrate it on that which is closed this side of it, by the very effect of demand, in order to give desire its proper place.

Indeed, it is quite simply, and I will say later in what way, as desire of the Other that man's desire finds form, but it does so in the first instance by representing need only by means of a subjective opacity.

I will now explain by what bias this opacity produces, as it were, the substance of desire.

Desire begins to take shape in the margin in which demand becomes separated from need: this margin being that which is opened up by demand, the appeal of which can be unconditional only in regard to the Other, under the form of the possible defect, which need may introduce into it, of having no universal satisfaction (what is called 'anxiety'). A margin which, linear as it may be, reveals its vertigo, even if it is not trampled by the elephantine feet of the Other's whim. Nevertheless, it is this whim that introduces the phantom of the Omnipotence, not of the subject, but of the Other in which his demand is installed (it is time this idiotic cliché was, once and for all, put back in its place), and with this phantom the need for it to be checked by the Law.

But I will stop there and return to the status of the desire that presents itself as autonomous in relation to this mediation of the Law, for the simple reason that it originates in desire, by virtue of the fact that by a strange symmetry it reverses the unconditional nature of the demand for love, in which the subject remains in subjection to the Other, and raises it to the power of absolute condition (in which 'absolute' also implies 'detachment').

For the gain obtained over anxiety with regard to need, this detachment is successful in its first, humblest form, that in which it was detected by a certain psychoanalyst in the course of his pediatric practice, and which is called 'the transitional object', in other words, the bit of 'nappie' or the beloved bit of material that the child never allows to leave his lips or hand.

This is no more than an emblem, I say; the representative of representation in the absolute condition is at home in the unconscious, where it causes desire according to the structure of the phantasy that I will now extract from it.

For it is clear that the state of nescience in which man remains in relation to his desire is not so much a nescience of what he demands, which may after all be circumscribed, as a nescience as to where he desires.

This is what I mean by my formula that the unconscious is *'discours de l'Autre'* (discourse of the Other), in which the *de* is to be understood in the sense of the Latin *de* (objective determination): *de Alio in oratione* (completed by: *tua res agitur*).

But we must also add that man's desire is the *désir de l'Autre* (the desire of the Other) in which the *de* provides what grammarians call the 'subjective determination', namely that it is *qua* Other that he desires (which is what provides the true compass of human passion).

That is why the question *of* the Other, which comes back to the subject from the place from which he expects an oracular reply in some such form as *'Che vuoi?'*, 'What do you want?', is the one that best leads him to the path of his own desire – providing he sets out, with the help of the skills of a partner known as a psychoanalyst, to reformulate it, even without knowing it, as 'What does he want of me?'

It is this superimposed level of the structure that will bring my graph (cf. *Graph III*) to completion, first by introducing into it as the drawing of a question-mark placed in the circle of the capital O of the Other, symbolizing by a confusing homography the question it signifies.

Of what bottle is this the opener? Of what reply is it the signifier, the universal key?

It should be noted that a clue may be found in the clear alienation that leaves to the subject the favour of stumbling upon the question of its essence, in that he cannot fail to recognize that what he desires presents itself to him as what he does not want, the form assumed by the negation in which the *méconnaissance* of which he himself is unaware is inserted in a very strange way – a *méconnaissance* by which he transfers the permanence of his desire to an ego that is nevertheless intermittent, and, inversely, protects himself from his desire by attributing to it these very intermittences.

Of course, one may be surprised by the extent of what is accessible to consciousness-of-self, providing one has learnt it elsewhere – which is certainly the case here.

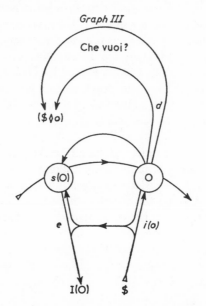

Graph III

Che vuoi?

($◊o)

d

s(O)   O

e   i(o)

I(O) $

For in order to rediscover the pertinence of all this, a fairly detailed study is required – a study that can only take place in the analytic experience – that would enable us to complete the structure of the phantasy by linking it essentially, whatever its occasional elisions may be, to the condition of an object (the privilege of which I have done no more than touch on above in terms of diachrony), the moment of a 'fading'[13] or eclipse of the subject that is closely bound up with the *Spaltung* or splitting that it suffers from its subordination to the signifier.

This is what is symbolized by the sigla ($◊o), which I have introduced in the form of an algorithm; and it is no accident that it breaks the phonematic element constituted by the signifying unity right down to its literal atom. For it is created to allow a hundred and one different readings, a multiplicity that is admissible as long as the spoken remains caught in its algebra.

This algorithm and the analogues of it used in the graph in no way contradict what I said earlier about the impossibility of a metalanguage. They are not transcendent signifiers; they are the indices of an absolute signification, a notion which, without further commentary, will seem appropriate, I hope, to the condition of the phantasy.

On to the phantasy presented in this way, the graph inscribes that desire governs itself, which is similar to the relation between the ego and the body image, except that it still marks the inversion of the *méconnais-sances* on which each is based. Thus the imaginary way, through which I must pass in analysis, and where the unconscious was *itself*,[14] is closed.

Let us say, borrowing the metaphor used by Damourette and Pichon about the grammatical 'I' and applying it to a subject to which it is better suited, that the phantasy is really the 'stuff' of the 'I' that is originally repressed, because it can be indicated only in the 'fading' of the enunciation.

So our attention is now drawn to the subjective status of the signifying chain in the unconscious, or rather in primal repression (*Urverdrängung*).

In our deduction it is easier to understand why it was necessary to question oneself regarding the function that supports the subject of the unconscious, to grasp that it is difficult to designate that subject anywhere as subject of a statement, and therefore as the articulator, when he does not even know that he is speaking. Hence the concept of drive, in which he is designated by an organic, oral, anal, etc., mapping that satisfies the requirement of being all the farther away from speaking the more he speaks.

But although our completed graph enables us to place the drive as the treasure of the signifiers, its notation as ($\lozenge$D) maintains its structure by linking it with diachrony. It is that which proceeds from demand when the subject disappears in it. It is obvious enough that demand also disappears, with the single exception that the cut remains, for this cut remains present in that which distinguishes the drive from the organic function it inhabits: namely, its grammatical artifice, so manifest in the reversions of its articulation to both source and object – Freud is un-failingly illuminating on this matter.

The very delimitation of the 'erogenous zone' that the drive isolates from the metabolism of the function (the act of devouring concerns other organs than the mouth – ask one of Pavlov's dogs) is the result of a cut (*coupure*) expressed in the anatomical mark (*trait*) of a margin or border – lips, 'the enclosure of the teeth', the rim of the anus, the tip of the penis, the vagina, the slit formed by the eyelids, even the horn-shaped aperture of the ear (I am avoiding embryological details here). Respiratory erogeneity has been little studied, but it is obviously through the spasm that it comes into play.

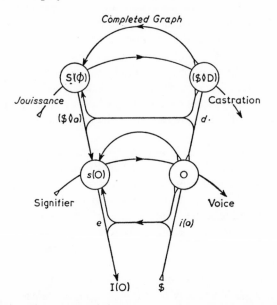

Observe that this mark of the cut is no less obviously present in the object described by analytic theory: the mamilla, faeces, the phallus (imaginary object), the urinary flow. (An unthinkable list, if one adds, as I do, the phoneme, the gaze, the voice – the nothing.) For is it not obvious that this feature, this partial feature, rightly emphasized in objects, is applicable not because these objects are part of a total object, the body, but because they represent only partially the function that produces them?

These objects have one common feature in my elaboration of them – they have no specular image, or, in other words, alterity.[15] It is what enables them to be the 'stuff', or rather the lining, though not in any sense the reverse, of the very subject that one takes to be the subject of consciousness. For this subject, who thinks he can accede to himself by designating himself in the statement, is no more than such an object. Ask the writer about the anxiety that he experiences when faced by the blank sheet of paper, and he will tell you who *is* the turd of his phantasy.

It is to this object that cannot be grasped in the mirror that the specular image lends its clothes. A substance caught in the net of the shadow, and which, robbed of its shadow-swelling volume, holds out once again the tired lure of the shadow as if it were substance.[16]

What the graph now offers us is situated at the point at which every signifying chain prides itself on looping its signification. If we are to expect such an effect from the unconscious enunciation, it is to be found here in S(Ø), and read as: signifier of a lack in the Other, inherent in its very function as the treasure of the signifier. And this is so even though the Other is required (*che vuoi*) to respond to the value of this treasure, that is to say, to reply, from its place in the lower chain certainly, but also in the signifiers that constitute the upper chain, in terms of drive, in other words.

The lack referred to here is indeed that which I have already formulated: that there is no Other of the Other. But is this mark made by the Unbeliever of the truth really the last word that is worth giving in reply to the question, 'What does the Other want of me?', when we, the analysts, are its mouthpiece? Surely not, and precisely because there is nothing doctrinal about our office. We are answerable to no ultimate truth; we are neither for nor against any particular religion.

It is already quite enough that at this point I had to situate the dead Father in the Freudian myth. But a myth is not enough to support a rite, and psychoanalysis is not the rite of the Oedipus complex – a point that I shall develop later.

No doubt the corpse is a signifier, but Moses's tomb is as empty for Freud as that of Christ was for Hegel. Abraham revealed his mystery to neither of them.

Personally, I will begin with what is articulated in the sigla S(Ø) by being first of all a signifier. My definition of a signifier (there is no other) is as follows: a signifier is that which represents the subject for another signifier. This signifier will therefore be the signifier for which all the other signifiers represent the subject: that is to say, in the absence of this signifier, all the other signifiers represent nothing, since nothing is represented only *for* something else.

And since the battry of signifiers, as such, is by that very fact complete, this signifier can only be a line (*trait*) that is drawn from its circle without being able to be counted part of it. It can be symbolized by the inherence of a (—I) in the whole set of signifiers.

As such it is inexpressible, but its operation is not inexpressible, for it is that which is produced whenever a proper noun is spoken. Its statement equals its signification.

Thus, by calculating that signification according to the algebraic method used here, namely:

$$\frac{S(\text{signifier})}{s(\text{signified})} = s \text{ (the statement), with } S = (-I), \text{ produces: } s = \sqrt{-I}.$$

This is what the subject lacks in order to think himself exhausted by his *cogito*, namely, that which is unthinkable for him. But where does this being, who appears in some way defective in the sea of proper nouns, originate?

We cannot ask this question of the subject as 'I'. He lacks everything needed to know the answer, since if this subject 'I' was dead, he would not, as I said earlier, know it. He does not know, therefore, that I am alive. How, therefore, will 'I' prove to myself that I am?

For I can only just prove to the Other that he exists, not, of course, with the proofs for the existence of God, with which over the centuries he has been killed off, but by loving him, a solution introduced by the Christian *kerygma*. Indeed, it is too precarious a solution for me even to think of using it as a means of circumventing our problem, namely: 'What am "I"?'

'I' am in the place from which a voice is heard clamouring 'the universe is a defect in the purity of Non-Being'.

And not without reason, for by protecting itself this place makes Being itself languish. This place is called *Jouissance*, and it is the absence of this that makes the universe vain.

Am I responsible for it, then? Yes, probably. Is this *Jouissance*, the lack of which makes the Other insubstantial, mine, then? Experience proves that it is usually forbidden me, not only, as certain fools believe, because of a bad arrangement of society, but rather because of the fault (*faute*) of the Other if he existed: and since the Other does not exist, all that remains to me is to assume the fault upon 'I', that is to say, to believe in that to which experience leads us all, Freud in the vanguard, namely, to original sin. For even if we did not have Freud's express, and sorrowful avowal, the fact would remain that the myth Freud gave us – the latest-born myth in history – is no more use than that of the forbidden apple, except for the fact, and this has nothing to do with its power as myth, that, though more succinct, it is distinctly less oppressive (*crétinisant*).

But what is not a myth, and which Freud nevertheless formulated soon after the Oedipus complex, is the castration complex.

In the castration complex we find the major mainspring of the very subversion that I am trying to articulate here by means of its dialectic. For this complex, which was unknown as such until Freud introduced it into the formation of desire, can no longer be ignored in any reflexion on the subject.

There can be little doubt that in psychoanalysis, far from there having been any attempt to carry its articulation further, it has been employed precisely in order to avoid any explanation of it. This is why this great Samson-like body has been reduced to turning the grinding wheel for the Philistines of general psychology.

Certainly there is in all this what is called a bone. Though it is precisely what is suggested here, namely, that it is structural of the subject, it constitutes in it essentially that margin that all thought has avoided, skipped over, circumvented, or blocked whenever it seems to succeed in being sustained by a circle, whether that circle be dialectical or mathematical.

This is why I am so anxious to guide my students over the places where logic is disconcerted by the disjunction that breaks through from the imaginary to the symbolic, not in order to enjoy the paradoxes that are produced in such a disjunction, nor to point out some 'crisis' in thought, but, on the contrary, to bring their false brilliance back to the gap that they designate, which I always find instructive, and above all to try to work out the method of a sort of calculation, the inappropriation of which as such would spoil the secret.

Such is the phantom of the cause, which I have followed in the purest symbolization of the imaginary through the alternation of the similar and the dissimilar.[17]

Let us observe carefully, therefore, what it is that objects to conferring on our signifier S($\emptyset$) the meaning of *Mana* or of any of its cognates. The fact is we cannot be content to articulate it from the poverty of the social fact, even if this is tracked down in some supposed total fact.

No doubt Claude Lévi-Strauss, in his commentary on Mauss, wished to recognize in it the effect of a zero symbol. But it seems to me that what we are dealing with here is rather the signifier of the lack of this zero symbol. That is why, at the risk of incurring a certain amount of opprobrium, I have indicated to what point I have pushed the distortion of the mathematical algorithm in my use of it: the symbol $\sqrt{-1}$, which is still written as '*i*' in the theory of complex numbers, is obviously justified only because it makes no claim to any automatism in its later use.

But we must insist that *jouissance* is forbidden to him who speaks as such, although it can only be said between the lines for whoever is subject of the Law, since the Law is grounded in this very prohibition.

Indeed, the Law appears to be giving the order, '*Jouis!*', to which the subject can only reply '*J'ouis*' (I hear), the *jouissance* being no more than understood.

But it is not the Law itself that bars the subject's access to *jouissance* – rather it creates out of an almost natural barrier a barred subject. For it is pleasure that sets the limits on *jouissance*, pleasure as that which binds incoherent life together, until another, unchallengeable prohibition arises from the regulation that Freud discovered as the primary process and appropriate law of pleasure.

It has been said that in this discovery Freud merely followed the course already being pursued by the science of his time, indeed, that it belonged to a long-standing tradition. To appreciate the true audacity of his step, we have only to consider his recompense, which was not slow in coming: failure over the heteroclite nature of the castration complex.

It is the only indication of that *jouissance* of its infinitude that brings with it the mark of its prohibition, and, in order to constitute that mark, involves a sacrifice: that which is made in one and the same act with the choice of its symbol, the phallus.

This choice is allowed because the phallus, that is, the image of the penis, is negativity in its place in the specular image. It is what predestines the phallus to embody *jouissance* in the dialectic of desire.

We must distinguish, therefore, between the principle of sacrifice, which is symbolic, and the imaginary function that is devoted to that principle of sacrifice, but which, at the same time, masks the fact that it gives it its instrument.

The imaginary function is that which Freud formulated to govern the investment of the object as narcissistic object. It was to this point that I returned myself when I showed that the specular image is the channel taken by the transfusion of the body's libido towards the object. But even though part of it remains preserved from this immersion, concentrating within it the most intimate aspect of auto-eroticism, its position at the 'tip' of the form predisposes it to the phantasy of decrepitude in which is completed its exclusion from the specular image and from the prototype that it constitutes for the world of objects.

Thus the erectile organ comes to symbolize the place of *jouissance*, not in itself, or even in the form of an image, but as a part lacking in the desired image: that is why it is equivalent to the $\sqrt{-1}$ of the signification produced above, of the *jouissance* that it restores by the coefficient of its statement to the function of lack of signifier (—I).

If its role, therefore, is to bind the prohibition of *jouissance*, it is nevertheless not for these formal reasons, but because their supersession (*outrepassement*) signifies that which reduces all desired *jouissance* to the brevity of auto-eroticism: the paths laid out by the anatomical conformation of the speaking being, that is, the already perfected hand of the monkey, have not, in effect, been ignored in a certain philosophical ascesis as paths of a wisdom that has wrongly been termed cynical. Certain individuals, obsessed no doubt by this memory, have suggested to me that Freud himself belongs to this tradition: the technique of the body, as Mauss calls it. The fact remains that analytic experience demonstrates the original character of the guilt that its practice induces.

Guilt that is bound up with the recall of *jouissance* that is lacking in the office rendered to the real organ, and consecration of the function of the imaginary signifier to strike the objects of prohibition.

This, indeed, is the radical function for which a more primitive stage in the development of psychoanalysis found more accidental (educative) causes, just as it inflected towards the trauma the other forms in which it had the merit of interesting itself, namely, those relating to the sacralization of the organ (circumcision).

The passage from the (—φ) (small phi) of the phallic image from one side to the other of the equation, from the imaginary to the symbolic, renders it positive in any case, even if it fulfils a lack. Although a support of the (—I), it becomes Φ (capital phi), the symbolic phallus that cannot be negated, the signifier of *jouissance*. And it is this character of the Φ that explains both the particularities of the woman's approach to sexuality, and that which makes the male sex the weak sex in the case of perversion.

I will not deal with the question of perversion here, in as much as it accentuates to some extent the function of desire in the man, in so far as he sets up dominance in the privileged place of *jouissance*, the object *o* of the phantasy (*objet petit* a), which he substitutes for the Ø. Perversion adds a reabsorption of the φ that would scarcely appear original if it did not interest the Other as such in a very particular way. Only my formulation of phantasy enables us to reveal that the subject here makes himself the instrument of the Other's *jouissance*.

It is all the more important for philosophers to grasp the relevance of this formula in the case of the neurotic, precisely because the neurotic falsifies it.

Indeed, the neurotic, whether hysteric, obsessional, or, more radically, phobic, is he who identifies the lack of the Other with his demand, Φ with D.

As a result, the demand of the Other assumes the function of an object in his phantasy, that is to say, his phantasy (my formulae make it possible to know this phantasy immediately) is reduced to the drive ($◊D). That is why it was possible to draw up the catalogue of drives in the case of the neurotic.

But this prevalence given by the neurotic to demand, which, for an analysis declining into facility, shifted the whole treatment towards the handling of frustration, conceals its anxiety from the desire of the Other, anxiety that is impossible not to recognize when it is covered only by the phobic object, but more difficult to understand in the case of the other two neuroses, when one is not in possession of the thread that makes it possible to present the phantasy as desire of the Other. One then finds its two terms shattered, as it were: the first, in the case of the obsessional, in as much as he denies the desire of the Other in forming his phantasy by accentuating the impossibility of the subject vanishing, the second, in the case of the hysteric, in as much as desire is maintained only through the lack of satisfaction that is introduced into it when he eludes himself as object.

These features are confirmed by the fundamental need of the obsessional neurotic to stand in the place of the Other, and by the disbelieving side of hysterical intrigue.

In fact, the image of the ideal Father is a phantasy of the neurotic. Beyond the Mother, the real Other of demand, whose desire (that is, her desire) one wishes she would assuage, there stands out the image of a father who would close his eyes to desires. The true function of the Father, which is fundamentally to unite (and not to set in opposition) a desire and the Law, is even more marked than revealed by this.

The neurotic's wished-for Father is clearly the dead Father. But he is also a Father who can perfectly master his desire — and the same can be said of the subject.

This is one of the dangers that analysis must avoid, the interminable aspect of the transference principle.

That is why a calculated vacillation of the analyst's 'neutrality' may be more valuable for a hysteric than any amount of interpretation – though there is always a danger of frightening the patient. Provided, of course, that this fright does not lead to a breaking off of the analysis, and that he becomes convinced by what follows that the analyst's desire was in no way involved. This, of course, is not a piece of technical advice, but a view that is opened up to the question of the analyst's desire for those who would not otherwise know about it: how the analyst must preserve for the other the imaginary dimension of his non-mastery, of his necessary imperfection, is as important a matter to settle as the intentional consolidation in him of his ignorance of each subject who comes to him for analysis, of an ever renewed ignorance that prevents anyone becoming a 'case'.

To return to phantasy, let us say that the pervert imagines himself to be the Other in order to ensure his *jouissance*, and that it is what the neurotic reveals when he imagines himself to be a pervert – in his case, to assure himself of the existence of the Other.

It is this that gives the meaning of the perversion that is supposed to lie in the very principle of neurosis. The perversion is in the unconscious of the neurotic as phantasy of the Other. But this does not mean that in the case of the pervert the unconscious is 'open ended'. He, too, after his fashion, defends himself in his desire. For desire is a defence (*défense*), a prohibition (*défense*) against going beyond a certain limit in *jouissance*.

In its structure as I have defined it, the phantasy contains the $(-\varphi)$, the imaginary function of castration under a hidden form, reversible from one of its terms to the other. That is to say, like a complex number, it imaginarizes (if I may use such a term) alternatively one of these terms in relation to the other.

Included in the *objet* a is the ἄγαλμα, the inestimable treasure that Alcibiades declares is contained in the rustic box that for him Socrates's face represents. But let us observe that it bears the sign $(-)$. It is because he has not seen Socrates's prick, if I may be permitted to follow Plato, who does not spare us the details, that Alcibiades the seducer exalts in him the ἄγαλμα, the marvel that he would like Socrates to cede to him in avowing his desire: the division of the subject that he bears within himself being admitted with great clarity on this occasion.

Such is the woman concealed behind her veil: it is the absence of the penis that turns her into the phallus, the object of desire. Draw attention to this absence in a more precise way by getting her to wear a pretty wig and fancy dress, and you, or rather she, will have plenty to tell us about:

the effect is guaranteed 100 per cent, for men who go straight to the point.

Thus by showing his object as castrated, Alcibiades presents himself as he who desires – a fact that does not escape Socrates's attention – for someone else who is present, Agathon, whom Socrates, the precursor of psychoanalysis, and confident of his position in this fashionable gathering, does not hesitate to name as the object of the transference, placing in the light of an interpretation a fact that many analysts are still unaware of: that the love–hate effect in the analytic situation is to be found elsewhere.

But Alcibiades is certainly not a neurotic. It is even because he is *par excellence* he who desires, and he who goes as far as he can along the path of *jouissance*, that he can thus (with the help of a certain amount of drink) produce in the eyes of all the central articulation of the transference, made present by the object adorned with his reflexions.

Nevertheless, he projected Socrates into the ideal of the perfect Master, whom, through the action of $(-\varphi)$, he has completely imaginarized.

In the case of the neurotic, the $(-\varphi)$ slides under the $\math$ of the phantasy, to the advantage of the imagination that is peculiar to it, that of the ego. For the neurotic has been subjected to imaginary castration from the beginning; it is castration that sustains this strong ego, so strong, one might say, that its proper name is an inconvenience for it, since the neurotic is really Nameless.

Yes, it is beneath this ego, which certain analysts choose to strengthen still more, that the neurotic hides the castration that he denies.

But, contrary to appearances, he clings to it.

What the neurotic does not want, and what he strenuously refuses to do, until the end of the analysis, is to sacrifice his castration to the *jouissance* of the Other by allowing it to serve that *jouissance*.

And, of course, he is not wrong, for although, at bottom, he feels himself to be what is most vain in existing, a Want-to-be (*un Manque-à-être*) or a Too-much-of-it (*un En-Trop*), why should he sacrifice his difference (anything but that) to the *jouissance* of an Other, which, let us remember, does not exist. Yes, but if by some chance it did exist, he would 'enjoy' it (*il en jouirait*). And that is what the neurotic does not want. For he imagines that the Other demands his castration.

What analytic experience shows is that, in any case, it is castration that governs desire, whether in the normal or the abnormal

Providing it oscillates alternately between $\mathⅩ$ and *o* in the phantasy, castration turns phantasy into that supple, yet inextensible chain by which the arrest of the object-investment, which can hardly go beyond certain natural limits, takes on the transcendental function of ensuring the *jouissance* of the Other, which passes this chain on to me in the Law.

To whomsoever really wishes to confront this Other, there opens up the way of experiencing not only his demand, but also his will. And then: either to realize oneself as object, to turn oneself into a mummy, as in some Buddhist initiation rite, or to satisfy the will to castration inscribed in the Other, which culminates in the supreme narcissism of the Lost Cause (this is the way of Greek tragedy, which Claudel rediscovers in a Christianity of despair).

Castration means that *jouissance* must be refused, so that it can be reached on the inverted ladder (*l'échelle renversée*) of the Law of desire. I won't go any further here.

>>≪≪

This article is now appearing for the first time: an unexpected shortage of the funds that are usually lavished on the publication, even in their entirety, of such 'round-table' conferences having left it in abeyance, together with all the fine things that adorned this one.

I should mention, for the record, that the 'Copernican' development was added later, and that the end of the article, on castration, was never delivered owing to lack of time, and was replaced in fact by a few remarks on the machine in the modern sense of the word, from which the relation of the subject to the signifier can be materialized.

From the fellow feeling natural in any discussion, I should not like to exclude that which was aroused in me by a particular disagreement. The term 'a-human' which someone wished to attribute to what I said did not cause me the least distress, since the element of the new that the category implies gave me, on the contrary, a certain pleasure. I noted with no less interest the crackling that followed soon afterwards at the word 'hell', since the voice that pronounced it gave it, owing to the speaker's declared allegiance to Marxism, a certain piquancy. I must admit that I am partial to a certain form of humanism, a humanism that comes from an area where, although it is not used with any less cunning than elsewhere, nevertheless has a certain quality of candour about it: 'When the miner comes home, his wife rubs him down ...' I am left defenceless against such things.

In a private conversation someone asked me (this was how he put it) whether to speak for the blackboard did not imply belief in an eternal scribe. Such a belief is not necessary, I replied, to him who knows that all discourse has its effect through the unconscious.

Notes

1. Or even from attempting to interest people, under the heading of *Psi* phenomena, in telepathy, or in the whole Gothic psychology that a Myers is capable of reviving. The most vulgar quack will be able to uncross the field in which Freud has contained him in advance, by presenting what he accepts of these phenomena as requiring translation, in the strict sense of the term, into contemporary forms of discourse.

Even when prostituted, psychoanalytic theory remains prudish (a well-known characteristic of the brothel). As we say since Sartre, she's a respectable girl [*une respectueuse*, a reference to Sartre's play, *La putain respectueuse* – Tr.]: she won't walk in any old street (note added, 1966).

2. The original reads: 'le rapport de travers (en anglais on dirait: skew) . . .' [Tr.].

3. I have translated *énoncé* as 'statement' and *énonciation* as 'enunciation', the former referring to the actual words uttered, the second to the act of uttering them [Tr.].

4. English in the original [Tr.].

5. The English 'was' translates the French '*fut*' (*passé simple*, past historic) and *était* (*imparfait*, imperfect) [Tr.].

6. *G.W.*, VIII: 237–8; *Standard Edition*, 12: 225–6.

7. I am referring here to the friend who invited me to this conference, having, some months before, revealed to me the reservations that he derived from his personal ontology against 'psychoanalysts' who were too 'Hegelian' for his liking, as if anyone except myself in that assembly could be accused of this.

This in the confusion of pages from his journal cast to the four winds (no doubt by accident) that had snatched them from him.

At which I made him agree that, in order to interest this ontology of his in the, even entertaining, terms in which he clothed it in familiar notes, I found its

'certainly not, but perhaps' procedure doomed to mislead.

8. '*Le chien fait miaou, le chat fait oua-oua*'. A nursery song in which various animals are attributed with the wrong sound [Tr.].

9. I leave this paragraph only as a monument to a battle long since forgotten (note added, 1962: where was my head?).

10. The words in brackets have been added, with a view to pinpointing later developments on identification (1962).

11. This, too, refers to what I said in my seminar, 'L'Éthique de la psychanalyse' (1959–60), on the second death. Like Dylan Thomas, I don't want there to be two. But is the Absolute Master, therefore, the only one that remains?

12. That I should have said this at the time, even in more vigorous terms, in this détour, serves as a meeting-point by virtue of the fact that, three years later, on the subject of the Name-of-the-Father, I took the opportunity of abandoning the theses that I had promised in my seminar, on account of the permanence of this situation.

13. English in the original [Tr.].

14. 'là où s'était', thus making the verb 'to be' reflexive – an allusion to Lacan's gloss on Freud's '*Wo es war soll Ich werden*' [Tr.].

15. Which I have since justified by means of a topological model borrowed from surface theory in *analysis situs* (note added 1962).

16. In French, '*proie*' is usually 'prey', but it is also used in the phrase '*lâcher la proie pour l'ombre*' ('to drop the substance for the shadow') [Tr.].

17. More recently, in the opposite direction, in the attempt to make homologous surfaces topologically defined in the terms employed here in the subjective articulation. Cf. the simple refutation of the supposed paradox 'I am lying' (note added 1962).

Classified index of the major concepts

≫≫≪≪

Note

1. The reader will find in this index, drawn up according to an order that I have established, the major concepts of Lacan's theory, referred to the contexts in which they occur – these contexts themselves providing their essential definitions, their functions and their principal properties.

2. In the pages referred to after each term in the index, it is the concept, not the word, that is to be looked for. I have chosen to designate the classified concept by the expression that seemed to me most adequate and most comprehensive, usually proceeding by retroaction from the latest stage in the development of the theory.

3. I am well aware that with such an articulation what I was offering was necessarily an interpretation. It seemed to me, therefore, to be opportune to explain it in a few words, so that one may, after following my reasoning, deduct it from the sum of the index.

4. I have chosen to isolate the concepts which, concerning the theory of the subject, are of interest, if only by denying them their names, to the human sciences as a whole, with the effect of stressing the specificity of the analytic experience (in its Lacanian definition: the bringing into play of the reality of the unconscious, the introduction of the subject to the language of his desire).

5. If the signifier is constituent for the subject (I, A), one may follow, through its defiles, the process of transformation (of mutilation) that makes a subject of man, through the obliquity of narcissism (I, B). The properties of symbolic overdetermination explain why the logical time of this history is not linear (I, C).

6. One must then take again in their simultaneity the elements successively presented (II, A, B, C). One will observe that the topology of the subject finds its statute only by being related to the geometry of the Ego (II, B, 4 and II, C, 3). One is now in a position to grasp the functioning of communication: in its structure, all the pieces of the game find their place (II, D).

7. From the structure of communication, one will deduce what is the power of the treatment, with what ear to listen to the unconscious,

what training to give analysts (III, A, B). The last part (III, C) is centred on the eminent signifier of desire. The following section (IV) is clinical (the account of it is very succinct).

8. As for the Lacanian epistemology, it marks, I believe the position of psychoanalysis *in* the epistemological break, in as much as through the Freudian field the foreclosed subject of science returns into the *impossible* of its discourse. There is, therefore, a single ideology of which Lacan provides the theory: that of the 'modern ego', that is to say, the paranoiac subject of scientific civilization, of which a warped psychology theorizes the imaginary, at the service of free enterprise.

Jacques-Alain Miller

>>≪≪

I. THE SYMBOLIC ORDER

A. The Supremacy of the Signifier
(see: *The place of the Other*)

1. The exteriority, autonomy and displacement of the signifier; its defiles.
a. Exteriority: *64–66*.
b. The defiles: *65–66*, 126–127, *147–148*, *158* (and the proper name), *255–256*, *310–311*.

2. The signifying unit.
a. Symbol, letter, signifier: *61–65*, 82, *104*, *152–153*, *183–184*, 233–234, 263, 316–317.
b. Articulation: *126*.
c. Materiality and locus of the letter: 87, *147–148*.

3. The structure: the symbolic, the imaginary, the real: 65 (production of the real by the symbolic), *180–187* (hallucination), *191* (supremacy of the symbolic over the imaginary), *195* (supremacy of the symbolic over the real), *197* (intrusion of the imaginary in the real).

4. The supremacy of the signifier over the signified: *150–154*, 160, 284, *289–290*.

B. The Defiles of the Signifier

1. The genesis of the ego: imaginary identification (see: *The function of the ego*).
a. Primordial symbolization and primary identification (the demand for love and the 'Fort-Da'): *103–104*, 207, *233–234*, *255*, *285–286*.
b¹. The mirror-stage: *1–7*, 42, *54–55*, *137–139*, *196*, 209, 211–212.

b². Narcissism: *16–25*, *123*.
b³. Aggressivity: *8–29*, 42 (see: *The fragmented body*).
c¹. The superego: 21, 143, *255–256*.
c². The ideal ego: 2, *307*.

2. The production of the subject: symbolic identification (see: *The structure of the subject*).

C. The Structure of the Subject

D. Intersubjective Communication

III. DESIRE AND ITS INTERPRETATION

A. The Formations of the Unconscious
(see: *Communication*)

B. The Analytic Experience

1. Technique: 33–36, *45*, *48–49*, 75–76.

2. a. Empty speech (the discourse of the imaginary): *41–42*, *45–46*, *139* (see: *Narcissism, The illusion of autonomy*).
b. Abjection of the theory of the ego in analysis (splitting of the ego and identification with the analyst): 44–45, *90–91*, *119* (abjection) (see: *The theory of ideology*).
c. 'Frustration': *41–42*.
d. Resistance: 13, 23–24, 79, 129–131, *142*, 235.

3. a. Neutrality and the analyst's response: *12–16*, *43*, *89–90*, *93*, *95–96*, *139–140*, 229–230.
b. The transference: 14 (negative), *58*, *166–167*, *170*, 235–237, 241–250, *261*.

c. Intransitive demand and suppression: *41–49*, *254–256*, *270–274* (see: *The locus of the Other, Repetition, Need, demand, desire*).

4. a. Punctuation, interpretation: *44*, 81, *95–96*, *98–99*, *154* (see: *Repetition*).
b. The purpose and end of analysis (full speech, the language of desire, the subjectification of death): 7, *43*, *80–83*, 88, *105*, *171*, 281 (see: *Death, Castration*).

5. The training of analysts.
a. The knowledge (*savoir*) of the analyst and the training analysis: 82–83, 144–145, 147 (see *Epistemology*).
b. Psychoanalytic associations: 30–36, 226–228 (see: *The theory of ideology*).

C. The Phallus

1. The drives: 189–190, 236–237, *314–316*.

2. L'objet *a*: *197–198*, *220–221*, *239*, *243–244*, *250*, *251–252*, *265*, *274–275*, *314–316*, *322–324*.

3. Jouissance, *Castration*: *198–199*, *206–207*, 246, *262–269*, *281–291*, 316–318.

4. Desire.
a. 'Man's desire is the desire of the Other': 5–6, *58*, 67, 288–289.
b. Desire and the Law; need, demand, desire; desire and phantasy: *166–167*, *175*, 244, 252, *258–259*, *263–265*, 269, 272, *275–276*, *285–288*, 310–313, *322–323*.

IV. CLINICAL PRACTICE

A. Freud's Cases

1. Dora: 77–78, 91–92, 236, 274.

2. The Rat Man: 77–79, 88–89, 235–238.

3. The Wolf Man: 48, 77–78, 87, 117.

4. Judge Schreber: 36, 93, 183–192, 199–221.

5. Little Hans: 36, 168.

6. The dream of the butcher's wife: 257.

B. Psychiatric Practice

1. Neurosis
a. Neurosis; in general: 28–29, 168; hysteria: 5, 14, 89–90; phobia: 14, 248–249.
b. Obsessional neurosis: 5, 14, 89–90, 99, 199, 236–238, 247, 268.

2. Perversion: in general: 197–198; sado-masochism: 25; scoptophilia: 25; homosexuality, 25, 55.

3. Psychosis (see: *Verwerfung*).
a. Psychosis (in general): 179–221.
b. Paranoia (in Kraepelin's sense): 5, 16–17.

V. EPISTEMOLOGY AND THE THEORY OF IDEOLOGY

A. Epistemology

1. The epistemological break (the example of physics): 9–10, *72–73*, 114, 179, 294–296.

2. Truth
a. Truth as fiction, as secret, as symptom: *47, 74–75* (opposed to exactitude), *98* (opposed to exactitude), 123, *305–306*.

b. Psychoanalysis and science: *56–57, 72, 76–77, 162, 174.*

3. Conjecture
a. The conjectural ('human') sciences: *66, 73–77,* 148–150.
b. Psychology as science; its object: 130.

B. The Theory of Ideology

1. The ideology of freedom: theory of the autonomous ego, humanism, rights of man, responsibility, anthropomorphism, ideals, instinctual maturation, etc.: 26–27, 53–55, 132, *165, 216,* 230–231, 306.

2. The ideology of free enterprise: the American Way of Life, human relations, human engineering, success, happiness, pattern, etc.: 37–38, 115–116, 127–128, 231, *243.*

Commentary on the graphs

❯❯❮❮

If it is true that perception eclipses structure, a schema will infallibly lead the subject 'to forget in an intuitive image the analysis on which it is based' (p. 214).

It is the task of symbolism to forbid imaginary capture – and, indeed, its difficulty follows from the theory.

When gaining some illumination from Lacan's schemata, we should not forget this warning.

Such a precaution reveals the inadequation in principle between the graphic representation and its object (the *object* of psychoanalysis). Moreover, all the constructions gathered together here have no more than a didactic role: their relation with the structure is one of analogy.

On the other hand, *there is no occultation of the symbolic* in the topology that Lacan sets up, because this space is the very space in which the relations of the logic of the subject are schematized. The inadequation of the analogies is pointed out by Lacan quite unambiguously on the optical model of the ideals of the person, precisely in the absence of the symbolic object *o* (*objet petit* a). From the note added to Schema *R* (note 18, p. 223), one may learn the rules of transformation of intuitive geometry in the topology of the subject.

J.-A. M.

❯❯❮❮

I *The schema of the intersubjective dialectic*
('Schema *L*', p. 193)

The schema shows that the dual relation between the ego and its projection *o o'* (indifferently its image and that of the other) constitutes an obstacle to the advent of the subject S in the locus of its signifying determination, A. The quaternary is fundamental: 'a quadripartite structure has, since the introduction of the unconscious, always been required in the construction of a subjective ordering' ('Kant avec Sade', *Écrits*, p. 774). Why? Because to restore the imaginary relation in the structure that presents it involves a duplication of its terms: the 'small other' being exponentiated into 'capital Other', the undoing of the subject of the signifying chain coming to double the ego. The symmetry or reciprocity belongs to the imaginary register, and the position of the Third Party implies that of the fourth, which is given according to the levels of the analysis, the name of 'barred subject', or dummy (*mort*). (Cf. p. 229, psychoanalytic bridge).

⋙⋘

II *The structure of the subject*
('Schema *R*', p. 193; 'Schreber's Schema' (I), p. 212)

1. *Composition of the symbolic, the imaginary and the real ('Schema R')* 'Schema *R*' is made up of the meeting of two triangles, the symbolic ternary and the imaginary ternary, delimited in a square by the base of each triangle. If the triangle of the symbolic occupies half of the square to itself, the other two figures sharing the other half, it is because, in structuring them, it must make them overlap. The dotted line stands for the imaginary.

This construction requires a double reading:

1. It may be read as a representation of the statics of the subject. Thus it consists of: (a) the triangle *I* resting on the dual relation between the Ego and the Other (narcissism, projection, captation), with, for its apex, the phallus, the imaginary object 'in which the subject identifies himself ... with himself as a living being' (p. 196), that is to say, the species under which the subject represents himself to himself; (b) the field *S*, with the three functions of the Ego Ideal I in which the subject is mapped in the register of the symbolic, of the signifier of the Object M, of the Name-of-the-Father F in the locus of the Other O. The line I M may be regarded as doubling the relation between the subject and the object of desire through the mediation of the signifying chain, a relation that the Lacanian algebra was to write as $orall o$ (but the line immediately proves to be an inadequate representation); (c) the field *R*, framed by the imaginary relation and the symbolic relation.

2. But it is also the history of the subject that is notated here: on the segment *i* M are placed the figures of the imaginary Other, which culminate in the figure of the mother, the real Other, inscribed in the symbolic under the signifier of the primal object, the first exterior to the subject, which bears in Freud the name of *das Ding* (cf. *Écrits*,

p. 656); on the segment *m* I follow the imaginary identifications that form the Ego of the child until he receives his statute in the real and form the symbolic identification. One finds once again, therefore, a specified synchrony of the ternary *S*: the child in I is linked to the mother in M, as desire of her desire; in the third position is the Father, transmitted by the speech of the mother.

In his note of 1966, Lacan shows how to translate this square into his topology. The surface *R* is to be taken as the 'flattened form' (*mise-à-plat*) of the figure that would be obtained by joining *i* to I and *m* to M, that is, by the torsion that characterizes the Moebius strip in complete space: the presentation of the schema in two dimensions is to be referred, therefore, to the cut that spreads the strip out. This explains why the straight line I M cannot refer to the relation between the subject and the object of desire: the subject is simply the cut of the strip, and what falls from it is called the object *o* (*objet petit* a). This verifies and complements Jean-Claude Milner's formula on '$\mathcal{S} \Diamond a$': 'the terms are heterogeneous, whereas there is homogeneity attached to the places' (*Cahiers pour l'analyse*, no. 3, p. 96). That is the power of the subject.

2. Schreber's schema (I)

('Schema of the structure of the subject at the termination of the psychotic process.')

This schema is a variation of the preceding one: the foreclosure of the Name-of-the-Father (here F*o*), which involves the absence of the representation of the subject *S* by the phallic image (here Φ), throws the relation of the three fields out of alignment: the divergence of the imaginary and the symbolic, the reduction of the real to their disalignment.

The point *i* of the delusional ego is substituted for the subject, while the Ego Ideal I takes the place of the Other. The trajectory S*oo'*O is transformed into the trajectory *ioo'*I.

❧❧❧❧

III *The graphs of desire*
(*Graph 1*, p. 303; *Graph 2*, p. 306; *Graph 3*, p. 313; *Graph 4*, p. 315)

On *Graph 1*, one may read the inversion that constitutes the subject in his intersection of the signifying chain. This inversion takes place by *anticipation*, whose law imposes at the first intersection (on the vector S–S') the last word (that is to say, punctuation) and *retroaction*, enumerated in the formula of intersubjective communication, which necessitates a second intersection, in which is situated the receiver and his battery. *Graph 2* composes, on the basis of the elementary cell, the imaginary identification and the symbolic identification in the subjective synchrony; the signifying chain is here given its specification as speech. It becomes the vector of the drive, between desire and phantasy, in the complete graph – the intermediary graph simply punctuating the question of the subject to the Other: 'What does he want of me?' to be inverted in its return, 'What do you want of me?'

Index of Freud's German terms

꒷꒷꓋꓋

Index of proper names

≫≫⋘⋘